# FROM PEARL HARBOR TO HIROSHIMA

*Also by Saki Dockrill*

BRITAIN'S POLICY FOR WEST GERMAN REARMAMENT, 1950–55

# From Pearl Harbor to Hiroshima

## The Second World War in Asia and the Pacific, 1941–45

Edited by

**Saki Dockrill**
*Lecturer in War Studies*
*King's College London*
*University of London*

MACMILLAN

First published 1994 by
THE MACMILLAN PRESS LTD
Houndmills, Basingstoke, Hampshire RG21 2XS
and London
Companies and representatives
throughout the world

ISBN 0-333-57722-1

A catalogue record for this book is available
from the British Library.

Printed in Great Britain by
Ipswich Book Co Ltd
Ipswich, Suffolk

To the memory of Louis Allen, Lord Cheshire
and Christopher Thorne

# Contents

# Maps

# Acknowledgements

This collection of essays is based upon papers given at the Conference on 'The Pacific War: A Reappraisal after Fifty Years' held at the Imperial War Museum, London, on 5 and 6 December 1991. The Conference was sponsored by the Japan Foundation, the *Asahi Shimbun*, the *Daily Telegraph* and the Department of War Studies, King's College London, and was attended by more than a hundred historians and students from Britain and overseas.

The editor of the current volume would like to thank the Japan Foundation, the *Asahi Shimbun* and the *Daily Telegraph* for their invaluable help which enabled this Conference to take place. It resulted from close collaboration between the Department of War Studies and the Imperial War Museum and I wish to thank the Imperial War Museum and especially its Director, Dr Alan Borg, and Mrs Gill Smith of the Museum, for helping to make the Conference so successful. Special thanks also due to Professor Freedman, Head of the Department of War Studies, for his patient encouragement and support of the project.

I would also like to thank the contributors to this volume for their cooperation while I was preparing it for publication. Mr David Steeds kindly volunteered to edit the summary of the paper which was written and sent to me by the late Louis Allen prior to the opening of the Conference and appears here as Chapter 6.

I am grateful to Vice-Admiral Sir Ian Hogg for permitting Ian Nish to quote from the H.W. Gwynne papers in Chapter 1, and due appreciation should also go to the Bodleian Library, Oxford, for allowing Ian Nish to consult these papers. My thanks also to Colonel Ōya and the Archival Section of the Institute for National Defence Studies for kindly allowing the use of Colonel Ōya's Oral History in Chapter 11. On behalf of the contributors I would also like to thank the staff of the various archives that were consulted. Copyright material from the Public Record Office, Kew, appears by permission of the Controller, Her Majesty's Stationery Office.

Finally, I wish to thank Tim Farmiloe, Director, and Belinda Holdsworth, Editor, at Macmillan for their help in preparing the manuscript for publication. I am also grateful to Anne Rafique of Anne Rafique Editorial Services for her editorial work on the text.

Shortly after the end of the Conference, Mr Louis Allen, who gave a paper, Group Captain Lord Cheshire, who attended the Conference, and Professor Christopher Thorne, who had initially hoped to speak at the Conference and who was my tutor when I studied at the University of Sussex during the academic year 1981–2, died. This book is therefore dedicated to the memory of these three distinguished people.

November 1992                                                                  Saki Dockrill
                                                                      King's College London

# Foreword

The fiftieth anniversary of the Japanese attack on Pearl Harbor and the consequent linkage of the Pacific with the Atlantic, Soviet Russia and North Africa as theatres of the Second World War, gave rise to several important international historical conferences. This volume records the papers given at one of these conferences, held in Britain at the Imperial War Museum and organised by the Department of War Studies at King's College London. Though small-scale by the standards of those held in Japan and Hawaii, it was attended by historians from the United States, Japan, China and Germany, as well as from the United Kingdom. Discussion at the Conference was lively, and marked a continuation of a move away from the earlier established approach to the subject, with its exclusive focus on the Japanese–American confrontation. With Dr Drea's paper and the spirited discussion which followed it, there was a continuing intrusion of historians into the one area excluded, deliberately we are told, from the official histories, including the volumes on British intelligence, that is, the field of intelligence, especially signals intelligence and cooperation between the major belligerents on both sides in the Pacific War.

Discussion of responsibilities and war guilt has come a long way from the not altogether satisfactory view of the Far Eastern Pacific War as having arisen from a single 'conspiracy to commit aggressive war' which was imported into the proceedings of the International Military Tribunal for War Crimes in the Far East from the proceedings made against selected survivors from the Nazi leadership at Nuremberg at the end of the war. There is, nevertheless, still an element of self-willed hubris in the historiographical view of the drive which dominated Japanese policy from 1937 onwards, a hubris the more easily conceptualised by the ultimate vengeance which descended from the air on Tokyo, Hiroshima and Nagasaki. From the vantage point of 1991, with the Cold War and its threat of thermonuclear Armageddon apparently ended, that historical view which sees the dropping of the atomic bomb on two Japanese cities as the end of the world wars of the first half of this century rather than the first shot in the 'Cold War' of the second half can be put with solidarity and conviction, as it was by Professor Freedman and Dr Dockrill in Chapter 11 of this volume.

The location of the Conference made it possible to discuss the links between the European and Far Eastern wars free of the understandably nationalist orientation of so much earlier American writing on the subject. The late Christopher Thorne used to point out that the American intervention against Japan's demands on French Indo-China which marked the final stages in the escalation of Japanese–American hostilities, was linked not to Roosevelt's anxiety about Japanese expansion in the Far East, but to his anxiety about its effects upon British resistance in Europe. Roosevelt saw a threat to the British position in Malaya and Singapore as a gross distraction from Britain's efforts in Europe, and something which might very well take Britain out of the war. This point was made repeatedly in discussion at the Conference. The view that the Japanese élite themselves bore much of the responsibility for linking the conflict in the Far East with that in Europe by yielding to the temptation to capitalise on the Axis victories in Europe emerged from the discussion on Professor Martin's paper. Perceptions of the Second World War as global were, however, confined to the Commonwealth and the United States where the existence of an agreed common German–Japanese strategy was assumed. This assumption has died hard; despite the clear evidence now available that no such coordinated strategy existed and that serious earnest confrontation between the Axis states had no place in the way their governments operated.

In this debate the Chinese historian insisting that the Second World War began with the openings of the Sino-Japanese conflict in 1937 struck an inevitably discordant note. Certainly the Big Three, who were to emerge victorious in 1945, found very soon that strengthening China against Japan, even Kuomintang China, made overall sense in their global strategy, since, faced with the threat of Hitler's reckless expansionism in Europe, none of them wished to be involved in a second conflict in the Pacific. But Chinese motives for resisting Japan were different, as were those of the Japanese expansionists, and represent a linear development from the 1890s onwards which has nothing to do with Europe. That is to say, its motivations and causes are native to the Far East. Even if Japan had not felt cribbed, confined and threatened by the two great Anglo-Saxon naval powers; even if Japanese propaganda had not tried to rally Asian hostility to white imperialism behind it; even if those Chinese who thought that China should compromise with Japan had been successful, there would still have been a Sino-Japanese conflict and a war in the Far East which had nothing to do with that in Europe.

The link between the two wars in the end comes down to the American determination not to see Britain weakened, so that her resistance to Hitler would crumble; and the Japanese decision to take advantage of the distraction of Britain and America in Europe to pursue their long-standing aims for the Japanese Imperial way in the Far East. But in the end the responsibility, as it was left by the Conference on the outbreak of the Second World War, seems to come down finally onto Japan and onto the Japanese leadership. That many were reluctant to take the final step has much to do with the manner in which American pressure drove Japan into a corner. That would nowadays be generally accepted, but the corner was one of Japanese making and one which arose inevitably from the American and British view that war is an unnatural state of affairs and that war in the Far East threatened everybody's long-standing interests. That this view prevailed, that the Japanese have been the greatest beneficiaries from that, is one of the ironies of history.

Donald Cameron Watt
The London School of Economics
University of London

# Notes on the Contributors

The late **Louis Allen** was Reader in French at Durham University and Honorary Fellow at the East Asia Centre, Northumbria Universities, and was well known for his *Singapore 1941–1942* (1977) and *Burma: the Longest War* (1984).

**Nigel Brailey** is Lecturer in History, University of Bristol, and has written numerous articles on Thailand and South-East Asia. Dr Brailey is the author of *Thailand and the Fall of Singapore* (1986) and is currently working on a biography of Sir Ernest Satow.

**Saki Dockrill** is Lecturer in War Studies, King's College London, and the author of *Britain's Policy for West German Rearmament, 1950–55* (1991) and of a number of articles on the Cold War and the origins of the Pacific War. Dr Dockrill is now completing a study on *Eisenhower's New Look National Security Policy, 1953–61*.

**Edward Drea** is Chief, Research and Analysis Division, US Army Centre of Military History, Washington DC, and the author of *The 1942 Japanese General Election* (1979) and many articles on American and Japanese intelligence. Dr Drea has recently published *MacArthur's ULTRA: Codebreaking and the War Against Japan* (1991).

**Lawrence Freedman** is Professor of War Studies and Head of the Department of War Studies, King's College London. His major publications include *US Intelligence and the Soviet Strategic Threat* (1977), *The Evolution of Nuclear Strategy* (1983) and *War, Strategy, and International Politics* (editor; 1992).

**Ikuhiko Hata** is Professor of the History of Modern Japan, Takushoku University, Japan, and his major studies include *The Sino-Japanese War* (Tokyo, 1961), *Japan Examined* (Hawaii, 1983), and *The Nanjing Incident* (Tokyo, 1986).

**Peter Lowe** is Reader in History in the University of Manchester and his major studies include *Great Britain and the Origins of the Pacific War* (1977) and *The Origins of the Korean War* (1986). Dr Lowe now completing a study of *British Policy in East Asia, 1948–54*.

**Bernd Martin** is Professor of Modern History, Historisches Seminar, Albert-Ludwigs-Universität, Freiburg, and Dr Martin's major publications include *Deutschland und Japan im Zweiten Weltkrieg* (Göttingen, 1969) and *Weltmacht* *oder niedergang? Deutsche Großmachtpolitik im 20. Jahrhundert* (Darmstadt, 1989).

**Ian Nish** is Emeritus Professor of International History and taught in the Department of International History at the London School of Economics until 1991. His major publications include *The Anglo-Japanese Alliance* (1966), *Alliance in Decline* (1972) and *Japan's Struggle with Internationalism: Japan, China and the League of Nations 1931–3* (1992).

**John Pritchard** was a Research Fellow in War Studies at King's College London. He has compiled *The Tokyo War Crimes Trials* (1981) and is co-author (with P. Calvocoressi and G. Wint) of *Total War* (1989). Dr Pritchard is currently compiling *The British War Crimes Trials in the Far East*.

**Ronald Spector** is Professor of History and International Relations at the George Washington University and is well known as the author of *Advice and Support: The Early Years of The US Army in Vietnam, 1941–60* (1983) and *Eagle Against the Sun* (1984).

**David Steeds** is Senior Lecturer in Far Eastern Studies and acting head of the Department of International Politics, University College of Wales, and the author (with Ian Nish) of *China, Japan and 19th Century Britain*.

**Wenzhao Tao** is Senior Research Fellow and Chief, the Division of History of China's Foreign Relations, at the Chinese Academy of Social Science. He was a visiting scholar at the Georgetown University, Washington DC, 1982–4, and is the co-author of *History of the Imperialist Aggression in China* (Beijing, 1986) and of a forthcoming book on the *History of Sino-American Relations, 1911–1950*.

**Donald Cameron Watt** is Stevenson Professor of International History at the London School of Economics and his major publications include *Personalities and Policies* (1965), *Too Serious a Business* (1975), *Succeeding John Bull: America in Britain's Place, 1900–1975* (1984) and *How War Came* (1989).

# Introduction: One Step Forward – A Reappraisal of the 'Pacific War'
## Saki Dockrill

Historians have not yet reached a consensus as to what the war between Imperial Japan and the Allies between 1941 and 1945 should be called. The Japanese General Headquarters–Cabinet Liaison Conference on 10 December 1941 decided that Japan's wars, including that with China, should collectively be called 'The Greater-East Asian War' or *Daitō'a Sensō*. In the aftermath of the war on 15 December 1945, the General Headquarters (GHQ) of the Supreme Commander for the Allied Powers (SCAP) ordered the Japanese Government not to use the term 'Greater-East Asian War' in any official documents. This was because the term was understood to have been employed by the Japanese leaders to justify Japan's invasion of China and South East Asia.[1]

Since then, the title 'Pacific War' or '*Taiheiyō Sensō*' has generally been used in publications and in school textbooks. However, Japanese historians have debated for some time whether 'the Pacific War' is an accurate description of the 1941–5 conflict, since it tends to concentrate attention on the Japanese–US war in the Pacific, thereby obscuring the fact that the war was also fought extensively in East Asia, and particularly in China. One school of historians has suggested that it should be called 'the Asian-Pacific War' or 'The Second World War in Asia and the Pacific'.[2]

On the other hand, the term 'the Pacific War' remains popular in the West. The Conference at the Imperial War Museum in London, whose papers are the basis for this volume, was entitled 'The Pacific War' with a subtitle – 'World War II in Asia and the Pacific, 1941–1945'. This was intended to be a compromise, but some British historians are not quite comfortable with either 'World War II in Asia and the Pacific, 1941–1945' or 'the Pacific War'. In their view, the conflicts on the other side of the Eurasian continent, as opposed to the war in Europe, should be called 'The Far Eastern War'. The late Christopher Thorne in his book *The Far Eastern War* explained that the Far East 'embraces not only the Pacific but East Asia, Southeast Asia, and Australia', while the use of the term 'the Far East' implies 'Eurocentric' attitudes.[3] Moreover, Britain and her European allies were heavily engaged in fighting Nazi Germany between 1939 and 1945, and the war in Asia, which began in 1941, took place, in the words of D. Cameron Watt 'too far' to the east of their main battlefields to be discussed in the context of the Second World War.[4] Of course, these perceptions would have altered significantly if the Axis powers had attained any meaningful cooperation comparable to the Allied powers and if Germany and Japan had been

1

able to achieve a concerted war effort, for instance in Soviet Russia in 1941–2 or in the area of India and the Middle East in 1942. However, Britain, by virtue of her imperial holdings and her ties with the Commonwealth countries, was already linked to the 'Far East' and India. Moreover, the Pacific War might not have taken place at all if the European imperial powers (the Netherlands, Britain and France) had not been so distracted and nearly destroyed by the German offensives which swept over Europe in 1940. Japan, in turn, wanted to make use of the vacuum then created in Asia in order both to achieve her 'Greater East Asia Co-Prosperity Sphere' (although it is debatable whether she invaded these countries as 'the liberator of Asia from the West' and/or as 'a Machiavellian hoax'[5]) and to obtain much-needed raw materials which might enable her to win the war in China. From these perspectives, it could be said that Japan's war in Asia is closely linked to, or was even the consequence of, the conflict in Europe, as has been demonstrated by some of the chapters in this volume.[6] One could therefore argue that 'The Second World War began in Europe in the first days of September 1939 (despite the cataloguers of the Library of Congress who date its beginning to December 7, 1941)'.[7]

Moreover, Admiral Yamamoto's immediate military goal, which was finally approved by the Chiefs of the General Staff, was not to fight the Americans, but to demoralise them so that they would not become engaged, at least for a year or so, in the war with Japan on the side of Britain, France and Holland and China. Hence, there is some truth in stating that Pearl Harbor was 'a side show' to Japan's main aim of seizing the European imperial holdings.[8]

However, American historians are most unlikely to accept the British view that the war should be called the 'Far Eastern War' and that the Far Eastern War was different and therefore separated from the war in Europe. It is true that prior to Pearl Harbor, President Franklin D. Roosevelt was more concerned about the growing threat from Nazi Germany to the security of Europe and about its influence in Latin America than that posed by Japan to the Pacific and Asia. He was more anxious to assist the British and French war efforts against Germany than about China's predicament. However, once the war with Japan broke out and Germany subsequently declared war on the United States, the situation changed completely. A similar pattern evolved when the Korean War broke out in June 1950. Despite the United States' Europe-first strategy, she became heavily involved in the fighting in Korea.

After Pearl Harbor, the Americans, as Ronald Spector convincingly argues in this volume, were literally fighting the world war on two fronts. The order of priorities, despite America's acceptance of a Europe-first strategy, became a matter of contention in view of the size of the manpower commitments to, and the massive military operations in the Pacific War and the anxiety of the American military to defeat Japan as quickly as possible.[9]

Alternatively, given that the Manchurian crisis in 1931 and the Sino-Japanese war which began in 1937 had already involved the two countries in lengthy conflict before the outbreak of the Pacific War or the Far Eastern War, it might be more sensible to argue from the Chinese perspective that the Pacific or Far Eastern War was merely an extension of the military conflict against the Japanese which commenced in 1928 or 1931 or at the latest in 1937.[10]

Not only do historians across the Atlantic differ in their assessments of the 1941-45 war, but there is also a notable gap between the interests of the academic community and those of the general public in the Pacific War between the United States, Japan, China, and other Asian countries on one hand and Europe and Britain on the other. The former countries overwhelmingly outweighed the latter in their preoccupation with the Pacific War.

Under these circumstances, two things can be said. First, it is remarkable that there have recently been two conferences on the subject of the 'Far Eastern War', both at the Imperial War Museum in London in 1979 and in 1991.[11] Given the financial limitations, neither of these conferences could be described as international in a true sense in terms of the range and number of speakers the conference organisers could afford to invite to London.

Secondly, the fact that historians could not even agree on when the war started or what it should be called, suggests that the title of the 1991 conference – 'The Pacific War: A Reappraisal After Fifty Years' – might have been too ambitious. Nevertheless it is hoped that the conference was at least a step towards a reappraisal of the Pacific War.

Studies in English on the causes of the Pacific War and the outbreak of the war at Pearl Harbor have recently increased in number, especially in North America. However, historians are unable to agree on a number of key issues: the impact of Japan's decision to conclude the tripartite pact in September 1940 on her subsequent decision to go to war with the Western allies or the importance to be attached to the proposed and abortive summit conference between Prince Fumimaro Konoye, the Japanese Prime Minister and President Roosevelt during the summer and autumn of 1941. Whether in fact the war between Japan and the United States which started in December 1941 was inevitable or when Japan had reached the point of no return remain contentious issues. There are a number of other possible turning points – Japan's invasion of Indo-China in 1940–41, the American imposition of a total oil embargo on Japan on 1 August 1941 and the failure of Japanese–American diplomacy with the despatch of the 'Hull Note' of 26 November 1941.[12]

While these questions remain unanswered in this relatively well-researched area, it is not surprising that the Pacific War, which has received less attention than the war in Europe, has left historians with many opportunities for research. Ronald Spector persuasively argues the need for more scholarly attention to the subject, while Edward J. Drea examines a new area of study – the US Army's breaking of the Japanese Imperial Army's codes. Studies of the Grand Alliance between Britain, the Soviet Union and the United States, or on the Anglo-American 'special relationship', are more popular than those on the relations between the Axis, for two main reasons. First, as discussed earlier, there was little anxiety in Berlin or Tokyo for concerted efforts between Germany and Japan, by contrast with the close collaboration between Britain and the United States. Second, the development of the Cold War after 1947 encouraged historians to examine the wartime relations between the Soviet Union, Britain and the United States. This volume benefits from Bernd Martin's study on the German–Japanese alliance during the Second World War. By the same token, little is known in Europe about Chinese perceptions of the role of China during the war with Japan or her relations with Britain and the United States during the Pacific War. Wenzhao Tao's chapter has thrown some light on this 'unknown' area. The role of Thailand is another area neglected by the historians of the Second World War. While the concept of the Greater East Asia Co-Prosperity Sphere has been generally regarded as Japan's justification for fulfilling her imperial goals, there was also a genuine, if naive, pursuit of Japanese pan-Asianism. Nigel Brailey has discussed this in Chapter 7, 'Thailand, Japanese Pan-Asianism and the Greater East Asia Co-Prosperity Sphere'.

Whether or not Admiral Yamamoto's surprise attack on Pearl Harbor was a viable strategy remains contentious. However, not much is known in the West about the origins of Yamamoto's ideas and the evolution of the Japanese Navy's thinking. Moreover, it is interesting, as Ikuhiko Hata points out in Chapter 3, that Japanese veterans now think Yamamoto was wrong and that Japan should have followed a more conventional strategy of countering and destroying the enemy's main battlefleet after it had been 'lured' into Japan's home waters.[13] Hata also asks 'what if Japan had not attacked at Pearl Harbor, had restrained itself from further expansion of its battlefront, and had massed the full strength of its Combined Fleet in the western Pacific to await and intercept the advance of the US Navy?'[14]

The United States went to war simply because Japan attacked Pearl Harbor. Without such a self-evident Japanese challenge to the United States, it would have been very difficult for President Roosevelt to go to Congress with a proposal to declare war on Japan. However, the situation would have been equally frustrating for Japan if she had merely waited for the US main fleet to be decoyed into the western Pacific, while she was starved of US oil and in the middle of her war with China. Alternatively, even if Japan had attacked Britain and Dutch imperial holdings in Asia, but not American territories in the Pacific, it remains debatable whether the United States would have gone to war for the sake of the European imperial powers. Roosevelt later told Churchill that if 'it had not been for the Japanese attack [on Pearl Harbor, he] would have had great difficulty in getting the American people into the war'.[15] Indeed, if the Americans had been willing to attack Japan mainly to help the British and Dutch, there would seem to have been little reason why they did not help the Allies by declaring war on Nazi Germany in May 1940 when Britain, the Netherlands and France were in dire straits as a result of the successful German offensive in western Europe.

By comparison, Anglo-Japanese relations before Pearl Harbor seemed to have been more straightforward. Ian Nish explains how and why the relationship between these countries, despite some lingering interest among a few decision-makers and diplomats in London and Tokyo in coordinating their mutual interests in China, did not improve during the 1930s. That Britain's leadership regarded the threat from Germany as more serious and urgent, while hoping that 'Japan could be and must be "pacified"', as the Cabinet Defence Requirements Committee agreed in February 1934, has been well researched;[16] however, historians remain divided about the role of Churchill in executing his Nazi-first strategy. John Pritchard argues in Chapter 2 that Churchill 'belittled' the strategic importance of the Pacific and Asia, for instance by diverting Britain's precious resources to Soviet Russia in September 1941.[17] Churchill was determined to give 'any help we can spare to the Russians following [the] principle that Hitler is the foe we have to beat'. It was therefore important for Britain to entangle the USSR in the Allied war effort, with the Anglo-American 'special relationship' intended to be the mainstay of the alliance.[18] Japan launched her attack on Malaya and Singapore on 7 December 1941 and by the end of the month Japanese forces were overwhelming Britain's resistance. Churchill telegraphed the Deputy Prime Minister, Clement Attlee, from Canada on 30 December 1941,

If Malay Peninsula has been starved for sake of Libya and Russia...no one is more responsible than I, and I would do exactly the same again.[19]

Churchill remained faithful to his strategic priorities, but Britain's relative neglect of the defences of her Commonwealth and Imperial territories in Asia, which was exposed in the early stages of the war with Japan, has been the source of much bitterness in the minds of Australians in particular. A statement by Australian Prime Minister Keating in February 1992 demonstrated that Australian feelings on this subject remain sore.[20] British–Commonwealth relations are dealt with by Peter Lowe in Chapter 10. On the other hand, as the late Louis Allen and David Steeds show in Chapter 6, Britain's determination to recover Burma from Japan, which was achieved in May 1945, once again reminds us of the close links between the war in Europe and in the Asian Pacific. Britain's ultimate victories in Asia and the Pacific were reflected in her insistence on remaining a global power after the Second World War.

Similarly historians have debated intensively the question of the American use of atomic bombs against Japan in 1945. Lawrence Freedman and Saki Dockrill here examine this long-debated issue from a different angle and try to assess American strategic aims in the use of this immensely destructive weapon and to analyse the effect of these bombs on the minds of the Japanese military and civilian leaders. As more information becomes available from Japanese sources in future, it is hoped that Japanese perceptions at the time will be clarified further.

Overall, while this volume does not pretend to be a comprehensive account of the Pacific War, it has at least marked a step forward in reappraising the Pacific

War from an international perspective. This has been done by involving not only Far Eastern diplomatic historians but also military and international historians in the Conference. It has entailed a turning away from the tendency of concentrating on the study of the causes of the Pacific War solely from the perspectives of diplomatic historians. A study of the history of international relations during this century inevitably involves an analysis of wars – their causes, courses, and consequences. Moreover, during military conflicts, even in countries controlled by civilians, military leaders tend inevitably to be given a larger role than in peacetime in influencing the civilian decision-making process regarding the nation's military requirements. In Imperial Japan, the military leaders of the Imperial Army and Navy were leading members of the cabinet, while the importance of the Foreign Ministry was increasingly becoming marginal in the decision-making process. Japan thus requires a quite different approach to the study of British or United States diplomacy during the same period.

On the other hand, a study of war should embrace many academic disciplines. However, this volume has not covered sociological, ethnic, cultural or philosophical factors pertaining to the Pacific War, nor has it dealt with the experiences of the war from the point of view of combatants or from that of civilians who suffered during the war. Perhaps there is a need for more conferences, workshops and publications to evolve a more comprehensive examination of the Pacific War.

NOTES

1.  J. Kisaka, *Taiheiyo Sensō* (The Pacific War), (Tokyo: Shogakkan, 1989) p. 18.
2.  For instance, Akira Iriye's book entitled *The Origins of the Second World War in Asia and the Pacific* (London and New York: Longman, 1987); Kisaka, *Taiheiyo Sensō*, pp. 18–19.
3.  Christopher Thorne, *The Far Eastern War* (London, Boston and Sydney: Unwin Paperbacks, 1986) pp. x–xi.
4.  D. Cameron Watt's remarks during the Imperial War Museum Conference in December 1991.
5.  Louis Allen, 'The Campaigns in Asia and the Pacific', *Journal of Strategic Studies* 13:1 (March 1990) p. 164.
6.  See chapters by Ian Nish, John Pritchard, Louis Allen and David Steeds, and Peter Lowe.
7.  D. Cameron Watt, *How War Came* (London: Heinemann, 1989), p. xii.
8.  The late Louis Allen discussed this issue in such terms in his speech at an annual conference of the International History Group, British International Studies Association (BISA), Durham, 20 September 1991.
9.  Russell Weigley, *The American Way of War* (Bloomington: Indiana University Press, 1973) pp. 270–1.
10. See, Wenzhao Tao, Chapter 8 in this volume.

11. The first was 'the Anglo-Japanese Conference on the History of the Second World War' in 1979; the second was the source of the present book.

12. For instance, see a recent study, Hilarly Conroy and Harry Wray (eds), *Pearl Harbor Reexamined: Prologue to the Pacific War* (Honolulu: University of Hawaii Press, 1991).

13. See Hata, Chapter 3; and S. Toyama, 'The Outline of the Armament Expansion of the Imperial Japanese Navy During the Years 1930–1941' *Revue internationale d'histoire militaire* 73 (1991) p. 55.

14. See Hata, Chapter 3.

15. Robert Dallek, *Franklin D. Roosevelt and American Foreign Policy 1932–1945* (New York and Oxford: Oxford University Press, 1979) p. 307; see also Warren F. Kimball, *The Juggler – Franklin Roosevelt as Wartime Statesman* (Princeton: Princeton University Press, 1991) p. 13.

16. Michael Howard, 'British Military Preparations for the Second World War' in David Dilks (ed.) *Retreat from Power – Studies in Britain's Foreign Policy of the Twentieth Century, 1906–1939* (London: Macmillan, 1981) p. 109; see also Brian Bond, *British Military Policy between the Two World Wars* (Oxford: Clarendon Press, 1980).

17. See also, Dick Wilson, 'Churchill Belittled Threat of Pacific War', *Japan Times*, 27 August 1992.

18. Martin Gilbert, *Finest Hour: Winston S. Churchill 1939–1941* (London: Heinemann, 1983) p. 1118.

19. Martin Gilbert, *Road to Victory: Winston S. Churchill 1941–1945* (London: Heinemann, 1986) p. 34; Eliot A. Cohen, 'Churchill and Coalition Strategy in World War II' in Paul Kennedy (ed.), *Grand Strategies in War and Peace* (New Haven and London: Yale University Press, 1991) p. 55.

20. See, for instance, *The Guardian* 29, February 1992.

# Part I
# The Road to Pearl Harbor

# 1 Anglo-Japanese Alienation Revisited
## Ian Nish

In 1979 we held in London the Anglo-Japanese Conference on the history of the second world war. Its papers and proceedings were published in English as *Anglo-Japanese Alienation, 1919–52*, while in Japan they were published under the more academically respectable title of *Nichi-Ei kankeishi, 1917–49*.[1] The alienation discussed in that volume was of two kinds. The first was the deteriorating relationship between Britain and Japan in the 1930s which eventually led to war in 1941. The second was the post-war alienation which was a global phenomenon whereby Britain acknowledged that she could no longer sustain a major role in east Asia. Aspects of the first will be dealt with by other authors in this volume. My concern in this chapter is to consider the thinking on both sides between 1931 and 1937 as politicians in Britain and Japan became aware that the two countries were voluntarily or involuntarily being pulled apart. What form did the alienation take in this period? And how did it fit in with (what some scholars call) the proposals for an Anglo-Japanese rapprochement? During the early 1930s Britain increasingly had her back to the wall in east Asia, which was an area remote from her homeland and of lesser interest to her than some parts of the British Commonwealth where she had major problems at the time. She still had a formidable presence in Asia, both naval and commercial; but her status there was beyond the strength which she could devote to maintaining it. The result was a series of attempts by Britain to seek accommodation with Japan, a country whose political stance she did not like. On Japan's side also, there was a series of approaches, often rather shadowy, by which she sought to cut free from her isolation in the world.

An idea which comes through from the 1979 conference is Professor Hosoya's idea of the 'afterglow' of the Anglo-Japanese alliance.[2] Though there is a good deal of contemporary evidence to the contrary, there is also much that confirms his view that, while the alliance ended, it cast a long shadow over the next decade. The draft tripartite arrangement which A.J. Balfour put before Secretary Hughes after the consultations with his secretaries on the *Empress of France* openly mentioned the word 'alliance' and argued that any two of the parties should, in the event of their being threatened, 'be at liberty to protect themselves by entering into a military alliance' of a defensive sort. After discussion in Washington, Balfour discovered the strength of Hughes' personal resistance and the intensity of public opinion against any continuation of the alliance. He altered 'alliance' to 'arrangement'.[3] It remained in this watered down form in the four-power pact which emerged. But the incident suggests that Britain, like Japan, was not inclined to 'ditch' the alliance unless outside pressure was exerted.

'Afterglow' in an imprecise concept, but it exists nonetheless. If we attempt to draw up a balance sheet, the ending of the alliance closed some doors: Japanese officers could no longer come so freely to British naval colleges and attendance at manoeuvres was restricted. On the other hand, the men who ruled – and administered – Britain and Japan had grown up in the alliance period and were used to this nexus. Had Japan been able to form an alternative alliance it might have been different, but relations with the United States continued to be strained because of the immigration issue and she was preoccupied with domestic issues after the Great Kantō earthquake of 1923. Britain, like the United States, contributed generously to the cause of earthquake relief.[4]

The 'afterglow' does not wholly apply to China. After the 1910s when Japan had secured special rights in China and had striven to establish hegemony in certain areas, the period from 1924 to 1927 – Shidehara's tenure of the Foreign Ministry – was a more conciliatory one. Big business cooperated with the government in a non-interventionist policy in China. This did not mean, of course, that Britain and Japan would work together there. They were after all trade rivals; and there were many disputes between them, notably at the Peking Tariff conference of 1925. Eventually Britain chose to act alone and to publish the 'December memorandum' around Christmas 1926. This was a measure to clarify Britain's policy towards the Nationalist forces which were gaining ascendancy in China. It was an attempt to recognise these forces, give them generous assurances and answer the (to London) wrong-headed criticisms which were being made of Britain. The December memorandum, the work of Austen Chamberlain as foreign secretary, was not aimed against Japan. It was seen in Whitehall exclusively in terms of Anglo-Chinese relations.[5]

This approach to China poisoned Anglo-Japanese relations. In a later Japanese cabinet minute of August 1932, the following assessment is made:

> Since the first world war Anglo-Japanese cooperation in the east has come to nothing in terms of the international situation. As a result of Britain's adoption of the so-called new China policy which was extremely ingratiating to the Chinese, any return to Anglo-Japanese cooperation over the China question has been made much more difficult.[6]

From 1927 onwards the paths of the two countries diverged, and collaboration over long-term policy was unlikely. But it has to be said that on the ground Minister Yoshizawa cooperated with Sir Miles Lampson in Peking and with the Diplomatic Body there.[7] Moreover there was more evidence of Japan's wish to cooperate with Britain under the Tanaka government (1927–9) than there had been under its more liberal predecessor. When the special emissary, Count Uchida Yasuya, was sent round the world to sign the Kellogg–Briand Pact in 1928, he was given the brief to sound out the British government. But he had a cool reception, because Britain was in no mood to cooperate with Japan in China at that stage. So the state of affairs in China blotted out some of the 'afterglow' as it had earlier weakened the alliance.

The afterglow of the alliance did not outlast the outbreak of the Manchurian crisis, which is clearly a subject too large to deal with in a short essay of this kind.[8] How did Britain view the crisis in Manchuria and China? As usual Sir Victor Wellesley was called upon to draw up for the cabinet the Intelligent Woman's Guide to the Crisis in China. Usually moderate in his judgements, he is fairly savage in his assessments here, admittedly written at the peak of frustration caused by the Shanghai crisis on 1 February 1932:

> the events of September 1931 were precipitated by a military-fascist plot in Japan to eject the rather liberal Minseito Government and set up a government which would settle the Manchurian business once and for all. The Government however did not try to check its military dictators, though the (at times) complete divergence between Foreign Office assurances and actual happenings in Manchuria, showed that Japan was in a state of divided rule. The Minseito government has now fallen, and with a septuagenarian Premier, an insignificant Foreign Minister and a public opinion favourable to a strong policy, the military and naval politicians have the country's destiny at their disposal.[9]

The underlying idea here would seem to be that Britain had little confidence in the Seiyūkai ministry of Prime Minister Inukai, then 77, and Foreign Minister Yoshizawa, well known to European diplomats as Japan's representative at Geneva during the early months of the crisis. But Britain for the sake of her interests in Shanghai had to try to resolve the conflict there (though leaving the League of Nations to seek for a Manchurian solution). Her problem was to find an associate ready to work with her to resolve the issue. On this point the assessment was gloomy:

> We must eventually be done for in the Far East, unless the United States are eventually prepared to use force. It is universally assumed here that the US will never use force... The Japanese are more afraid of the US than of us, and for obvious reasons. At present, however, they share our low view of American fighting spirit.[10]

Enquiries in Washington did not suggest that it was ready for effective resistance.

As the above quotation suggests, there is a natural triangularity in the approach to the problem of east Asia at this period. Professor Hosoya has favoured such an approach when discussing 'Britain and the US in Japan's view'.[11] This was true also of Britain. There were those in Britain who, conscious of Britain's weakness in the aftermath of the depression, wondered what arrangement could be negotiated with the United States over east Asian problems. But even this group in the Foreign Office felt that, however desirable such a cooperative venture was in principle, Britain was likely to be exploited by a reluctant America and that she could not afford in the depressed state of the British economy to suffer this fate. On the other hand, there were those in the British establishment who drew the conclusion from the Manchurian crisis that the 'Washington system' and the Kellogg–Briand Pact were not working and would not solve world crises. This circle, which took in Neville Chamberlain, the chancellor of the exchequer in the National government, and Sir Warren Fisher, the permanent secretary to the Treasury and a senior civil servant, was distrustful of Washington which tended, in its view, to entangle Britain in crises and then left Britain, in the hoary phrase, to pull American chestnuts out of the fire for her. It shared the low view of America's fighting spirit quoted above; it tended to favour a much more straightforward solution, namely some sort of negotiations to revive an agreement with Japan. This was, to be sure, one aspect of the afterglow of the alliance. But it was probably a minority standpoint. Washington warned Britain against any rapprochement of this kind. Likewise Tokyo, in the repeated assertions of Ambassador Matsudaira, warned Britain against an Anglo-American rapprochement for east Asia. It was, he said, 'not conducive to world peace if an Anglo-American entente is urged primarily with a view to checking other nations'.[12] In short, an anti-Japanese entente would be deeply resented by Japan. There was no ready-made proposal of a bilateral or trilateral nature which would carry overwhelming support.

It is also ludicrous to try to analyse Japanese thinking towards Britain during the Manchurian crisis on the basis of a single document. But the Japanese did try to crystallise their British policy in a cabinet memorandum of 27 August 1932 (from which we have already quoted). By this time the government of Admiral Saitō was in power and had appointed Uchida Yasuya as foreign minister on 6 July. Treaties were being negotiated with the government of Manchukuo, and the ministers had announced to the Diet that they proposed to recognise Manchukuo in the face of the known opposition of world opinion. On 27 August the cabinet endorsed a memorandum by the secretariat entitled 'a draft policy for dealing with the situation from the viewpoint of international relations'.[13] After discussing the League and the China problem, it passed to relations with individual countries and tried to define policy towards Britain, France, the US, the USSR, Holland (in that order) and others. On Britain, it wrote:

A return to cooperation with Britain over China is something much to be desired because Britain's interests and power there are still firmly established today. We have tried in the past to take any suitable occasion to work for the restoration of cooperation but have not seen it come to fruition.... There are doubts about whether Britain would be enthusiastic for negotiations [after the Shanghai incident]. We should take the first appropriate step to restore Anglo-Japanese cooperation either by opening negotiations or by using the question of the follow-up to the Shanghai incident.... If we now move in this direction, we may assume that it will advance a little the prospect of a restoration of

Anglo-Japanese cooperation. Bearing in mind that the important points for Britain exist in China proper [Shina hombu], especially Shanghai, Canton, and the areas of the Yangtse valley and south China, it may be considered that we could, by respecting Britain's concerns appropriately, advance the cause of cooperation and thus create a favourable climate for our position over the Manchurian question.[14]

This was a small extract from a much larger document but it has great significance. It is surely significant that the advisers to the Japanese government at the height of the Manchurian crisis should be writing so optimistically of the possibility of cooperation with Britain.[15] Historians who have had the benefit of seeing the British archives would have to conclude that the Japanese perception of possible *cooperation* was wide of the mark. Official British opinion was on the whole solidly in favour of China. It is conceivable that the Japanese understanding of British attitudes may have been distorted by statements of Ambassador Lindley in Tokyo and by the reports of Ambassador Matsudaira in London. But it is hard to assess the impact their reports had. Then there was the question of 'expert opinion'. Colonel Homma, the military attaché, speaking to the Japan Society of London, said: 'We are grateful and indebted to those who, with Far Eastern knowledge, lead the public opinion of this country in the right direction'.[16]

Again there are reports in the Foreign Ministry archives around August 1932 that 'the Conservative party in the House of Commons will strongly support the policy of Japan in Manchuria'.[17] In short, the Japanese may have had some grounds for believing that they were securing support in influential circles, but there was also a strong element of wishful thinking in their deductions. However one explains it, the Foreign Ministry officials were under a serious misapprehension if they believed that Britain could have entertained any suggestion for cooperation in China in 1932. In Britain as a parliamentary democracy it would have led to a tremendous outcry of indignation from all shades of the political spectrum.

Yet the ideas contained in this document seem to have become a sort of blueprint for Japan's foreign policy and there are recurring references to it. This was natural enough since the government of Admiral Saitō continued in office until July 1934. A new foreign minister, Hirota Kōki, came to power in September 1933 and reiterated the same views in his interviews and speeches. In private, the senior officials were taking a similar line. In a note of April 1933 Tōgō Shigenori, the head of the Europe-American Division, had written that Britain and Japan had much in common in China and there were good grounds for the two to cooperate there.[18] Shigemitsu, who became vice-minister in May 1933, put forward similar sentiments, though he sometimes spoke against undue involvement with Britain. So the theme of Anglo-Japanese cooperation was not infrequently heard in 1933–4.

But how did Britain react? In the first place, Britain was pleased that the animus which she had attracted because many Japanese assumed that the Lytton report had been drafted in a way that reflected Britain's anti-Japanese sentiments had proved to be short-lived.[19] She was also gratified that there was a lull in the Sino-Japanese fighting following the Manchurian incident, despite the anxieties in the other direction at the time of the Jehol operation. But this has to be set against the hostility to Britain (among others) implied in the Amō declaration of 17 April 1934.[20] This incautious statement seemed to suggest that Japan was anxious to establish hegemony in China. Simultaneously there were the difficult negotiations in 1933–4 over the Indian commercial treaty. Nonetheless Britain did respond to the various voices favouring Anglo-Japanese cooperation, largely because it suited her to do so in the context of defence, and especially the naval limitation treaties (for which the preliminary talks were due to open in London in October 1934).

The story of the so-called Anglo-Japanese 'rapprochement' of 1934 has been the subject of many great studies. D. Cameron Watt, Ann Trotter, Stephen Endicott, Hosoya Chihiro, Stephen Pelz and Kibata Yōichi have each contributed to the understanding of the problem.[21] Professor Trotter has edited the Foreign Office Confidential Print for both Japan and China and the volumes for Japan in the 1930s are eagerly awaited by all students of eastern affairs. The focus of research has tended to move on to more recent periods. But, in an important new study of the period using the personal papers of Neville Chamberlain, Gill Bennett, one of the editorial assistants for the *Documents on British Foreign Policy*, analyses how a rift developed within the cabinet and government over their perceptions of the proper course for east Asia. The fundamental cause was the difference between the sources of information available to the Treasury and the Foreign Office.

> The Foreign Office, naturally, paid attention to their representatives in the field, even if they were not always guided by them: most of the Chancellor's information came from London, filtered through from the Far East. The views of British firms in China were put by their influential but London-based directors: the views of the Japanese Government found their way through the somewhat shady figure of A.H.F. Edwardes... If more localized information was required, the Treasury had to send someone to get it: hence the Federation of British Industries Mission of 1934, and the Leith-Ross Mission of 1935–6.[22]

But the competing policies that emerged resulted in compromises. In the end Chamberlain 'could not achieve the impossible by sheer force of will [within Britain] and it was not possible to force either China or Japan to conform to a line of policy merely because it was reasonable or sensible, or even advantageous'.[23] This view accords well with that of the older study by Ann Trotter, 'Backstage Diplomacy: Britain and Japan in the 1930s', and by the more general study of British foreign policies in the 1930s by Brian McKercher which argues that Britain was still pre-eminent in the world, even if not powerful.[24] It seems to be a natural deduction from this that Britain was inclined on the whole to uphold her standing in the east, even if her power to do so was limited or even illusory.

To aid our understanding, three volumes in the series, *Documents on British Foreign Policy, 1919–39*, second series, volumes XIII, XX and XXI, have appeared in recent years. It is perhaps true that they do not radically alter the profile of the relationship between London and Tokyo as depicted by earlier writers. But they are notable for their masterly prefaces by Professor W.N. Medlicott. It is worth quoting, from the preface to volume XX, his authoritative view:

> [When the present Volume closes] at the beginning of November 1936, British attitudes on Far Eastern policy remained basically the same as they had been in 1933: a desire for friendly relations with Japan, tempered by annoyance at Japan obstruction to British interests in the Far East, and alarm at her aggressive stance towards China.[25]

It was a time when Britain was probing – perhaps blindly and certainly not unanimously – into the nature of Japanese internationalism.

The Foreign Office did not move in reaction to Hirota's statements of goodwill when he took up office in September 1933. Its officials had the feeling that they contained more rhetoric than substance. In December, it was concluded that Britain should hold fast to her policy of non-recognition of Manchukuo and should not risk antagonising the United States, as was inevitable if she were to toy with the idea of reverting to the Anglo-Japanese alliance.[26] But this diplomatic line had to be considered in the light of Britain's defence requirements which had taken on top priority because the Washington and London naval treaties could be denounced in December 1934 subject to two years' notice being given. At the cabinet on 14 March of that year there was some support for the idea of an Anglo-Japanese non-aggression pact, especially if Japan could thereby be induced not to press for equality in naval armament.[27] But Prime Minister J. Ramsay MacDonald felt that the American Democratic leaders would not take such a pact at face value and would treat it merely as an alliance. MacDonald, however, was ailing and was shortly to make way for Neville Chamberlain, his able and opinionated Chancellor of the Exchequer, who was to serve as acting prime minister during the critical months of August and September.

The issue was unresolved and continued in the background of discussions on defence topics throughout the summer. Meanwhile a new ambassador, Sir Robert Clive, took up his appointment and was told on 3 July that Japan was prepared to conclude non-aggression pacts with America and Britain.[28] It would appear that Clive's report was studied in greater detail because the ministers were on holiday, clear of parliamentary business. Sir John Simon, the foreign secretary, seems to have come round to seeing the advantages of a non-aggression pact, and Neville Chamberlain came out very strongly in favour of what he mischievously called a 'Simon–Hirota pact'.[29] He clearly implied that it was a Japanese initiative that Britain was taking up. Simon, however, encountered resistance from Far Eastern experts in the Foreign Office. Eventually at a Cabinet meeting on 25 September after the parliamentary vacation it was agreed to proceed circumspectly with further enquiries from Hirota.[30] The latter, however, seems to have been using the British 'overtures' as a countermove against the navy and had already conceded defeat when the Cabinet on 7 September decided to go into the naval talks on the basis of a 'ceiling' for naval strength of all signatories, a solution which was known to be unacceptable to the US. The domestic battle had been lost; and the British talks consequently lapsed.[31]

The failure of the preliminary naval discussions led to Japan's decision to give notice of quitting the naval limitation schemes. This was followed by a number of reverses for Anglo-Japanese reconciliation. There was first the snub to Sir Frederick Leith-Ross during his sojourn in Tokyo in September 1935 on his way as emissary to China in order to assist in clearing up her financial problems.[32] Then the Japanese negotiators withdrew from the London naval conference in January 1936.[33] In the autumn there was a serious episode at Keelung in Taiwan when three British naval ratings were arrested; and the announcement was made of the anti-comintern pact between Germany and Japan which was suspected (rightly) of having secret clauses.[34] It was possible to explain these episodes as actions of the Japanese army and navy designed to embarrass the more discreet civilians. But it was generally felt in Britain that 'the military party' was in the ascendant and did not want to make a deal.

Ambassador Matsudaira returned to Tokyo in August 1935 with the expectation that he would return to London once again. Given the fact that he had already served at the Court of St James for six and a half years, it would have been exceptional for him to receive an extension of appointment. But he genuinely felt that his years in London had been successful, that the relationship was critical and that his experience would be valuable for his country in riding the storm. Before his departure he had been well briefed on Britain's ideas for improving relations and there is evidence that he conscientiously took these matters up in the appropriate quarters.[35] One thing that obstructed a return to cordiality was the presence in China of Leith-Ross, which was regarded in Japan with excessive suspicion. It was, of course, a strange irony that the Leith-Ross mission – in some ways the brainchild of the Chamberlain–Fisher circle, which might be described as 'pro-Japanese' – was widely regarded in Tokyo as an example of confront-ation. Eventually, however, as a result of Matsudaira's efforts at persuasion in Kasumigaseki and Neville Chamberlain's pressure on Leith-Ross, the latter was induced to pay a second visit to Japan which was several degrees more profitable than the first. By the time he returned in June 1936 to Shanghai (shortly before his return to Britain), the awkwardness was appreciably overcome. Meanwhile on 9 March it was gazetted that Matsudaira had been appointed Minister of the Imperial Household. It was with genuine surprise that he had to tell Britain of his change of plans.[36] But there was a genuine desire that the improvement that he had initiated should be pursued.

The approach came from an unexpected quarter. Shigemitsu, who gave up his functions as vice-minister for foreign affairs in April wrote a letter to Arthur Edwardes, the agent for the Manchukuo government in London, the following month. Shigemitsu had known Edwardes in Shanghai when the former had been consul-general and the latter officiating Inspector-General of the Chinese Maritime Customs Service. They had subsequently met and had important conversations when Edwardes timed a visit he was making to the east to coincide with the FBI visit to Japan and Manchukuo in September 1934. (It seems more appropriate to describe it as a 'visit' since the use of the word 'mission' suggests the existence of some government mandate.) Edwardes reported with particular optimism to Sir Warren Fisher, the permanent secretary to the Treasury, on his parleys with Shigemitsu and others.[37]

The role of Edwardes in London is shrouded in obscurity. Arthur Edwardes, a long-term member of the Maritime Customs Service since 1904, had been appointed to head the organisation *ad interim* in 1927. A casualty partly of revolutionary nationalism which gripped China around 1928 and partly of tensions between north and south, he was forced to retire in January 1929 at the age of 45. Though in receipt of a pension from China, he accepted a position as a sort of consultant to the government of Manchukuo after its creation in 1932 and assisted its delegation in Geneva at the meetings of the League of Nations Assembly before the crucial vote on 24 February 1933.[38] He then spent time in Manchukuo and Japan before returning to London for duties, the nature of which is far from clear. Suffice it to say that at the start of 1934 he was operating from an office in central London with the telegraphic address 'MANCAGENT'. From this it may be deduced that he was acting as the agent for the Manchukuo government. It would appear that his remit was primarily to deal with businessmen and the Federation of British Industries who were hopeful of an open door into Manchukuo. From there it spread naturally to the Treasury where Edwardes seems to have struck up a special relationship with Fisher. While it was slightly irregular for an agent of Manchukuo, which was not recognised by the British government, to be associated with a senior official, Edwardes was able to make his approaches through the Japanese embassy.[39]

In the light of this, Shigemitsu's letter to Edwardes deserves to be reproduced in full:

...During these several weeks past since I was relieved of the Vice-Ministership I have been taking rest – a much-needed rest. At the same time, I have been unable to keep my mind off the many and varied questions pending between Japan and other countries – especially the British Empire. To you as a personal friend and as a staunch supporter of Anglo-Japanese cooperation I feel I may be allowed to state freely and frankly my private thoughts regarding such matters.

The traditional friendship between England and Japan since the days of the Alliance is a most precious link between East and West and a mainstay of world peace. This is not diplomatic rhetoric but a literal truth as you and I honestly believe with thousands of our fellow-countrymen. While the warm and fraternal sentiments between our peoples are as much in evidence as ever, a sincere desire for close unity and collaboration finds expression in various ways on both sides – such as for instance in the discussion of the question of the renewal of the Anglo-Japanese Alliance, which is still kept up in certain quarters.

On the other hand, there exist, one must admit, clashes of material interests, which give rise to mutual distrust and apprehensions. You are no doubt aware of the prevailing impression in this country regarding the British activities in China, which are branded here as political manoeuvres directed against Japan. I know my country is being accused by some prominent Englishmen of scheming to drive British influence from China, although, as a matter of fact, the British foothold has been strengthened recently in China. These charges and counter-charges, however unjust and baseless, indicate the existence of an unwholesome atmosphere created by misunderstanding and mistrust.

In the commercial field, the conflicts of interest are as certainly visible as they are real – in India, in Canada, in Egypt, in Australia and practically in all parts of the globe. The Japanese are extremely irritated under the pressure of British policy against the legitimate expansion of their trade, which is of vital necessity to their national existence and growth, and which, despite the alarm so loudly sounded, constitutes only 3 or 4 per cent of world trade. Here our grievances are justified, I believe, to a large extent.

Then, there is the naval question, although in this case the difficulties may not prove too serious.

A general conversation between the two Governments on the subject of the Anglo–Japanese relations as a whole may be quite valuable; it may help pave the way for an amicable solution of individual questions as these are more or less inter-related. What do you think of such a conversation? A general readjustment and rehabilitation of British–Japanese relations should not prove too difficult if only the traditional sentiments of amity and goodwill between our two peoples were properly mobilized and the spirit of equity and fair play kept alive.

This is of course my private idea and as such I am passing it on to you. But I can assure you that many Japanese are anxious to see something done. The only thing that can be done, to begin with anyway, appears to be that the two Governments come together and talks [*sic*] the whole matter over...[40]

It is unclear how and when this personal letter reached its destination. But we know that on 11 July Edwardes prepared a typed copy of it and passed it to Howell Arthur Gwynne (1865–1950), the venerable editor of the *Morning Post*, with the suggestion that 'much valuable use can be made of it if it is shown to the *select few*'. Gwynne replied on 13 July that it was something which 'I can make good use of quietly and confidentially'.[41] The meaning of this exchange is by no means clear. It is not certain who were 'the select few'. Gwynne was famous as a person close to the right wing of the Conservative Party (though not to Winston

Churchill). It may be deduced that he was in some way close to the Chamberlain–Fisher circle.

It is too much to imagine that Shigemitsu sent this unsolicited private letter without some specific purpose. Despite the disclaimer, we have to assume that it had been officially approved. There had been much havoc in the Foreign Ministry following the mutiny of 26 February and the fall of the ministry which resulted. The new prime minister, Hirota, had himself taken over as foreign minister and continued to serve until the appointment of Arita on 2 April. Shigemitsu appears to have stayed in office until the nomination of his successor on 10 April. It would seem likely that the letter had been in contemplation while Shigemitsu was still in office. Two factors could have brought it to the fore: one was Matsudaira's return to Tokyo; the other – and more likely – was the decision of Hirota to send Yoshida Shigeru as ambassador to London. Hirota was ashamed that he had not been able to get his way with the army over the appointment of Yoshida to the cabinet as foreign minister and offered him instead the opportunity of going to the Court of St James.[42] Yoshida had no hesitation in accepting on 9 April, because he felt it was desirable both from Japan's domestic crisis and from the depressing international situation. He told correspondents when he went to report his departure to the Ise shrine that he had high expectations of what he could do in London.[43] He also wanted to have an exchange of views en route, with the administration in Washington. He met Secretary Cordell Hull on 12 June. So Yoshida was carefully preparing the ground in advance for a new diplomatic 'offensive' when he reached London.

The new Japanese ambassador showed the accustomed shrewdness in settling in at his post. He reached London on 23 June and went to Buckingham Palace to present his credentials three days later. After being introduced to Foreign Office staff, he lunched with Neville Chamberlain on 20 July and met Sir Horace Wilson, the chief industrial adviser. There was a special luncheon also for Yoshida to meet members of the Barnby mission. These were persons identified by the Japanese as their natural friends. They deduced – and their friends did not dispute the notion – that the Foreign Office was by and large hostile to Japan and that their allies were to be found in the Treasury, the Board of Trade, the Conservative party and the Federation of British Industries. It was naturally in that direction that they pushed their initiatives, spurred on by a press campaign in the *Asahi*.[44]

The press was not neglected. Even before the Shigemitsu letter arrived, Edwardes wrote to Gwynne on 15 June as follows:

> [Yoshida] is intensely pro-British and believes that the only solution of the Far Eastern problem is cooperation between Japan and ourselves, and, as you know, he was the 'fons et origo' of the conversation of [?at] your dinner party. Although this fact is manifestly unpublishable, I think it would be an excellent idea to refer to Yoshida's definite policy as expressed by him on his departure from Tokyo.[45]

It is difficult to judge whether this letter led to any press campaign in the *Morning Post*. But Yoshida did meet Gwynne shortly afterwards.

In due course at the end of October Yoshida through Edwardes passed over a draft memorandum to Neville Chamberlain. It was to serve as the basis for discussions leading to an Anglo-Japanese understanding. In the end, the negotiators could not find a satisfactory formula and it lapsed. This is not the place to follow this personal initiative by a purposeful and determined ambassador who was probably not influential enough to carry the proposal with his own government. The story has been well told elsewhere;[46] and need not be repeated here. Our purpose has been to show how many-sided were the approaches between the two nations to prevent alienation at this time.

We have tried in this paper to analyse some aspects of the Anglo-Japanese relationship before the breakdown around the start of the Sino-Japanese war. There is much truth in Dr Lowe's description of this period when he writes, 'the demands on British resources were so formidable that diplomatic ingenuity offered the only realistic way of resolving issues and of averting confrontation'.[47] In the period between 1937 and 1941 Britain used 'diplomatic ingenuity' to ensure that the concessions she made were minimal, that is, a vulnerable Britain conceded enough to avoid forcible confrontation. Before 1937 Britain was not inclined to make concessions. Thus, when it was decided to send out Sir Frederick Leith-Ross to China in May 1935, Britain did not seek Japan's permission in advance.[48] It was an independent action which was in the nature of a challenge to Japan and the Amō declaration, despite the fact that the idea originated with the Chamberlain–Fisher group. It was the last occasion when London would be so imprudent and incautious.

The gradual alienation which has been the subject of this paper began with the two countries keeping their distance in the 1920s, respecting each other's positions at the naval conference and to a modest extent cooperating in China. But Britain would not entertain talk of a return to the alliance, though the idea popped up informally from time to time. The drift received a jolt with the Manchurian and Shanghai crises. These exposed the fallibility of government in both countries. On the one hand, civil government in Japan which still had the upper hand in the days of the alliance was shown to have yielded power in effect to the service leaders. On the other, the vulnerability of Britain's imperial territories and world-wide commercial and investment interests was revealed. The exploration of positions which is sometimes given the title of the 'Anglo-Japanese rapprochement' took place between two countries which were 'estranged' but felt it to be in their interest to seek out a workmanlike formula for damage limitation.

Multiple Diplomacy was a factor which existed in both Britain and Japan and is a fertile area for research. In Britain, when a foreign secretary is not assertive, other ministers in the financial or trade departments may well encroach on his functions. This was true especially in a time of depressed trading like the early thirties. Outside government, others were also chipping away at the walls of Anglo-Japanese estrangement (though not in a coordinated campaign): Sir Harry MacGowan of ICI, A.H.F. Edwardes, the Federation of British Industry, and some right-wing newspapers. In the long run, these attempts at outflanking the Foreign Office all failed, though they may have had an influence on thinking in Japan. In that country there was a similar pattern. Within the ministry General Araki, the war minister, often interfered with foreign policy.[49] Within the Foreign Ministry there was the rivalry between factions seeking to hi-jack the making of policy, the pro-British group being the Shin-Ei-Beiha. Then there were the court officials presided over by Count Makino with his long-term claim to be an Anglophile.[50] Ambassador Matsudaira Tsuneo whose return to Tokyo in August 1935 left the London embassy dangerously empty for a year became a valuable addition to the court party as Minister to the Imperial Household. And what of Yoshida Shigeru? It seems unlikely that a self-confident, innovative and influential diplomat like Yoshida did not have some plan underlying his secret visit to the UK in October 1934.[51] So the story of Anglo-Japanese relations in the 1930s has many instances where individual initiatives played a part. But in most cases they had only peripheral influence on policy-making. On the other hand, there were few who predicted outright war between Britain and Japan before Japan's war with China began. There was of course Ishimaru Tōta, author of *Japan Must Fight England* (1934) but the sensational English title reflects neither the Japanese title (*Nichi-Ei hissenron*) nor the contents of the work.[52] There was certainly a wide and widening gulf between the two in the 1930s; but they were trying to live with their differences and contain their disagreements.

## NOTES

1. I.H. Nish (ed.), *Anglo-Japanese Alienation, 1919–52: Papers of the Anglo-Japanese Conference on the History of the Second World War* (Cambridge, 1982) p. 279.
2. C. Hosoya in Nish, *Alienation*, p. 10.
3. D. Dakin (ed.), *Documents on British Foreign Policy, 1919–1939*, 1st series, vol. xiv, nos. 415–16 (hereafter cited as DBFP).
4. I.H. Nish, *Alliance in Decline: A Study in Anglo-Japanese Relations, 1908–23* (London, 1972) p. 387; A.J. Bacevich, *Diplomat in Khaki: Major General Frank McCoy and American Foreign Policy, 1898–1949* (Lawrence, Kansas, 1989) pp. 107–8.
5. Bamba Nobuya, *Japanese Diplomacy in a Dilemma: New Light on Japan's China Policy, 1924–9* (Kyoto, 1972) pp. 264–8.
6. Cabinet resolution of 27 August 1932, in *Nihon gaikō nempyō narabi ni shuyō bunsho* 2 vols. (Tokyo, 1955) vol. ii, p. 208. (Hereafter cited as NGNB).

7.   W.J. Oudendyk, *Ways and By-ways in Diplomacy* (London, 1939) passim, esp. p. 369; Yoshizawa Kenkichi, *Gaikō 60-nen* (Tokyo, 1958) p. 92ff.
8.   For the outbreak of the Manchurian crisis, see I.H. Nish, *Japan's Struggle with Internationalism: Japan, China and the League of Nations 1931–3* (London, 1992).
9.   Note by Wellesley, 'Anglo-Japanese Relations and the Present Crisis in China', 1 Feb 1932, in *DBFP*, 2 (ix), no. 239.
10.  *DBFP*, 2 (ix), no. 238 fn.
11.  Hosoya, in Nish, *Alienation*, chs. 1 and 3.
12.  *The Times* (London) , 24 October 1935.
13.  'Kokusai kankei yori mitaru jikyoku shori hōshin an', in *NGNB*, ii, 206–10.
14.  *Ibid*, esp. p. 208.
15.  Ogata Sadako, *Defiance in Manchuria, 1931–2* (Berkeley, 1964) p. 164; Hosoya, in Nish, *Alienation*, p. 17.
16.  General Homma, address to Japan Society of London, quoted in F.S.G. Piggott, *Broken Thread* (Aldershot, 1950) pp. 239–40.
17.  Japan, Foreign Ministry archives, A.1.1.0.21-12-2.
18.  Tōgō Shigenori, *Jidai no ichi-men* (Tokyo, 1951) pp. 82–98, esp. 85–8.
19.  This point is hard to document, but was mentioned to the author by F.T. Ashton-Gwatkin, CMG.
20.  *DBFP*, 2 (xx), no. 107.
21.  D. Cameron Watt, 'Britain, the United States and Japan in 1934', in *Personalities and Policies* (London, 1965); Ann Trotter, *Britain and East Asia, 1933–7* (London, 1975); S.L. Endicott, *Diplomacy and Enterprise: British China Policy, 1933–7* (Manchester, 1975); C. Hosoya, '1934 -nen no Nichi-Ei fukashin kyōtei mondai' in *Kokusai Seiji*, 58 (1977) pp. 69–85; S.E. Pelz, *Race to Pearl Harbor* (Cambridge, Mass., 1974); Y. Kibata, 'Igirisu no tai -Nichi seisaku 1934' in Tokyo University *Kyoyo gakka kiyō* 1977, pp. 1–26.
22.  Gill Bennett, 'British Policy in the Far East, 1933–6: Treasury and Foreign Office', in *Modern Asian Studies* 25 (1991).
23.  Bennett, *ibid*.
24.  A. Trotter, 'Backstage Diplomacy: Britain and Japan in the 1930s', *Journal of Oriental Studies* (Hong Kong), 15 (1977), pp. 37–45; B.J.M. McKercher, 'Our Most Dangerous Enemy: Great Britain Pre-eminent in the 1930s', *International History Review* 13 (1991), pp. 751–9.
25.  *DBFP*, 2 (xx), xv.
26.  Memo by C. Orde, 14 Dec 1933 in *DBFP*, 2 (xx), no. 64.
27.  *DBFP*, 2 (xiii), pp. 2–3 and 2 (xx), no. 97.
28.  *DBFP*, 2 (xx), nos. 148–9 and 2 (xiii), no. 8, note 1, which seems to confirm that Clive's message was sent telegraphically but did not immediately attract attention.
29.  *DBFP*, 2 (xiii), nos. 8 and 14.
30.  *DBFP*, 2 (xiii), nos. 19 and 21.
31.  *DBFP*, 2 (xiii), nos. 22 and 29. The best Japanese account is in *Gaimushō no 100-nen* (Tokyo, 1969), ii, pp. 515–19, which documents the considerable Foreign Ministry opposition to ending the treaty system.
32.  *DBFP*, 2 (xx), no. 343 and pp. 1003–43.
33.  *Gaimushō no 100-nen* ii, pp. 520–2; Admiral Nagano to Foreign Office, 15 January 1936 in *DBFP*, 2 (xiii), no. 622.
34.  *DBFP*, 2 (xx), nos. 593 and 597; DBFP, 2 (xxi), no. 5.
35.  Sir Samuel Hoare, speech, 19 June 1935 in *Proceedings of the Japan Society* (London), 33 (1936), p. 32.
36.  Matsudaira to Japan Society, 9 March 1936, *ibid*., p. xxi.
37.  *DBFP*, 2 (xx), no. 174.

38. South Manchuria Railway, *Fourth Report on Progress in Manchuria*, Dairen, 1934, p. 91.
39. Trotter, 'Backstage Diplomacy', p. 44 and fn. 57. Trotter gives evidence that Edwardes had by 1936 become liaison officer with the Japanese embassy.
40. Shigemitsu to Edwardes, May 1936, box 18, H.A. Gwynne papers, Bodleian Library, Oxford.
41. Author's italics. Edwardes to Gwynne, 11 July; Gwynne to Edwardes, 13 July 1936 both in box 18, Gwynne papers.
42. *The Times* (London), 7 and 20 March 1936.
43. *The Times*, 21 May 1936.
44. *The Times*, 8 August 1936.
45. Edwardes to Gwynne, 15 June 1936, box 18, Gwynne papers.
46. *The Times*, 8 August 1936, endorsed the idea editorially: 'This country would welcome the friendship of Japan, a proud and gallant young nation for whom we have always had respect'. Inoki Masamichi, *Hyoden Yoshida Shigeru* 4 vols (Tokyo, 1981), vol. 3, pp. 24ff; articles by Murashima in Kurihara Ken (ed.) *Ningen Yoshida Shigeru* (Tokyo, 1991); I.H. Nish, 'Mr Yoshida at the London Embassy, 1936–8' in *Bulletin of the Japan Society*, (London, 1979), 87, pp. 3–7; John Dower, *Empire and Aftermath* (Cambridge, Mass., 1979) ch. 5.
47. P.C. Lowe in Nish, *Alienation*, p. 103.
48. *DBFP*, 2 (xx), nos. 270 and 325; Hatano Sumio, 'Leith Ross no Kyokuto hōmon to Nihon' in *Kokusai Seiji* 58 (1977) pp. 86–104.
49. M.D. Kennedy, *Estrangement of Great Britain and Japan, 1917–35* (Manchester, 1969), pp. 269–72; A.M. Young, *Imperial Japan, 1926–38* (London, 1938), pp. 182–7.
50. Sir Francis Lindley in Yuki Yoshida, *Whispering Leaves in Grosvenor Square, 1936–7* (London, 1938), p. 7.
51. Cf. Sugiyama in *DBFP*, 2 (xxi), no. 10.
52. Taking up journalism on his dismissal from the navy after the First World War, Lieut. Commander Ishimaru published his *Nichi-Ei hissenron* as one of a large number of alarmist publications. While he was probably an unrepresentative minority voice within the circle of defence writers, the book had a wide readership in Japan and ran to many editions. It was translated into English and published as *Japan Must Fight Britain*. But Japanese newspapers suggested that it should not be taken seriously.

# 2 Winston Churchill, the Military, and Imperial Defence in East Asia
## John Pritchard

As Lord Tedder once remarked, *pace* Ronald Spector's criticisms elsewhere in this volume:

> Surely it is the problems of the early stages of the war which we should study. Those are the difficult problems, those are the practical problems which we and every democratic nation have to solve. There are no big battalions or blank cheques then. Here is the real and vital test of our defence policies.[1]

This chapter deals with the period between September 1939 and December 1941 and examines the military and political qualities of Prime Minister Winston Churchill and of his immediate predecessor.[2]

### CHURCHILL AND THE PHONY WAR

The British declaration of war against Germany on 3 September 1939 did not immediately affect the balance between Eastern and Western imperial strategy. That had already been tipped towards the European theatre. Nevertheless, the seriousness of Britain's imperial liabilities in the Far East continued to alarm British strategists.

On 5 September 1939, the Joint Planning Staff (tellingly characterised as 'the masters of negation' by Arthur Marder,[3] although the phrase scarcely does them full justice) presented the Chiefs of Staff with memoranda concerning what Australia and New Zealand might contribute to the European War. Despite the recent change of government in Japan brought about by the Molotov–Ribbentrop Agreement in mid-August against the background of the Nomonhan Incident, it would, agreed the Joint Planners, be 'unwise' for either of the Antipodean Dominions to despatch an overseas expeditionary force unless Japan declared both her neutrality and her policy in the European conflict.[4] On the other hand, two days later, the Chiefs of Staff were pressed by the Admiralty to leave *only* a light screen of forces in the Mediterranean and in the Far East: almost all of Britain's naval forces ought to be concentrated upon Germany.[5]

There were four major flashpoints where there were acute dangers that an open conflict might erupt between British and Japanese forces and set off a Pacific War.

The first, Hong Kong, was for all intents and purposes a complete write-off, although it had been decided at the time of 1939–40 European Appreciation back in February 1939, to devote at least some effort towards increasing Hong Kong's ability to withstand a light scale of attack and to deny its port facilities to the enemy. In that period, it should be recalled, the British community in Hong Kong was not so large as to distort British appreciations as to that colony's importance as a defence priority.[6]

By contrast, at the second and third flashpoints, Shanghai and Tientsin, it was recognised that the British government was in no position to do anything at all short of committing the Empire to a long-term Pacific war should the British garrisons there be overrun. In the event, the epicentre of that war should lie in South-East Asia.

It was upon Singapore, indeed, where Britain had constructed the largest military base in the Southern Hemisphere, that the security of the eastern half of the British Empire was felt to depend, and where the *Admiralty* now in September 1939 believed that serious thought should be given to doubling the period before relief from three to six months.[7] Remember that from about the time of the German invasion of Austria in March 1938 until the beginning of June 1939, the period before relief had been set at just 70 days (to which was added a further fortnight in calculating the period before reprovisioning).[8] The Chiefs of Staff, therefore, had only recently been persuaded that any increase in the period before relief was necessary at all,[9] so the Admiralty's sudden proposal to double the latest figures was a rather breathtaking increase. Upon closer investigation afterwards, grave doubts arose about whether it was remotely possible to accumulate, much less hold, sufficient military stores and foodstocks (which *inter alia* would include warehousing for 406 006 tons of *padi* rice at a cost of Malayan $25 million).[10] The direct and indirect expenses inherent in doubling the period before relief would be more or less equivalent to half the cost of building another battleship,[11] the sum of all the Imperial contributions which had been made to the defence of Singapore in the entire period up to 1939.[12] This (although it may be vexatious for a later generation of Australians to admit the fact) puts the Antipodean dependency upon others for regional 'self-defence' into its rightful historical perspective and, to an accountant's eye, was £4 788 750, 42 per cent of the total, the equivalent in value to the cost of couple of county-class cruisers.

Logically, if such a step was regarded as necessary, then the strengthening of the garrison and air defences of Malaya and Singapore – with its further costs – ought to have been regarded as relatively high priorities. The Air Staff estimated that its share in increasing the period before relief to six months would cost the Royal Air Force £1.25 million. The War Office, however, evidently regarded doubling the period before relief as a cloud-cuckoo exercise, and given that the Army lacked the resources to make any contribution towards it, the Chief of the Imperial General Staff did not even bother to put a figure on the purely hypothetical cost of supplying non-existent military hardware and stores to augment what was already in place.[13]

The changes in the Admiralty's policy recommendations on this occasion did not proceed, however, from any fundamental change in its perception of the risk that the British Empire might find itself at war against Japan. In fact, during the weeks ahead, the Japanese Prime Minister, General Abe Nobuyuki, did announce his country's non-belligerency and called upon all of the European belligerents to withdraw their forces from China, but Tokyo fell short of declaring Japan's neutrality, and the British Foreign Office, at least, took this to mean that Japan wished to keep her options open.[14] However, the American attitude appeared to be stiffening towards Japan: by the end of September, even Lord Chatfield, Britain's Minister for the Co-ordination of Defence and a man with an excellent memory of American volatility in the Far East,[15] credited the United States with having restrained any temptation that the Japanese might have felt to join forces with Germany in the war against Britain and France.[16] Naturally, the American attitude would have a crucial bearing upon the extent to which the threat of a Japanese mad-dog act ought to be taken seriously.[17]

It therefore comes as no surprise that in a report on 25 September 1939 which the Chiefs of Staff endorsed[18] and passed on to the Cabinet three days later,[19] the Joint Planning Staff looked hard at the Sino-Japanese stalemate in China and came to the conclusion that Japan was unlikely to succeed in winning the war against Chiang Kai-shek by military means and on present form also appeared unlikely to consolidate her economic position in regions already occupied by Japanese forces.[20] So far as the Chiefs of Staff and their Joint Planners were concerned, it would suit Britain well for the Sino-Japanese conflict to continue indefinitely. Throughout the autumn and winter of 1939–40, the Chiefs of Staff and the Foreign Office seemed to concur that it was 'highly unlikely' that Japan would move southward before the China War was under control and Japanese relations with the United States improved. 'The conclusion is that Japan will concentrate all her efforts on the solution of the China Incident,' the Foreign Office predicted on 13 November 1939: 'She will sit on the fence as far as the war in Europe is concerned, keeping her hands free to pick up whatever trade advantages it may offer.'[21]

The War Cabinet, however, while accepting this advice, also recognised that prolongation of the China Incident might have disastrous consequences.[22] There was a clear danger – had been for years – that under the pressure of that war, Anglo-Japanese relations might deteriorate to the point where it might make sense for the Japanese to join Germany and break out into the Pacific. But early in November, perhaps galvanised by the shock of the German submarine attack at Scapa Flow and the loss of the *Royal Oak* on 14 October (which had political repercussions that lasted over the next several weeks), the Cabinet headed the advice of their three Service chiefs and decided to inform the Australian and New Zealand governments that Japanese and Italian neutrality seemed sufficiently secure to permit the Pacific Dominions to despatch troop reinforcements to Europe in relative safety.[23]

Only eleven days later, however, the British and French governments seemed to be sending quite different signals to Tokyo. On 13 November they informed Japan that they intended to withdraw all but token forces from their stations in north China, just as Japan had demanded.[24] News came that a sizeable expedition of Japanese troops had crossed the waters of the Gulf of Tonkin from Hainan north-west to the Chinese mainland at Pakhoi, from whence they began to advance swiftly northward to the railhead at Nanning, once the northern terminus of the French supply route to Chiang Kai-shek's forces. The Dutch, meanwhile, had become so alarmed by the extent to which they believed themselves vulnerable to any impending Japanese attack in the Dutch East Indies that all leave for Dutch troops in Indonesia was cancelled. None of this, however, induced the British Chiefs of Staff to reconsider their conclusion that there was no immediate emergency in the Far East.[25]

At the end of that week, Winston Churchill, as First Lord of the Admiralty, tabled a memorandum for the Cabinet, crafted ultimately for Australian consumption but setting out his own views about Britain's Imperial Defence priorities. With a characteristically rhetorical flourish he explained why he believed Japan would not dare to attack Singapore:

> Singapore is a fortress armed with five 15-inch guns, and garrisoned by nearly 20,000 men. It could only be taken after a siege by an army of at least 50,000 men, who would have to be landed in the marshes and jungle of the isthmus which connects it with the mainland. As Singapore is as far from Japan as Southampton is from New York, the operation of moving a Japanese Army with all its troopships and maintaining it with men and munitions during a siege would be forlorn. Moreover, such a siege, which should last at least four or five months, would be liable to be interrupted if at any time Great Britain chose to send a superior fleet to the scene.... It is not considered possible that the Japanese, who are a prudent people and reserve their strength for the command of the Yellow Seas and China, in which they are fully occupied, would embark upon such a mad enterprise.[26]

Churchill moved on to declare that by the same logic Australia was even less likely than Malaya to be exposed to the risk of a Japanese invasion. He admitted that things might have been different if the Fleet were tied to the European theatre, but Italian neutrality, now assured (as it then seemed), had changed all that: 'The British Fleet,' he said, 'has become again entirely mobile.' Even if Britain could not smash the Japanese fleet in its home waters, a battle squadron could be sent to the East which would be adequate to defend Australia and Singapore. 'The Admiralty,' he declared, 'accepts the *full* responsibility of defending Australia or Singapore from a Japanese attack on a *large* scale.'[27]

Churchill's words on this occasion were in sharp contrast to what he had advocated as recently as 25 March 1939, when, out of political office, he had written Prime Minister Chamberlain as a back-bench MP to suggest that no anxiety in the Far East must deflect His Majesty's Government from its 'prime objective':

> If Japan joins the hostile combination, which is by no means certain, for she has her hands full, all our interests and possessions in the Yellow Sea will be temporarily effaced. We must not be drawn from our main theme by any effort to protect them.[28]

He had added, as an afterthought, 'Only if the United States comes in against Japan could we supply even a squadron of cruisers to operate with them'. From a strategical point of view, this was the stark truth. Yet there was an element of faith in Churchill's remarks that should not escape our notice. It took time for Churchill – like Chamberlain before him – to learn how strongly the United States resisted the commitment of defence forces against Japan prior to the end of 1941. Meanwhile, his delusions about America – which seem genuine enough – helped to steady his Cabinet's resistance to Hitler. He was not, however, the only one prone to such wishful thinking. The British Ambassador in Washington, Lord Lothian, wrote to Lord Halifax on 10 November 1939:

> If the United States is to rely upon Great Britain to prevent totalitarian Europe from entering the Atlantic through the Straits of Gibraltar and the exits from the North Sea, the United States must themselves underwrite the security of the British Empire in the Pacific because they cannot afford the weakening of Great Britain itself which would follow the collapse of her dominions in the Pacific.[29]

Lothian's appreciation did coincide with the grave concern felt by informed circles in Washington about the pattern of change in the world's strategical balance of power. It lacked, however, a realistic appreciation of the verities of political life in Capitol Hill with its vast and myopic hinterland.

Churchill's far too ambitious proposals in November 1939, however, when their implications were understood, all but doomed plans to send precious modern RAF land-based aircraft to bolster Far Eastern defences. If the Admiralty were willing to devote themselves to Far Eastern defence out of existing forces (as they had been hesitant to do in the recent past, in the second quarter of 1939, up to the worst moments during the Tientsin Crisis),[30] then why should the Air Staff divert carefully hoarded squadrons of aircraft to a distant and now quiescent theatre? On the outbreak of the European war, there were only six (some say seven) squadrons of aircraft in the whole of Malaya, 30 per cent below the lower approved scale and 42 per cent below the number which had been accepted by the Committee of Imperial Defence at the time of the European Appreciation in February 1939. There were no fighter aircraft, only two squadrons of torpedo bombers, two squadrons of flying-boats, and two squadrons of Blenheim bombers: hardly a deterrent to the Japanese.[31] What then would become of the decision to double the period before relief from three months to six? Was there to be any substance to it?

At the end of 1939, the Chiefs of Staff and their Joint Planners believed that a thousand Japanese aircraft were involved in active operations in China and Formosa, but a further 1100 frontline aircraft were available for deployment elsewhere. Moreover, the main elements in the Japanese battlefleet had not been engaged at all in the China war, nor, thought the Chiefs of Staff, had more than a minor fraction to the Japanese naval air forces.[32]

A year later, British aircraft production had increased to about 2000 a month, about a quarter of which were contributed by the United States. The overall number included more than a thousand fighter aircraft a month, over 600 bombers a month, about 30 reconnaissance aircraft, and over 80 army co-operation aircraft a month. But the air situation in Malaya since the outbreak of the European war had scarcely improved at all, either qualitatively or numerically.[33] By mid-July 1940, at which time Britain and Australia together had stationed eight squadrons comprising 88 first-line aircraft in Malaya, the Joint Planning Committee had become convinced that an air strength of 22 squadrons comprising 336 first-line aircraft were required to safeguard the defence of Malaya, the north-eastern half of the Indian Ocean, and British North Borneo, 'a very substantial addition to any programme hitherto contemplated'.[34] It was a target which came to be widely approved but never achieved, and for that Churchill has to accept a good deal of personal responsibility. The figure of 336 aircraft was by no means regarded as a conservative one. In a tactical appreciation prepared by the three Service Commanders-in-Chief in the Far East on the eve of the Singapore Defence Conference of October 1940 and only circulated to the Joint Planners in full on 19 December 1940, it was baldly stated that in their opinion 336 aircraft 'would not be adequate' and that they regarded 566 deployed in 29 squadrons (all but six of which would be deployed in Malaya itself) as 'the minimum necessary for adequate defence' of Malaya and the immediately surrounding area necessary for its security.[35] After considering the matter further at the Singapore Defence Conference, they and strong visiting delegations representing the views of Commonwealth defence authorities in the region recommended in their report on 31 October that British air strength in the region should be increased even further, by another squadron of sixteen aircraft (a fighter squadron to be deployed for the defence of Burma).[36]

To return to that very day in November 1939 on which Churchill prepared to submit his grand review to the War Cabinet for approval, his Director of Naval Intelligence, Rear-Admiral John Godfrey, cautiously put an estimate on Japan's *current* naval construction programme at four capital ships, three aircraft carriers, six cruisers, nine destroyers of 1500 tons, fourteen large submarines of about the same displacement, and several minor warships. Moreover, Churchill was informed that Naval Intelligence now anticipated that Japan was likely to spend a further 50 million Yen (£3.31 million) during the current financial year on new construction about which Britain had no further information.[37] It was a sobering portent.

Churchill had the weekend to mull over this advice. He evidently returned on the Monday, 20 November, undeflected by thought. Pressing his memorandum upon his colleagues in the War Cabinet, he demanded their agreement to giving Far Eastern defence a higher priority than British defence interests in the Mediterranean.[38] This was a recommendation which recalls the basic principles of British strategy during the middle years of the thirties, principles that had been fudged as a result of the zigzag course produced by the Admiralty's two 'palace revolutions' in the spring and summer of 1939.[39] Neville Chamberlain, indeed, was quick to point out to Churchill that the First Lord had gone

> rather further than anything agreed upon by the Government in recent discussions before the war, or communicated to the Dominions. The Government had not been prepared to decide, in advance of the event, whether the Mediterranean should be abandoned to allow a Fleet to go to the Far East. In this they had particularly borne in mind the possibility of Italian hostility. They had, however, given the Australian Government the assurance given in [Chamberlain's] telegram of the 20th March, but had not gone further in specifying the action [Britain] should take. It was, of course, true that the neutrality of Italy altered the circumstances envisaged before the war, and on which that telegram was based.[40]

In fact, Chamberlain's remarks were somewhat disingenuous, for he knew full well that one of Churchill's predecessors as First Lord of the Admiralty, Sir Samual Hoare, had given absolute assurances to the Dominion prime ministers at the time of the 1937 Imperial Conference, that in the event of impending hostilities with Japan, Britain would despatch a sufficiently powerful fleet out to Singapore to guarantee the protection of the Dominions. Those assurances, made quite unconditionally and backed by the whole of the Chamberlain Cabinet, were not offered lightly and became, as intended, the bailing wire that kept the self-interests and sentimental attachments of the Dominions tied together in a unified Imperial Defence System.[41] When making this commitment, Britain had made no provision for having to fight more than one European enemy at the same time, but when Churchill now echoed the same sentiments just two and a half years later, the circumstances were roughly comparable to the scenario anticipated by Whitehall in 1937.

Responding to the Prime Minister, Churchill denied having gone beyond Chamberlain's telegram of March 1939. If an attack on Australia should come, he saw no option to sealing the ends of the Mediterranean and going to the Far East. Admiral Lord Chatfield, as Minister for the Co-ordination of Defence, emphatically agreed: this was the line upon which he had staked his own career through thick and thin, ever since being appointed First Sea Lord and Chairman of the Chiefs of Staff in 1933, and, as the unofficial historian of the War Cabinet, he reminded his colleagues that the present situation did indeed fit the conditions foreseen by the Chiefs of Staff and by their ministers in answering the Australians at the 1937 Imperial Conference. Naturally, Britain's new Balkan commitments, agreed by the politicians in the intervening period (and without the benefit of strategical advice, although Chatfield omitted to say so), 'made it very difficult for us to give any specific and detailed assurances to the Dominions'.[42] As Sir Maurice Hankey had occasion to recollect in a diary entry dated 25 August 1939, 'I shivered down my spine when we gave provisional guarantees to Poland and Roumania, because I knew we could not make them good.[43] What had followed there, and subsequently in Greece and elsewhere, was entirely predictable and more of the same. So Chatfield came pretty close to the bone when he reminded the Cabinet on that late November morning, that 'It was evident that we could not give a 100 percent guarantee. Much must depend on the actual situation.[44]

Chamberlain replied that the Churchill memorandum allowed far too much to be read into it: it could be interpreted as 'an announcement of our intention to send a Fleet to Singapore the moment Japan declared war'. But Churchill rather lamely argued that the Dominions would understand the true position if they read his memorandum alongside previous papers. He explained that:

> It was important to reassure the Dominions, so they would consent to the despatch of their forces [to Europe]; and he thought it was right, in present circumstances, in telling the Australians that we should come to their aid in the event of a great invasion – a contingency which he thought extremely remote.[45]

On this basis, the War Cabinet approved Churchill's paper but added a rider that in its exposition to the Dominion Ministers in the afternoon, it should be emphasised that the policy iterated in Chamberlain's 20 March telegram still remained valid.[46] When Churchill returned to the Cabinet three days later, on Thursday, 23 November, he reported that Richard Casey, leader of the Australian Delegation, had been warmed by the memorandum and chilled by the explanations. Stanley Bruce, the Australian High Commissioner, had protested that Britain had promised to send seven capital ships to Singapore once Japan entered the war (an undertaking repeated as recently as the time of the Tientsin Crisis), but Churchill had wriggled out of this with an argument that Japan would have to do more than merely declare war before Britain could 'immobilize a large portion of our fleet' by despatching it to the Far East.[47] Because of the Australian objections, however, Churchill drafted a new version in consultation with the two successive Ministers for the Co-ordination of Defence, Lord Chatfield and Sir Thomas Inskip, together with the Permanent Head of the Foreign Office, Sir Alexander Cadogan. Extended to include New Zealand, too, and as slightly modified and approved by the War Cabinet, it now read in part:

> we wish to make it plain that we regard the defence of Australia and New Zealand, and of Singapore as a stepping stone to these two Dominions, as ranking next to the mastering of the principle fleet to which we are opposed, and that if the choice were presented of defending them against a serious attack, or sacrificing British interests in the Mediterranean, our duty to our kith and kin would take precedence.[48]

This reassurance sufficiently satisfied the Australian delegation that afternoon for Casey to inform the British that he would wire Canberra recommending the dispatch of an Australian Expeditionary Force, and that he hoped it might set sail as early as mid-December.[49] And so, at the end of November, there was a remarkable unanimity in policy statements which papered over the grave uneasiness which all concerned felt about the ability of the British Government to deliver the goods in the event of a war against Japan. The Joint Planners, for instance, in a report on future military policy in the Middle East noted (with an eye on the possibility of Italian intervention in the war) that 'it must be remembered that our interests in the Middle East, important as they are, are not as important as the security of France, Britain, or of Singapore.[50] And the Chiefs of Staff, in their subsequent Review of the Middle East, declared that the sea route through the Mediterranean, the Suez Canal and the Red Sea to the East, was Britain's 'primary' strategic interest in that theatre, followed by the Anglo-Iranian oilfields and the Indian Northwest Frontier. But they also emphasised, 'We require depth to defend these interests,'[51] and there, of course, lay the rub.

Certainly, at the time of the outbreak of the European War, and notwithstanding the alarm that the Tientsin Crisis had produced only three months earlier, the naval defences of Malaya and Singapore were in a deplorable state. Six motor torpedo boats had been expected that had not yet arrived; six destroyers had been allocated, but two were on loan to Hong Kong, one was at its home port (although ready for sea), and the other three were not expected to arrive until February 1940 at the earliest! There were no crews for the minesweepers and other auxillary anti-submarine vessels, and there were only two submarines to patrol the Straits of Malacca. Force Emu, which had been sent out from India during the Tientsin Crisis, it was a lightly armed mobile force intended for jungle warfare. The defence of northern Malaya had been left to the Federated Malayan Straits Volunteers, the defence of Johore was down to the local sultan's people, there was a Malay battalion at Port Dickson, one Indian battalion at Taiping and another at Penang. And that was all there was, apart from woefully inadequate British and Indian forces cooped up in the Singapore garrison.[52] There was no proper civil defence organisation, no air-raid warning system worthy of the name, no sense of urgency in civil administration, and perhaps worst of all, no provision had been made for the coordination of the three services at Singapore. Governor Sir Shenton Thomas, for all of his faults, did try to get Lieutenant-General Bond and Air Vice-Marshal John Tremayne Babington, the two men upon whose judgement, as the commanders of the British Army and Air Forces in Malaya, so much would depend prior to the arrival of the Fleet, to agree on a common strategy. Sir Shenton was totally unsuccessful. The Secretary of Defence in Malaya, C.A. Vlieland, known as 'Starchy Archy', prepared an appreciation in July 1940 which went much further than the more famous appreciation made by Lieutenant-General Sir William Dobbie in 1937–38 and described in considerable detail how the Japanese would, and did, attack. Vlieland's advice was ignored and he resigned.[53]

Provided that the real defence of Malaya and Singapore could be left to the main fleet upon its prompt arrival at Singapore, all this might not have mattered. But Churchill circulated a note to the War Cabinet prepared by the Naval Staff which pointed out that the recent modernisation of the Japanese battlefleet had increased its efficiency to the point where any British fleet sent to the Far East must be composed of the most up-to-date vessels possessed by the Royal Navy. In particular, the four Royal Sovereign-class battleships were now regarded as entirely unsuitable for operations in the Far East, given their low speed and comparatively short gun-range. Provided the French could be counted upon to stand firm, 'it might be considered that it would be sufficient to retain the *R*-class battleships in home waters and send the *whole* of the remainder of the Fleet to the Far East.'[54] Given the uncertainty that all three services felt about the likelihood that the fleet could be spared in sufficient time and strength, this was all pretty appalling for the defence of what had long been regarded as one of the two 'keystones' upon which the very survival of the British Empire depended.[55] Two months later, staring invasion in the face as the prospect of the collapse of French drew nigh, the Chiefs of Staff were to report on 25 May 1940 that if France were overrun, '*we do not think we could continue the war with any chance of success*' [their italics] unless the United States were 'willing to give us full economic and financial support'.[56] And far more than this was likely to be necessary in the Far East, as the Chiefs of Staff made abundantly clear:

> The retention of Singapore is very important [*sic*: the word 'vital', previously attached to Singapore's priority in Imperial defence, now seems to have been dropped from their vocabulary!] for economic control, particularly of rubber and tin. To counter Japanese action in the Far East, a fleet, adequately supported by airforces, is necessary at Singapore. It is most improbable that we could send any naval forces there, and reliance would have to be placed upon the United States to safeguard our interests.[57]

The sense of helplessness among the Chiefs of Staff increased as the next few weeks passed. On 13 June, with a candour born of black despair and in compliance with instructions from the War Cabinet, the Chiefs of Staff prepared an *aide mémoire* for Ambassador Lothian in Washington. 'The collapse of France would provide Japan with the temptation to take action against French, British or Dutch interests in the Far East,' they wrote; 'We see no hope of being able to despatch a fleet to Singapore. It will therefore be vital [ah, that word, again!] that the United States of America should publicly declare her intention to regard any alteration of the *status quo* in the Far East as a *casus belli*.'[58] It is difficult to conceive of a more direct or desperate appeal. The British Empire, staring into the abyss of defeat, was clutching at a last straw to save its very existence. It is important to preserve our sense of that moment, and to recall it, as we turn our attention to a new storm that now threatened to sweep Britain into that defeat: the Burma Road crisis.

## THE BURMA ROAD CRISIS

Before the European campaigns had opened in the spring of 1940, Britain had steadfastly ignored Japanese demands to stop the flow of supplies to China except when Japanese troops physically block the roads beyond British territory. However, with the onset of the spring campaigns in Europe, followed by the collapse of France in May and June, and a decision by Marshal Petain's government to close the road and rail links from the port of Haiphong in Indo-China to the province of Yunnan in southern China, Britain's position on the Burma Road became a burning issue. Directly after the evacuation of the British Army form Dunkirk ended on 4 June, the British had yielded to Japanese pressure and yet managed to extract a reasonable compromise agreement which finally settled the long-running Tientsin dispute. It was hoped that this sop would appease the Japanese, particularly as Britain could not possibly hope to gain from the continuance of friction there.[59] However, a week later, Japan presented Britain with what amounted to an ultimatum on a much more important issue: the Burma Road. The Japanese had decided that the time had come to sever the West's last remaining major supply line to China. There was still a small trickle of European and American supplies reaching the Chinese, smuggled through the Japanese forces surrounding Hong Kong. And arms continued to flow from the Soviet Union to China across the desolate wastes of Sinkiang. But the volume of traffic on the Burma Road was about twenty times greater than that.

Warned correctly by Ambassador Sir Robert Craigie in Tokyo that although the present Japanese government did not seek to make the Burma Road issue a *casus belli* Japanese extremists were absolutely determined to close the supply route whatever the consequences, London reluctantly accepted the need for compromise despite the symbolic importance of the Burma Road in gaining or retaining American sympathy for Britain.[60] After discovering that the United States would not promise active support to Britain if the Burma Road issue escalated to the point where war might become inevitable, the British and Japanese agreed to a proposal, first recommended by Ambassador Craigie, to suspend traffic over the road for three months in exchange for a Japanese promise to seek a prompt Sino-Japanese peace settlement. The Burma Road Agreement is usually regarded as a major setback for British prestige and an example of perfidious Albion's habitual appeasement of aggressors at the expense of those who depended upon British help: American isolationists made great play with these themes and claimed that it proved the British Empire was beyond redemption physically and spiritually. This affair had finally brought down the moribund Cabinet of Admiral Yonai Mitsumasa on 16 July 1940, but, as he was enabled to do under the Japanese Constitution, the outgoing Foreign Minister, Arita Hachiro, signed the Burma Road Agreement on the 17th, five days before his successor, Matsuoka Yosuke, took office under the incoming prime minister, Prince Konoye Fumimaro, on the 22 July.

The Agreement was no less unpopular in leading Whitehall circles. Lord Halifax, although generally regarded as an 'arch appeaser', had resisted the Burma Road Agreement and, with the Foreign Office as a whole, regarded the Agreement as deplorable and evidently did his best to block it. For a time Prime

Minister Winston Churchill – and the governments of Australia and New Zealand – shared the Foreign Office's view. At first they saw no real advantages in the Agreement and anticipated that it would have a deplorable effect on American, Soviet and Chinese opinion as well as upon domestic morale in Britain. The crisis came at a time when leading members of Churchill's Cabinet and senior politicians of all parties were far from convinced that they should follow Churchill in rejecting German peace initiatives that had been extended through the channels of King Gustav of Sweden, Pope Pius XII, and the Swiss and Spanish governments. The Americans, too, were known to have been sounded out by the Germans about offering their services as mediators (frustrated mainly, it would appear, by Roosevelt's anxieties about whether an armistice would result in German control of the British and French fleets).[61]

The Chiefs of Staff, however, and not for the last time, put the case for 'appeasement' with vigour and intelligence: the one thing that Britain must do everything to avoid was a three-enemy war without the wholehearted support of a first-class ally.[62] Admiral Sir Dudley Pound had fought this corner hard ever since his appointment as First Sea Lord and Chief of Naval Staff in June 1939.[63] Pound had been out-gunned by his distinguished predecessor, Lord Chatfield (then Minister for the Co-ordination of Defence) at the height of the Tientsin Crisis while still new to the job,[64] but on this occasion, scarcely a month after the Italian declaration of war, in the immediate aftermath of the fall of France and while a German invasion of the United Kingdom itself was impending, Pound was determined to force ministers to abandon all hope of Far Eastern naval action.[65] Not surprisingly, since Chatfield had resigned at the beginning of April 1940 and was no longer present to oppose him, and since Churchill had demoted the three Service ministers from the War Cabinet, Pound succeeded. The crisis came as the Joint Planning Committee and the Chiefs of Staff were preparing a new Far Eastern Appreciation.[66] The issue became bound up with the attitude of the Antipodean Dominions towards the escalation of Japanese pressure upon the Dutch administration in the Dutch East Indies. The War Cabinet were informed that Australia and New Zealand were prepared to halt the flow of convoys to Europe unless the British undertook to send a fleet to the Far East in response to any Japanese attack on the Dutch East Indies. The War Cabinet refused to give way to the Dominions over the question of guarantees to the Dutch, and eventually the Dominions, Churchill and Halifax finally conceded to the expert advice of the military (and Craigie) on the Burma Road issue as well, although Churchill grumbled that the blame should be pinned on the Americans (who had also fallen into line after recognising that the British lacked the power to do otherwise).[67] Churchill had an unhappy tendency to seek scapegoats for disasters or shortcomings in which he was implicated.

In truth, the British gave the Japanese almost nothing at all. London's pragmatic refusal to underwrite the defence of the Dutch East Indies was overshadowed by Britain's neutralisation of the French fleet which had taken place at

Mers-el-Kebir near Oran in the opening days of July (Operation Catapult) and the ensuing break in diplomatic relations between Britain and the government of Marshal Petain, and this, together with speculation about the pending invasion of Britain, made it difficult for the Japanese (or Churchill's critics) to read any significance in rumours of a possible rift between the remaining partners of the Alliance.

It took time for the second Konoye Cabinet to establish itself, but Japanese extremists soon realised, even if most Western observers did not, how cleverly the Burma Road Agreement suited both the British and Japanese governments. Although Japanese extremists expressed their pique by promptly arresting a large number of British residents in Japan on trumped-up charges of espionage and propaganda, the Burma Road Agreement effectively neutralised Japan at a critical time. As for the British hostages taken by Japan, representations by Ambassador Craigie in Tokyo failed to produce results, but when Japanese residents throughout the British Empire were arrested by local governments in a carefully orchestrated demonstration, a tacit agreement was soon reached by both sides which led to the release of all who had been held.

As the British and Japanese governments each looked at it, Japan would have the Burma Road for the asking if the Germans successfully invaded Britain. The Battle of Britain, long awaited, commenced on 8 August. Provided Britain could survive until the Spring of 1941, the intervening winter weather over the English Channel and unfavourable conditions in the south-west Pacific Ocean and the South China Sea would afford protection both to Metropolitan Britain and to Singapore, the two 'keystones' of the Empire. Thus the Burma Road Agreement would come to be reviewed at a time when the Germans might be running into difficulties or the Americans might be more prepared to stand together with the British Empire. Furthermore, Japan's signature on the Agreement implied a tacit confidence in Britain's ability to survive at least through the summer months, since Japan might expect far more sweeping changes in Britain's attitude if Germany were to win the European War. The masterstroke of the Agreement, however, was that the period between mid-July and mid-October during which the road was closed to military (although never to civil) traffic happily coincided with the monsoon season when traffic on the Burma Road would anyway have dropped by some 90 per cent.

As it happened, Japanese forces were unable to take advantage of the Burma Road Agreement in pressing forward to success in China, Franklin Roosevelt declared that his Administration planned to lend 'all aid short of war' to Britain, Anglo-American accord was reached in principle on the exchange of American destroyers for the lease of air and naval bases in British territories at home and overseas, while the Americans chose this time to remind the Japanese that the conclusion of any new trade treaty with them would depend upon Japan's behaviour as a responsible member of the world community. British troops garrisoned in China began withdrawing during August. During September, as the

US Congress approved a $5.25 billion defence budget, paid attention to Roosevelt's address to Congress on 16 May 1940 calling for an increase in annual aircraft production to 50 000 new warplanes, and made provision for the construction of seven 55 000-ton battleships, the Americans began conscripting an Army of two million men. Even 10 per cent of the first year's projected American aircraft production, 5000 warplanes, amounted to more than twice what Britain estimated to be the size of the entire Japanese air forces and, if stationed in the Philippines for instance, would have changed the strategical balance of power for the whole of South-East Asia. In fact, according to evidence produced at the Tokyo War Crimes trial, the real annual military and naval aircraft production target in Japan for 1941 was about five times larger than what Britain had imagined was the entire air strength of the country. But it was still a comparatively paltry programme, 12 866 aircraft, compared to the stupendous American programme. The numbers Japan actually produced monthly in each of the years 1940–43 declined from 1390 to 1380, 1220 and 1050, respectively.[68] So all of this and news of Roosevelt's transfer of 50 American destroyers to the Royal Navy in September 1940 naturally produced a strong, lingering but not compelling incentive for caution on the part of the Japanese.

Throughout the period during which the Burma Road Agreement ran, Admiral Yonai's successor as prime minister, Prince Konoye, chafed over it. Not surprisingly, the new Cabinet was opportunistic, zealously pro-German and intensely active diplomatically. As early as 6 August, the Japanese informed the Governor-General of French Indo-China that they expected the French to grant the Japanese army the right to station troops and aircraft in northern Indo-China, on the pretext of stabilising the region and isolating Indo-China from the Sino-Japanese war zone in south China, but with the thinly veiled ulterior motive of projecting Japanese influence over Thailand and establishing strong Japanese forces within easy striking distance of Malaya and its air corridor from India through southern Burma. It was a less propitious moment than the Japanese knew. Within a month Hitler had concluded that the Germans were losing the Battle of Britain against the Royal Air Force, although the terror of the Blitz over British cities was yet to come. And on 17 September Hitler ordered German preparations for the invasion of England to be postponed indefinitely. The Blitz, however, developed with a vengeance, and the Americans did not get the message. Therefore, notwithstanding warnings from Secretary of State Cordell Hull at the beginning of September that American public opinion would not tolerate Japanese aggression in Indo-China, Japanese troops attacked the French garrison at Langson (until forced to break off on the direct orders of the *Showa* Emperor), after which the Japanese army then peacefully occupied the northern half of the country in strength from 22 September, encountering no further resistance from the Vichy French authorities there.

It was, indeed, the change in atmosphere generated by the cascade of events since the fall of France that produced Japan's advance into French Indo-China, a logical although foolhardy response that made the Pacific War almost inevitable. Four days later, President Roosevelt imposed an embargo, to become effective from 15 October, on the export of American iron and steel scrap to all countries outside of the Western Hemisphere apart from Britain. In the months that followed, the list of embargoed commodities denied to Japan was to be greatly extended until that nation's entire economy threatened to collapse.

In London, these developments were carefully watched, and during inter-departmental discussions it was generally concluded that Britain's interests would not be well served by a renewal of the Burma Road Agreement. Appeasement of Japan would have alienated opinion in the United States and several of the Dominions at a time when Britain's only hope of turning a stalemate into victory against Germany rested upon Imperial manpower and the flow of American arms, food and money. A general settlement with Japan could not possibly succeed without direct American participation, and this remained highly unlikely. The price which Britain would have had to pay for a stable, unilateral agreement with Japan would have had serious economic and political repercussions upon Britain's ability to sustain the European war effort. This muddled pessimism about the bleak outlook for diplomatic appeasement gradually gained wide acceptance within the British government outside of military circles, who remained prepared to appease Japan at almost any price.[69] But before interdepartmental differences could be resolved by the British War Cabinet, Japan concluded a political, military and economic pact with Germany and Italy on 27 September 1940.

From that moment, Appeasement was more or less a dead issue in Washington and London. The British and American ambassadors in Tokyo, Craigie and Grew, predicted that none of its signatories was likely to gain much from the Tripartite Pact. Nevertheless, United States officials used the Pact as a pretext, informing the Japanese that it must be repudiated before America would agree to conclude any new trade treaty with Tokyo.

So it was that when the time finally came for the Burma Road Agreement to expire at the end of the monsoon season, Britain had passed through her most despairing hours in the war against Germany and had avoided an unwinnable war with Japan, an eventuality which might well have led to the collapse of Churchill's premiership and his replacement by a government of a quite different character under Lord Halifax. For their part, the British scored a propaganda victory by announcing that the Burma Road would re-open at the end of its three-month closure, explaining that the main reason for taking this step was Japan's failure to abide by her promise to seek an early end to the war in China. It was not a step taken without attendant risks. To a large extent the British were blind to Japanese intentions and their real military and naval capabilities, for the Service attachés in Japan had long been seriously hampered in their attempts to acquire reliable information and the British Secret Intelligence Service in Japan was not functioning.[70]

Meanwhile, a few days earlier, the British War Cabinet had taken an important step towards enhancing its preparedness for the outbreak of war in the Pacific by establishing an interdepartmental Far Eastern Committee, of permanent officials rather than of ministers, to keep Britain's Far Eastern policy under constant review, to liaise with the United States and affected Imperial governments, to encourage and to coordinate appropriate countermeasures against Japan within British government departments, and to study every conceivable method by which Britain might meet Japan's military challenge to the British Empire in case of war. The establishment of this major Cabinet Committee, although it carried out its work under the chairmanship of a succession of senior Foreign Office officials and was undoubtedly dominated by these chairmen and other Foreign Office members, was another nail in the coffin of Lord Halifax's own pretension to set the tone in British foreign relations. Strictly speaking, the Far Eastern Committee was an advisory rather than a policy-making body, but it was a body which reported to the Cabinet, not only to and through the Foreign Secretary. The independence and influence of the Far Eastern Committee is also, paradoxically, indicative of Winston Churchill's personal indifference towards almost anything connected with Far Eastern affairs with the notable exception of an abiding interest in any direct threat to the Dominions: as he himself acknowledged, the defence of the Dominions was a matter of great moment to him, but with a strange mathematical precision, he confesses in his memoirs that he came to regard the security of Suez, Egypt and the Middle East as five times more important than the defence of Malaya.[71] This was a matter he was content to delegate – without interference – on a month-to-month basis. The Prime Minister simply did not believe, until perhaps very late in the day, that the Japanese would be so bold as to dare to take on the might of the Anglo-Saxon world.

THE APPROACH OF WAR

The persistence of the strategic idea of sending the main fleet to Singapore is one of the more remarkable things in British contingency plans to deal with Japan during the period leading up to the Pacific War. Admiral Pound's longstanding reservations about the concept have already been noted but were far from constant. As late as 29 October 1940, Rear-Admiral Roger Bellairs of the Admiralty handed a memorandum to Admiral Bailey of the US Navy to be given to President Roosevelt personally. In it the Americans were told that to oppose the Japanese fleet in the event of a crisis in the Far East, it would be necessary to dispatch a force of eight or nine battleships, three aircraft carriers, and a balanced number of cruisers, destroyers and submarines to Singapore. Bellairs recognised that for Britain to attempt this singlehandedly, it would be necessary for her to abandon the Eastern Mediterranean, fatally weakening the Home Fleet and the force protecting the Atlantic convoys.[72] Clearly, this could not be done under present circumstances.

In the ensuing discussions, it became clear that the United States was quite unwilling to move all or even a detachment from its own Pacific Fleet to Singapore, even if that meant that the Japanese would breach the Malay Barrier. Eventually, a kind of compromise was reached, and in February 1941 the Chiefs of Staff advised the Americans that if the United States Navy were prepared to offer immediate cover in the Atlantic and Mediterranean waters as envisaged during the Anglo-American Staff Conversations in Washington (or if in the absence of such an arrangement London reached a political decision to abandon the Mediterranean), then they expected to be able to send out a force of about six capital ships and their attendant escorts to the Far East. It was fully appreciated that if it had to operate without active American cooperation, this force would be too small to undertake any offensive action against the Japanese and would leave Britain too weak nearer home to adopt a forward position. As their representatives expressed their dilemma directly to Secretary of War Henry Stimson, Secretary of the Navy Frank Knox, the US Army Chief of Staff and the American Chief of Naval Operations as late as 26 March 1941, 'Under the dispositions proposed the Japanese Navy would be containing a superior force of United States and British heavy ships'.[73] Even so, they were quite unwilling to accept American arguments that the loss of Singapore would not be an irremediable catastrophe, and in the following week it was agreed that 'in the event of war with Japan the necessary naval reinforcements for the Far East should be found by us, in which event we shall be able to take account of US reinforcements in the Atlantic.'[74]

The Japanese had made the potentially disastrous mistake of completely discounting the resolve of the British Government to send a major fleet out to Singapore in the event of war at the time of the Tientsin Crisis in the summer of 1939. After war was declared in Europe, the Japanese saw no reason to take the British in isolation more seriously than before. However, they did become increasingly alarmed at what they saw as a definite pattern of encirclement by the British Commonwealth in collaboration with the Dutch and Americans. Reference has already been made to the Commonwealth Defence Conference at Singapore in October 1940.[75] From November 1940 to January 1941, Japanese newspapers reported the establishment of a unified General Headquarters for British Commonwealth forces in the Far East and speculated that the deployment of US naval forces to Singapore was under consideration.[76]

The sweeping November victories gained by the Democrats in general and more particularly by Franklin D. Roosevelt gave a great fillip to those who wanted, and now expected, the American administration to take a firmer stand against aggression in the spring and summer of 1941. On 20 November 1940, the United States agreed to grant Chiang Kai-shek a new loan of $50 million for currency stabilisation, which was interpreted as a response to an announcement earlier that day in Tokyo that Japan had concluded a treaty with Wang Ching-wei's breakaway regime in China. The Americans further indicated that another $50 million might be made available to China if required. The Japanese watched as London followed this up with its own announcement of a one million grant to China. By January 1941, in Roosevelt's budget speech to Congress, the President called for another $11 billion to be allocated on national defence expenditure, bringing the total defense appropriations since May 1940 to $28 billion,[77] a message that no one could ignore. Soon there were reports reaching Whitehall that supplies were beginning to reach Japanese troops operating in south China from the railway running from French Indo-China up to Nanning, while the Japanese accused Britain of authorising the shipment of large quantities of arms and military equipment to flow directly to the Kuomintang up the Burma Road.

However, at the Anglo-American Staff Conversations in Washington DC during February and March 1941, Britain failed to obtain a US commitment to underwrite the defense of Singapore.[78] Despite this setback, and doubtless having regard for President Roosevelt's request to Congress for a $7 billion appropriation of Lend-Lease Aid early in March 1941, General Sir John Dill, Chief of the Imperial General Staff and a man who was to become nearly the ideal Senior British Officer during subsequent 'Conversations' in Washington, now recommended that the reinforcement of Britain's position in the Far East should take place almost immediately, during the spring of 1941.[79] Churchill, however, opposed this, siding with the Foreign Office in arguing that the Japanese were unlikely to move against Singapore before the Russians were defeated by Germany.[80]

Churchill, writing not altogether comfortably after the war, insists, 'I am sure that nothing we could have spared at this time, even at the cost of wreaking the Middle East theatre or cutting off supplies to the Soviet, would have changed the march of fate in Malaya.'[81] How strange, when he also declares that the events of December 1941 were an 'unforeseeable climax' to the year![82]

Vital time had been lost, earlier that year, and when the die was cast by the Japanese advance into southern Indo-China in July 1941, it was perhaps already too late. In April 1941, Japanese anxiety about their military as well as their economic encirclement by the 'Associated Powers' grew even more acute when they learned of a high-level defence conference in Manila attended by the British Commander in Chief, Far East, the United States High Commissioner in the Philippines, the C-in-C of the US Asiatic Fleet, and the Dutch Foreign Minister. The outcome of the Manila consultations was in a sense less important than the fact that Japan would feel impelled to take defensive countermeasures. In mid-May 1941, the question of Anglo-Dutch cooperation in case of Japanese aggression once again returned to the fore, surfacing in the Defense (Operations) Committee together with the issue of the despatch of a fleet to the Far East.[83]

This came at an inopportune time. The Russo-Japanese Non-Aggression Treaty signed in Moscow during April had been read as a sign that Japan had chosen to throw her weight into the Southern Advance, Churchill had not had an easy time during a vote of confidence over his handling of the Greek crisis, and on 24 May the Royal Navy had been shaken by the loss of HMS *Hood* and the mauling of the *Prince of Wales* by the guns of the *Bismarck*, events not altogether redeemed by the destruction of the *Bismarck* three days later.[84] Despite the intimations from the United States during the recent defence conferences that they were prepared to provide naval cover in the Atlantic, this was felt to be no time to renew Britain's reliance upon her naval resources to secure the defence of Singapore, and indeed during this period the defence of Malaya was felt to devolve, by default, upon a build-up of its air defences until such time as a fleet could be spared for Singapore.[85] It was all rather late in the day, however, and little was done to rectify the deficiencies in British imperial defence preparedness against the Japanese.

It was on the economic and diplomatic encirclement of Japan and the natural momentum of events that the British Government chose principally to rely; the freezing of Japanese assets by the United States, the British Commonwealth and the Dutch East Indies began to bite hard. An inevitable dialogue of the deaf took place in Washington between Japanese and American negotiators, in which the United States overplayed its hand, whether deliberately or not, and, with serious results, failed to have regard to the practicality of what amounted to an American ultimatum: a demand that the Japanese must agree to accept the US 'bottom line' or face the certainty of economic strangulation. Meanwhile, a high-level Japanese economic mission to the Dutch East Indies, led first by the Japanese Minister of Commerce and Industry, Kobayashi Ichizo, and then by Ambassador Yoshizawa Kenkichi, was frustrated in its aim of 'persuading' the Dutch to provide oil and other supplies required by the Japanese Empire. The military problem re-emerged in an more acute form in mid-October 1941, after General Tōjō Hideki became Minister of Japan, from which time the issue was rarely off the agenda until the outbreak of the Pacific War.

In the last few days of peace, the prospect of war grew into a certainty. Churchill's own account – and his papers in the 'Premier' files – on the state of British intelligence concerning Japanese dispositions on the eve of the Pearl Harbor attack and during the advance of Japanese seaborne assault forces heading across the Gulf of Siam are far from satisfactory.[86] Much of the relevant intelligence documentation is not available at the Public Record Office, but it would appear that air intelligence assessments of the Japanese threat were still lamentable even at this late stage and that the higher echelons in Malaya Command (if not the C-in-C, Far East) were lulled into a false sense of security by believing that Japan would require eight to ten divisions of troops to seize Malaya and that she was not yet in a position to transport or support such a force.[87]

Apportioning appropriate responsibility for the failure of the British to launch *Operation Matador*, the pre-emptive strike across the Kra Isthmus intended to forestall a Japanese attack upon Malaya from the foot of Thailand is still difficult. Although the Joint Intelligence Committee had anticipated a Japanese invasion of Thailand since 2 August, and the Australians had become alarmed about the same prospect since late November, Churchill told Anthony Eden, his Foreign Secretary, on 2 December 1941 that

> An attack on the Kra Isthmus would not be helpful to Japan for several months. In any case we should not take forestalling action without a definite guarantee of United States support.[88]

One hopes that Prime Minister John Major's recently expressed intention to liberalise freedom of access to Government papers will bear fruit in this as well as in other areas of historical rumour and speculation. Certainly, whatever the shortcomings of the Royal Air Force command in Malaya, Churchill cannot escape a major share of blame for consistently downgrading the number and type of aircraft available to them. While the imminence of war in the Far East remained very much in doubt, it is scarcely fair to speak of anyone's neglect in this matter: the conflicting demands of other theatres were of surpassing importance. However, by September to December 1941, the threat of Japanese entry into the war became too acute for anyone to underrate. And in that period Churchill and his old crony Lord Beaverbrook, the Minister of Supply, have to share much – although not all – of the blame for diverting hundreds of aircraft to the Soviet Union (numbers which the United States had offered to make available to the Soviets instead and which Britain donated only to uphold the prestige of the British Empire in Stalin's eyes), thus depriving Malaya Command of both the 'higher' and 'lower' approved scales of air reinforcements which the Chiefs of Staff and the Allied defence conferences insisted were essential to its defence.

What is indisputable is that there were no more than 167 frontline aircraft in Malaya when the Japanese finally attacked, and in just one day of action the British lost 55 per cent of those few aircraft they had there: proof, if it were needed, of the utter inadequacy of the provision that had been made for the air defence of such a vital theatre. The shortage of tanks in Malaya, which was also down to Beaverbrook and Churchill's insistence on giving priority to the reinforcement of Russia, was to prove no less instrumental in the rapid collapse of British resistance to the Japanese invasion.[89] The story of Churchill's despatch of the small naval detachment of the *Prince of Wales* and the *Repulse* is too well known to bear repeating here[90]: it is clear that he and others failed to recognise how vulnerable these ships would be, particularly to well-handled land-based enemy aircraft. Churchill's reputation is further stained by his failure to appreciate that Singapore was not in fact a citadel at all (although he had spent nigh on two decades of effort in promoting and proclaiming its strength). It is hard to imagine how he and his military advisers in London should have been completely ignorant of its limitations until the last minute, as he sought to maintain.[91] It seems to me indisputable that he simply gambled on bluffing the Japanese – and lost. As for his insistence on the landing of the 18th Division at Singapore, straight into certain captivity, he rightly believed that Yamamoto's front-line forces, vastly outnumbered by the defenders, must be nearly exhausted, and since it was believed that continued resistance in Malaya – even for another month – might well throw off the Japanese timetable and save Burma, there was a balance of risk which in the event was decided by pressure exerted from the Dominions.[92] In this regard it is therefore ironic that if one prominent researcher in this field is correct, there were approximately 6000 Australian deserters who had fled from their units by the time the British commander was obliged to withdraw to Singapore Island. At Singapore, with better intelligence (and less treachery perhaps), there might have been more reason than merely Churchill's military and political instincts for resisting to the bitter end: General Yamashita was all but out of ammunition, had Lieutenant-General Arthur Percival but known the fact.

However, Churchill's orders to Major-General Christopher Maltby, requiring a fight to the death of every last man at Hong Kong, when his more humane course would have been to have surrendered after little more than a token resistance against the overwhelming forces which the Japanese had brought to bear there, cannot be regarded as rational. Churchill, having given them too little, asked too much of them: ever conscious of history and propaganda, he was inclined to forget that for troops under fire, valour and vainglory truly are poles apart. Scarcely anyone who had studied the Japanese war in China had any illusions about how badly the Japanese might treat those who surrendered, but the great pity is that the average British soldier never really thought about the Chinese at all and certainly would not have imagined that he was no better in Japanese eyes.

It is therefore consistent if ironic that at the very closing stages of the war, from the summer of 1944 to early August 1945, one sees Churchill and the Chiefs of Staff rather high-handedly united in trying to ensure that the British Pacific Fleet, together with a Very Long Range Bomber Force (of up to 20 squadrons) and as large a British and Commonwealth land component as possible (quite apart from the forces already committed in South-East Asia Command), should play a major part in the closing stages of the war.[94] And we find, right up to the last, that the regard felt by Churchill and the Chiefs of Staff for their Antipodean 'kith and kin' did not stretch so far that they would bear to listen to complaints which the Australian and New Zealand authorities voiced about Britain's dictatorial heavy-handedness and the future risk of a confrontation between the imperial aspirations of Britain and the United States in the South China Seas and south-west Pacific. The words in which Churchill explained his feelings towards Japan before Pearl Harbor might have passed for those of Chamberlain on the eve of the German adventure in Europe, with only the substitute of a single word: namely, the word 'Japan' for 'Germany':

A declaration of war by Japan [said Churchill] could not be reconciled with reason. I felt sure she would be ruined for a generation by such a plunge, and this proved true. But Governments and peoples do not always take rational decisions. Sometimes they take mad decisions, or one set of people get control who compel all others to obey and aid them in folly. I have not hesitated to record repeatedly my disbelief that Japan would go mad. However sincerely we try to put ourselves in another person's position, we cannot allow for processes of the human mind and imagination to which reason offers no key. Madness is, however, an affliction which in war carries with it the advantage of surprise.[95]

Chamberlain, I may say, would not have made this mistake about Japan any more than Churchill would have made it with Germany. Chamberlain thought Japan would listen only to the self-interests dictated by international balances of power: if Japan thought she could gain by extending the war to include Britain or France, words would fail to stop her, palliatives would fail to charm her. However, Chamberlain had hopes to buy time with negotiations and concessions to Germany and Italy. It worked to some degree with Germany for the six months between September 1938 and March 1939. Against Italy the same policy had succeeded until 10 June 1940. Six days after the British retreat from the Continent ended at Dunkirk, Mussolini took the only rational course he could have chosen in an attempt to safeguard the future independence of his country in circumstances where it seemed any further delay would be worse than imprudent. Churchill's policy was diametrically opposed to Chamberlain's in Asia as well as Europe, and despite recognising his duty to protect the Dominions, he did not bear the cross which burdened Chamberlain: the paralysing consciousness of the global requirements for adequate Imperial defence when there was no realistic prospect for strong Allied support and, as F.S. Northedge expressed the dilemma in other terms a quarter-century ago, 'British policy was in a maze in which every path led nowhere'.[96] Nevertheless, of the two prime ministers, Churchill's was the more permanent failure for British fortunes, for Britain, as the Chiefs of Staff had always forewarned, was never to recover from the loss of the East.

Moreover, Chamberlain was not a man to forsake the strategic advice given to him by Britain's professional soldiers and economists. That he was often wrong, as they were, cannot be doubted. But it is well to remember that much of Churchill's interference in the economic and strategic direction of the war led to disasters which reached right round the world. The diarist Chips Channon put his finger on the mistrust that individuals who knew the Prime Minister well bore against Churchill. When Singapore fell, Channon reflected, 'I fear he has the evil-eye, or ill-luck; certainly nothing that he ever touched – Dardanelles, abdication, India Bill – has come off well.'[97] On the economics side, Churchill had sacked an unsuccessful team and brought in new men who bore out in practice the unforgiving truths of virtual bankruptcy predicted by their predecessors: only the strength of the American economy could stave off Britain's financial collapse. On the military side, although he was a capricious master, Churchill was to retain throughout the war generals and admirals to whom Chamberlain had listened intently and who had been the backbone of Appeasement until Britain declared war on Germany. Men as far removed in experience and temperament as Lord Chatfield and Alec Cadogan despaired of what Chatfield called Churchill's 'height of inefficiency and bad administration', which stood in such contrast to their high regard for Neville Chamberlain's more methodical, composed and cerebral leadership.[98] Reading the papers at the Public Record Office, one feels compelled to agree. 'It's no use sitting upon me,' Churchill reportedly said of himself, to other subalterns at Meerut in 1898, 'for I am india-rubber – and I bounce!' How right! And yet, despite disasters, prevarication and shortcomings, Churchill stands, and remains undiminished in the mind, as the one indispensable giant of the war.

## NOTES

1. Lord Tedder, *Air Power in War* (Lees-Knowles Lecture, London: Hodder & Stoughton, 1948), cited by J.R.B. Butler, 'Introduction' in T.K. Derry, *The Campaign in Norway* (London: HMSO, 1952) and in Butler, *Grand Strategy*, vol.II (London: HMSO, 1957) p. xvii.
2. For Britain's pre-war period, see R.J. Pritchard, 'The Far East as an Influence on the Chamberlain Government's Pre-war European Policies', *Millennium: Journal of International Studies*, II:3 (1973–74) 7–23, and *Far Eastern Influences upon British Strategy towards the Great Powers, 1937–1939* (London: Garland 1987) *passim*.
3. A.J. Marder, 'Winston is Back': Churchill at the Admiralty, 1939–1940', *English Historical Review*, Supplement V (London: Longman, 1972).
4. JP(39)7 and JP(39)8, both 5 September 1939, Cab 84/7; WP(G) (39)5, 6 September 1939, Cab 67/1.
5. COS(39)16, 7 September 1939, Cab 80/1.
6. The 'British' included 1800 service families, 3000 European civilian families, 700 Indian Families, and 1100 Eurasian families. In addition there were 11 000 foreign women and children of whom approximately 1000 were Americans. COS187(40)4, 20 June 1940, Cab 79/5, and COS(40)477, 19 June 1940, Cab 80/13. For a major effort to evacuate these women and children from 25 June 1940, see WM181(40)7, 25 June; WM183(40)13, 26 June; WM187(40)6, 29 June 1940; all in Cab 65/7, and WP(40)250 [=COS(40)534], 5 July 1940, Cab 66/9.
7. COS7(39)3, 8 September 1939, Cab 80/1; COS(39)49, 26 September 1939, Cab 80/3. See also an excellent essay by Y.M. Streatfield, 'Singapore Defences, 1921–1939', unpublished monograph, Cabinet Office Historical Section, Cab 101/294, *passim*.
8. Ibid., Streatfield, and R.J. Pritchard, *Far Eastern Influences, passim*.
9. The decision to increase the period before relief to 90 days (with an extension of the period before reprovisioning to 105 days) was taken by the Chiefs of Staff on 1 June 1939, COS299(39), Cab 53/11. See also COS848(JP), 27 February 1939, Cab 53/45; COS901(JP) [=ODC898-M], 10 May 1939, Cab 53/48; and COS920 [=CID502-C], 6 June 1939, Cab 53/50. The decision was approved by the CID at CID364(39)2.

10. This involved extra reserves of food, ammunition, aircraft, anti-aircraft measures, coal, petroleum supplies, etc., which lumped together would cost approximately £4–5 million. To extend the period before relief to 90 days (105 days for reprovisioning) would cost a further £913 900 for additional reserves of food, £130 000 in naval expenditure with possibly another £200 000 for a naval victualling store ship (and an annual running cost of £20 000 to maintain it), and £1.25 million for the additional requirements of the Royal Air Force, not to mention whatever the Army [did not] have to spend. See COS32(39)3, 29 September 1939, Cab 79/1.

11. Pritchard, *Far Eastern Influences*, pp. 239, 241.

12. See Streatfield, 'Singapore Defences', p. 182.

13. See note 8 above.

14. F1549/972/23, Tokyo despatch 328, Political Diary for September 1939, 31 December 1939, FO 371/24742; F10130/456/23, 11/14 September 1939, and minutes, FO 371/23562.

15. Pritchard, 'The Tientsin Crisis: Bluff, Bluster and Blunderbuss Policies on the Eve of the European War' in *Proceedings of the British Association for Japanese Studies*, VII:1, *History and International Relations* (1983) *passim*.

16. Ge/39/4, Chatfield to Lord Lothian, 26 September 1939, and report by Lothian, 15 September 1939, FO 800/397. Compare T.A. Bisson, 'Japan's Position in the War Crisis', *Foreign Policy Reports*, XV:16 (1 November 1939) pp. 202–3.

17. For an excellent recent review of the pre-war limitations on FDR, see D. Cameron Watt, *How War Came* (London: Heinemann, 1989) pp. 255–70.

18. COS(39)52, 28 September 1939, Cab 80/3.20.

19. WP(39)56, Covering Note by E.E. Bridges, 28 September 1939, Cab 66/1.

20. JP(39)43 [=COS(39)48(JP], 25 September 1939, Cab 84/8.

21. COS(39)52, 28 September 1939, Cab 80/3; WP(G) (39)92, 15 November 1939, Cab 67/2; WP(39)114 [=COS(39)112], 3 November 1939, Cab 66/3; F11621/456/23, Tokyo tel.1454, 6/7 November 1939, and minute by A. Clarke, 8 November 1939, FO 371/23562. The quotation is from WP(G) (39)92.

22. WM68(39)6, 2 November 1939, Cab 65/2; WP(39)103 [=COS(39)102], 28 October 1939, Cab 66/3.

23. WM68(39)6, 2 November 1939, Cab 65/2.

24. WP(39)125, 17 November 1939, Cab 66/3; F2415/972/23, Japanese Political Diary for October–December 1939, 31 December 1939, FO 371/24742.

25. WP(39)129 [=COS(30)124], 17 November 1939, Cab 66/3.

26. WP(39)125, 17 November 1939, Cab 66/3. See also WM90(39)4, 21 November 1939, Cab 65/2.

27. Ibid., WP(39)125. Author's emphasis.

28. Prem. 1/345. See also R. Hough, *Former Naval Person: Churchill and the Wars at Sea* (London: Weidenfeld & Nicolson, 1985) pp. 156, 169.

29. Annex to WP(G)(39)92, 10 November 1939, Cab 67/2.

30. Pritchard, 'The Tientsin Crisis'.

31. The number of front-line aircraft available for the defence of Malaya at the outbreak of the Second World War in September 1939 was six squadrons comprising 58 aircraft: four Singapore flying boats, six Sunderland flying boats, 24 Vildebeest torpedo-bombers and 24 Blenheim bombers. This was 20 more aircraft than the maximum front-line forces available six months earlier (well before the Tientsin Crisis in the summer of 1939). A further two squadrons comprising 32 Blenheims were sent from the United Kingdom and arrived on 22 September 1939. At that time there were no fighter aircraft available for the defence of Malaya. See S. Woodburn-Kirby et al., *The War Against Japan*, I, (London: HMSO, 1957) p. 21. Since the summer of 1937 it had been anticipated that the ultimate air strength in

Malaya should stand at 10 squadrons and a spotter/reconnaissance flight. For the 1939/40 European Appreciation, see DP(P)44 [=COS 843], 20 February 1939, Cab 16/183A.

32.   See Streatfield, 'Singapore Fortress'.
33.   DO(40)38th Mtg., 29 October 1940, Cab 69/1.
34.   COS(40)555(JP), 19 July 1940, Cab 80/15.
35.   JP(40)746(S) [=COS(40)1053], 19 December 1940, Cab 84/24.
36.   COS(40)1054, 31 October 1940, Cab 80/24.
37.   NID/0982/39, minute by DNI, 20 November 1939, Adm 1/9973.
38.   WM89(39)7, 20 November 1939, Cab 65/2.
39.   Pritchard, 'The Tientsin Crisis'.
40.   WM89(39)7, 20 November 1939, Cab 65/2.
41.   Pritchard, *Far Eastern Influences*, pp. 8–26, 39–41; ibid., 'The Far Eastern Influence'.
42.   Ibid., and WM89(39)7, 20 November 1939, Cab 65/2.
43.   Diary entry for 25 August 1939, cited in S.K. Roskill, *Hankey: Man of Secrets*, III, *1931–1963* (London: Collins, 1974) p. 415.
44.   WM89(39)7, 20 November 1939, Cab 65/2.
45.   Ibid. Author's emphasis.
46.   Ibid.
47.   WM92(39)5, 23 November 1939, Cab 65/2.
48.   WP(39)135, 21 November 1939, Cab 66/3; WM90(39)4, 21 November 1939, Cab 65/2.
49.   WM93(39)7, 24 November 1939, Cab 65/2.
50.   JP(39)74 [=COS(39)137(JP)], 28 November 1939, Cab 84/8.
51.   WP(39)148 [=COS(39)146], 28 November 1939, Cab 80/5.
52.   Streatfield, 'Singapore Fortress'. The Singapore garrison consisted of three British battalions, a local Malay battalion, two heavy coastal defence regiments, three anti-aircraft artillery regiments, and four fortress companies of Royal Engineers, but the delegates at the 1940 Singapore Defence Conference reported that the ground forces in Malaya needed twelve more infantry battalions, six more field artillery regiments, three more anti-tank regiments and three more companies of Royal Engineers. They were short by 120 heavy anti-aircraft guns, 98 light anti-aircraft guns, 138 searchlights and three light tank companies, so that altogether the GOC Malaya Command was under-strength by nearly the equivalent of two full divisions. The Conference also agreed that the defence forces in Burma required seven more infantry battalions (it already had six trained and a further four in various stages of recruitment) and the equivalent of about one and a half more artillery regiments, just in the short term: COS(40)1054, 19 December 1940, Cab 80/24. The delegates did not propose to add any medium tank units, an omission that played a large part in the subsequent defeat of the British by the Japanese. The American military attaché in Bangkok attended the Conference as an observer and it is scarcely surprising that during 'technical' staff discussions which followed between the British and American strategical authorities in London and Washington, serious doubts were expressed about whether the weak forces in Malaya and the surrounding area could resist a Japanese attack sufficiently long for a fleet to reach Singapore even if there were no undue delay in despatching the necessary naval reinforcements.
53.   H. Humphreys, letter to R. Lamb, 19 April 1990. I am indebted to R. Lamb for sharing this letter with me during the several months in which we collaborated in the research for his recent book, *Churchill as War Leader: Right or Wrong* (London: Bloomsbury, 1991). See also B. Montgomery, *Shenton of Singapore: Governor and Prisoner of War* (London: Leo Cooper/Secker & Warburg, 1984), *passim*; I.

Simson, *Too Little, Too Late* (London): Leo Cooper, 1970), *passim*; S. Woodburn-Kirby et al., *The War against Japan*, pp. 24–33. The Papers of Col. G.T. Wards, Imperial War Museum, 92/24/1, are also pertinent concerning Gen. Bond's flat contradiction of Ward's prescient warnings concerning the fighting qualities of the Japanese in May–June 1941.

54.   WP(40)95, 12 March 1940, Cab 66/6. Author's emphasis.

55.   Pritchard, *Far Eastern Influences, passim.*

56.   WP(40)168 [=COS(40)390], 25 May 1940, Cab 66/7. Emphasis in the original source.

57.   Ibid. See also S. Woodburn-Kirby, *The War Against Japan*, I, pp. 24, 478–9.

58.   WP(40)203 [=COS(40)455], 13 June 1940, Cab 66/8.

59.   F3103/972/23, Japanese Political Diaries for June 1940, 11 September and 11 October 1940, FO 371/24742; F2417/2417/23, Tokyo Annual Report for 1939, 1 January 1940, FO 371/24743; and F821/821/23, Craigie's Final Report, 4 February 1943, with F2602/821/23G, Response of Far Eastern Department, 23 April 1943, with minutes, FO 371/35957.

60.   P. Lowe, *Great Britain and the Origins of the Pacific War: A Study of British Policy in East Asia, 1937–1941* (Oxford: Clarendon, 1977) pp. 136–75; N.B. Clifford, *Retreat from China: British Policy in the Far East, 1937–1941* (London: Longmans, 1967) pp. 141–6, 150; and P. Calvocoressi, G. Wint and J. Pritchard, *Total War: The Causes and Courses of the Second World War*, 2nd rev. edn. (London: Viking, 1989) pp. 907–9.

61.   See B. Gardner, *Churchill in his Time: A Study in a Reputation, 1939–1945* (London: Methuen, 1968) pp. 65–92; R. Lamb, *The Ghosts of Peace, 1935–1945* (Wilton: Michael Russell, 1987) pp. 130–46. For a particularly interesting recent discussion of the significance of the 'peace' overtures, see J. Costello, *Ten Days that Saved the West* (London: Bantam, 1991) *passim.*

62.   WM181(40)7, 25 June 1940, Cab 65/7; WM187(4), 29 June, WM189(40)12, 1 July, WP193(40)5, 4 July, WM194(40)1, 5 July, WM195(40)9, 6 July, WM199(40)4, 10 July, WM200(40)13, 11 July, WM203(40)2, 14 July, WM204(40)5, 15 July, WM205(40)2, 16 July, and WM206(40)2, 17 July 1940, all in Cab 65/8; WP(40)227 [=COS(40)499], 28 June, WP(40)234, 29 June, WP(40)242, 2 July, WP(40)249 [=COS(40)532], 4 July, WP(40)256, 9 July, and WP(40)263, 12 July 1940, all in Cab 66/9; and WP(40)297, 31 July 1940, Cab 66/10; COS195(40)1, 26 June, COS203(40)3, 1 July, COS207(40)3, 4 July, COS209(40)2 and 3, 5 July, COS230(40)2, 23 July, COS231(40)2 & 3, 24 July, COS233(40)3, 26 July, COS234(40)3, 27 July, COS239(40)1, 30 July, and COS240(40)1, 31 July 1940, all in Cab 79/5; JP(40)298 [=COS(40)506(JP)], 29 June 1940, Cab 80/14; COS(40)528, 3 July 1940, Cab 80/14; WO 32/9366 (file). See also P. Cosgrove, *Churchill at War*, I, *Alone, 1939–40* (London: Collins, 1974) pp. 272–3, 321–31.

63.   Pritchard, 'The Tientsin Crisis'.

64.   Ibid.

65.   See Note 63.

66.   JP970(40)d, 6 July, and JP77(40)1, 1 August 1940, both in Cab 84/2; JP(40)359, July, and JP(40)365, 1 August 1940, in Cab 84/17; COS230(40)2, 23 July, COS234(40)3, 27 July, and COS236(40)3, 27 July 1940, all in Cab 79/5; COS(40)563, 21 July 1940, Cab 80/15; COS(40)592 [=WP(40)302, with covering memorandum, 5 August 1940], 31 July 1940, Cab 66/10.

67.   Ibid.; Cosgrove, *Churchill at War*, p. 272; COS289(40)1, 31 August 1940, Cab 79/6.

68.   Affidavit [PX 840] and Testimony by J.G. Liebert, 22 October 1946, R.J. Pritchard and S.M. Zaide (eds) *The Tokyo Trial: Proceedings of the International Military*

*Tribunal for the Far East* [hereafter *IMTFE*] (New York: Garland, 1981), 4, T. 8371–82; Testimony by Okada Kikusaburo, 13 March 1947, Ibid., 8, T18292–3, 18297–304.

69.  Cosgrove, *Churchill at War*, pp. 325–31.

70.  Regarding the SIS and the state of British intelligence on Japan, see JP(40)590(S), 31 October 1940, Cab 84/21. See also PX 628, Tentative Plan for Policy towards the Southern Regions, 4 October 1940, Pritchard and Zaide, *IMTFE*, 5, T. 11722–28, especially T. 11724, and Affidavit [DX 3013] and Testimony by Sawada Shigeru, 27 August 1947, Ibid., 11, 26848–62.

71.  W.S. Churchill, *The Second World War*, III, *The Grand Alliance* (London: Cassell, 1950) p. 379.

72.  Bellairs to Bailey, 29 October 1940, in Adm. 205/6 (file). See also ADA(40)10, 17 October, ADA(40)13 [=COS(40)856], 22 October, ADA(40)18, 29 October, and ADA(40)22 (Revise), 14 November 1940, all in Cab 99/8; ADA(J) (40)1, 20 October, ADA(J) (40)2, 20 October, ADA(J) (40)7, 9 November 1940, all in Cab 99/8.

73.  BUS(J) (41)1st Mtg., 29 January, and BUS(41)32, 26 March 1941, Cab 99/5.

74.  BUS(41)33 [=COS(41)250], 2 April 1941, Cab 99/5. In this connection it is particularly significant that the British were to leave the Americans in no doubt that 'On a long-term view the Far East is to the British Commonwealth of greater importance than the Middle East'. BUS(J) (41)6, 31 January 1941, Cab 99/5.

75.  For the British delegation's terms of reference and instructions at the Singapore Conference, see COS(40)802, 4 October, COS(40)802(JP) [=JP(40)517], 5 October, COS(40)804, 6 October, COS(40)807, 6 October, COS(40)815 (Revise), 10 October, COS(40)831 [=ADA(40)3], 14 October and COS(40)836, 16 October 1940, all in Cab 80/20.

76.  DD 1900-A-4, 13 November, DD 1900-A-6, 13 November, DD 1900-A-5 and 15 November, DD 1900-A-7, 24 November 1940, Pritchard and Zaide, IMTFE, 11, T. 25486–90; DD 1900-A-8, 13 January, DD 1900-A-11, 15 January 1941, Pritchard & Zaide, *IMTFE*, 11, T. 25501, 22504–8. Cf. Affidavit [DX 3655] and Testimony by Tojo Hideki, 29 December 1947, Pritchard and Zaide, *IMTFE*, 15, 36244–54. A useful source is *Japan Surveys the European War* (Tokyo: Tokyo Press Club, 1940), a copy of which is in FO 371/24730. For British documentation, see COS(4)835(JP) [=JP(40)556], 16 October and COS(40)839 (Revise), 22 October 1941, Cab 80/20; COS(40)857, 22 October, COS(40)873, 27 October, COS(40)880, 30 October and COS(40)895, 2 November 1940, Cab 80/21; COS(40)1023, 8 December 1940, Cab 80/24.

77.  DX 2847, Excerpt from *Peace and War* (Washington, DC: US State Department), in Pritchard and Zaide, *IMTFE*, 11, T. 25493.

78.  See Notes 75 and 76; ADA(J)(40)1, 20 October, ADA(J)(40)2, 20 October, and ADA(J)(40)7, 9 November 1940, all in Cab 99/8; BUS(J)(41)13, 11 February, BUS(41)12, 12 February, BUS(J)(41)16, 19 February, BUS(41)16, 25 February, BUS(J)(41)28, 4 March, BUS(J)(41)11th Mtg., 26 February, and BUS(41)33 [=COS(41)250], 2 April 1941, all in Cab 99/5, as well as the final Report, BUS(J)(41)30 [=ABC-1], 27 March 1941, also in Cab 99/5. I can find no evidence to support T.B. Kittridge, *Historical Monograph: U.S.–British Naval Cooperation, 1940–1945* (TS, Washington Navy Yard, *n.d.*) I, Sec. 4, Pt. B, which I suspect is also the unidentified and not always unimpeachable source for S.E. Morison, *History of United States Naval Operations in World War II*, III: *The Rising Sun in the Pacific* (Boston: Little, Brown, 1968) p. 50, Note 3. They in turn are followed by W.H. Heinrichs, 'The Role of the U.S. Navy' in D. Borg and S. Okamoto, *Pearl Harbor as History* (New York: Columbia, 1973) p. 222. C. Thorne, *Allies of a Kind*

(London: Hamish Hamilton, 1978) p. 77, is far more satisfactory and consistent with the documentary record. If one were to believe Kittridge, the British delegation effectively sabotaged their chief objectives at an early stage: I simply disbelieve him. See also COS(41)387, the Report of the American–British–Dutch Conversations held at Singapore in April 1941, 21 June 1941, Cab 80/28.

79. Dill to Churchill, 15 May 1941, printed in J.R.M. Butler, *Grand Strategy*, II (London: HMSO, 1957) pp. 580–1. See also DX 2848, Extract from *Peace and War*, in Pritchard and Zaide, *IMTFE*, 11, T. 25493–500.

80. Churchill, *The Second World War*, III, p. 379.

81. Ibid., p. 523.

82. Ibid., p. 458.

83. For instance, see DO(41)21st Mtg., 1 May 1941, DO(41)30th Mtg., 15 May 1941, and DO (41)31st Mtg., 19 May 1941, all in Cab 69/2.

84. Gardner, *Churchill in his Time*, pp. 110–20.

85. For the development of British plans to overcome existing deficiencies in measures intended to protect Singapore before the arrival of an adequate fleet, see COS(40)893, 2 November 1940, Cab 80/21; COS(40)908, 6 November, COS(40)921, 8 November, COS(40)924, 9 November, COS(40)940, 14 November and COS(40)950, 18 November 1940, all in Cab 80/22; COS(40)955, 19 November and COS(40)970, 22 November 1940, all in Cab 80/23; COS(40)1011, 4 December and COS(40)1032, 11 December 1940, both in Cab 80/24.

86. Churchill, *The Second World War*, III, pp. 532–6. See also miscellaneous papers collected by Group-Captain K. Darvall, Senior Air Staff Officer, GHQ Singapore, in Air 23/1865 (file), Air 23/1970 (file) and Air 23/3575 (file).

87. The PRO does not hold the records of the Security Services and much of the relevant raw intelligence files from various agencies are still withheld from public inspection. However, see Air 23 papers cited in Note 87.

88. S. Woodburn-Kirby, *Singapore: The Chain of Disaster* (London: Cassell, 1971) pp. 121–5, 128; Churchill to Eden, 2 December 1941, *et. seq.*, Prem. 3/156/5; R. Parkinson, *Blood, Toil, Tears and Sweat* (London: Hart-Davis MacGibbon, 1973) pp. 325–6, 330. See also DO(41)54th Mtg., 5 August 1941, DO(41) 56th Mtg., 8 August 1941, Cab 69/2; DO(41)23, 20 October 1941, Cab 69/3; COS 39(O)(42), 1 December 1941, Cab 79/55, and its Confidential Annex, Cab 79/86; COS411(41)1, 7 December 1941, Cab 79/16; COS44(O)(39)1, Cab 79/55. Compare Japanese Imperial General Headquarters Orders 556 and 558–560, 6 November 1941, 561, 8 November 1941, 564–565, 15 November 1941, 569–579, 27 November–3 December 1941, US Navy History Division, Washington Navy Yard.

89. Lecture by H. Probert, Post-Graduate Seminar on the History of Southeast Asia, School of Oriental and African Studies, 26 May 1992. See also M. Tsuji, *Singapore, The Japanese Version* (London: Constable, 1956) *passim*.

90. B. Bond (ed.), *Chief of Staff: The Diaries of Lieutenant-General Sir Henry Pownall*, II, *1940–1944* (London: Leo Cooper, 1974) pp. 65–87, 94–100. See also DO(41)38th Mtg., 29 October 1940, Cab 69/1; DO(41)65th Mtg., 17 October 1941, Cab 69/2; DO(41)66th Mtg., 20 October 1941, Cab 69/8; DO(41)71st Mtg., 3 December 1941, Cab 69/2; Prem. 3/156/1 (file), and Air 23/4745 (file) on Air Inquiry into the loss of the *Prince of Wales and Repulse*.

91. Woodburn-Kirby, *The War against Japan*, I, pp. 213–17, 254–5; Bond, *Chief of Staff*, pp. 82–7, 96–100; See also DO(41)75th Mtg., 27 December 1941, Cab 69/2, and Prem. 3/156/3 (file).

92. Ibid., Woodburn-Kirby, pp. 162–3, 182–4, 212, 214–17, 251–5; Bond, pp. 94–5; Churchill, *The History of the Second World War*, IV, *The Hinge of Fate* (London, Cassell, 1951), pp. 47–52. See also Prem. 3/156/3 (file).

93. Conversation with Captain P. Elphick on 28 April 1993, concerning the forthcoming publication of his second book on the fall of Malaya, and his first, *Odd Man Out*.
94. Prem. 3/142/5; 3/149/7; 3/149/9–3/149/11; 3/159/7; 3/160/6–3/160/8& 8/29 (files).
95. Churchill, *The Second World War*, III, p. 536. See also COS41(O) (41)2, 2 December 1941, Cab 79/55.
96. F.S. Northedge, *The Troubled Giant: Britain among the Great Powers, 1916–1939* (London: LSE/Bell, 1966) p. 471.
97. H. Channon, *Chips: The Diaries of Sir Henry Channon* (London: Weidenfeld & Nicolson, 1967) p. 322; Cosgrove, *Churchill at War*, p. 19; R.R. James, *Churchill: A Study in Failure* (London: Weidenfeld & Nicolson, 1970) *passim*.
98. D. Dilks (ed.), *The Diaries of Sir Alexander Cadogan, 1938–1945* (London: Cassell, 1971) pp. 290, 300–1, 347, 392; Gardner, *Churchill in his Time*, p.166.

# 3 Admiral Yamamoto's Surprise Attack and the Japanese Navy's War Strategy

## Ikuhiko Hata

### A FICTIONAL 'DECISIVE BATTLE IN THE PACIFIC'

'The place: the seas south of the Ryūkyū Islands. The time: mid-August.... The victorious enemy fleet steams westward with a victorious cry, pausing only to rescue our drowning sailors! Ah, the entire Japanese fleet annihilated in these waters....leaving a resentment that will burn for generations.'

These lines are from the conclusion of *Tsugi no issen* (The Coming Battle), published in 1914 by 'A Certain Commander', the anonymous pen-name adopted by Commander Mizuno Hironori of the Imperial Japanese Navy.

Mizuno was already famous for his documentary account of the Battle of Tsushima, entitled *Kono issen* (This Battle), which had established him, along with Army Lieutenant Sakurai Tadayoshi (author of *Nikudan* (Human Bullets), an account of the Japanese attack on Port Arthur) as one of the foremost literary chroniclers of the Russo-Japanese War of 1904–5. Mizuno would later retire with the rank of captain and go on to make a career for himself as a liberal commentator on naval affairs, but at the time he wrote *The Coming Battle* he was still on active duty as a commander in the Imperial Navy. Even though he published anonymously, the story line of his novel – detailing a crushing defeat of the Japanese fleet by American warships – was sufficiently shocking that it may surprise some readers to learn that Mizuno escaped any disciplinary action for having written it. Yet there was a hidden motive concealed in the plot of Mizuno's novel.

By 1914, when the book was written, the Russo-Japanese War had been over for nearly a decade, and the United States had been officially designated by naval planners as Japan's number two hypothetical enemy after Imperial Russia (promoted to number one in 1923). Positing war with the United States, the Japanese Navy was developing the concept of an '8–8 Fleet', a force built around eight battleships and eight battle cruisers. The Navy was convinced that if the Diet did not approve the naval budget for this build-up, an inferior Japanese fleet risked being crushed by US naval forces in a battle somewhere in the seas east of the Philippines, and was determined not to allow this to happen.[1]

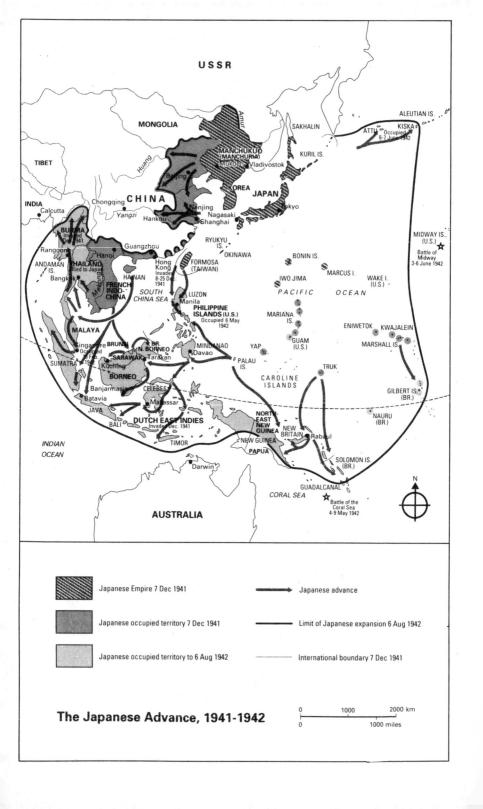

The Japanese Advance, 1941-1942

| | Japanese Empire 7 Dec 1941 | | Japanese advance |
|---|---|---|---|
| | Japanese occupied territory 7 Dec 1941 | | Limit of Japanese expansion 6 Aug 1942 |
| | Japanese occupied territory to 6 Aug 1942 | | International boundary 7 Dec 1941 |

USSR

MONGOLIA

TIBET

INDIA
Calcutta

SAKHALIN

ALEUTIAN IS.

ATTU Occupied
KISKA 6-7 June 1942

MANCHUKUO
(MANCHURIA)
Mukden Vladivostok

KURIL IS.

Beijing

KOREA JAPAN

CHINA

Chongqing

Yangzi
Hankou

Nanjing
Nagasaki
Shanghai

Tokyo

MIDWAY IS.
(U.S.)
Battle of
Midway
3-6 June 1942

BURMA
Invaded
Dec 1941

RYUKYU
IS.

OKINAWA

BONIN IS.

Rangoon

Guangzhou

ANDAMAN
IS.
Allied to Japan

THAILAND

Hanoi

Hong
Kong
Invaded
8-25 Dec
1941

FORMOSA
(TAIWAN)

IWO JIMA

MARCUS I.

WAKE I.
(U.S.)

Bangkok

HAINAN

LUZON

PACIFIC OCEAN

FRENCH
INDO-
CHINA

SOUTH
CHINA SEA

Manila

PHILIPPINE
ISLANDS (U.S.)
Occupied 6 May
1942

MARIANA
IS.

ENIWETOK

KWAJALEIN

MALAYA

BRUNEI

BR.
N. BORNEO

MINDANAO

YAP

GUAM
(U.S.)

MARSHALL IS.

Singapore
Occupied
Feb 1942

SARAWAK

Tarakan

Davao

PALAU
IS.

SUMATRA

Kuching

BORNEO

TRUK

GILBERT IS.
(BR.)

Banjarmasin

CELEBES

CAROLINE
ISLANDS

Batavia

Makassar

JAVA

BALI

DUTCH EAST INDIES
Invaded Dec 1941

TIMOR

NORTH-
EAST
NEW
GUINEA

NAURU
(BR.)

INDIAN
OCEAN

Darwin

NEW GUINEA

PAPUA

NEW
BRITAIN

Rabaul

SOLOMON IS.
(BR.)

AUSTRALIA

GUADALCANAL

CORAL SEA
Battle of the
Coral Sea
4-9 May 1942

N

0          1000          2000 km

0                1000 miles

Mizuno's novel was based on this perception of the situation, and the inflammatory nature of its plot was designed to stimulate patriotic anxiety in his readers in order to win public support for naval policy.

In fact, Japan's politicians and mass media tended to be more sympathetic to the Navy's desire for a naval build-up versus the United States than they were to the Army's insistence on military preparations against Russia, and in 1920 the budget supporting the 8–8 Fleet finally passed the Diet.

In the years after Mizuno's *The Coming Battle*, a spate of similar fictional accounts of a future war between Japan and the United States were published in Japan.[2] Two of the most influential were by Westerners. The first was Homer Lea's *The Valor of Ignorance* (1909), which went through three different Japanese translations and was reprinted even during World War II. The second was Hector C. Bywater's *The Great Pacific War* (1929), which caused a sensation when first published because its powerful realism spurred accusations of the leaking of military secrets. One of the most popular Japanese works of this kind was *Beikoku osoruru ni tarazu* (Why Fear America?) by Ikezaki Tadataka, which went through 68 printings in the first year and a half after its release in 1929.

With the exception of Mizuno's novel, accounts of future war written by Japanese all ended in victory for Japan; Western accounts divided the fate of battle more equally. In any case, there is little doubt that the theme of naval warfare in the Pacific between Japan and the United States was one which exerted a powerful fascination over many readers.

First of all there was the immense scale of the setting. The largest ocean on the planet, dotted with its innumerable islands, became a vast and glittering chessboard with warships arrayed as in a complex game: battleships as kings and queens, heavy cruisers as rooks, light cruisers as bishops, aircraft carriers as knights, and light cruisers, destroyers, and other auxiliaries as pawns, small but potentially deadly as they closed within range of the torpedoes they carried.

Aboard the flagship *Yamato* during the Pacific War, Admiral Yamamoto Isoroku never missed his lightning games of Japanese-style chess with his favourite staff officer, Watanabe, and was frequently heard to remark, 'A bad chess player doesn't have a chance at beating the Americans'.

Just as chess has its standard gambits, the fiction of future war developed certain standard scenarios. Young naval officers who read Homer Lea and Hector Bywater with enthusiasm later went on to serve as strategic planners, drafting the annual war plans, teaching strategy and tactics at the Naval War College, rising through the ranks to command their own ships and direct them on manoeuvres. In the process, the line between fiction and reality began to blur.

Recently a number of historians have come to question the notion that war between Japan and the United States in the 1940s was really inevitable.[3] This doubt seems reasonable, and the present writer, too, has come to wonder if perhaps thirty years of imaginary war games, played with relish by both amateurs and professionals alike, finally resulted in the tragedy of the real war.

## OFFENSIVE AND DEFENSIVE STRATEGIES

My first visit to the US Naval War College in Newport, Rhode Island, was in the autumn of 1963. Founded by Alfred Thayer Mahan, the world-renowned naval strategist, the halls of this institution were the training ground for the famous admirals whose names punctuate the history of the Pacific War: Nimitz, Spruance, King. The instructor who guided me on a tour of the college showed me a lecture hall whose floor had been used for games simulating naval warfare with Japan. Before World War II there had been no official war-games room, so student officers had crawled across this floor, moving model warships across an imaginary Pacific.

Commander Akiyama Saneyuki, Admiral Tōgō Heihachirō's planning officer for the Battle of Tsushima, had applied to the US Naval War College at the turn of the century but had been refused admission; in compensation, Mahan offered him private instruction. In a broad sense, the Pacific War was fought between men on both sides who had been trained by Mahan's disciples.

In the archives of the Naval War College there is a file containing the problem-sets given to the officers in training and their answers to them. The folder for 1933 contains a set of these practice manoeuvres in which the 'Blue' (US) fleet commander, Captain Ernest King, chose a northern attack route advancing along a Hawaii–Midway–Wake–Marianas line. The president of the War College, Rear Admiral Laning, preferred a southern route, beginning with the Japanese Mandate islands of the South Pacific (now Micronesia) and then advancing westward along the northern coast of New Guinea. He criticised King's plan as 'the worst possible'.

Not quite a decade later, King, as Chief of Naval Operations, was in charge of planning a two-ocean strategy for a global conflict. In the Pacific, he employed his 'worst possible' plan, bypassing Micronesia in favour of an advance through the central and northern Pacific – and achieved a stunning success.[4]

In the autumn of 1927, six years before Captain King's student exercise, Lieutenant Commander Takagi Sōkichi engaged in his graduation manoeuvres at the Japanese Naval War College in the Tsukiji district of Tokyo. Takagi, as commander of the 'Blue' (Japanese) fleet, attacked Pearl Harbor with two aircraft carriers. The attack met with little success, Takagi lost one of his carriers, and his effort was branded as 'rash' by both the instructors and his fellow students. Takagi's opponent, a student officer commanding the 'Red' (US) fleet, launched a hit-and-run raid on Tokyo with two carriers, and got away unscathed.

Surprise carrier assaults of this kind across the breadth of the Pacific were favourite gambits by ambitious student officers at both the US and Japanese naval war colleges. Yet in these exercises, air attacks on Hawaii most frequently ended in heavy losses inflicted by the counterattack of the defending forces, and a Pearl Harbor attack was never included in the official annual war plan approved by the Japanese emperor.[5]

In a Japanese Navy dominated by men who liked to play the role of the English-style officer and gentleman, Yamamoto Isoroku, like Takagi, stood out for his boldness. It seems no mere coincidence that in a lecture that he delivered at the Naval Torpedo School in the summer of 1928, soon after his return from service as naval attaché in Washington, Captain Yamamoto argued for the necessity of an attack on Pearl Harbor.[6] It seems safe to assume that the actual attack on Pearl Harbor in December 1941 was an idea that had begun to ferment in the brain of this unorthodox and unusually individualistic Japanese naval officer as early as the 1920s.

The war games played hundreds and thousands of times in Newport and Tsukiji may have been conducted on paper or with miniature models, but for the men involved this was no mere recreation: a war in the Pacific was, for all concerned, an event which could determine the very fate of their respective nations. The focus of attention was a clash between the main battlefleets of both countries somewhere in the western Pacific; a battle that, when it occurred, would prove as decisive as the Battle of Tsushima that won the Russo-Japanese War. To prepare for the possibility of this historic struggle, both Japan and the United States devoted something like a quarter of their national budgets to building up, maintaining, improving and training their fleets. In the phrase of the ancient Chinese military strategist Sun Tzu, 'Armies are nurtured for a century to be expended in a single day' – an unusually apt characterisation of the US and Japanese preparations for war in the Pacific.

In the years between the Russo-Japanese War and World War II, the unceasing research and practice of naval planners in both Japan and the United States produced at a fairly early juncture what might be called a 'classic' strategic scenario for war in the Pacific, which predicated an offensive strategy by the United States – a long-distance strike across the Pacific – which would be met by a Japanese strategy of defence.

In fact, this essential strategic picture, shared by both sides, hardened into a fixed idea that survived more or less unaltered for nearly 30 years – something rare in the annals of military planning. During this time, despite the agreements on naval armaments ratios at the Washington and London Conferences, despite Japan's acquisition of the mandate islands in the South Pacific as a result of World War I, and despite the revolution in technology represented by the growth of military aviation, the US Navy's continuing numerical superiority and the nearly universal acceptance of the Big Gun doctrine that saw battleships as the centrepiece of any navy acted to prevent any fundamental rethinking of the classic strategic vision.

Although it did not ground this notion on a particularly rigorous theoretical foundation, the US Navy believed that in order to make a cross-Pacific offensive strategy possible, it needed at least a 150 to 160 per cent superiority over the Japanese fleet. For its part, the Japanese Navy calculated that it needed a strength equal to at least 70 per cent of the US Navy's in order to mount a viable defence.

At the Washington Conference in 1922, a compromise was reached in which the United States was given the 10:6 ratio of capital ships that it demanded *vis-à-vis* Japan, but Japan received in return an advantageous agreement regarding the limitation of defensive installations in the Pacific islands. Admiral Katō Tomosaburō, the senior Japanese representative at the conference, reckoned that this compromise amounted in practical terms to the 10:7 ratio Japan desired. At the London Naval Conference in 1930, Japan was left disappointed by an agreement that barely met its minimal demands with respect to submarines, but at the same time secured a heavy cruiser ratio approaching 10:7. Moreover, aircraft, which Japan set great store by, were not affected by the treaty. As a result, neither the Washington nor London treaties upset the strategic balance or the strategic planning assumptions of either Japan or the United States.

In this context, the attention of naval planners in both countries shifted to the tactical aspects and concrete details of their respective grand strategies. As the writers of futuristic war fiction exercised their imagination to produce dramatic fantasies of Pacific conflict, the naval war colleges on both sides of the ocean were the scene of elaborate simulations, in which strange and brilliant gambits were played, rejected, and played again. Each year Blue and Red fleets wrangled and collided, won and lost, under the stern eyes of the admirals who evaluated the outcome of the games.

The staff officers must have felt a certain satisfaction at the magnificence and grandeur of their exercises, which must have exceeded the imaginative powers of even the most inventive writer of fiction. And indeed, the results of this ceaseless debate and experimentation were war plans that rivalled the famous Schlieffen Plan for Germany's 1914 invasion of France in their precision and polish.

The strategy developed with such painstaking attention by the numerically inferior Japanese Navy was based on the tactics of attrition. In essence, as the US fleet steamed forth from its bases on the West Coast and Hawaii on its way to the site of the decisive battle, Japanese forces would worry and hound it, chipping away at its fighting strength and morale in preparation for a knockout blow in the final confrontation between the two main battle forces.

This sort of defensive strategy was natural for an inferior opponent to adopt, and the US planners assumed as much. The problem was what specific tactics the Japanese would employ to carry it out.

A strategy of attrition is divisible into two distinct phases: Phase I is concerned with wearing down the enemy's strength, while Phase II involves the inevitable confrontation with what is left of the enemy's main force.

For Phase I, the Japanese Navy exercised considerable ingenuity in developing the tactics for submarine observation, pursuit, and harassment of the enemy fleet, as well as surprise night attacks by torpedo flotillas of cruisers and destroyers on the eve of the confrontation between the main battle fleets.

World War I had taught the effectiveness of submarines against an enemy's merchant marine, but the Japanese Navy, impressed by the capacity for stealth and mobility these vessels possessed, boldly decided to employ them as a main element of its attrition strategy. The plan was to encircle Hawaii with a powerful submarine force soon after the outbreak of hostilities, using them to monitor the departure of the US fleet, reporting periodically on its strength, disposition, and course while awaiting the opportunity to damage it with surprise attacks. For this purpose, the Japanese Navy developed large, high-speed submarines that were capable of making a round-trip voyage across the Pacific without refuelling.

For its surface torpedo flotillas, intended for night attack, the Japanese first employed light cruisers and destroyers, but then broke with convention by adding high-speed battle cruisers of the Kongō class, beginning in 1933.

In the days before radar, surveillance and recognition depended entirely on the powers of human eyesight. The Japanese Navy exerted itself to find and men with excellent eyesight to serve as its lookouts and give them special training. It succeeded in developing a cadre of specialists who could spot and differentiate a target at 10 000 metres even in the dead of night – even a cat would have envied their ability.

If all went as planned, the main elements of the Japanese Navy would be taking another page from Sun Tzu, who advised, 'Lie comfortably in wait to strike an exhausted enemy'. Delivering the *coup de grâce* to a US fleet damaged and worn down by the submarines and torpedo flotillas should not be too difficult.

At the time, naval officers the world over believed in the axiom that the outcome of any sea battle would be determined by the numerical ratio between the capital ships of the respective fleets. The strategic planners of the Japanese Navy, faced with the 6:10 ratio against the US Navy that had been established in the Washington Treaty, were hard pressed to invent some means for overcoming this fundamental disadvantage and give themselves a chance of victory. The bitter dispute within the Navy that was waged between the 'Disarmament Faction' and the 'Fleet Faction' over the terms of the London Treaty was largely based on various interpretations of how to deal with this basic issue.

The thinking of the Disarmament Faction was based on the implicit assumption that a so-called '60-Percent Navy' had no chance of winning against the Americans, and that a war with the United States must therefore be avoided. In contrast, the Fleet Faction believed that with fierce training and tactical ingenuity some avenue towards victory could be discovered, and made redoubled efforts to refine and improve the attrition strategy. As a result, in the course of the 1930s the initial emphasis on submarines as the main element in the attrition strategy began to shift towards night attacks by surface forces and then to the use of the new technology represented by aircraft.

Despite these efforts, the strategists of the Japanese Navy were still not fully confident of the effectiveness of the attrition strategy. Repeated simulation games and fleet exercises produced varying results depending on the conditions established as their premise. On the eve of the Pacific War, Yamamoto, now Commander-in-Chief of the Combined Fleet, expressed the following opinion in a letter to the Navy Minister: 'Given the fact that in repeated war games the Imperial Navy has yet to achieve a single decisive victory, and concerned about the erosion of morale that will result if this situation continues, we have given standing orders for the suspension of fleet exercises'.[7]

The last major set of special fleet exercises conducted by the Navy had taken place in the summer of 1936 in the waters south of the Japanese home islands. In these exercises, Blue Fleet (Japan) unleashed repeated night attacks at close quarters against Red Fleet (America), but was annihilated by the Red counterattack. Chief Umpire Admiral Suetsugu, seeing what was happening and fearing for the effect on morale of such a crushing defeat, advised the commander-in-chief to give the searchlight signal marking the termination of the exercise, but he was too late.[8]

There is also a famous episode concerning the war gaming preceding the Battle of Midway. When a throw of the dice had indicated nine direct bomb hits on a Japanese carrier, Rear Admiral Ugaki Matome, Chief of Staff of the Combined Fleet, intervened to say, 'I judge that only three direct hits were scored', allowing the carrier *Akagi*, which should have been sunk in this attack, to be used in the next phase of the operation.[9] From this one can see how rife the bad habit had become among Japanese naval planners to take gaming and exercises, which should have been conducted scrupulously, and rig them so that they ended either in Japanese victories or in draws.

Despite all this, in the absence of any other more reliable alternative, the attrition strategy continued to be adhered to without any major revaluations or revisions. Moreover, as the Disarmament Faction lost strength as a result of the dispute over the 'right of supreme command' which accompanied the signing of the London Treaty, the Fleet Faction, with its hardline approach to the United States, became the dominant force within the Navy, and anyone bold enough to question the viability of the existing strategic doctrine ran the risk of being branded a defeatist or a coward.

This climate of opinion even gave birth among some of the Navy's young officers to a vague belief in the 'inevitability of victory' against the United States, while at the same time generally contributing to an ossification of strategic thinking and a tendency toward irrational faith in the 'spiritual' superiority of Japanese forces. None of these developments boded well for the Navy as a whole. In 1940 the Office of the Chief of Naval Operations suddenly delivered itself of the judgement that Japan could win at even a 5:10 numerical ratio against the United States. This drastic downward revision of the classic 7:10 ratio became one of the theoretical underpinnings of the decision to go to war with America the following year: the only problem was that it had no rational basis.[10]


## WHAT WAS ADMIRAL YAMAMOTO THINKING?

It was against this background of events that Admiral Yamamoto appeared as the Commander-in-Chief of Combined Fleet, bringing with him the ambitious concept of a Pearl Harbor attack in bold defiance of traditional strategic doctrine.

Given its distaste for strong individual personalities, and with war on the horizon, it remains a mystery as to why the Navy gave the all-important position of fleet commander to Yamamoto, who not only rejected established doctrine but was also regarded as being opposed to war with the United States.

A look at Yamamoto's record shows that he attained the rank of vice-admiral without once serving as a bureau or section chief in either the Navy Ministry or the Office of the Chief of Naval Operations: a very unusual career pattern. If a number of talented officers among his peers had not been forced into early retirement as a result of the rivalry between the Disarmament and Fleet factions, it is unlikely that Yamamoto would have ever had the chance to rise to the position of Commander-in-Chief, Combined Fleet.

Yamamoto had in earlier days been one of the hawks associated with the Fleet Faction – to the extent that he had threatened to beat up a high official representing the Ministry of Finance at the London Naval Conference in 1930.[11] After a number of the officers who led the Disarmament Faction had been forced out of the Navy, Yamamoto was able to inherit their positions.

At the same time, Yamamoto had spent many years outside the mainstream of the Navy. Two tours of duty in Washington – first as a language officer and then as naval attaché – had turned him into something of an expert on America, while his involvement in aviation going back to his days as a captain won him the epithet 'father of the naval air forces'. Experiences such as these broadened his vision, and laid the basis for his innovations in strategic thinking.

After his appointment as Commander-in-Chief of Combined Fleet in September 1939, Yamamoto implemented a sweeping revision of Navy doctrine centring on the following points: (1) a shift from a defensive to an offensive strategy, (2) a priority given to the Navy's air forces, and (3) the new tactical concept of the use of carrier groups as main battle units. As innovative as these changes were, the highlight of the new Yamamoto strategy, for better or worse, was the Pearl Harbor attack.

As we have seen, the concept of an attack on Pearl Harbor was not in itself a startling idea, for it had been the imaginative fuel behind many a student exercise at the Naval War College and numerous works of popular fiction. However, in the more serious war-gaming conducted by the Office of the Chief of Naval Operations, the attacking force had frequently been decimated by the land-based aircraft of the defenders, and it had been determined that a raid on Pearl had very slim prospects of success.

Because of this, the idea had never even been considered for inclusion in the official annual war plan submitted for imperial approval. Moreover, years of adherence to a fundamentally defensive strategy meant that Japanese warships had been designed with only a limited cruising range in mind.

It was the autumn of 1940 when Yamamoto turned to his chief of staff, Rear Admiral Fukudome Shigeru, and said as if thinking aloud, 'I wonder if it would be possible to hit Hawaii with an air attack?' Fukudome later said that he believed exercises in which torpedo planes attained a high direct hit ratio of 77 per cent and demonstrated that they could be used effectively to sink battleships served as the hint which led Yamamoto to this remark.[12]

However, at this time the Japanese Navy did not possess a single aircraft carrier with the capacity to make it to Hawaii and back without refuelling. Nor did it have shallow-water torpedoes which could run at the 15-metre depth of the US battleship fleet's Pearl Harbor anchorage. Low-level horizontal bombing runs had demonstrated a hit ratio of less than 2 per cent. In other words, even if the Navy had wanted to attack Pearl Harbor, it was clear that the conditions for success did not exist, and initially no one supported the idea. In an effort to win approval, Yamamoto wrote to the Navy Minister, saying that he was 'convinced that victory or defeat will be determined on the first day' and that he was prepared to resign his position as commander-in-chief in order to 'assume personal command of the strike force'.[13]

For the next year, Yamamoto struggled to remove the material obstacles to his plan. Through his efforts, six aircraft carriers were prepared to make the voyage, shallow water torpedoes were developed, and the hit ratio of the low-level bombers was greatly improved through training. At last, in October 1941, the Office of the Chief of Naval Operations finally gave its grudging approval.

An additional factor influencing the decision was that the home base of the main US battlefleet had been shifted in May 1940 from the West Coast to Hawaii. A long lance now had some chance at striking at the heart of American naval power in the Pacific.

THE PHENOMENAL SUCCESS OF THE PEARL HARBOR ATTACK

The question of why the US Navy was caught by surprise at Pearl Harbor occasions heated debate even today, and has given rise to some wild theories, including accusations that Roosevelt himself was involved in a conspiracy to conceal foreknowledge of the raid. In my opinion, the question is best answered by an American failure to perceive the fact that Yamamoto had succeeded in the space of a single year in altering the conditions which had previously made such a raid impossible.

Despite the success of the attack in destroying the US battleship fleet, there is also debate over whether, in the long run, it ended up being a plus or a minus for the Japanese Navy. Representative of those whose assessment of Pearl Harbor is essentially negative is Samuel E. Morison's series *The History of US Naval Operations in World War II*. Morison rates the attack as ultimately a failure because (1) it unified American popular opinion and aroused public hostility against Japan, (2) it failed to find and sink the US carrier force, (3) it did not destroy the naval arsenal and fuel storage facilities at Pearl, and (4) the sunken battleships, with the exception of the *Arizona*, were all raised from the shallow waters of the anchorage, repaired, and returned to service. Moreover, deprived at least temporarily of its battleship force, the US Navy was forced to make the full transition to a carrier-centred strategy, which the Japanese Navy itself was slower to carry out.

These are arguments of hindsight, which might have assigned the raid a nearly perfect score if only the carriers had been found and sunk and if the planned second assault had been pushed through to destroy the harbour facilities as well as the ships. But given the overall strategic picture, in which the Pearl Harbor attack fulfilled its other function of securing the flank of the main Japanese thrust into South-East Asia to capture its raw materials, I would assign the raid a score of about 90.

According to the Rainbow V and OPL-46 strategic plans released after the war, the US Navy envisioned a classic strategy involving a sortie from Hawaii against the Marshall Islands on the fifth day of hostilities, followed by a sweep through the islands of Micronesia on the way to an assault on the Japanese home islands.[14] If this had been carried out, the Japanese would have found themselves fighting a two-front war in the Pacific – a continuation of their offensive in South-East Asia coupled with defensive operations in the Central Pacific – that would have placed an immense strain on their forces.

In other words, the Pearl Harbor attack, which delayed the ability of the United States to mount a trans-Pacific offensive campaign for two years, at the cost of only 29 planes and five midget submarines, should be rated a phenomenal success. The issue was whether or not the Japanese Navy could keep it from ending as a single spectacular burst of fireworks, and succeed in yoking it to a grand strategy that had similar prospects of success through the end of the conflict.

In April 1941 Yamamoto had already warned Prime Minister Konoye Fumimaro, 'We can give you a wild show for six months to a year, but if the war drags on to two and three years, I cannot be confident of the outcome'.[15] On another occasion, when a subordinate argued against the Pearl Harbor attack on the grounds that it would be risky, Yamamoto replied, 'If we don't succeed with the surprise attack, all we can do is say our luck was bad.' Behind these statements can be read an attitude of mind that was well aware of the United States' 10 to 1 superiority over Japan in total national resources, resigned to a brave but most likely vain display of valour and violence. If war with the United States was itself an immense gamble, why not begin the gambling at the very outset?

For a fleet commander upon whose shoulders rested the fate of the entire nation, this may seem a rather irresponsible frame of mind – but it resembles the thoughts that the sixteenth-century warlord Oda Nobunaga must have had as he set out for his miraculous victory over superior Imagawa forces at the Battle of Okehazama.

Nobunaga's closest advisers urged him to immure himself in Kiyosu Castle and fight a defensive action against the Imagawa armies, in much the same way that mid-twentieth-century Japanese naval strategy remained fixed upon the idea of fighting a holding action against the US fleet in waters close to the home islands. In both cases, however, no supporting forces existed to come to the relief of the besieged defenders.

Instead of following the advice of his retainers, Nobunaga mounted an attack which succeeded largely because of its implausibility, which gave him complete surprise. After Okehazama, however, Nobunaga never again resorted to such a gamble, sticking instead to orthodox strategies for the rest of his drive to unite Japan under his power.

Did Yamamoto learn from Nobunaga's example and his shift in strategy? In a letter to the Navy Minister he touched on the problem, saying 'We shall be driven into the unfortunate position of having to fight an Okehazama, a Hiyodorigoe, and a Kawanakajima all at the same time', citing three famous surprise victories by inferior forces from Japan's medieval past.[16] But in the final analysis, the answer must be 'no'.

## THE FAILURE OF THE SECOND GAMBLE

When Admiral Nagumo's task force returned from the Pearl Harbor raid in December 1941, Yamamoto addressed its commanders in the following manner: 'If you are puffed up with pride at the success of this single surprise attack, you are not real warriors. After a victory, one should merely tighten one's helmet straps once again.' To Captain Miwa Yoshitake, who stood nearby as Yamamoto spoke, these words sounded like a rebuke.[17]

Yet the unforeseen speed and smoothness of Japan's advance into South-East Asia and the Pacific had amazed even Combined Fleet and Imperial Headquarters; far from tightening their helmet straps, Japan's military planners were having trouble keeping their feet on the ground. 'Victory disease' was setting in.

Combined Fleet Chief of Staff Ugaki Matome's diary for 5 January 1942 displays the soaring spirits of the time: 'Where do we go from here? Advance on Australia? On India? Invade Hawaii? Watch for a good opportunity and strike the Soviet Union?' Spurred on by Ugaki, Combined Fleet staff planners drew up a number of ideas for follow-up campaigns. The most ambitious was that of Rear Admiral Yamaguchi Tamon, who later died at Midway, which called for the conquest of Fiji, Samoa, New Zealand, and Australia, then the seizure of Midway and Hawaii, all as preparation for an invasion of California in 1943 and massive air raids across the length and breadth of the United States.[18]

As one might expect, this plan of Yamaguchi's was treated as a wild fantasy, but both the Office of the Chief of Naval Operations and Combined Fleet judged that an invasion of Hawaii might be feasible. The first step towards this was the dispatch of Combined Fleet's main strength toward Midway in June 1942.

The Office of the Chief of Naval Operations had initially favoured an advance to Fiji and Samoa to cut the lines of communication between the United States and Australia instead of an attack on Midway, but Yamamoto overcame this, as he had done with the Pearl Harbor plan. The results were tragic. Failure of Japanese surveillance permitted a pre-emptive strike by the American forces; the

Japanese strike force lost the four aircraft carriers that constituted its main strength and was forced to withdraw. In the words of Admiral King, 'This was the most decisive defeat tasted by Japanese naval forces since the days of Toyotomi Hideyoshi'.[19]

With the loss of four of its principal aircraft carriers, the core of its offensive capacity, the Japanese Navy had no other choice but to adopt a defensive posture. For three years after Midway, without ever again regaining the initiative, it suffered a slow and painful attrition of its forces until it was finally pushed out of the ring altogether.

Yamamoto's prediction of a wild show for six months to a year had been correct. Yet some observers argue that if defeat was inevitable after the initial victories, it still should have been possible for the Japanese Navy to have found a way to end the struggle in a stalemate or a draw, rather than in complete destruction. And such criticism unavoidably turns against Yamamoto himself.

Perhaps because of his dramatic death in the air over the Solomons in April 1943, in the post-war era Yamamoto has been a popular figure both in Japan and the United States. Particularly among veterans of the Japanese Navy, criticism of Yamamoto has been taboo, but over the years a number of long-repressed complaints and grievances have occasionally broken into the open.

A number of years ago I organised a round-table discussion among veterans of the rank of captain to vice-admiral for a special issue of a magazine devoted to the history of the Pacific War.[20] I was startled to find that the entire conversation turned, from beginning to end, on reviling Yamamoto. The criticisms were many, but all of them shared the view that Yamamoto's fatal mistake had been the offensive strategy he adopted from Pearl Harbor onward, arguing that he should have followed the traditional defensive strategy instead. For example, the late Vice-Admiral Nakazawa Tasuku (who once headed the Operations Section and later the Operations Bureau of the Office of the Chief of Naval Operations) argued, 'It would have been much better to have enticed the advancing US fleet into Micronesia and then hit it with both carrier and land-based aircraft'. Nakazawa added that Shimada Shigetaro, a classmate of Yamamoto's who was given the post of Navy Minister in October 1941, would have been a better choice for the post of Commander-in-Chief, Combined Fleet – not because Shimada would have been a more brilliant commander than Yamamoto, but because Shimada's experience in the Operations Section would never have let him contemplate anything other than a defensive strategy of interception.

Former Captain Mayuzumi Haruo, an authority on naval gunnery who had dreamed of seeing an exhausted US trans-Pacific strike-force worn down by air attacks and then brought under the gigantic guns of the battleship *Yamato*, said bluntly, 'Yamamoto didn't know a thing about using battleships'.

Another Operations Section veteran, former Rear-Admiral Matsuda Chiaki, lamented, 'Yamamoto completely ignored the classic strategic planning that had resulted from more than 30 years of constant refinement by successive chiefs of Naval Operations and their staffs.... He didn't even try to make use of the military preparations that had at last made victory possible.' According to Matsuda's harsh assessment, 'It would be no exaggeration to conclude that [Yamamoto's strategy] was either the kind of hit-or-miss thing you would expect from an amateur ignorant of basic tactics, or else an ill-considered gamble.'

In all of these comments one can sense the chagrin and resentment that still festers among the more orthodox veterans of the Navy, and the way it tends to accumulate about the figure of Yamamoto, the Navy's most famous heretic.

## DID YAMAMOTO MAKE THE RIGHT DECISION?

In my belief that the Pearl Harbor attack itself was not a mistake, I differ from these veterans, but in principle I adhere to the position of the orthodox camp.

First of all, let me reaffirm the obvious principle that naval strategy should be subordinate to overall national strategic planning. For Japan on the eve of World War II, the national grand strategy was represented by a document adopted at the liaison conference between Imperial General Headquarters and the Cabinet three weeks before the fighting commenced, entitled *Tai Bei-Ei-Ran-Shō sensō shūmatsu sokushin ni kansuru fukuan* (A Plan for Completion of the War Against the United States, Great Britain, the Netherlands, and Chiang Kai-shek). Contained in it was the following passage:

> The Empire will...crush American, British and Dutch strongholds in East Asia and the Western Pacific...and secure major resource areas and lines of communication in order to prepare a posture of long term self-sufficiency. All available methods will be exerted to lure out the main elements of the US fleet at an appropriate time to attack and destroy them.[21]

In other words, for better or worse, the official assessment of the prospects for the coming war acknowledged the very high likelihood that it would be a protracted struggle, one which would require a swift occupation of the resource-rich areas of South-East Asia and their integration into an autarkic 'Greater East Asia Co-prosperity Sphere' capable of resisting the United States 'for an extended period without major defeats'.

What is frankly revealed by this document is that even if Japan did not think it could win the war outright, it hoped that it could avoid losing – a position quite at odds with Yamamoto's strategy commencing with the Pearl Harbor attack, an aggressive strategy predicated on an quick and decisive outcome. Moreover, the line in the official war plan which spoke of 'luring out the main elements of the US fleet at an appropriate time' was clearly a directive to adopt a defensive strategy.

Whether or not Yamamoto was aware of this decision by the Liaison Council, he staked his career on the idea for an attack on Pearl Harbor, pushing so hard that Admiral Nagano Osami, Chief of Naval Operations finally grudgingly acceded to his wishes.

The irresponsibility of Nagano and Navy Minister Shimada must also be noted, but this kind of *gekokujō* situation in which hotheaded subordinates overmastered their superiors was far from unusual in the Japanese military in the 1930s and 1940s, as the insubordinate behaviour of the Kwangtung Army in Manchuria indicates.

It might be said that Yamamoto was not immune to this malady, and managed to turn Combined Fleet into a second Kwangtung Army. Although the Pearl Harbor attack was a success that helped guarantee the rapid thrust to secure the resources of South-East Asia, thus benefiting Japan's grand strategy, the Navy should have considered it a lucky fluke and returned to its fundamentally defensive strategy.

A two-year period of grace had been created before the US Navy could mount a trans-Pacific campaign. In the interval, Japan should have expanded its lines no further, and concentrated instead on shipping the resources of South-East Asia to the home islands to transform them into war materiel and fighting power, concentrating on developing a posture that could survive 'for an extended period with no major defeats'.

The Combined Fleet could then lie in wait within Japan's defensive perimeter, and if an ill-prepared US force did come out to engage it, it could intercept it with the aid of land-based air forces. The Americans might be able to launch two or three carrier raids on Tokyo, but sporadic and limited attacks of this nature should not be a major cause for alarm.

The scenario outlined above is little more than a bundle of hypotheses, and no matter how much of an optimist I may be, this should not be taken as suggesting that I think the Japanese–American war in the Pacific could have ended in a Japanese victory or even a draw.

With the defeat of Germany, Japan would still have been left alone to fight the rest of the world. Sooner or later, it would have lost, and the atomic bombs would still have delivered the *coup de grâce*. In the final analysis, it would not have made a great deal of difference whether the Navy adopted Yamamoto's strategy or had stuck to its classic doctrine. Yet at the same time, there are lessons to be learned from that debate.


LESSONS AND CONCLUSIONS

The first lesson is that both in diplomacy and war, the details of policy and tactics must advance in directions congruent with an comprehensive national strategy.

Policy and tactics that violate such a grand strategy can only lead to catastrophe, no matter how brilliant they may be in and of themselves.

Second, the national grand strategy must be so clear that it allows no possibility of misinterpretation, and it must be predicated on the will to implement it. In Japan, when a decision is necessary on an issue on which it is difficult to achieve consensus, there is a habit of papering over differences by producing some pleasant-sounding but unintelligible document. The plan adopted by the Liaison Council was actually a fairly honest reading of the situation, perhaps because even today it is difficult to see any viable alternative once the crucial decision to go to war had been reached. The fact that both Yamamoto and Naval Operations gave it so little consideration may very well have been because they failed to realise it was more than the usual mealy-mouthed bureaucratic compromise.

Third is the risk that attends a sudden change in strategic doctrine. Well aware of America's enormous potential capability for waging war, Yamamoto felt that there was little prospect for success in a protracted struggle, and pinned his hopes instead on a quick strike that would bring a swift resolution. However, only a few of his closest associates really understood this. Even within Combined Fleet, the majority were not quick enough on the uptake to grasp Yamamoto's change in thinking, and merely followed orders blindly. Among this majority was the commander-in-chief of the First Air Fleet, Vice-Admiral Nagumo Chūichi. Assigned command of the task force attacking Pearl Harbor, he steamed off without much of a commitment to the gamble he was undertaking and missed his chance to deliver the second attack against the harbour facilities. Evidently not a gambling man, he was in command again at Midway, where he made mistake after mistake and suffered an irreversible defeat.

Whenever I review the history of Japanese and American naval strategy in the Pacific, I recall the fate of the Schlieffen Plan. Alfred Graf Schlieffen, Chief of German General Staff, was presented with the agonising dilemma of a two-front war with France on the west and Russia to the east. The plan he produced was to gather his main forces on his right flank in the west, march them across neutral Belgium, and in six weeks' time outflank and destroy the French armies from their rear. That accomplished, Germany's forces would then turn to confront their Russian opponent. Convinced that this was the only way Germany stood a chance of winning a European war, Schlieffen died in 1913, leaving a final command to 'Strengthen the right flank!' The German Army took this last testament of Schlieffen's as an iron rule, but his successor, 'Little Moltke' was a general of only mediocre ability. When the fighting actually began in 1914, Moltke became concerned about the security of his left flank, and drew forces off from the crucial right in order to reinforce it.

The result was that the German right advanced only a little further before stopping in exhaustion, and the protracted two-front war the Schlieffen Plan had been designed to prevent became a reality.

It is of course impossible to re-enact history under a different set of circumstances. Yet even today there are many people who wonder, in one of history's great 'ifs', what would have happened if Moltke had honored Schlieffen's testament and strengthened his right.

I close with another 'if' of history which seems worthy of debate: what if Japan had not attacked at Pearl Harbor, had restrained itself from further expansion of its battlefront, and had massed the full strength of its Combined Fleet in the western Pacific to await and intercept the advance of the US Navy?

## NOTES

1. Matsushita Yoshio, *Mizuno Hironori* (Tokyo, 1950) pp. 26–27.
2. Between 1911 and 1933 a total of 78 books (including translations) were published on the theme of war between Japan and the United States. See Hata Ikuhiko, *Taiheiyō kokusai kankei shi* (Reality and Illusion: A History of the Russo-Japanese and Japanese–American Crises, 1900–35), (Fukumura Shoten, 1971) pp. 224–8.

    Moreover, a report from the assistant US military attaché in Tokyo to the State Department mentions that 36 magazine articles of this nature were published in 1932 alone (Cranford Memorandum, 9 September 1932, *Foreign Relations of the United States*, 1932, vol. IV, pp. 706–15).
3. See, for example, the work of Akira Iriye, including *Nichibei sensō* (The Japanese–American War), (Tokyo, 1978).
4. King and Whitehall, *Fleet Admiral King*, (New York, 1952) p. 239.
5. Takagi Sōkichi, *Shikan Taiheiyō sensō* (A Personal View of the Pacific War), (Tokyo, 1969) p. 16.
6. Yamamoto Chikao, *Daihon'ei kaigunbu* (Navy Section, Imperial General Headquarters), (Tokyo, 1974) p. 54.
7. Letter from Admiral Yamamoto to Navy Minister Oikawa dated 7 January 1941.
8. Koyanagi Tomiji, article in the magazine *Maru*, May 1961.
9. Japanese Defence Agency, *Middouē kaisen* (The Battle of Midway), (Tokyo, 1971) p. 90.
10. Ōmae Toshikazu, 'Kyū kaigun no heijutsuteki hensen to kore ni tomonau gunbi narabi ni sakusen' (Strategic Developments in the Former Imperial Navy and their Effect on Military Preparedness and Operations), unpublished MSS, (Tokyo, 1956) p. 28.
11. Hata Ikuhiko, *Shōwashi no gunjintachi* (Army and Navy Men in the History of the Shōwa Era), (Tokyo, 1982) p. 15.
12. Fukudome Shigeru, *Shikan Shinjuwan kōgeki* (A Historical Perspective on the Pearl Harbor Attack), (Tokyo, 1955) p. 151.
13. Letter from Yamamoto to Navy Minister Oikawa, 7 January 1941.
14. Samuel E. Morison, *The Rising Sun of the Pacific*, pp. 88–90; see also Edward S. Miller, *War Plan Orange* (Annapolis, 1991).
15. Yamamoto to Konoye at Konoye's residence in April 1941. See Nomura Minoru, *Daihon'ei kaigunbu: rengō kantai (1)* (Navy Section, Imperial General Headquarters: Combined Fleet [1]), (Tokyo, 1975) p. 567.

16.   Letter from Yamamoto to Navy Minister Shimada, dated 24 October 1941.
17.   Miwa Yoshitake, unpublished memoirs. Yamamoto's helmet strap metaphor had been employed before, by Admiral Tōgō in 1905.
18.   John J. Stephan, *Hawaii Under the Rising Sun* (Honolulu, 1984) pp. 103–4.
19.   *The War Reports of Admiral King*, (New York, 1947) p. 525. Hideyoshi's attempts to invade Korea in the late sixteenth century led to several severe defeats of his naval forces by his Korean opponents.
20.   *Rekishi to jinbutsu* (Historical Personages), May 1981, pp. 58–80.
21.   Hattori Takushirō, *Dai Tōa sensō zenshi* (A Complete History of the Greater East Asian War), (Tokyo, 1953) p. 283 Shiryō-shū (Documents of Annual War Plans of the Imperial Japanese Navy) (Tokyo, 1986).

# Part II
# Conflicts in the Pacific

# 4 American Seizure of Japan's Strategic Points Summer 1942–1944

## Ronald Spector

In June 1944, a few days after the Allied landings in Normandy, an American armada of fifteen aircraft carriers with 900 planes embarked, seven battleships, 120 smaller warships, and a convoy carrying 127 000 men converged on the Marianas to begin one of the most complex and decisive campaigns of the Pacific War.[1] Less than four months later an even greater array of forces, including over 700 ships carrying 160 000 troops with all their supplies and equipment, sailed for an attack on the island of Leyte in the Philippines, protected by a fleet of over 40 battleships and aircraft carriers. Eventually the Philippine campaign was to involve over a quarter of a million men and witness some of the bitterest fighting of the war. The liberation of Manila, for example, caused greater loss and damage to that city than that suffered by any city in Britain or occupied Europe during the entire war.

Strangely enough these Pacific campaigns, which rival in size if not in duration the campaigns in Italy, the Mediterranean and North Africa, have received relatively little attention from historians. Nothing like the lengthy and continuing multinational debate about the merits and nature of various generals, strategies and battles in the North African, Italian and European campaigns exists for the campaigns and commanders of the Pacific War. General Douglas MacArthur, having attained near mythic status early in the 1940s is an exception. Aside from MacArthur, however, most of the other top generals and admirals of the Pacific War lacked scholarly biographies until the last decade, and many are still to be written.

The 1990 special issue of the *Journal of Strategic Studies* entirely concerned with the 'Decisive Campaigns of the Second World War', devotes only one essay in seven to the war with Japan and even here the author, a leading British authority, cannot resist devoting more than half of his brilliant and thought-provoking essay to the British and Indian operations in South-East Asia, operations which he characterises as 'either ancillary or a sideshow'.[2] Two recent and very lengthy general histories of World War II, Peter Calvocoressi and John Pritchard's *Total War*, and Martin Gilbert's *The Second World War: A Complete History*, barely mention the Pacific campaigns of 1944.[3] The campaigns in the Marshall Islands in January and February of 1944, for example, involved three major amphibious operations and the crippling of the major Japanese central

Pacific base at Truk, and resulted in a speed-up of the entire tempo of the Pacific War. They receive only one paragraph in Calvocoressi's 1300-page book. A single battle in North Africa receives four pages.

How do we explain this relative lack of interest in the strategy and operations of the Pacific War? I have previously suggested that the dramatic beginning of the Pacific War with the attack on Pearl Harbor and its even more dramatic and tragic end in the atomic raids on Hiroshima and Nagasaki have inspired so much research and controversy as to distract attention from the conduct of the war itself.[4] In any case, historians of foreign relations, who have been in the great majority among American writers about the war with Japan, always feel more comfortable describing the causes and conclusion of a war than its conduct.

Another possible explanation is the predominance or at least the prominence of British historians as leaders in the field of World War II historiography. From B.H. Liddell Hart to Chester Wilmott to Michael Howard to Donald Cameron Watt, British historians have exercised enormous influence in setting the agenda and asking the key questions for World War II research, and their interests, understandably enough, have not been in the Pacific War.

The irony of all this is that virtually every writer agrees that the campaigns in the South and Central Pacific during 1942–44 were the decisive element in bringing about the defeat of Japan, yet they remain among the least studied and least discussed aspects of World War II. In the discussion which follows I have tried to provide one interpretation of these campaigns and also to address the larger question recently raised by Professor Allen when he suggested that the war in Europe and the war in Asia 'were not just in different locations they were different wars'.[5]

American conduct of the Pacific War from 1942 to 1944 was primarily determined by four considerations. They were: the actions of the Japanese; the US relationship with her allies, especially Britain and China; the personal and doctrinal differences and rivalries between and among the various armed services, theatres and commanders; and finally the availability of scarce resources such as cargo shipping, carrier task forces, amphibious troops, transport planes, and landing-craft.

After the Allied defeats in South-East Asia which marked the first six months of the Pacific War, the multinational American, British, Dutch and Australian command was dissolved and the Pacific War became in fact, of not in name, an exclusive project of the United States. The British had passively acquiesced in this arrangement as early as March 1942, and while the Australians and New Zealanders complained loudly about this American monopoly from time to time there was little they could do to change the state of affairs. This despite the fact that during 1942 and 1943 Australia and New Zealand provided a substantial proportion of the forces arrayed against the Japanese in the South Pacific.[6] The Pacific and Japan had long been considered a special concern of the US Navy and the Navy continued to consider it as such. As late as 1957 the Navy's official unofficial historian, Admiral Samuel Eliot Morison declared, in a lecture at Oxford University that, 'The Pacific War was, by and large, the Navy's war to which the Army confirmed.'[7]

The Army, for its part, might have been well satisfied to leave the Pacific to the Navy except for two rather large considerations. The first was the need to guard the vital line of communications through the South Pacific to Australia, which, after the disasters of 1941–2, had become the major American base. To garrison the islands along this route nearly 80 000 troops sailed for the south west Pacific between January and April 1942: nearly four times the number sent to Europe during that period.[8]

The second factor was the presence in Australia of General Douglas MacArthur who had already attained the status of instant folk hero in the United States after his 'heroic' defence of Bataan (which he, in fact, visited only once) and his dramatic escape from the doomed fortress of Corregidor. It was inconceivable that a soldier of MacArthur's stature be denied a major command and since there was little desire in the White House or the Pentagon to have him brought to Washington, a command was created for him in Australia – the Southwest Pacific Area – comprising Australia, New Guinea, the Philippines, the Solomons, Borneo, the Bismarck Archipelago and much of the Dutch East Indies. Most of these exotic lands were, of course, now under the control of the Japanese. The Australians, who expected and had been promised that their country would form the nucleus of a major Allied theatre, were, for some time, happy to have MacArthur as supreme commander. They believed that they would benefit from his towering fame and what they took to be his great influence on Washington and that he could secure for them the attention and claim on war resources that they felt they required.[9]

The rest of the Pacific was left to the Navy whose vast domain, the Pacific Ocean Areas, was entrusted to Admiral Chester W. Nimitz who also commanded the Pacific Fleet. MacArthur and Nimitz received their orders from the Joint Chiefs of Staff, but Admiral Ernest J. King, the Chief of Naval Operations, had a 'direct line' to Nimitz, bypassing the other members of the JCS. This was because King also held the position of Commander in Chief, US Fleet (COMINCH) and thus could issue orders and advice to Nimitz as Commander in Chief, Pacific Fleet, through the 'operational' channel. General George C. Marshall, the Army Chief of Staff, had no such direct operational line to MacArthur and the latter also could not directly command the armies, air forces or fleets under him as Nimitz could command Pacific Fleet.

Because of this peculiar arrangement and because of the personalities involved, discussion of Pacific strategy often took the form of arguments between MacArthur and King with the Joint Chiefs and their strategic planners acting as final arbiters. At the beginning of 1944 much of the hard fighting and all of the large-scale land battles of the Pacific War still lay in the future. Yet most of the critical strategic decisions had already been taken during the course of the previous two years.

After the Japanese defeat at Midway, the JCS had approved a limited offensive in the South Pacific by MacArthur and Nimitz's forces aimed at the Japanese base at Rabaul. The first phase of this offensive resulted in the protracted and bloody campaigns of Guadalcanal and Papua. I have argued elsewhere that the struggle for Guadalcanal, far more than Midway, spelled the beginning of the end for Japan.

Richard B. Frank, an American historian, has powerfully reinforced this argument in his definitive account of the Guadalcanal campaign based on extensive research in both Japanese and American records.[10] Frank points that while the defeat at Midway turned back the Japanese offensive in the Central Pacific, Japan was still on the offensive in the South Pacific, where the Imperial Army had plans to seize Port Moresby in Papua New Guinea and sever the Allied lifeline to Australia. 'We cannot know,' he writes, 'whether the Japanese, undistracted by the landing on Guadalcanal, would have seized Port Moresby and whether they might have ventured in the South Pacific once in possession of that critical objective.' As it was, the Japanese were drawn into a fatal battle of attrition for Guadalcanal, a battle which cost them dearly in irreplaceable experienced aviators and ships' crews.

Not that American conduct of the Guadalcanal campaign was invariably brilliant. In fact had Congressional auditors or Pentagon systems analysts ever been turned loose on Guadalcanal the South-West Pacific War might well have been cancelled. Despite a clear American edge in such 'high-tech' areas as communications-intelligence, air search and surface search radar, and automatic rapid-fire naval ordnance, the US Navy still lost more sea battles around Guadalcanal than it won. In the final Battle of Tassafaronga a surprised and outnumbered force of Japanese destroyers managed to sink one US cruiser and cripple three others. At least three top US commanders were relieved for cause during the Guadalcanal campaign, including the overall theatre commander, Admiral Robert L. Ghormley, who was replaced by Admiral William F. Halsey; Admiral Richmond Kelly Turner, widely blamed for the disastrous Battle of Savo Island, narrowly escaped the same fate.

Yet the overall result of the bloody struggle for Guadalcanal was a defeat for Japan. The Japanese had been forced into a war of attrition with the greatest industrial power among all the belligerents – a type of war she could not win.[11] The Guadalcanal campaign also highlighted what was to be a persistent feature of the Pacific War, the struggle for resources. In the midst of the fighting bitter disputes had arisen between King and some of the other Chiefs as to the South Pacific's proper share of land-based Army fighters and bombers and the allocation of cargo shipping, disputes that in some cases had required the intervention of President Roosevelt to resolve.[12]

A kind of lull settled over the Pacific theatres in early 1943 as American commanders realigned and refitted their forces and integrated new units and equipment, and the Japanese attempted to shore up their defences and planned pre-emptive strikes against the steadily growing Allied forces on their perimeter. In Washington the battle of the strategists continued as heated as ever. No overall plan for the defeat of Japan had yet been agreed upon or even formulated. Nor had the American and British high commands agreed about the nature of the Allied effort to be made against Japan prior to the defeat of Germany. At Casablanca in January 1943 Marshall and King proposed that the combined Chiefs agree in principle to allocate 30 per cent of Allied resources to the war against Japan. The British refused to commit themselves to any specific formula but did agree that the Americans could go ahead with further offensive moves against Japan designed to retain the initiative.[13]

Back in Washington Army and Navy leaders sought, without success, to agree on a unified command for the Pacific theatres and on the implications of the Casablanca decisions for Pacific strategy.[14] All three Pacific commanders, MacArthur, Nimitz, and Admiral William F. Halsey, who exercised a quasi-independent command in the south-west Pacific under MacArthur's general direction, agreed that they lacked sufficient forces to complete the conquest of Rabaul begun in 1942. They especially wanted more long-range bombers, which could reach Rabaul. But the Army Air Forces, eager to begin the combined bomber offensive against Japan, also agreed on at Casablanca, were reluctant to make the bombers available for the Pacific.

In the end, the Pacific commanders did get some additional aircraft and troops, but not enough to meet their requirements for an attack on Rabaul. The Joint Chiefs of Staff accordingly modified their objectives to include only advance up the Solomons as far as Bougainville and a parallel advance by MacArthur's forces along the north coast of New Guinea, with both approaches converging on Rabaul. Although the decision settled nothing it did, as Robert Love points out, 'tie the War Department to specific allocations of shipping and aircraft to the Pacific in 1943 and satisfy, for the time being, Admiral King's persistent objections to the Pacific theatre being dependent on what was left over from the European theatre.'[15]

The long-planned American offences in the Pacific finally got under way in June 1943, as MacArthur and Halsey's forces moved north and west against Japanese bases at Munda, Vella La Vella, and on the New Guinea coast. Both MacArthur and Halsey came to employ the tactic known as leapfrogging, bypassing strongly held Japanese bases to attack weaker ones, while cutting off the bypassed bases through air and naval power.

Meanwhile, JCS planners had drafted a broad blueprint for an overall strategy for the war against Japan. The plan called for the continuation of MacArthur and Halsey's advances through the Solomons and along the New Guinea coast towards the Philippines. At the same time it also called for the opening of a new advance across the central Pacific, a region of thousands of tiny islands extending from the Gilberts, the easternmost chain, near the equator, north and west through the Marshalls, the Carolines and the Marianas. This was the route favoured in the pre-war American plans for war with Japan called the 'Orange Plans'. It was also the shortest route and one where the growing might of American naval and amphibious forces could be brought to bear most effectively.

At the Trident conference at Washington in May 1943, Admiral King explained to his doubting British colleagues the beauties of the new plan which would keep the Japanese off balance, further waste their forces, and enable the Allies to 'obtain positions of readiness for the final onslaught against Japan which was to follow the collapse of Germany. He urged the British to open still another front against the Japanese in Burma in order to facilitate land communication from India to China.

The British Chiefs were far from persuaded by King's presentation and they flatly refused to speed up their war in South-East Asia. Yet, American agreement to Churchill's proposals to invade Italy gave the British no choice but to accede to American wishes for the Pacific. In the end the combined Chiefs agreed that the US might 'simultaneously maintain and extend unremitting pressure against Japan with the purpose of continually reducing her military power and attaining positions from which her ultimate surrender can be forced'.[16]

The central Pacific drive did not begin until November 1943, and got off to a shaky start with the costly attack on Tarawa in the Gilberts. However, the second phase of the campaign, the capture of the Marshalls in early 1944 resulted in a change of pace of the entire Pacific War. Adopting leapfrogging on a giant scale, the central Pacific forces under Admiral Raymond Spruance struck directly into the heart of the island group by seizing the Kawajalein atoll. Kwajalein fell so swiftly that Spruance's forces were able to attack Eniwetok atoll at the extreme north-west end of the island chain six weeks ahead of schedule. In the process, Spruance's carrier task forces attacked and crippled the principal Japanese central Pacific base at Truk in the Carolines.

The swift and relatively easy capture of the Marshalls enabled the Americans to change the entire Pacific timetable and the assault on the Marianas was set for June 1944 instead of September. MacArthur, fearful of being relegated to a back seat in the Pacific drive, also speeded up his advance. In a daring gamble he seized the Admiralty Islands two months ahead of schedule, thus completing the encirclement of Rabaul and forcing the Japanese to yield more of the north coast of New Guinea. Then in their most brilliant campaign of the war, MacArthur's forces 'leapt' 580 miles to seize the Japanese base at Hollandia on the north coast of Dutch New Guinea.

At the Quadrant conference in Quebec in August 1943, the British and Americans put the final touches on a timetable for the planned two-pronged advance in the Pacific. Rabaul was crossed off the list of invasion targets; its neutralisation by air was to be completed by May 1944, followed by MacArthur's westward advance toward the Vogelkop Peninsula of New Guinea. Meanwhile, Nimitz would follow his Gilbert assault with attacks on the Marshalls, the Carolines and the Palaus. All this was to be completed by the end of 1944. The

Joint Chiefs failed to specify whether MacArthur's or Nimitz's campaign were to receive priority, simply declaring that 'due weight should be given to the fact that operations in the central Pacific promise more rapid advance'.[17]

More than a little puzzled by such circumlocutions, the British inquired whether it might not be better to limit MacArthur's operation in New Guinea to a holding mission and use the resources saved for Overlord. King and Marshall immediately rejected this suggestion which, while logical enough, struck at the heart of the delicate Army–Navy *modus vivendi* on Pacific strategy. Both advances were essential and mutually supporting, they declared, and in any case the forces for the south-west Pacific operations were already in place or en route. Any surplus in that theatre would have to be allocated to the central Pacific, not Europe.[18]

The British raised no more objections though their point was well taken; the two advances could be mutually competing as well as mutually supporting. As I have tried to show elsewhere, in critical operational situations such as developed on Bougainville and in the campaign at Biak the divided advance led to the edge of disaster.[19]

Shortly after the American landings on the large island of Bougainville in the northern Solomons, the Japanese assembled a naval striking force of seven heavy cruisers, a light cruiser and four destroyers to attack the American landing force at Empress Augusta Bay. As Samuel Eliot Morison noted, this relatively small force posed a deadly threat to the entire operation because Admiral William F. Halsey's forces at Bougainville had been denuded of warships to meet the demands of the impending attacks in the central Pacific. Consequently 'Halsey had not one heavy cruiser to oppose them; every capital ship in the Pacific was warming up for the Gilberts'.[20]

As it was, the threat to the landing force was eliminated by two daring carrier raids, the first since 1942 against heavily defended land bases. The brilliance (and good luck) of Halsey's daring raids should not obscure the fact that the American two-pronged offensive in the Pacific could, at times, create grave risks – even before the central Pacific thrust was even under way. Had the Japanese handled their forces more skilfully or been luckier, the entire Bougainville operation might have been defeated.

A similar situation developed in the spring of 1944, during the American conquest of Biak, a large island at the western end of New Guinea. The Japanese made serious errors in judgement during the campaign, first deciding that the island was not vital, then deciding that it was. First deciding to defend it only with the forces in place, then sending in powerful reinforcements. Yet, despite their vacillation, the Japanese succeeded in assembling an overwhelmingly superior naval force to attack the Allied landing force at Biak which had no warships larger than a destroyer.[21] Fortunately for the Americans, as the Japanese armada was about to set out, word was received of the American attacks on the Marianas. The Japanese immediately suspended the Biak operation and headed north to defend those vital islands.

The Biak episode provides an excellent illustration of how the American strategy of two different drives across the Pacific under independent command might easily have led to disaster. By dividing their forces the Americans had given the Japanese an opportunity to concentrate a locally superior force against one part of their advance, something the Japanese achieved at Biak. Had Combined Fleet proceeded with the third attempt to reinforce Biak, it would probably have inflicted a serious defeat on the inferior Allied naval forces, delivered a destructive bombardment of American positions on Biak, and succeeded in getting their much-needed reinforcements ashore.

As the official US Army history admits,

> the Allied Forces of the Southwest Pacific Area probably had little idea how potentially dangerous the situation was at Biak, and it remained for postwar Japanese reports to reveal how narrowly greater losses and strategic delays were averted. Without doubt, success for the Japanese during KON would have seriously delayed the pace of Allied operations in the Southwest Pacific Area, if not throughout the Pacific.[22]

Even in the absence of dramatic crises like Biak, competition for scarce resources, especially assault shipping, sometimes left one theatre with very meagre means to carry out its mission.

The Japanese alarm at the American attack on the Marianas in June 1944 is understandable. From those islands, Saipan, Tinian, and Guam, the new US heavy bomber, the B-29, could reach Japan itself. The Japanese combined Fleet, reorganised as a carrier striking force, challenged the American invaders in the series of actions known as the Battle of the Philippines Sea.

The Japanese naval historian Admiral Yōichi Hirama has recently argued that the Philippines Sea was the naval battle which most closely corresponded to prewar Japanese operational plans and concepts. The Japanese counted for victory on the strength of their land-based air groups in the Marianas, and in the Palaus on the longer range of their carrier-based aircraft. However, most of the Japanese land-based planes were lost to pre-emptive American air raids or fell victim to poor maintenance or inadequate base facilities. The Japanese carriers found the American fleet first and launched four waves of air attacks while still out of range of their opponents. Yet the battle ended in defeat for the Japanese whose aviators were no match for their more experienced American opponents expertly guided by radar to intercept positions. Japanese aircrews who survived the American combat air patrols found themselves subject to a hail of anti-aircraft fire employing the new proximity fuse.

On 20 June 1944 the American carriers finally located the Japanese fleet, sank one carrier and damaged three others. The two large carriers, *Shōkaku* and *Taihō*, had been sunk by submarines earlier in the battle.

With the Central Pacific Forces firmly lodged in the Marianas, and MacArthur completing his long advance through the south-west Pacific, only one major strategic decision remained: where should the two advances converge?

King argued that Luzon could be bypassed and American forces operating from bases in the Marianas could strike directly at Formosa or even the main islands of Japan. MacArthur, however, was outraged at the thought of leaving any part of the Philippines and the Filipinos under Japanese occupation until the end of the war.

Three developments finally settled the argument. Admiral Halsey, now in command of the fast carrier forces, raided the southern Philippines during September 1944 and found them to be only lightly defended. Acting on Halsey's report, Admiral Nimitz suggested to the Joint Chiefs that his previously planned, slow and deliberate approach to the Philippines be modified, and that the US forces strike directly at the island of Leyte. MacArthur quickly agreed, as did the Joint Chiefs of Staff, to set the new date for the Leyte invasion as 20 October 1944.

From that point on, events conspired to make a decision in favour of Luzon rather than Formosa all but inevitable. First, MacArthur informed the Joint Chiefs that the new invasion date for Leyte would enable him to invade Luzon two months ahead of schedule on 20 December 1944. Formosa could not possibly be attacked so soon. Then Washington planners discovered that the manpower needs for a campaign against Formosa far exceeded the number of troops actually available in the Pacific. The most glaring deficiency was in the category of service troops. Nimitz alone would require between 90 000 to 200 000 for a campaign against Formosa. To obtain so many new service troops, Nimitz would have to wait until the war in Europe was over. Finally, bad news arrived from China: major Japanese offensives overran most of the air bases in east China, bases from which the Joint Chiefs had planned to launch their aerial bombardment of Japan.

The loss of those airfields rendered the seizure of a port on the China coast less than urgent. In any case, the air forces had long since begun to look to the Marianas as the principal base for their B-29s.[23] By this point, also, Nimitz was urging King to consider an alternative plan: to neutralise Formosa by air attacks, then use the central Pacific forces to seize Iwo Jima and Okinawa, which would provide far better airfields than Formosa for a final assault on Japan.[24]

Finally, on 3 October, King gave in. The Joint Chiefs of Staff directed MacArthur to invade Luzon on 3 December. Nimitz's forces, after providing naval support to the Philippine invasion, would invade Iwo Jima and Okinawa. The final shape of Pacific strategy had at last emerged from the cross-currents of interservice and personality differences, improvisation and opportunism, conflicting demands on resources, luck, and timing.

To what extent then was the war with Japan a 'different war', a separate war? If we divide the war into its 'strategic', 'operational', and 'tactical' levels, in the manner beloved of military school instructors, we can say that at the operational level it was indeed almost a separate war. Victories and defeats in that theatre had relatively little, if any, direct impact on campaigns and battles in other theatres, especially after 1942. If we consider the year 1944, we behold the strange spectacle of Japan reeling from her loss of the Marianas, her lines of communication almost severed by air and submarine attacks, yet still able to launch a series of powerful attacks deep into the heart of China which brought an end to the American air threat from the mainland of Asia and threatened to bring about the collapse of the entire Nationalist war effort. Further American victories in the Pacific had little effect on the Japanese drive and, conversely, the near collapse of China hindered MacArthur and Nimitz not one whit in their conquest of the Philippines.

One reason for the separateness of the theatres, as D. Clayton James reminds us, was the utter failure of the Axis 'to develop strategic planning at the alliance level'. This failure, he argued, 'was almost as important to the final outcome as the success of America and Britain in molding their coalition strategy'.[25]

It is, in fact, at the strategic level that the concept of the Pacific War as 'a different war' tends to break down. Time and again the timing and direction of the Pacific War was influenced by the demands of other theatres for resources such as bombers, landing-craft, and cargo shipping. For example, in the autumn of 1942, the Americans decided to switch priorities in shipbuilding from landing craft to destroyer escorts because of the threat posed by the German U-boat campaign in the Atlantic. The programme was a success, and the first of nearly 500 destroyer escorts joined the fleet in early 1943. However, by the spring of 1944, a severe shortage of landing-craft and cargo shipping had developed.[26] The speed-up of the Pacific campaigns in early 1944 and General Eisenhower's decision to broaden the beachhead in Normandy also produced increased and competing demands for assault shipping. These in turn competed with and disrupted the building programme for cargo shipping also vital to the Pacific.[27] If strategy consists of reconciling ends with means then the strategy of the Pacific War was far from being that of a separate conflict.

During the fifty years since Pearl Harbor Americans have regarded the Pacific War as an exclusively and characteristically American triumph. Russell Weigley, in one of the most widely used books on American military history writes that 'the American victories before Hiroshima combined decisiveness with limited casualties and costs in proportions which had eluded every power since Prussia's victories of 1866 and 1870–71; and the American victories were won against a brave and skillful antagonist, not a decayed or incompetent power such as Prussia had overcome'.[28]

This happy outcome had a less happy legacy, for Americans have since 1945 regarded the Pacific War not has a highly unusual success but as the norm against which all subsequent wars and military commitments were to be measured. Hence, the frustration with the conflicts in Korea and Vietnam which combined indecisiveness with relatively high cost. Here lies also the reason for the American elation with the Gulf War which combined very low casualties with a seemingly decisive outcome and was quickly halted by President Bush before it could assume any other character.

The easy assumption of American invincibility left by the Pacific War was also a long time dying. In February 1942, Rear-Admiral Raymond Spruance commanded a cruiser division in a raid on Watje Atoll in the Marshalls. The nervous and inexperienced American crews literally couldn't shoot straight, expending over 190 shells to sink two small ships in the harbour and then were unable to silence Japanese shore batteries.[29] Just over two years later, Spruance's armada in the Marianas annihilated the Japanese naval air forces despite yielding the initiation to the enemy. Few Americans remembered the confusion and debacles of 1941-2, but many recalled the triumphs of 1944, successes brought about by American organisational ability, technology and production capacity. The frustration, consternation and anger of the Korean War six years later may be explained in large measure by the memory of these triumphs in the Pacific which, far from being viewed as exceptional, perhaps unique and unrepeatable were viewed as the norm to be expected when America went to war. Whether Americans have since come to accept a more realistic view of war is a question beyond the scope of this paper, but the popular reaction to the Vietnam War and the recent Gulf conflict suggest that the answer would probably be in the negative.

## NOTES

1.　J.P. Wilmott with customary hyperbole has called the Battle of the Philippines Sea, fought during the Marianas Campaign, 'One of the most comprehensive and complete victories won by a fleet in modern history, rivalling Tsushima and Trafalgar in its extent and one-sidedness'. See Wilmott, *The Great Crusade* (London, 1990) p. 337.

2.　Louis Allen, 'The Campaigns in Asia and the Pacific', *Journal of Strategic Studies* 13, March 1990, p. 165.

3.　Peter Calvocoressi, Guy Wint and John Pritchard, *Total War* (New York, 1989); Martin Gilbert, *The Second World War* (New York, 1989). I have given my views of these works in more detail in '50 Years Ago: Views of World War II', *Washington Post Book World*, XIX, 10 December 1989.

4.　Ronald Spector, *Eagle Against the Sun: The American War with Japan* (New York, 1985) p. xv.

5.　Allen, 'The Campaigns in Asia and the Pacific', p. 167. Wilmott similarly characterises the war with Japan and the war in Europe as 'two partially concurrent conflicts'.

6.　D.M. Horner, *High Command: Australia and Allied Strategy, 1939-1945* (Canberra, 1982) pp. 256-7, and *passim*.

7.　Samuel Eliot Morison, *Strategy and Compromise* (Boston, 1958) p. 85.

8.  Maurice Matloff and Edwin M. Snell, *Strategic Planning for Coalition Warfare, 1941–1942* (Washington, 1953) pp. 145, 162–4.
9.  Horner, *High Command*; Forrest C. Pogue, *George C. Marshall: Ordeal and Hope* (New York, 1967), pp. 373–5; D. Clayton James, *The Years of MacArthur, 1941–1945* (New York, 1975) p. 139.
10. Richard B. Frank *Guadalcanal* (New York: Random House, 1990).
11. Spector, *Eagle Against the Sun*, pp. xvi, 228, and *passim*.
12. Morton, pp. 325–40.
13. Matloff and Snell, op. cit., pp. 128–30; Louis Morton, *Strategy and Command: The First Two Years* (Washington, 1960) pp. 437–44, 447–53, 456–68.
14. 'Outline History of Effort to Gain Unity of Command', Attachment to Memo for COMINCH, 20 February 1943, Double Zero Files, Ernest J. King Papers, Naval Historical Centre, Washington, DC.
15. Robert W. Love, 'Ernest Joseph King, Jr.' in Robert W. Love, ed., *The Chiefs of Naval Operations* (Annapolis, Md, 1983) p. 160.
16. Final Report to the President and Prime Minister, 25 May 1943, CC242/6, JCS Records, Record Group 228, National Archives, Washington, DC.
17. Preparation of Plans for the Defeat of Japan, 7 July 1943; JPS 67/6, Specific Operations in the Pacific and Far East, 6 August 1943, JCS446. Both in Records in JCS, Record Group 228, National Archives.
18. Maurice Matloff, *Strategic Planning for Coalition Warfare, 1943–1944* (Washington, DC, 1958) p. 235.
19. Spector, *Eagle Against the Sun*, pp. 244–6, 292–3.
20. Morison, *Breaking the Bismarcks Barrier* (Boston, 1950) p. 324.
21. Robert Ross Smith, *The Approach to the Philippines* (Washington: Office of the Chief of Military History, 1953) pp. 346–612.
22. Ibid, p. 362.
23. Robert Ross Smith, 'Luzon Versus Formosa', in Kent Roberts Greenfield (ed.), *Command Decisions* (Washington, DC, 1960) pp. 463–72.
24. Love, 'Ernest Joseph King', p. 175.
25. D. Clayton James, 'American and Japanese Strategies in the Pacific War', in Peter Paret (ed.), *Makers of Modern Strategy* (Princeton, 1986) p. 713.
26. Love, 'Ernest Joseph King', p. 166.
27. R. Leighton and R. Coakley, *Global Strategy and Logistics, 1943–45* (Washington, DC, Government Printing Office, 1962) pp. 319–21.
28. Russell F. Weigley, *The American Way of War* (Bloomington, Indiana University Press, 1977) p. 311.
29. Thomas B. Buell, *The Quiet Warrior* (Boston, 1974) pp. 105–6.

# 5 US Army Codebreakers and the War against Japan
## Edward Drea

Perhaps the most fruitful approach to reassessing the Pacific War is from the viewpoint of the accomplishments of US Army codebreakers. Since the mid-1970s, accounts of the exploits of Allied codebreakers during World War II have focused on successes against the German Enigma cipher systems, the Japanese Foreign Ministry's machine cipher, and the Imperial Japanese Navy's codes. The contributions of British cryptanalysts at Bletchley Park to the war against Nazi Germany are well known. The story of the deciphered Japanese diplomatic codes – MAGIC – is also a familiar one and underpins the continuing controversy over American unpreparedness on 7 December 1941 when Japanese naval aircraft attacked Pearl Harbor. Well publicised too are the brilliant feats of US naval cryptanalysts whose decryptions revealed the Japanese navy's plans at the Battle of the Coral Sea (May 1942) and Midway (June 1942). Numerous authors have recounted the role of navy cryptanalysts in laying the aerial ambush of Fleet Admiral Yamamoto Isoroku in April 1943. Yet relatively little is known about the US Army's cryptanalytic assault on the variety of codes or ciphers that Japan's military forces employed during the Pacific War. Recognition of the scope of US Army codebreakers' contributions to victory over Japan is long overdue.

This is not a neatly defined subject that lends itself to a simplistic evolutionary progression. American army cryptanalytic efforts against Japan's military codes proceeded by fits and starts. For eighteen months after Pearl Harbor, US Army cryptanalysts could not decipher a single high-grade encrypted Japanese military message. Even when they became able to read secret messages, there was no unified system for handling army-generated decryptions of Japanese military messages, much less for disseminating the invaluable intelligence derived from this source to the field commanders who needed it most. This study is representative rather than comprehensive. It highlights the technical achievements of US Army codebreakers and, for illustrative purposes only, shows how the Allies exploited various Japanese code or cipher systems at specific moments during the Pacific War.

The US Army's achievement against Japan is all the more remarkable when one understands its shoestring operation during the interwar years. The War Department, Military Intelligence Division (MID), MI-8 had broken Japanese naval and diplomatic codes in the early 1920s and the State Department had used the resulting intelligence windfall to great advantage during the Washington Naval Conference in 1922.[1] Afterwards State and MID both funded MI-8 until a series of parsimonious budgets, capped by the State Department's decision in 1929 to withdraw all funding, put the small codebreaking cell out of business.

With MI-8 closed, the Army transferred its cryptanalytic functions to the Code and Cipher Section, Office of the Chief Signal Officer, Signal Corps, which already was responsible for compiling codes and ciphers (cryptology) for the army. In December 1929, William F. Friedman took charge of the newly created Signal Intelligence Service (SIS) then located in the rear wing of the second floor of a decrepit wooden structure, the Munitions Building in Washington, DC. Friedman recruited a few brilliant young assistants, among them Abraham Sinkov, into SIS. Meanwhile, the Japanese Foreign Ministry had replaced its existing manual encoding systems with a newly developed cipher machine, leaving SIS with the unenviable task of solving a sophisticated mechanical cipher system.[2]

Throughout the 1930s, Friedman's small group operated under restrictive federal legislation and was further hampered by a budget that was miserly even by the standards of the depression-era army. Despite these handicaps, by 1936 Friedman's nine cryptanalysts had solved the machine-encrypted Japanese diplomatic system, the so-called RED Machine.[3] Then, in 1939, the Japanese Foreign Ministry introduced its 'B', or more famously PURPLE, machine cipher. Colonel Spencer B. Akin, took command of Signal Intelligence Service in August 1939 and headed the effort to solve PURPLE, which the Chief Signal Officer, Brigadier General Joseph O. Mauborgne, told him was SIS's most important mission.[4] The outbreak of war in Europe in September 1939 did not improve SIS's budget or staff but did increase demands for a solution to PURPLE. Thus the Army had to concentrate the work of its few cryptanalysts on the solution of the Japanese diplomatic ciphers. Similarly US Navy cryptanaylsts working in Washington found themselves tracking German submarines and working with the army against PURPLE.[5] After eighteen months of intensive effort SIS crypt-analysts did crack PURPLE, though at the expense of painstaking study of the Japanese Army's codes. Together with the US Navy, SIS developed a system for decrypting and sharing PURPLE and other diplomatic material. Within the army, the resulting decryptions of Japanese diplomatic traffic were known as MAGIC because General Mauborgne referred to his cryptanalytic team as 'magicians'.[6]

The US Army built eight PURPLE analog machines one of which was under Navy control on Corregidor in the Philippine Islands.[7] In the summer of 1941, Douglas MacArthur, Commanding General of the newly established US Army Forces in the Far East, personally asked for Colonel Akin as his chief signal officer. Although he was aware from his SIS days that the army's Station 6, just outside the gate of Fort McKinley in the Manila suburbs, intercepted Japanese diplomatic radio traffic and that the navy operated a PURPLE machine, Akin had no authority over these hush-hush units. Only MacArthur and Admiral Thomas C. Hart, Commander, US Asiatic Fleet, Manila, were privy to MAGIC, which special couriers hand-carried to their offices.[8]

On 7 December 1941, Station 6 had two officers and 16 enlisted men of the 2nd Signal Service Company engaged in intercepting Japanese diplomatic communications. Station 6 dispatched its re-enciphered, transcribed intercepts to SIS headquarters and provided copies for the navy detachment on Corregidor. It neither intercepted Japanese military communications nor carried out cryptanalysis.

This brief overview makes plain that the US Army entered the war against Japan woefully unprepared to solve the Imperial Army's secret radio communications. Without the continuity of effort essential for such a project – the collection of repetitious codegroups by constantly monitoring communications' networks – army cryptanalysts found themselves starting from scratch. MacArthur's Station 6, for example, had to recover the Japanese Army Air Force's air to ground code system and begin its analysis of Japanese military codes under fire.

On 7 December, 1941 all of Signal Intelligence Service (SIS) numbered only 330 personnel, roughly half of whom were stationed at radio intercept sites in the Panama Canal Zone, the Philippine Islands, and Hawaii. Few trained Japanese linguists were available to translate enemy messages so Japanese-Americans or sons of American missionaries who had proselytised in Japan were hurriedly pressed into service. In March 1942 a slowly expanding SIS began shifting its operations to Arlington Hall, Virginia, in the Washington DC suburbs and added two more intercept sites, one at Petaluma, California, and the other at Vint Hill Farms, Warrenton, Virginia.[9] Moreover the army assumed the entire MAGIC mission from the navy, ensuring a steady flow of intelligence throughout the war years unwittingly supplied by Japan's diplomats. The solution of Japan's military codes and ciphers, however, now became SIS's top priority.

The Army had to accumulate sufficient quantities of Japanese military messages to enable cryptanalysts to discern repetitive patterns that would lead them to solutions. Collecting the raw data was the first hurdle. Intercept operators had to discover the enemy's major radio frequencies that carried significant military communications so that they would not waste their time monitoring routine broadcasts. Traffic analysis and radio direction finding techniques were used to identify radio message traffic network patterns.

Successful traffic analysis depended on the solution of the code numbers used to conceal the message-centre place-names that appeared on all Japanese military messages. The first success in this area came in September 1942 and by the following June traffic analysts had reconstructed all twelve Japanese main military systems. Able to locate and map Japanese army radio stations and network broadcasting circuits, the Allies identified four distinct major military networks: that used by GHQ in Tokyo; by Southern Army which controlled army operations from Burma to New Guinea; by the Water Transport organisation which had charge of army shipping and convoys; and by the Army Air Force.[10] The sum of this traffic analysis and radio direction finding data was codenamed

THUMB. By knowing what to listen to, intercept operators gradually amassed sufficient quantities of radiograms for cryptanalysts to unravel the contents of the enemy messages.

In April 1942, shortly after arriving in Australia, MacArthur organised Central Bureau and placed it under Akin's command. Central Bureau was a combined American, Australian and British decryption centre with headquarters initially in Melbourne. About 70 Australians just returned from service in the Middle East provided traffic analysis expertise while SIS in Washington sent two levies of cryptanalysts, headed by Abraham Sinkov, now a Major, to Australia. A handful of British enlisted intercept operators and one officer of the Far East Combined Bureau (the British cryptanalytic centre all of whom who had escaped from their base in Singapore), and the survivors of Station 6 also joined Central Bureau.[11]

Station 6 had already identified rudiments of the Japanese Army Air Force's air to ground (pilot to ground controller) radio network with the aid of a codebook recovered from the wreckage of a Japanese Army bomber which crashed on Luzon. Lax security practices of Japanese air to ground radio operators, like transmitting identical messages in encrypted and unencrypted versions or in two different codes, facilitated additional code recoveries.[12] Central Bureau solved the army air to ground system during 1942 and the resulting decoded messages were codenamed PEARL. When MacArthur arrived in Australia in the spring of 1942, however, the air threat that he faced was from the Japanese Navy's land-based aircraft.

During these early months of the Pacific War, the Australians made the greatest contributions to the new decryption centre. Especially prominent was the work of Commander T.E. Nave, RN, who was posted to Central Bureau in May 1942. Nave's extensive background in solving Japanese naval ciphers made it natural for him to lead the solution of the Japanese naval air to ground codebook. He capitalised on the collection efforts of the Australian intercept site that had opened at Darwin in 1941, as well as the Australian navy's small direction-finding unit and cryptographic unit which he had previously directed.[13]

The Japanese Navy's air to ground code employed a *katakana* (one form of the Japanese syllabary) substitution system. For example, '*kore*' equated to 'such and such bridge is completely destroyed and passage difficult' while '*moi*' meant 'enemy strengthening positions on front'. The British operators from Singapore trained Australian intercept operators in the complexities of recording Japanese *kana* broadcasts and the Australians quickly became adept at copying the *kana* variation of the Morse code.

Nave's cryptanalysis and Australian intercept capabilities enabled Central Bureau to break the Japanese naval air to ground code during 1942, the first to be solved by Central Bureau.[14] Nave also instructed a select group of Australian officers how to unravel the naval air codes so effectively that when the codes changed, as they regularly did, they could be reconstructed with minimum delay. The resulting decoded messages fell under the PEARL rubric and were read regularly throughout the war.

Australian and British expertise in traffic analysis, the naval air to ground code and American skill in cryptanalysis largely determined the division of labour at Central Bureau. The Australians became responsible for traffic analysis (THUMB) and codebreaking (PEARL) and the Americans for cryptanalysis (ULTRA).[15]

During 1942 and 1943, the US Army expanded the number of cryptanalysts, technicians and support staff assigned to Central Bureau from 40 in May 1942 to 1000 by the end of 1943. Americans at Central Bureau focused on the Japanese Army's three-digit and four-digit ciphers and studied new or revised ones like the army Water Transport system or the army geographic name code. SIS also analysed these systems, studied the Japanese military attaché cipher, and maintained the flow of MAGIC from Japan's compromised diplomatic messages. To accomplish these multiple missions, the US Army commenced mass-producing intercept operators, cryptanalysts, Japanese linguists, and intelligence specialists. But it took time for these specialists to reach the Pacific theatres, so until help could arrive, during 1942 and early 1943, the Army depended on Australian codebreakers and traffic analysts and on US Navy cryptanalysts for its main sources of signal intelligence about its Japanese enemy.

Central Bureau did not, however, exchange cryptanalytic data with the US Navy's nearby Fleet Radio Unit, Melbourne, or elsewhere, because the Japanese navy encrypted its radio communications on entirely different cryptographic principles than its army counterparts. In short, an exchange of such data would be more confusing than enlightening. Instead the navy provided MacArthur with its decrypted intelligence by daily courier who orally briefed the general on the latest developments.[16] So from 1942 until mid-1943, the Navy was MacArthur's source for ULTRA.

Japan's early victories against the Allies extended the Empire's boundaries over 20 million square miles through Asia and the Pacific and unintentionally opened one avenue for exploitation of the Imperial Army's secret messages. The Japanese Army's geographic name code book (used to encode the location of the sender and receiver of messages) had no entries for such exotic and unanticipated proper names like Rabaru (Rabaul, New Britain), Pooroto Morosubi (Port Moresby, Papua New Guinea), or Guadakanaru (Guadalcanal, Solomon Islands) because they never expected to fight in such places. Wartime necessity forced them to issue an expanded geographic code book that included the new names. In June 1942 SIS tackled this revised geographic name code, the so-called DD number (*den dai* or telegram number), by matching intercepted Japanese army messages with those addressed to army units but relayed on previously compromised Japanese naval radio networks. By September 1942, with only 23 cryptanalysts, SIS solved the geographic name code and could now identify locations, but not yet units.[17] Thus DD 5391–9834 equated to Davao, Philippine Islands (5391), the place of the message's destination and Rabaul (9834), the place of origin. SIS shared its find with Central Bureau. Indeed throughout the

Pacific War Central Bureau and SIS (and its successors) exchanged technical data related to cryptanalysis on a daily basis.

Now able to identify the location of the message sender and the location of the receiver, Allied cryptanalysts moved against the encrypted address code that disguised army units. For instance the codename of the 237th Infantry, 41st Division was 'kawa 3564' whose enciphered address form might appear as 1791 4229 6580. The British Wireless Experimentation Centre (WEC) in India initially worked on the solution of the address system. By the summer of 1943, WEC had reached a point where it could read the unit addresses on current intercepts. Reconstruction of the entire address code book was then undertaken by SIS at Arlington Hall.[18]

Central Bureau and Arlington Hall had also been unravelling unit address ciphers to reach the second-level unit codename. Thus, in the fall of 1942, traffic analysts at Central Bureau could identify the first-level cipher, say 4901 1572 2233 as a unit codenamed Akatsuki 6168. Traffic analysis revealed that this was a major headquarters whose radio network (its span of command and control) stretched from Hiroshima, Japan (its location) to the Palaus and Rabaul (both large Japanese bases). Until Central Bureau solved the unit codename, however, intercept operators could not know that they were listening in on messages from HQ, First Shipping Transport Command.

Work against these sophisticated ciphers progressed in 1942 and 1943, but for defensive and offensive advantages the Allies capitalised on compromised Japanese army and navy air–ground codes. Australian Army 51 Wireless Section deployed to Darwin, Australia, in June 1942 to monitor Japanese naval land-based air force communications, particularly from Timor, Portugese East Indies, whose airfields served as staging bases for air attacks on Darwin. Traffic analysis in combination with codebreaking enabled 51 Wireless to forecast accurately Japanese land-based naval air raids. The unit also eavesdropped on naval air to ground communications, thereby detecting movements of Japanese aircraft from Singapore to the Philippines to Rabaul or to New Guinea airfields like Lae or Wewak.[19]

Central Bureau's knowledge of the Navy's air to ground code also proved valuable in detecting Japanese Army Air Force deployments to the south-west Pacific theatre. Because Japanese army pilots lacked over-water flight training and navigation skills, they depended on navy-piloted transport planes to shepherd them to their destinations. In late December 1942, for instance, a message from a navy transport plane revealed that 57 Japanese aircraft were flying to Rabaul as part of the aerial build-up in the theatre.[20] The ability to read Japanese naval ciphers also provided tactical advantages to MacArthur. In late December 1942 a deciphered naval message transmitted by the Eleventh Air Fleet on Rabaul announced a 37-plane attack against Allied positions at Buna, Papua New Guinea. When the raid came, American P-38s, waiting in ambush, shot down 11 Japanese warplanes.[21]

At the ULTRA level, US naval cryptanalysts at Melbourne repeatedly unravelled Japanese navy ciphers forecasting resupply or invasion convoys sailing from Rabaul to New Guinea ports like Buna or Lae during the heavy fighting from July 1942 to January 1943. It is true that most of these convoys reached their destinations intact, but several suffered losses from Allied air or submarine attacks made possible because of foreknowledge of the convoy's destination and sailing time. Decrypted Japanese naval messages supplied by Melbourne filled in the larger strategic picture for MacArthur who knew from naval ULTRA that the enemy occupation of Wewak and Madang in December 1942 was part of a more ambitious scheme to construct a series of airfields along New Guinea's north coast.[22] The greatest triumph of the navy cryptanalysts in MacArthur's theatre, however, was the forecasting of the major Japanese sealift to Lae scheduled for March 1943.

After the Allies drove the Japanese from Buna and Australian forces checked the enemy's advance at Wau, Eighth Area Army on Rabaul dispatched reinforcements to New Guinea. In early February 1943, US Fifth Air Force photo interpreters discerned Japanese deployments similar to those used previously to escort a major convoy to New Guinea ports. Allied aerial reconnaissance over Rabaul was accordingly increased and the resulting photography showed a concentration of 79 vessels, including 45 merchantmen and six transports in the massive harbour.[23] These large numbers of ships bespoke a major convoy forming, yet photographs could not tell MacArthur the time or place of the Japanese destination. Navy cryptanalysts could. On 19 February, 1943 Melbourne analysts handed MacArthur unimpeachable intelligence that the Japanese planned to land at Lae in early March.

Eleventh Air Fleet was the source of this intelligence. Headquarters, Eleventh Air Fleet was charged with providing air cover for the convoy. It broadcast numerous coordination messages and transmitted orders to its subordinate land-based air squadrons. One such decrypted radiogramme mentioned that about 5 March a six-ship convoy would land the 51st Division at Lae.[24] Later decryptions supplied by the US Navy increased the number of ships in the reinforcement convoy and laid out precise convoy routes. By this time, Lieutenant General George C. Kenney, Commander, Fifth Air Force, and his deputy commander Brigadier General Ennis C. Whitehead were rehearsing the new low-level tactics that they would use against the convoy.

Forewarned of the convoy's route and destination by naval ULTRA, Allied pilots opened their attack on 2 March. After a three-day running battle, the Japanese had lost eight transports and four destroyers. Of the 6912 troops of the 51st Division; about 3900 survived, but only 1000 shocked and oil-soaked survivors reached Lae, while the remainder were returned to Rabaul. The lopsided victory, directly attributable to cryptanalysis, shifted the strategic initiative in the south-west Pacific to the Allies. They never relinquished it.

Reading the army air force code enabled Kenney to turn to the offensive with a vengeance. Messages addressed to the commanders of newly deployed Japanese army air force regiments and brigades identified lucrative Japanese airbase targets and exposed the enemy order of air battle in New Guinea. Traffic analysts tracked Japanese army pilots flying into New Guinea airfields and, through direction finding, often uncovered recently constructed airfields in the process. By late June 1943, the broken army air to ground code made the Allies aware that the Japanese Army Air Force was taking control from the navy of air operations in New Guinea. This major command change accompanied a further influx of army air units to eastern New Guinea. By early August Kenney knew from PEARL data the extent of the Japanese aerial reinforcements that were flowing into the theatre. The compromised air to ground system betrayed Japanese 6th Air Division, 13th, 59th, and 78th Air Regiments concentrated at Wewak.[25] Armed with this knowledge of his opponent's dispositions, Kenney meticulously plotted a devastating attack against his unsuspecting, but exposed, enemy. On 17 August, 1943, Allied airmen caught the Japanese planes on the ground. B-25 bombers struck from 300 feet dropping parachute-retarded fragmentation bombs on rows of neatly parked Japanese aircraft. P-38 and P-39 fighters swooped in to complete the destruction. Of 120 aircraft at Wewak; only 38 were left intact. The raid ensured Allied local air superiority for their imminent amphibious landing north of Lae on 4 September and their parachute assault in Nadzab scheduled for the following day.

These codebreaking successes were offset by Central Bureau and Arlington Hall's inability to pry open the secrets embedded in the Japanese Army's three and four-digit ciphers. The Army enciphered its most secret communications in a two-step process. First a code clerk substituted the appropriate four-digit number groups for specific words or phrases. The resulting code was then enciphered by means of another four-digit group of numbers taken from a key register which contained ten thousand random groups of numbers. The key changed daily, and false addition was used to complicate a cryptanalyst's task.[26] To further conceal a message's contents, radiomen divided messages into separate parts of fifty four-digit groups each and then juxtaposed the parts for transmission. The message header might appear in the third or fourth group of fifty while the final paragraph might be placed first. Nevertheless, even allowing for daily key changes, frequently used common military words – *shidan* (division), *butai* (unit), *hikōki* (airplane) – resulted in repetitions of code groups every two hundred or so messages. An army headquarters normally transmitted 200 or 300 messages daily, so cryptanalysts had access to the repetitions that they needed to identify patterns of encipherment and eventually to recover sufficient code group meanings to solve the message. However, it took time to establish the sequence of the series of key register numbers through the accumulation of sufficient quantities of radio intercepts.

Central Bureau first attacked the Japanese Army's three-digit cipher system which was used by echelons below a division – regiment, battalion, and company – for secure communications. Although these lower echelon messages might not contain high grade intelligence embedded in army or area army level communications, Central Bureau's rationale was that solving and understanding the cryptographic principles of the apparently simpler system would facilitate a later penetration of the more complex four-digit cipher. The structure of Japanese army communications, the excellent radio discipline of army signalmen, the low-powered transmissions, and the great distances separating the adversaries, that rendered intercepting signals difficult thwarted Allied attempts to break this three-digit cipher throughout the war.

Amidst this frustration, the US Army scored its first true cryptanalytic victory. The navy originally handled the cryptanalytic attack against Japanese water transport codes, but when they discerned the existence of separate codes for the Navy and the Army, it passed the work on the Army Water Transport Code, known as 2-4-6-8, to Arlington Hall for solution. 2-4-6-8 was a variation of the mainline army cipher and had been rushed into service to conceal the messages of water transport units proliferated in late 1942 to support Japanese Army advances into the Solomons and New Guinea. Imperial Army Headquarters used the Army Water Transport Code to control the army ships transporting troops and cargo to these far-flung units. A Shipping Command and a Shipping Force Headquarters in Tokyo controlled three major water transport commands which in turn commanded a multitude of port operations, anchorage, transportation, construction, stevedore and shipping engineer units that were in continual radio communication to keep the convoys moving smoothly. This major radio network stretched from Tokyo to the front lines.

Besides the routine administrative information and the conditions at various anchorages, the 2-4-6-8 code also carried messages about the departure and arrival time of individual transports or convoys, noon positions during their voyage, and occasionally detailed cargo lists. Anchorage directors across the Pacific needed these details in order to schedule and organise the barges that shuttled the men and cargo ashore from the transports.

In February 1943 certain inconsistencies in the cipher caught the eye of an enlisted cryptanalyst at Central Bureau, Sergeant Joseph E. Richard. He approached Sinkov and asked for permission to study the problem further. Richard's labour made it possible for cryptanalysts in Brisbane and Washington to identify further connections and, by using IBM sorters, to correlate a series of intercepted messages. In such fashion, Central Bureau and Arlington Hall broke 2-4-6-8 almost simultaneously on 6 April 1943.[27] Convoys betrayed by the compromised Water Transport Code fell victim to carefully crafted Allied submarine or aerial ambushes. The heavy losses of merchantmen and troop transports destined to resupply forward units at Rabaul or Wewak eventually forced Tokyo to suspend convoys to those destinations, in effect abandoning the now isolated garrisons. The Allies quickly learned that messages in the Water Transport Code often detailed specific unit movements that, in effect, provided an accurate and timely Japanese ground order of battle in the south and south-west

Pacific. By August 1944, the US Army had translated 75 000 WTC messages (10 per cent of those intercepted); 25 000 of them were shipping and 3750 convoy-related. Furthermore the understanding of the cryptographic principles and encryption methods that Central Bureau and Arlington Hall cryptanalysts gained in solving the Water Transport Code was applicable to other Japanese army cipher systems.[28]

On 18 September 1943 Arlington Hall unravelled the principal Japanese military attaché cipher. From then until 5 March 1945, when the Japanese introduced new variations to the cipher, US Army cryptanalysts read all military attaché traffic and made nearly half of the decrypted messages available to translators within a few hours of the time the signal was intercepted.[29] This cryptanalytic feat enabled the Allies to peer figuratively over their enemies' shoulders as Japanese officers wrote cables analysing political developments in occupied Europe and neutral capitals. Army attaché reports from Bucharest to Lisbon, Stockholm to Tangier, Berlin to Buenos Aires and anywhere else Japanese attachés might roost were goldmines of strategic intelligence about activities in Axis and neutral countries. Small wonder that the Americans described Japanese military attachés as 'the most efficient spies working for the United States in Europe'.[30]

The attaché evaluations, coupled with the uninterrupted flow of Japanese diplomatic message traffic (MAGIC) provided by cryptanalysts at Arlington Hall, offered otherwise completely inaccessible information to the Allies. Intelligence in these decrypted cables candidly evaluated economic conditions in enemy-held territory, revealed knowledge of enemy awareness of Allied operations, assessed production of armaments and data about new weapons, produced eyewitness accounts of the effectiveness of Allied air attacks, and recounted personal conversations with Adolf Hitler.[31]

Besides updating developments in Europe, the military attaché and Foreign Ministry cables revealed Tokyo's perspective on the war in Asia to the Allies. Each week Tokyo dispatched a circular message to its military attaché designed to acquaint them with the latest battlefield situations. The weekly report supplied key intelligence for the US Sixth Army during its bitter large-unit battles on Leyte in the Philippines, in 1944. For several months in 1945, the weekly bulletin was the main ULTRA sources available to the Americans fighting on Luzon because of the February 1945 change in Japanese army codebooks.[32] However, I am getting ahead of my story.

On 2 January 1944, MacArthur's forces leapfrogged past Japanese troops who were stubbornly clinging to Sio and landed at Saidor in eastern New Guinea. The envelopment cut off the Japanese 20th Division, whose forces withdrew westward pursued by the 9th Australian Division. An Australian patrol working its way through Sio discovered a trunkful of Japanese documents in a shallow stream. The document covers were missing, evidently to 'prove' to headquarters that the materials had been destroyed. But the many pages of multiple columns of Japanese *kanji* (Chinese-derived characters used in writing Japanese) aligned to four-digit numbers were intact. Thus the entire cryptographic library of the 20th Division, less covers, passed into Central Bureau's hands.[33]

Technicians at Brisbane used the data in the Japanese army's four-digit code book and its accompanying key register to program IBM sorters to decrypt the cipher. The machine solution proved so successful that the three fluent Japanese-language translators at Central Bureau found themselves overwhelmed with suddenly readable Japanese radio messages. MacArthur promptly requested translation assistance from the navy's cryptanalytic centre at Melbourne. Two naval officers who were cryptanalysts and Japanese linguists were immediately sent to Central Bureau. In a huge pile of decrypts they discovered a lengthy message that detailed the Japanese Second Area Army, Eighth Area Army, and Eighteenth Army's defensive plans for blocking MacArthur's expected offensive.[34]

From 20 January to 2 April 1944, US Army codebreakers read the Japanese Army's four-digit cipher – its most important top-secret messages – with clarity and accuracy. ULTRA's precise identification of the the otherwise hidden dispositions of Japan's Eighteenth Army in eastern New Guinea enabled MacArthur to bypass and isolate this opponent. He could plan the entire operation secure in his knowledge of his opponent's dispositions because his analysts were now able to read the four-digit cipher. In preliminary operations, Allied bombers and submarines, aimed at convoys betrayed by broken Water Transport Code messages, cut off the Japanese garrisons in eastern New Guinea from resupply. ULTRA from the four-digit cipher and PEARL (the compromised Army Air Force air to ground code) guided Kenney's massive air strikes that wiped out the Fourth Air Army on the ground at the sprawling Japanese airbase complex near Hollandia, Dutch New Guinea. ULTRA also confirmed the efficacy of the Allied deception campaign designed to make the Japanese believe that MacArthur intended to land next at Madang. ULTRA underpinned MacArthur's 400-mile leapfrog to Hollandia and Aitape, north-east New Guinea, that occurred on 22 April 1944 and was his outstanding use of ULTRA during the Pacific War.[35]

Two weeks before these multiple amphibious assaults, however, the Japanese Army changed its high-level cryptographic system, thereby denying US Army and Allied codebreakers access to its secrets.[36] How Central Bureau reconstructed the new key register is a model of cryptanalytic detective work.

A deciphered Water Transport Code message mentioned that a small cargo vessel, the *Yoshimo Maru*, was en route from Wewak to Hollandia carrying a party from Eighteenth Army's communications group. On 13 February 1944 American warplanes attacked the barge, setting it ablaze and then sinking it in shallow water within sight of the pier at Aitape harbour. Soon after, the 31st Anchorage Headquarters at Hollandia (identified by the compromised message place-name and unit codes) reported its concern about the fate of valuable code material aboard the 900-ton barge. One message, for example, was a addressed to a lieutenant who had survived the sinking and exhorted him about proper codebook security. Unfortunately for the Japanese, the anchorage command's deciphered admonitions pinpointed the time and place of the *Yoshimo Maru*'s sinking. After American troops secured Aitape in late April, Central Bureau arranged for an underwater diver to be flown to the site of the wreck. Under the eyes of Japanese infantrymen hiding in the hills east of the harbour, the diver salvaged a seared metal box that had wedged itself between the steps of a bulkhead ladder on the *Yoshimo Maru*. Back in Brisbane, technicians and cryptanalysts painstakingly reconstructed the key register from the grey ashen pages that had incinerated, but not decomposed, inside the box.[37] Armed with the latest key register, US Army codebreakers were soon reading Japan's four-digit cipher. A few months later American troops captured an intact copy of the key register when on 16 August they overran a handful of Japanese defenders at Sansapor, Dutch New Guinea.[38] These captured documents enabled army cryptanalysts to contribute to MacArthur's preparations to return to the Philippines by keeping him informed about the state of Japanese plans and dispositions in the islands.

One reason that MacArthur could move swiftly to the Philippines was that he did not have to fight his way through Japanese defences-in-depth in western New Guinea. American submarines had already sunk the troop transports bringing the reinforcements who were intended to defend the final barrier to the Philippines. In early April 1944, US navy cryptanalysts reported that a major convoy carrying the 35th Division was bound for Geelvink Bay, Dutch New Guinea.[39] Subsequent decryptions by army analysts of Water Transport Code messages disclosed that the 32nd Division was also en route to the area from Shanghai via the major Japanese base at Davao in the Philippines. By early May, US Army codebreakers knew that this so-called TAKE convoy consisted of nine transports and seven escorts carrying more than 12 000 troops of the two divisions. Water Transport Code decryptions provided the convoy's scheduled noontime positions between 2 and 9 May. Guided by this intelligence, American submarines sank four troop transports and deciphered WTC messages confirmed the disastrous losses of four ships and nearly 4000 soldiers.[40] The shaken survivors had seen the majority of their heavy equipment sink into the sea and were in no shape to defend anything. They found themselves speedily bypassed.

Through ULTRA the Allies knew that Japan was reinforcing the Philippines at a feverish rate. At least 20 000 troops were known to be in transit to the archipelago to upgrade four independent mixed brigades to full division-size formations. Army Water Transport messages transmitted from Army Shipping HQ at Hiroshima explained imminent plans to dispatch additional troop transports to Manila. ULTRA confirmed the 30th Division's arrival at Davao from Korea, the transfer of the 26th Division from North China to Manila, and the deployment of army air units from as far away as Burma and Manchuria to the Philippines as 300 warplanes of the 2nd and 4th Army Air divisions reinforced the islands. A message in the Water Transport Code betrayed the existence of newly formed Thirty-Fifth Army in the central Philippines while traffic analysis and compromised message unit codes uncovered the formation of a Fourteenth Area Army in Manila within three weeks of its formation.[41]

Naturally the Japanese build-up was not allowed to proceed unimpeded. Unrelenting attacks against Japanese shipping headed to the Philippines were coached on by ULTRA which assumed a dual role of identifying targets and then confirming their destruction. A note of caution; although ULTRA often validated a reported sinking, it could not always identify the cargoes stored in the enemy holds. ULTRA also missed major deployments, most notably the transfer of the entire 1st Division from Manchuria to Leyte during September and October 1944.

When the US Sixth Army landed on Leyte on 20 October 1944, deciphered Japanese army messages had provided an accurate order of battle not only on Leyte but throughout the Philippines. Moreover the complementary nature of various compromised codes greatly assisted the liberation of Leyte. Allied ability to read the air to ground code alerted them to the massive Japanese air attacks that soon followed the landings, and knowledge of the main army air force system provided the first definitive data about the new special attack corps or kamikaze tactics. Reading both these systems enabled MacArthur to plot Japanese staging areas, keep count of their operational aircraft, and detect the frenzied enemy efforts to tip the balance on Leyte by throwing 219 more warplanes into the battle during the first two v.eeks of the fighting.[42]

Imperial General Headquarters' decision to fight the main battle on Leyte radically altered the campaign in the Philippines. Deciphered military attaché cables made known to the Allies Tokyo's mistaken belief that an overwhelming Japanese victory in the battle for Leyte Gulf had isolated MacArthur's forces on Leyte. Vice Chief of Staff Lieutenant General Hata Hikosaburō boasted, for example, 'that the army and navy units had inflicted tremendous losses on the enemy in both day and night attacks'.[43] Acting on such wildly exaggerated battle claims, Southern Army ordered ground reinforcements to Leyte in an effort codenamed TA.

With one major exception, that of the 1st Division, broken Army Water Transport Codes and compromised army and navy air–ground codes divulged every TA sailing. Australian 6 Wireless Unit repeatedly identified convoy sailing times and destinations by the simple expedient of reading coded naval air–ground messages. Pilots flying air cover above the vessels routinely transmitted situation reports to their bases on the progress of the convoys, especially during the ships' final dash in or out of the port of Ormoc on Leyte's west coast.[44] They might just as well have advertised the convoy's position with neon lights.

The Japanese lost 24 ships, more than 3000 men, and about 130 000 tons of shipping during the two months of convoy runs to Leyte. Deciphered military attaché weekly reports and decrypted Foreign Ministry cables (faithful old MAGIC) revealed the magnitude of the TA reinforcement effort and verified its heavy losses en route to Ormoc.[45] Had all these Japanese units reached their intended destination unhindered, they surely would have prolonged the vicious fighting that characterised the Leyte campaign.

As fighting on Leyte entered its notorious 'mop-up' phase, MacArthur was anticipating his return to Luzon. ULTRA was a poor servant during the Luzon operation. On 1 February 1945 the Imperial Army introduced the fifth edition of its code book. The change left US Army codebreakers unable to read the four-digit cipher until such time as Central Bureau and Arlington Hall could gather sufficient code groups to solve the new system. Compromised military attaché messages and some MAGIC, which cryptanalysts continued to read without interruption, provided the main data about Fourteenth Area Army's forces on Luzon.

The steady destruction of General Yamashita Tomoyuki's Fourteenth Area Army mitigated against extensive Japanese radio communications thus denying the Allies the raw material to generate ULTRA. Some Japanese units destroyed their radios and communications equipment as they girded themselves for a last suicidal stand; others lost or abandoned their radio gear during pell-mell retreats; still others discarded damaged radios because they had no spare parts to repair them; others just ran out of batteries or fuel for generators. The end result was the same – a gradual, but steady, diminution of tactical radio message traffic. Communications between Imperial Headquarters and Yamashita also dried up because Tokyo regarded Luzon, much as Washington had three years earlier, as a lost cause. No relief convoys sailed for Manila, so few water transport encrypted messages were broadcast. Imperial Headquarters was hoarding aircraft for the defence of Japan, so very few air to ground transmissions near Luzon were overheard. Most of the Japanese navy had been sunk during the defence of the Philippines, so the volume of navy messages transmitted to Luzon dropped off precipitously.

The numbers of Allied cryptanalysts on Luzon increased inversely to the decrease of Japanese army messages. Headquarters, Central Bureau, had followed MacArthur to Hollandia in the late summer of 1944 and thence to Leyte in October 1944. This small advance echelon eventually established itself in the Manila Waterworks building, but the main cryptanalytic centre remained in Brisbane, now thousands of miles behind the fighting fronts. Since only MacArthur's General Headquarters received Central Bureau's ULTRA by radio, lesser headquarters had to await the arrival of a Central Bureau courier carrying ULTRA dispatches in a sealed pouch. Flying from Brisbane to Manila in 1945 was a slow, sometimes dangerous, and often unreliable means of travel. Field commanders were unable to accept a lack of timeliness in the delivery of perishable intelligence so Central Bureau displaced forward in June 1945. By this time, MacArthur's cryptanalytic centre had about 4000 personnel (about 50 per cent of them American) assigned to detachments throughout the Southwest Pacific Area. When cryptanalysts arrived at Central Bureau's new home in San Miguel, about thirty miles north of Manila, they had little to do but read old messages in hopes of discovering previously overlooked intelligence.[46]

The capture of numerous Japanese army and navy code books and key registers from the disintegrating enemy forces on Luzon and on Okinawa infused new life into Central Bureau. By 1 July 1945, the Allies were again reading all Japanese high command messages, including air force headquarters systems.[47] In other words, as the great showdown with Japan loomed, ULTRA reasserted itself as the premier source of intelligence not only about Japanese dispositions for the defence of her homeland, but also about enemy intentions. It was a crescendo performance where all the instruments – cryptanalysis, codebreaking, traffic analysis, direction-finding – blended together in an symphony which startled its audience.

On 20 January 1945 the emperor approved and the army promulgated the overall defensive plan for Japan's home islands. By mid-February a three-stage mobilisation commenced that aimed to field forty new divisions by August that year. Four other divisions from Manchuria were transferred to Japan to defend the homeland. Also in February, the American Joint Chiefs of Staff started planning for the invasion of Japan's southernmost main island of Kyushu. By late May, the JCS directed that the invasion – codenamed Operation OLYMPIC – be launched on 1 November 1945.

In April 1945, General MacArthur's intelligence experts originally predicted that six enemy combat and two depot divisions would defend Kyushu. At most, they thought, Imperial Headquarters would commit ten divisions to the island's defence. Decrypts of four-digit army ciphers revealed that the Japanese high command expected an invasion some time after the middle of the year and that Tokyo had alerted its major commands to watch for indications of such an operation.[48]

The Army Water Transport Code called attention to large numbers of troops shifting from Korea to Kyushu. Anchorage command messages similarly foretokened the destinations of the arriving units. Readable addresses on Army Air Force messages uncovered a new central command, General Air Army Command, in Tokyo. Compromised unit codes exposed the formation of newly designated armies and area armies which implied the existence of more subordinate divisions and brigades. Navy decipherments spoke of centralised command to repel an invasion, while naval air to ground codes gave away large-scale tactical deployments into southern Kyushu. Direction-finding bearings taken on various radio transmitters located newly established division head-quarters and the general disposition of Japanese units. From air to ground decrypts and deciphered army and naval air force messages cryptanalysts compiled a total of 1885 aircraft on Kyushu. In early July, American pilots flew hundreds of reconnaissance sorties to photograph every one of the 243 known airfields in Japan. Photographs of Kyushu revealed 1807 aircraft, a tribute to the accuracy of the ULTRA-derived figures.[49]

New unit code names and code numbers of the mobilised divisions began appearing in message traffic during late May as Japanese defensive preparations gained momentum. The appearance of more and more Japanese army and navy units in radio signals emanating from Kyushu concerned Allied intelligence.

ULTRA made plain that the Japanese were fortifying the very beaches that the Americans would have to seize and that more enemy troops were arriving daily. ULTRA also laid bare Imperial Headquarters brutal strategy – to inflict such severe damage on the invaders that the Allies would sue for a negotiated peace.[50]

The massive military build-up continued apace with Japanese diplomatic efforts to secure a negotiated peace. MAGIC exposed these peace initiatives.[51] Surely this reminded some old hands of Japanese negotiating duplicity in Washington while plotting the surprise attack on Pearl Harbor. More to the military point, by mid-July ULTRA showed that since early June roughly 100 000 troop reinforcements arrived in Kyushu bringing the garrison there to 380 000. A day later that figure leapt to 455 000 when Arlington Hall accepted three new unit code names as division-size formations.[52] Four days before the first atomic bomb attack (6 August 1945), Washington intelligence estimated that 545 000 Japanese were on Kyushu and by 7 August had increased that total to 560 000 troops. ULTRA and all its handmaidens correctly identified and located 13 of 14 enemy divisions defending Kyushu, and also provided specific details of the Japanese plan of defence.[53] Did this tremendous cryptanalytic victory affect the American decision to attack Japan with atomic bombs?

At the outset, I said that my essay was representative, not comprehensive. By discussing the technical achievements of US Army codebreakers to the Pacific War, I have necessarily presented a black and white picture of events. The grey areas – human failings, gross errors of interpretation, outright stupidity, and simple miscalculations – are missing and that omission skews any conclusion. In other words, the technical achievements of Army codebreakers in the Pacific War do not automatically equate with battlefield success or even to accurate assessments by intelligence agencies. Those are the grey areas that historians must address in order to reappraise the Pacific War.

A final thought is that the technical achievements of US Army codebreakers against Japan were not infallible. According to a Japanese authority, the Imperial Army might transmit about 2500 messages daily. Nowhere near that number were intercepted let alone translated every day. Instead scanners screened decrypts searching for key words that made the message significant enough to merit a complete translation. This filter eliminated more than 90 per cent of available intercepts. In August 1944, for instance, Translation Section, Central Bureau, was translating an average of 50 complete messages daily – many being multiple-part messages. This rose to 53 daily in September 1944 and peaked in July 1945 with an average of 76 messages per day or possibly 0.03 per cent of the potentially available radio traffic.[54]

Within these definite limitations, ULTRA and its various sub-categories do offer us an unparalleled opportunity to reappraise the Pacific War. Where else do we find the on-the-spot assessments and interpretations of Japan's generals and admirals, unclouded by fifty years of sometimes unreliable, sometimes dubious, and sometimes conveniently failed memories to protect reputations? The exploitation of the ULTRA documents to re-evaluate the Pacific War is the challenge that awaits historians.[55]

## NOTES

1. Herbert O. Yardley, *The American Black Chamber*, (New York: Ballantine, 1981). Chapter XIV discusses this feat.

2. 'History of the Signal Security Agency', vol. 2, 'The General Cryptanalytic Problems', 15 January 1947, Registry Group (RG) 457, SRH-361, 035. (Hereafter cited as SRH-361.) National Archives and Records Administration, Washington, DC, (Hereafter cited as NARA.)

3. Ibid., 035–036.

4. Spencer B. Akin, 'MacArthur's Signal Intelligence Service World War II', draft MS. MacArthur Memorial Bureau of Archives, Norfolk, Virginia, RG 15, Box 11, Folder 4, 'Papers of Major General B.H. Pochyla', 3. General Pochyla was Akin's deputy in SWPA during World War II. Also see David Kahn, *The Codebreakers: The Story of Secret Writing,* (New York: MacMillan, 1967), chapter 1, 'One Day of Magic'.

5. Frederick D. Parker, 'The Unsolved Messages of Pearl Harbor', *Cryptologia*, October 1991, pp. 296–7.

6. Thomas Parrish, *The Ultra Americans: The US Role in Breaking the Nazi Codes* (New York: Stein & Day, 1984) p. 56.

7. Dundas P. Tucker, 'Rhapsody in Purple: A New History of Pearl Harbor (1)', (edited and annotated by Greg Mellen), *Cryptologia*, (July 1982) p. 204.

8. Jack Finnegan, 'Grim Fate for Station 6', *Military History* (October 1986), 10; Akin, 'MacArthur's Signal', 7; 'Reminiscences of Lieutenant Colonel Howard W. Brown', Registry Group (RG) 457, SRH-045, 11 and 13, NARA; 'US Comint Policy Pearl Harbor to Summer 1942, Registry Group (RG) 457, SRH-269, 9, NARA.

9. 'History of the Signal Security Agency, vol. 3, The Japanese Army Problems: Cryptanalysis, 1942–1945', Registry Group (RG) 457, SRH-362, 031–032, 035, NARA (Hereafter cited as SRH-362.)

10. 'The Achievements of the Signal Security Agency in World War II', Registry Group (RG) 457, SRH-349, 015, NARA (Hereafter cited as SRH-349.)

11. Geoffrey St. Vincent Ballard, *On ULTRA Active Service: The Story of Australia's Signals Intelligence Operations during World War II* (Richmond, Victoria, Australia, 1991), pp. 145–7. Ballard served at Central Bureau during the war.

12. Ibid., p. 172.

13. As an officer in the Australia Royal Navy, Nave had studied Japanese in Japan from 1921 to 1923 and had then been seconded to the Royal Navy where he was a premier cryptanalyst between the wars. Nave served in Hong Kong, on flagships of the China Station, and the Far East Combined Bureau. Declared medically unfit for further service in the tropics, in February 1940 Nave was back in Australia. Recognising Nave's unique talents, the Chief of the Australian Naval Staff, Admiral Sir Ragnar Colvin, arranged for him to head a small navy cryptographic office in Melbourne in July 1940 which together with a small cell of cryptanalysts and

academics, had been deciphering Japanese diplomatic and commercial radio traffic passing between Tokyo and Japanese embassies in various countries of the Pacific region. Ibid., pp. 145, 164.

14.   Ibid., p. 172.
15.   Interview with Dr Abraham Sinkov, 23 February 1989, Phoenix, Arizona. My use of these codewords is anachronistic because they were neither widely nor uniformly employed in the Pacific theatres until mid-1944.
16.   'Memorandum for Director Naval Communications', 9 March 1943, 1. This memorandum is attached as an enclosure to 'Memorandum Admiral E.J. King, U.S.N., Subject: Merger of Army and Navy Radio Intelligence Activities', 10 March 1943 in 'Army-Navy Collaboration, 1931–1945', SRH-200, 155 and 157 Registry Group (RG) 457 NARA (Hereafter cited as SRH-200.) King was Commander, US Fleet.
17.   SRH-349, 015; SRH-362, 031, 034. An explanation of the *den-dai* system appears in Henry D. Ephron, 'An American Cryptanalyst in Australia', *Cryptologia*, October 1985, p. 340.
18.   SRH-349, 027.
19.   Ballard, *On ULTRA Active Service* pp. 178, 180.
20.   T2W (Fleet Radio Unit, Melbourne) 14/0221 December 1942, and T2W 18/0056 December 1942, 'Radio Intelligence in World War II Tactical Operations in the Pacific Ocean Area, December 1942', Registry Group (RG) 457, SRH-136, 349 and 514, NARA (Hereafter cited as SRH-136.)
21.   NPM (Pearl Harbor) –23/2032–December DI, et seq., SRH-136, 601–6.
22.   T2W, 1802 13 December DI, SRH-136, 518. 'Commander in Chief, Pacific (CINCPAC) Intelligence Bulletins', #277, 19 December 1942, Registry Group (RG) 457, SRMN-013, 260, NARA.
23.   Headquarters, Allied Air Forces, SWPA, Intelligence Summary #76 and #78, 10 and 13 February 1943 respectively.
24.   'Memorandum for Director Naval Communications', 9 March 1943, SRH-200, 1–2. NSS (Washington) –170036–February-DI, 'Radio Intelligence in World War II Tactical Operations Pacific Ocean Area, February 1943', Registry Group (RG) 457, SRH-144, II, 446. 'CINCPAC Intelligence Bulletin', #339, 19 February 1943, NARA.
25.   'GHQ, SWPA, Military Intelligence Section, Special Intelligence Bulletin', 28 and 30 June; 8, 10, 11, 15 July; and 2 August 1943, Registry Group (RG) 457, SRH-203, NARA (Hereafter cited as SIB and date.)
26.   Kamaga Kazuo, Fujiwara Kuniki, Yoshimura Akira, 'Zadankai: Nihon rikugun angōsho wa naze yaburarenakatta', (Discussion: Why couldn't the Japanese army codes be broken?) *Rekishi to jimbutsu: Nihon rikukaigun kaku tatakaeri* (The war between the Japanese army and navy) (December 1985), pp. 155–7. Kamaga and Fujiwara are former Imperial Army signal officers who devised army codes.
27.   Interview with Mr Joseph E. Richard; SRH-349, 026; 'An Exhibit of the Important Types of Intelligence Recovered through Reading Japanese Cryptograms', Registry Group (RG) 457, SRH-280, 1 and 2, NARA. (Hereafter cited as SRH-280.)
28.   SRH-280, 2. The 'Japanese Water Transport Translations,' are available as a discreet collection, Registry Group (RG) 457, SRR-001–44326, NARA.
29.   SRH-361, 083.
30.   SRH-280, 12.
31.   Ibid., 5.
32.   *Rikugun angōsho* 4 (Army code book, 4th edition) was valid from 1 June 1943 to 31 January 1945. SRH 362, 139.
33.   Ibid., pp. 139–41; Ballard, *On ULTRA Active Service*, p. 194.

34. 'The Pacific War through the Eyes of Forrest R. "Tex" Biard', *Cryptolog: Naval Cryptologic Veterans Association*, vol. 10, no. 2, winter 1989, pp. 20–2. Biard was one of the US Navy officers sent to MacArthur's headquarters.

35. For an account of the Hollandia operation see Edward J. Drea, 'Ultra Intelligence and General Douglas MacArthur's Leap to Hollandia, January–April 1944', *Intelligence and National Security*, vol. 5, no. 2 (April 1990), pp. 323–49.

36. '"MAGIC" Summary – Japanese Army Supplement', 8 April 1944, Registry Group (RG) 457, SRS 001/547, NARA (Hereafter cited as MSJAS and date.)

37. SIB, 17 March 1944; SRH-059, 027; Ballard, *On ULTRA Active Service*, p. 196; Richard interview. Ballard states that the *Yoshino Maru* was the victim, but that ship was actually sunk north of Luzon by the USS *Parche* on 31 July 1944. Incidentally ULTRA confirmed the *Yoshino's* loss (MIS Jul 31/Aug 1) carrying troops of 26th Division to the Philippines.

38. SRH-362, 147–148.

39. SIB, 13 April 1944.

40. MSJAS, 10 May.

41. SIB, 15/16 June; 7/8, 8/9 July; 2/3, 21/22 August; MSJAS, 5, 17, and 27 July; 8 August.

42. MSJAS, 2 November 1944.

43. 'Joint Intelligence Centre, Pacific Ocean Area (JICPOA), Summary of ULTRA Traffic, 11 September–31 December 1944, October 27, 1944', Registry Group (RG) 457, SRMD-007 (Part 1) 136, NARA (Hereafter cited as JICPOA and date.)

44. Ballard, *On ULTRA Active Service*, p. 222.

45. MSJAS, 17 November 1944.

46. Information from a former officer who served in Central Bureau who prefers anonymity. The Central Bureau strength figure appears in General Headquarters, Far East Command, Military Intelligence Section, General Staff, 'A Brief History of the G-2 Section, GHQ, SWPA and Affiliated Units', Introduction to the Intelligence Series, 1948, 69. Copy at US Army Centre of Military History.

47. Memorandum A.W. Sanford, Lt. Colonel, GS, to C-in-C., A.M.F. (Blamey), 30 June 1945, 'Ultra Material in the Blamey Papers', Registry Group (RG) 457, SRH-219, 064, NARA. Sanford was one of the Australian directors of Central Bureau.

48. MSJAS, 15 April 1945; SIB 27/28 April 1945.

49. MSJAS, 13, 20, and 21 April 1945; SIB, 7/8 July 1945.

50. MSJAS, 29 June 1945.

51. For examples of decrypted Japanese Foreign Ministry cables concerning peace overtures see US War Department, Office of the Assistant Chief of Staff, G-2 (Intelligence), '"MAGIC" – Diplomatic Summary' 5 and 18 May; 5, 6, 14, 22, 25, 30 June; 11 and 18 July, Registry Group (RG) 457, SRS-1534/1837, NARA.

52. MSJAS, 21 July 1945.

53. Compare GHQ, US Army Forces in the Pacific, Military Intelligence Section, General Staff, 'Amendment No. 1 to G-2 Estimate of the Enemy Situation with Respect to Kyushu (Dated 25 April 1945)', 29 July 1945, 1 and Bōeicho, Bōei kenshūjo senshishitsu, (Defence agency, national defence college, war history office) ed., *Senshi sōsho* (Official military history) vol. 57 *Hondo kessen jumbi (2) Kyūshū no bōèi* (Preparations for the decisive battle of the homeland (2) Defence of Kyūshū) (Tokyo: Asagumo shimbunsha, 1972) p. 597.

54. Kamaga Kazuo, 'Nihon rikugun angō wa 'antai' datta', (The Japanese army codes were secure), *Shogen: Rekishi to jimbutsu: Hiroku: Taiheiyō sensō* (Testimony: The Pacific War) (September 1984), 281; Ballard, *On ULTRA Active Service*, p. 195. Even when scanners knew exactly what they were looking for in piles of intercepts,

the percentage meriting full translation did not rise appreciably. After World War II, for instance, the US Navy re-examined Japanese cipher messages broadcast between July and December 1941 searching for references to the Pearl Harbor attack. Of the 26 581 messages intercepted during that period, analysts considered 2413 (about 9 per cent) important enough for translation. Among these, 188 (0.007 per cent) related to Pearl Harbor. See SRH-406, 1.

55.    Edward J. Drea, *MacArthur's ULTRA: Codebreaking and the War Against Japan* (Lawrence, Kan.: University of Kansas Press, 1992) analyses ULTRA's influence on operations and decision-making in the Southwest Pacific Area Theatre. However, no systematic account of ULTRA's role in the South or Central Pacific or China, India, Burma theatres is available for the air, ground, and naval phases of those campaigns.

# Part III
# Conflicts in Asia

# 6 Burma: The Longest War, 1941–45
## Louis Allen and David Steeds

Louis Allen was a brilliant lecturer, who, over the years, at conferences, seminars and other academic gatherings, delivered papers which were informative, provocative, often entertaining, and revealed always enormous knowledge of and infectious enthusiasm for the topic under consideration. His last performance, the paper on *Burma: The Longest War*, which he presented from his wheelchair at the Imperial War Museum on 5 December 1991 was vintage Louis, and those who were there will long remember it. It was, as Ian Nish observed in an obituary published in the *Newsletter* of the British Association for Japanese Studies, 'a moving account which combined the knowledge which comes from direct experience and that which comes from books'.

In the paper, Louis Allen displayed all his skill, and above all his easy mastery of an enormous subject, a mastery based on the breadth and depth of his knowledge of the source material, Western and Japanese. The notes he left behind, which are presented here, are but the bare framework for a paper which was a joy to listen to. Two weeks later he was dead.

## NATIONAL STRATEGIES

### Japan

Japan's purpose in Burma was to close the Burma Road, thus severing the supply route to Nationalist China. Burma also constituted the westernmost bulwark of the Co-Prosperity Sphere and, later, was considered as a stepping-stone for the invasion of India.

### Britain

The British intended to recover their colonial territory and its economic riches which had been seized by force. They were successful, but had neither the military strength nor the political motivation to retain it after their victory of 1945.

### USA

The purpose of the United States in Burma was to ensure the reopening of the supply line to Nationalist China. This they did by flying aircraft across the mountainous 'Hump' of the Himalayas and by building a road between Assam and Yunnan. They employed only a very small force of US infantry under Stilwell in Northern Burma, but their combat and transport aircraft were an absolutely vital part of the South-East Asia Command (SEAC) strategy.

## China

Chinese troops entered Burma to rescue the beleaguered British and Indian forces in 1942, but, like them, were soon defeated by the Japanese invaders. Chinese troops, reconstituted, trained and equipped by the Americans, later invaded Burma from the north under Stilwell; but the Chinese were chiefly concerned to keep these valuable forces intact for internal political reasons.

## India

India was the reservoir for the main body of troops in Burma (the Indian Army) and the base for the British counter-offensive. But India's views about the strategy and politics of the war were not consulted. They were taken for granted. Similarly, Burma's representatives in exile played little or no part in deciding the orientation of the campaign, even though their territory was twice ruthlessly fought over by both British and Japanese.

## THE CAMPAIGNS

### Narrative of Events

During the Second World War, Burma was the venue of the most extensive and most intense conflict between the British Empire and the Japanese Empire. On 11 December 1941, a unit of 143 Infantry regiment of 55 Division crossed over from Thailand to occupy Victoria Point and deny its airfield to the British, cutting the air reinforcement route between India and Malaya. And, at the war's end, occasional fighting in south-west Burma continued after the official surrender on 15 August 1945, because by that time the Japanese were so shattered by defeat that they had in many cases lost touch with outlying units. This combat period of three years ten months is the longest continuous period of fighting in any World War II theatre.

Burma witnessed a spectacular Japanese victory in 1942. By June 1942, the British-Indian forces were driven back from almost the entire territory of Burma, and in their retreat were accompanied by scores of thousands of Indian refugees who (justifiably) feared the reprisals of the Burmese once British government restraints were removed. They died in their thousands in the passes leading to Assam.

1943 was occupied on both sides by preparations for counter-offensives, involving the restructuring of command: the creation of Burma Area Army under General Kawabe by the Japanese, and of South-East Asia Command under Admiral Mountbatten by the Allies. The relative pause in hostilities enabled the Japanese to grant Burma a restricted form of political independence under Ba Maw (premier under British rule in 1937), with its own military force under the young student revolutionary Aung San, whom the Japanese made a major-general.

In 1944, the Japanese determined to push back the front line and pre-empt a British invasion of Burma. Officially, at the level of Imperial General Head-quarters in Tokyo, the strategic intention was to capture British stores and the British base at Imphal, capital of Manipur State; but the instrument was XV Army, and its C-in-C had other ideas. He was General Mutaguchi Renya, who had been a divisional commander at the fall of Singapore, and intended to round off his defeat of the British by expelling them from India and so taking them out of the war. Japanese forces would break into Assam, and then the Bengali nationalist revolutionary, Subhas Chandra Bose, would rouse the people of Bengal against British rule.

Mutaguchi willed the end, but not the means. His force was only three divisions strong, and had rations for only three weeks, on the supposition that they would live on captured British rations once Imphal fell. He came within an ace of success. Starting in early March, his 31 Division was soon astride the supply road from Kohima to Imphal, which led back to the railhead at Dimapur and so into India. Two other divisions, 33 and 15, cut off the north–south lines of communication of IV Corps, putting the whole Imphal area in a state of siege. A feint attack in Arakan by 55 Division was almost successful in surrounding and annihilating 7 Indian Division but, contrary to what the Japanese expected from past British behaviour, the British did not run back once their lines of communication were cut, but stood their ground and were supplied by air. This was Japan's first major defeat in South-East Asia.

XIV Army's defeat of Mutaguchi's invasion of India affected British strategy too. London had never wanted to fight a campaign back through the jungles of Burma, overland to Rangoon; it seemed much more sensible to hook round the Bay of Bengal and take Rangoon by sea. Indeed it was, but the landing craft for such an operation were never available, and General Slim, C-in-C of the XIV Army, followed up the defeated Japanese into Burma, and between December 1944 and April 1945 gradually reconquered the territory lost in 1942. At the same time the United States and US–Chinese forces in Northern Burma gradually pushed back Japanese 18 and 56 Divisions to take the town of Myitkyina, enabling the Burma Road to be re-opened and supplies to be brought through to Chiang Kai-shek's beleaguered forces in Chungking.

This was, in fact, the chief reason for the United States' presence in Burma. The US C-in-C, General Stilwell, built a road from Ledo in Assam to meet the old Burma road once Myitkyina was recaptured; once the Ledo road started to function, the United States lost interest in supporting the British effort to regain its former colonial territory. Fortunately, there were still enough USAAF elements to ensure that British forces could operate, firstly, in support of Stilwell, behind the Japanese lines in Northern Burma (the second Wingate expedition was to do this) and secondly, in the Arakan to fly in troops, ammunition and rations to 7 Indian Division when cut off. Likewise, at Meiktila in March 1945, Slim's bold stroke to grasp the jugular of Japanese communications in central Burma would have been impossible without adequate air support from both RAF and USAAF.

Meiktila was Slim's master-stroke. He put IV Corps and XXXIII Corps across the Irrawaddy, and deceived the Japanese into thinking that he was making for the old capital, Mandalay. Instead, IV Corps and 255 tank Brigade were pushed down the Myittha Valley in great secrecy, and burst across the Irrawaddy at Nyaungu. Meiktila was defended by a scratch garrison, soon overwhelmed. Aware of its crucial importance to their communications to the rest of Burma, the Japanese sent every available division against it. But Meiktila held, and from it, like a spring-board, the Allied divisions rolled down the road to Rangoon. Slim needed to be doubly sure of Rangoon so he put in an amphibious landing from the Arakan which narrowly beat the cross-country divisions to it. The Japanese XXVIII Army, cut off by the retreat of the main Japanese forces towards Tenasserim and Thailand, attempted to break out across the British lines after the fall of Rangoon and was decimated.

Japan's seizure of Burma, like her conquest of Malaya and Singapore, had not been expensive: a matter of two thousand lives; but to stay in Burma and retain her conquests cost her over 185 000 lives, one twelfth of the casualties she sustained throughout the war. The Indian Army was Britain's chief weapon of retrieval, and lost nearly 7000 men in the reconquest of Burma. Only two British divisions were involved, and UK casualties numbered only 4037. It was conditions and climate rather than battle casualties which made Burma such a fearsome theatre, for both sides. The British felt they were as far from home as they could possibly be, and that they were always last when it came to allocation of supplies and reinforcements: hence the epithet 'Forgotten Army'. For the Japanese, likewise, Burma was *jigoku*, 'hell'. Lethal diseases were endemic: malaria, amoebic dysentery, scrub typhus. Communications were non-existent to start with – India was linked with Burma by a couple of jungle tracks. So the military effort was also a medical effort, and an engineering effort (the Japanese had their own engineering triumph to correspond with Stilwell's Ledo Road in the railway linking Thanbyuzayat in Burma with Bampong in Thailand, but at a fearful cost of lives in the labour force of native coolies and Allied POWs). The north–south configuration of the mountain chains in Burma and the utility of the great rivers had always meant that Burmese commerce used the river courses. In some cases both sides did the same, but not all Burma was navigable river: central Burma, a dry dustbowl in the spring heat, was ideal tank country, and it was tanks and aircraft which made the victory of Meiktila possible.

Transport aircraft radically altered the field of battle: the Dakota carried everything from food to mules and field artillery; the light aircraft L-5 ensured that casualties, instead of being left behind to the tender mercies of the enemy, were flown out to hospitals. The Japanese were less lucky: their airforce, a potent factor in the first few months of 1942, soon relinquished mastery of the air to the RAF and USAAF.

## Tactics

The Japanese had a fondness for night attacks, and the gambit of encircling the enemy and cutting his retreat. This worked well in Malaya and in the early days in Burma. But Allied ability to supply forward troops by air, shown in the first Wingate expedition of 1943 and the second one in 1944, the supply of 81 West African Division in the Arakan, and the Battle of the Admin Box at Sinzweya in 1944, destroyed the effectiveness of this tactic.

Japanese infantry defence was tenacious, relying heavily on the use of mortars and on the construction of deeply entrenched and heavily protected bunker systems, which even tanks found hard to winkle out.

## Air

Japan's mastery of the air in 1942 brought about the first British defeats, but from 1943 onwards Allied air superiority enabled not merely supplies but whole formations to be flown to distant battlefields: General Wingate's Special Force into North Burma, 5 and 7 Indian Divisions to Imphal and Kohima, 99 Brigade to Meiktila in March 1945. This was made possible by the RAF and USAAF use of the Dakota, the workhorse of the battlefield.

Control of the air also transformed the medical situation. This medical/logistical triumph was made possible by the inability of the Japanese air force to respond in kind. In June 1944 the four air regiments of 5 Air Division could muster 129 aircraft of all kinds, of which only 80 were capable of flying. In contrast, between 18 April and 30 June, 19 000 Allied reinforcements and 13 000 tons of supplies were flown into Imphal and 43 000 noncombatants and 13 000 casualties were flown out. The lift involved ten US and five RAF squadrons, 384 (C-47) Dakotas in all, plus 20 (C-46) Commandos.

The Allies' advantage is shown by the contrast in casualty figures. In the invasion of India (February to July 1944) Japanese casualties numbered 65 978 and Allied casualties 27 776. Japanese casualties were nearly always fatal because of inadequate hospitalisation. Allied sick and wounded in contrast could expect to be ferried to base hospitals and survive.

## Medical

Climate, disease and distance were the three major impediments to campaigning in Burma. A stunningly beautiful country, it was nevertheless a place where amoebic dysentery, malaria, and scrub typhus flourished. Malaria was conquered by the use of the suppressive drug mepacrine, so effectively that to catch malaria became a military offence. Again, the casualty contrasts between Japanese and British/Indian are instructive.

The Japanese took Burma in 1942 at the cost of 2000 dead. Added to the 3500 killed in the Malaya campaign, this means it cost Japan 5500 men to destroy the British Empire in the Far East. Not, surely, an inordinate price.

On the other hand, *to stay* in Burma cost them far more. From start to finish, they despatched 303 501 troops to Burma. 118 353 returned to Japan after 1945, leaving a total casualty figure of 185 149 dead, thirteen times the British and Commonwealth losses. Three-fifths of Japan's soldiers never came back from Burma, one-twelfth of their losses in the war as a whole. These died from bombing, disease, and the cruelties of the Burmese climate and terrain. British and Commonwealth casualties numbered 73 900, but superior medical facilities meant that of that number only 14 326 died. If that figure is further broken up into British and Commonwealth casualties, the result is startling:

| | | |
|---|---|---|
| Indian troops | 6599 | (46%) |
| African troops | 858 | ( 6%) |
| UK troops | 4037 | (28%) |

That is, the number of UK troops killed in Burma was less than 5000 i.e. two-thirds of Indian troops killed, and one-twelfth of the fatal casualties in air-raids at home (60 595), or one-sixth of the war's casualties in the Merchant Navy (30 248).

Of the ground troops available to South-East Asia Command, which numbered well over a million men in 1944 and 1945, British and Commonwealth losses represented one-thirteenth.

United States forces were much smaller. US land forces in South-East Asia Command numbered 12 097 in April 1945, mostly engaged in road-building. The fighting component (GALAHAD in 1944. MARS force later) was less than 3000-strong and lost heavily. In its major engagement, the battle for Myitkina, casualty figures are as follows:

| | *Killed* | *Wounded* | *Sick* |
|---|---|---|---|
| Chinese | 972 | 3184 | 188 |
| US | 274 | 955 | 980 |

This major battle therefore cost 2209 US casualties.

## Engineering

Distance and climate produce problems which in turn can be solved only by a complex engineering structure. The Allies improvised a great deal, and the Japanese did without. Roads had to be built from scratch by both sides, and the ambitious road from Ledo in Assam to Myitkyina to link up with the former 'Burma Road' to China was built by US engineers and local labour. The road down the Myittha Valley, which was to carry Slim's blitzkreig force against Meiktila, made extensive use of 'bithess', hessian strips 50 yards long by a yard wide, treated with bitumen and packed tight. Every yard of road cost a gallon of petrol and a gallon of diesel, but 100 miles of bithess carried 1000 vehicles a day. The Myittha road took 42 days to build and carried 800 tons a day.

Oil pipelines came with the roads. A six-inch US pipeline ran from Calcutta to Tinsukia and later on to Mogaung; another from Chittagong to Tinsukia. A four-inch US pipeline and a four-inch British pipeline ran between Tinsukia and Bhamo, whence a single US four-inch pipe carried oil from India right to Kunming in China.

Japan's problems derived from the vulnerability of her shipping between Indo-China, Singapore and Rangoon to attacks from Allied aircraft and submarines. The solution was an imaginative one, to succeed where British and German engineers had, years before, decided a railway was impracticable. In June 1942, Southern Army GHQ ordered a railway to be built linking Non Pladuk in Thailand with Thanbyuzayat in Burma, 250 miles of track at a cost of seven million yen. But the real cost was human. The railway was completed by 23 October 1943. 'Few enterprises', wrote the Burmese premier and Japanese collaborator Ba Maw, 'during the war showed more essential vision than the construction of this railroad.' But the appalling working and camp conditions, and outbreaks of cholera and dysentery cost the lives of 12 000 British, Dutch and Australian POWs and at least 90 000 coolies from Burma, Java and Sumatra.

The Allies built 407 airstrips and 180 miles of paved runway, and 1300 military bridges, including the 1154-foot bridge at Kalewa, put up by British and Indian engineers in 28 hours, and the 4000-foot US-built suspension bridge across the Shweli River.

**Intelligence**

Japanese intelligence profited initially from knowledge of long-range British plans (and inadequacies) derived from documents seized from the Blue Funnel vessel, *Automedon*, which was sunk by a German surface raider in the Indian Ocean, after being searched. Documents passed to the Japanese included the British War Cabinet's detailed forecasts for 1941. An espionage network operated by the Japanese military attaché in Bangkok made contact with Sikh liberation movements in northern Malaya and with Japanese organisations intended to subvert the colonial regimes in Burma (Minami Kikan) and India (F Kikan).

Japanese codebreaking capacities do not seem to have affected the Burma campaign much, although traffic was read between Chiang Kai-shek and Mountbatten's headquarters. Some Japanese formations, believing in the strength of 'Japanese spirit' (*seishin* or *yamato damashii*) affected to disregard intelligence – this was true of Mutaguchi and XV Army; others, such as XXVIII

Army in the Arakan, were very intelligence-minded and generated whole hosts of small networks using native agents.

Britain's initial failures seemed to indicate inadequate intelligence, but the British in fact successfully used stay-behind parties in Karen territory, parties of agents under a British officer close behind the Japanese lines (V Force), and the longer-term use of behind-the-lines parties provided by Force 136, the Asian equivalent of Special Operations Executive (SOE) whose role in Asia as distinct from Europe, was intelligence rather than sabotage. Codebreaking had some considerable successes, based on the Wireless Experimental Centre in Delhi, a source available to Army commanders and above.

Combined Services Detailed Interrogation Centre (CSDIC) with headquarters at the Red Fort in Delhi, derived information from POW interrogation. But the source was limited by the small number of POWs taken (for example 130, including 12 officers, on the whole of IV Corps front between March and June 1944), and the low quality of their information. Of a total of under 3000 POWs taken in the whole campaign, the highest rank was captain. Captured documents provided a richer source and played a major role in the battles of the Admin Box, Kohima, Imphal, Meiktila and the Sittang breakout.

## Role Reversals

The campaign produced some interesting reversals of fortune.

(i)    The Japanese triumph of 1942 turned into the greatest defeat in Japanese Army history in 1945.

(ii)   The British catastrophe of 1942 turned into the massive victory of 1945.

(iii)  The myth of the ubiquitous Japanese superman of 1942 turned into the shattered, diseased, starving and ragged reality of 1945. The POW rate shows this vividly: six prisoners were taken in 1942, and at least 1500 in 1945.

(iv)   The image of omniscient Japanese intelligence during the invasion, combined with British ignorance and mismanagement, turned by 1945 into the British intelligence feat of knowing Japanese dispositions and strengths better than the Japanese themselves. Current Japanese historiography stresses this, emphasising poor military management and intelligence.

## Reversal in Politics

The British freed Burma from the Japanese in 1945, only to find the Burmese did not want them back; precisely as, three years before, the Japanese freed the Burmese from the British only to discover that the Burmese did not wish them to prolong their stay.

For reasons of expediency, the young men (Thakins) who sided with the Japanese in 1942 were welcomed back later by Mountbatten and, to a lesser extent,

Slim. When the war was over it was ultimately the Thakins who ruled Burma, in spite of the surface apparatus of a British return. Many of the hill tribes who sided with the British during the war found they were expected to compound with a new and unsympathetic regime. So when independence finally came on 4 January 1948, they faced rebellion or exile. The Karen people in particular felt the British had left them to the tender mercies of a party which had come to power by collaborating with the Japanese. It is a strange paradox that the totalitarian regime which even today impoverishes and tyrannises Burma is led by Ne Win, one of the original 'Thirty Comrades' who received military training at the hands of the Japanese; and his most bitter opponent is the daughter of his colleague, Aung San. She returned to Burma after many years in England and an English marriage, and led a freedom movement which won elections but was powerless to prise away the grip of a cruel and relentless army, even though her father is revered as the hero of Burmese liberation.

## THE BURMA CAMPAIGN: A WAR OF EXTREMES

- Extremes of hatred on both sides which, in many cases, still lingers.
- Extreme distance from home on both sides.
- Extreme views on the nature of the battlefield held by both sides. The British viewed themselves as the 'Forgotten Army'; the Japanese saw Burma as 'the hell' of the war in Asia.
- The Burma campaign was the longest fought by the British Army in World War II.
- It produced the longest retreat in the history of the British Army: Rangoon to Imphal.
- 1945 saw the British operating in the narrowest salient in the history of warfare: along the Mandalay–Rangoon Road, 250 miles in length, and a few hundred yards wide.
- Extremes of contrast in casualties: in July 1945, 17 000 Japanese were killed against a loss of 95 British during the battle of the Sittang breakout.
- Extreme racial variety of troops. The Japanese used Korean guards in their camps, Burmese and Javanese labourers on their railway, and some hill tribesmen from northern Burma (one tribe elected a Japanese soldier as its chief). The British forces contained UK soldiers, East and West Africans, Chinese, Burmese, Kachins, Chins, Nagas, Gurkhas, Pathans, Punjabis, Bengalis, Madrassis, and Rajputs, with all the dietary problems this, and religious differences, implied. And it must be remembered always that the Japanese were defeated in Burma not by the British but by the Indian Army.
- Extreme variety in types of warfare:
  - (a) Broken Arakan coastline, creeks and mangrove swamps, exploitable by Royal Navy and Royal Indian Navy small boats and marine commando warfare.

(b) Jungle and mountain warfare, transformed by the use of air transport and supply. The best illustration of this is that seven months before Arnhem – a failure, whatever the courage expended – IV Corps had created the success of Second Wingate, an entire division moved by glider hundreds of miles behind enemy lines, bringing its own artillery with it.

(c) The longest exposed river crossing in any theatre of the Second World War took place when XIV Army crossed the Irrawaddy in 1945. In five weeks, two Army Corps were transported over one of the widest rivers in the world: between 1000 and 4500 yards at some points.

(d) Desert warfare:
It is wrong to consider either the Burma campaign or the Malaya campaign as being lost or won in the jungle. Roads were vital, and tanks played an essential part at Kohima, at the relief of Imphal, in the capture of Meiktila, and the dash to Rangoon.

(e) From the British side, it was also a gunner's war, for example, the defence of Kohima by remote control by 161 Brigade's artillery firing from Jotsoma; and the artillery harrassment of 28 Army in the Sittang breakout.

As whole, the operations can be seen as a rapid evolution from a Rorke's Drift style of colonial warfare to the threshold of the modern age, won by aircraft and brought to an end by the atomic bomb.

## FURTHER READING – A SELECT BIBLIOGRAPHY

Allen, Louis, *Sittang The Last Battle* (London: Macdonald, 1973).
Allen, Louis, *The End of the War in Asia* (London: Hart-Davis, MacGibbon, 1976).
Allen, Louis, *Burma. the Longest War, 1942–45* (London: Dent, 1984).
Barker, A.J., *The March on Delhi* (London: Faber & Faber, 1963).
Bidwell, Shelford, *The Chindit War. The Campaign in Burma, 1944* (London: Hodder & Stoughton, 1979).
Callahan, Raymond, *Burma 1942–1945* (London: Davis-Poynter, 1978).
Calvert, Michael, *Prisoners of Hope* (London: Jonathan Cape, 1952).
Evans, Geoffrey and Brett-James, Anthony, *Imphal: A Flower on Lofty Heights* (London: Macmillan, 1962).
Kinvig, Clifford, *River Kwai Railway. The Story of the Burma–Siam Railroad* (London: Brasseys, 1992).
Lewin, Ronald, *Slim The Standard Bearer: A Biography of Field Marshal The Viscount Slim* (London: Leo Cooper, 1976).
Masters, John, *The Road Past Mandalay* (London: Michael Joseph, 1961).
Slim, Field-Marshal Sir William, *Defeat into Victory* (London: Cassell, 1956).
Swinson, Arthur, *Four Samurai. A Quartet of Japanese Army Commanders in the Second World War* (London: Hutchinson, 1968).
Sykes, Christopher, *Orde Wingate* (London: Collins, 1959).

# 7 Thailand, Japanese Pan-Asianism and the Greater East Asia Co-Prosperity Sphere

Nigel Brailey

Whatever one's thoughts about it currently, as it struggles to renew its democracy, Thailand has been most consistently prominent in modern times as a kind of arbiter of international affairs. In the 1960s, it was probably the most significant part of the South-East Asian 'audience' the United States was trying to impress through its opposition to communism in Vietnam.[1] In the 1890s, it was already the object of Japanese pan-Asianist initiatives designed to halt the spread of Western empire in Asia. And between 1941 and 1945, its loyalty was being competed for by the United States and Japan as the one never-colonised state in South-East Asia, and therefore the nearest to being the true, authentic and representative voice of the region.[2]

Its verdict nonetheless remains unclear, because its own interests did not fully correspond with those of either of the competitors, in 1941–45 as on the other two occasions. It consented to the Japanese use of its territory as a launch-pad for what was probably the critical campaign of the early days of the war, the attack on Singapore. And it was only used as a base for Japan's invasion of Burma, which cut China off from its Indian source of supplies, and might, if not set off, like Pearl Harbor, at half-cock, have destroyed the British Indian empire. But on the morning after the night which featured the commencement of both the Pearl Harbor and Malayan assaults, Thailand's police chief and deputy premier, Luang Adun, declared simply that: 'It was better to lose our sovereignty to this extent than to lose it completely by being taken over as a Japanese colony. Should Japan lose the upper hand ... England and the United States ... should still be able to be sympathetic to us as a small country.'[3] And in 1944, with the war already swinging conclusively against Japan, Adun inserted himself as deputy leader and probable real moving-spirit in the so-called Free Thai, to cooperate with and prepare the ground for the arrival of the forces of the victorious allies in 1945.

Similarly, Adun's friend and boss up to 1944, premier Phibun, openly declared war on Britain and the United States in January 1942, but was already asking rhetorically a few months later: 'Which side do you think will lose this war? That side is our enemy.'[4] Subsequently he refused to attend Greater East Asia Co-Prosperity Sphere meetings in Tokyo despite his pre-war willingness to deal with the Japanese. And his temporary ousting in 1944 would seem principally to have been due to Allied determination to refuse an accommodation with him.

Yet however apparently opportunist, Phibun was arguably the most representative leader of Thailand up to 1973, concerned above all with his country's
national interest. In these terms he expressed most clearly his compatriots' desire
to stand aside 'while the elephants fought'. And despite the influence of *force
majeure*, there must be a strong suspicion that, if forced to choose between the
Western empires and Japan, he necessarily would have inclined towards the latter,
while the no less patriotic contrary line adopted by Adun and Phibun's old rival,
Dr Pridi, in the last year of the war, was as much the consequence of the above
influence, when a non-apologetic Thailand might have faced severe punitive
treatment at the hands of the victorious Western powers. There is reason to
suppose that it was this that obscured the sympathy they had previously shown for
the anti-colonialism espoused by Tokyo, and in Dr Pridi's case were to display
again subsequently, evidence that has been lost in the general post-war 'fudge'.[5]

Modern Japan's pan-Asianist professions have hitherto gained little credit in
the West. Although the language employed by Western writers has been
markedly inconsistent,[6] the net effect has been to equate Japanese pan-Asianism
explicitly with 'imperialism', little different from 'yellow peril' attitudes going
back to the time of Sir Henry Norman in 1895.[7] However, before the arrival of
Commodore Perry in 1853, it cannot be claimed that Tokugawa Japan in its
*sakoku* isolation showed any significant wider Asian concern, so much so that
major theorists like Adam Smith and Karl Marx, who discussed both India and
China at length, saw fit to ignore its very existence as irrelevant to their purposes.
Post-1853, and particularly after the fall of the Shogunate government in 1868,
contacts with neighbours were developed, but often in an openly competitive
way. The ruling interests in Korea, the self-proclaimed guardian of true Confu-
cian principles, and in China itself, the original progenitor of Confucianism, both
sought to evade any serious accommodation with the West. By contrast, the Meiji
oligarchs running Japan after 1868 generally asserted the imperative need for
such accommodation and, at times, as in Korea in the early 1880s, afforded
support to local radicals who agreed with them. Indeed, Japan's ability to sustain
such movements in its neighbours had the added advantage of enlarging support
for reformist policies at home where obscurantist opposition remained quite
strong, and some of the oligarchs themselves, most notably the tragic Saigo
Takamori, expressed ambivalence.[8] By contrast, however, many, including as
eminent as progressive as Fukuzawa Yukichi, at times advocated even more total
commitment to Westernisation, to the extent of trying to deny that Japan was
even part of Asia.

1891 represents a major turning-point in this story. In May of that year, as a
culmination of efforts over the previous year, the Toho *Kiōkai*, or Oriental
Society, was inaugurated in Tokyo. The end of *sakoku* had led to growing
numbers of Japanese travelling abroad, initially mainly to the West, but by the
1880s increasingly through other parts of Asia, and they wanted at least a forum
through which they could report their experiences and disseminate their know-

ledge. And by 1891, figures as eminent as former foreign ministers Soejima Taneomi and Okuma Shigenobu, future Foreign Minister Komura Jūtarō, populist politicians such as Itagaki Taisuke and Inukai Tsuyoshi, and the widely-respected and influential aristocrat Prince Konoye Atsumaro, were prepared to lend their patronage to the new society.[9]

From the start, it seems that this society represented an accommodation of Japanese self-assertion and pride in their own cultural traditions, and an interest in making common cause with other Asians against the only force that seriously threatened them, namely the West. This would have applied at least to its more prominent figures. But the recruitment as its secretary in 1895 of the Cambridge-educated Inagaki Manjiro also brought to its ranks an individual with an unusual world-view and experience for a Japanese of his time, interested in opening up links with other oriental polities outside East Asia, for instance Siam, Persia and the Ottoman Empire. What is more, in his writings he was already anticipating Japan's still far-in-the-future international commercial and economic role, oblivious to the prospects of intervening military conflict.[10]

Inagaki's career, with its important diplomatic phase after 1897 when he was sent to Bangkok, was nonetheless to be overtaken by some of these conflicts, the first Sino-Japanese War of 1894–5, and particularly the Russo-Japanese War of 1904–5. For one thing, Japan's success in the latter war in halting Russian expansionism and creating a stalemate, if not a power vacuum, in East Asia, gave its armed forces unprecedented prestige in relation to the country's politicians and diplomats, and also largely eliminated the motivation for cooperative, common-cause relationships with other Asian countries. Additionally, it deprived Inagaki personally of his next logical posting, to Seoul in Korea, in consequence of Korea's subordination to direct Japanese control.[11] Thus an emergent Japanese special oriental diplomatic service, not to be revived until 1942, lost one of its plum postings. And Inagaki, who might have featured so prominently in it, was sent off instead to Madrid where he soon died.

Thus in so far as it survived into the Taishō era (1912–26) at all, Japanese pan-Asianism came to focus almost exclusively on China. Interest was boosted by the overthrow of the Manchu dynasty in 1911, but thereafter most Japanese reverted to increasing impatience and anger as one weak Chinese regime was succeeded by another, civil war and general chaos developed, and anti-Japanese feeling was promoted as the best rallying-cry to restore some degree of unity. Similarly, self-interested American support for China against Japan from the time of the so-called Twenty-One Demands did nothing but exacerbate the deterioration in relations.[12] And with the death in 1925 of Dr Sun Yat-sen, the outstanding pan-Asianist, anti-Western imperialist Chinese leader, and the general decline of Britain and the other old European colonial powers' ability to interfere actively in Asia, the ideology and enthusiasm of the years before 1904 seem to have become little more than a memory. But then in the early 1930s, the West's Great Depression began to have its impact in Eastern Asia, bringing to

Japan renewed economic and political instability.[13] The limitations of the security won in 1905 were exposed, and the West, through discriminatory import restrictions applied as much in its Asian colonies as in the metropolitan countries, emphasised the extent to which Japan was still very much 'on its own'.[14]

The aforementioned Inagaki, in particular, also serves to link these themes with the case of Thailand. There has been growing research interest in recent years in the story of the historical relationship with Japan of Thailand, or 'Siam' in its pre-1939, Western-named existence.[15] Subsequent to contacts in the early seventeenth century, there is little of interest in the relationship prior to the 1860s and 1870s. But not only did a limited commercial relationship emerge thereafter: there were important political contacts, involving a joint declaration or proto-treaty in 1887, and genuine treaties in 1898 and 1924, which prefigure the issue of a common-cause link in the 1930s and 1940s. Particularly in the mid-1890s, both Japan and 'Siam' felt severely threatened by Western imperialism. On the other hand, perhaps partly due to misunderstandings, Japan did see fit to pursue the benefits of extraterritorial legal jurisdiction over its citizens in 'Siam', and a generally unequal relationship with the latter in its early treaty negotiations. This was also the case in its relations with other oriental states, and can be said to have been indispensable in sustaining its claims to equality with Western powers.[16] In this respect as well, Japan can be said to have been caught on the horns of a Western-created dilemma. But Inagaki, who was responsible for negotiating the 1898 treaty, thereafter, until his departure in 1905, established a place of special affection amongst the Thai, and was succeeded in this – as he was also, after an interval, as Japanese Minister – by the legal adviser Dr Masao Tokichi. Thus even during the reign of King Wachirawut (1910–25), Japan generally commanded Thai friendship, and it was only during the final decade of its 'absolute monarchy' up to 1932, having at last secured a kind of conditional tolerance on the part of the Western powers involving their acceptance of its legal independence, that 'Siam' began to become generally apprehensive of involvement with Japan in any common-cause approach. As most 'Siamese' viewed it, such a stance might undermine Western tolerance, and drag them into a dangerous and undesired confrontation with the West.[17]

However, the 1932–3 Thai revolution which finally swept away the absolute monarchy, and nearly the monarchy as such, quite altered the situation. It was a revolution stemming almost entirely from domestic circumstances, political and economic, albeit exacerbated, particularly in the latter respect, by the World Depression. But especially in such economic terms it paralleled circumstances in Japan.[18] And there can be no question that the Thai revolutionary leaders, who divided into civilian and military factions, saw in their country's international situation similarities with that of Japan. Also, in China, they had in a sense a common enemy.

With respect to China, by the 1930s, the Japanese had simply begun to despair of the willingness of the Chinese to make common cause with them against the

West. Indeed, it appeared that the Chinese were interested in little else than fighting each other in endless warlord quarrels, so-called 'bandit-suppression' campaigns, and peasant revolts, interspersed by the occasional anti-Japanese commercial boycott as a warning that they wanted no distraction. A feature of Japanese documentation on this period is reference to Chinese 'insincerity.'[19] This apparently signified a Japanese belief that the real reason for the failure of the Chinese Kuomintang so-called 'nationalist' leadership to join them against the Western powers still so dominant in the Treaty Ports down the China coast was self or factional interest. Clearly it was particularly galling that a Japanese-educated and trained figure such as Chiang Kai-shek, when forced to commit himself in the matter, showed himself still wedded to expelling the Japanese from China, and depriving them of their many long-established economic interests as if they were not merely as objectionable as Westerners, but even worse. Even then, in 1937, following the Marco Polo Bridge Incident and the outbreak of the Second Sino-Japanese War, as eminent a Japanese general as Ishiwara Kanji, Chief of Operations on the Japanese General Staff, effectively put an end to his career by seeking to oppose this war.[20] Also, that same year saw the execution for supposed complicity in the 1936 Tokyo Army Garrison rebellion of Kita Ikki, forever described as Japan's ultranationalist of the inter-war period, yet someone profoundly interested in China since before 1911, and a resident in Shanghai and other places for some years afterwards.[21] And a whole series of other Japanese radical figures, nationalist and 'liberal', many of them undoubtedly anti-Western, including Toyama Mitsuru, *Oue* Kentarō, Miyazaki Toten, Ōkuma Shigenobu, Inukai Tsuyoshi, Uchida Ryōhei, and Ōkawa Shūmei, all viewed themselves as, if anything, pro-Chinese, on the assumption that real Japanese and Chinese interests were not in conflict.[22]

By contrast, almost from the start nationalism in Thailand had cut its teeth on the large Chinese community which was economically dominant in the country.[23] Fear of a parallel Chinese *political* takeover had been a reason cited by King Prachathipok, the last of the 'absolute' monarchs, for not making the sort of constitutional concessions he was reputed otherwise to favour.[24] And even though many of the 1932 revolution's 'promoters' had some Chinese blood coursing through their veins, they seem to have been almost as concerned to restrict the role of the Chinese economic élite as that of the royal family and its hangers-on in the political sphere.[25]

Yet how did the Thai really view the increasingly overt anti-Western expression of Japanese pan-Asianism in the 1930s? If anything Western observers of the time seem to have exaggerated the sense of common feeling, and the closeness of Japan–Thailand political and economic relations right up to 1940–1. A popular rumour had it that the Japanese were interested in building the long-bruited but always unlikely Kra Isthmus canal which would have enabled international shipping to bypass Singapore, and were likely to meet with Thai cooperation. A powerful faction amongst the Thai leadership of the 1930s was viewed as downright 'pro-Japanese'. And the United States Minister at the end, Dr H.C. Grant, argued that Thailand was already in Japan's pocket, and even urged a Washington that needed little persuading, to cancel delivery of some modern military aircraft already paid for by the Thai, on the grounds that it amounted virtually to a sale to the Japanese. Alone in South-East Asia not closed to the Japanese by Western imperial preference schemes, to the bitter resentment of Western commercial interests, Thailand proved a rapidly expanding market for the highly competitive exports of the former.[26]

But despite being identified early on by the Japanese themselves as a natural sympathiser of theirs, Dr Pridi Phanomyong, the real moving-spirit behind the revolution of 1932–3, took the opportunity of his visit to Japan at the beginning of 1936, to warn the Japanese against their 'pseudo-philosophy of pan-Asianism'. Thereafter, as Thai Foreign Minister, he outwardly insisted on Thai neutrality in Japan's relations with the West, although again in 1937 as in 1931 and 1932, Thailand saw justification in abstaining in a League of Nations vote on Japan's China policy. But he may have been influential in lucrative government contracts going to Western companies rather than their Japanese rivals. And during the summer of 1941, as Finance Minister, he actively resisted further integration of the Thai economy with that of its prospective ally, particularly in terms of Thailand's main raw material exports, rubber and tin. In this he was supported by such as Prince Wiwatthanachai, Thailand's leading financial expert and future founder-governor of the Bank of Thailand, and the long-time foreign affairs adviser and future Foreign Minister, Prince Wan Waithyakon. Luang Sin, the chief of the navy, and some other Thai organisations such as the State Railways, were influential in offering contracts and developing contacts, but Phahon, premier in 1933–8, who had pre-revolutionary experience of Japan, seems to have taken no initiatives at all, and Thailand as a whole seems to have been little involved. Thus with the apparent promise of being still left alone by the Western powers, notwithstanding a brief scare in 1934, [27] there was little more reason for Thailand's new ruling interests to risk the destruction of the established relationship than there had been for the more genuinely client-state of the absolute monarchy.

What had Japan to offer as an alternative to this established relationship? Yatabe Yasukichi, Japanese Minister in Bangkok 1928–36, talked mainly of a Japanese 'cultural' programme, though he was undoubtedly interested also in commercial links.[28] But in 1933, Tokyo still insisted on closing the Japanese market to Thailand's rice exports. And if during 1936–8, Japan's high command was beginning to view Thailand as prospectively important, it was only in a strategic sense, in the context of a war with the Western colonial powers, and above all as a corridor for an attack on British Singapore. The growing threat of a Japanese resort to force, albeit not specifically aimed at Thailand, seems nonetheless, right up to the autumn of 1941, to have stimulated a Thai inclination to resist. In September 1940, Japanese troops spilled across the border from China into northern Vietnam. And in July 1941, they also moved down into southern

Indo-China, even occupying bases along the Cambodian–Thai frontier. Moreover Japan's mediation of a Thai–French Indo-China border dispute in January–February 1941, viewed by the Thai as inordinately favourable to the French colonial regime, seemed totally in conflict with its pan-Asian professions.[29]

These, such as they were, had found expression back in 1938 in the proclamation of a Japanese 'New Order', inspired by the German plan for Europe, for *East* Asia; i.e. initially not conceived as extending into South-East Asia, although Shigemitsu Mamoru, as vice-foreign minister, had revived the concept of a 'Japanese Monroe Doctrine' as early as 1934.[30] And then, following the political negotiations in Tokyo that produced in July 1940 the second cabinet of Prince Konoye Fumimaro, Matsuoka Yosuke, the new Foreign Minister, announced apparently without warning a plan for a Greater East Asia Co-Prosperity Sphere, which was to comprise at least those parts of South-East Asia about to become 'ownerless' due to the German conquest of their colonial masters in Europe.[31] Mere 'cooperation' for mutual prosperity seems always to have been its main theme, but how this was interpreted was inevitably much affected by the exigencies of war, and of Japan as its chief Asian belligerent, in the aftermath of the attack on Pearl Harbor. At all events, the Sphere's principal institution, the Greater East Asia Ministry, not established until late 1942, seems to have had as its main responsibility the supervision of political and diplomatic links between the constituent territories of the Sphere, which in the case of previously independent or semi-independent countries such as Thailand, Manchukuo and Nanking China, were transferred from the Foreign Ministry. Needless to say, these links involved a variety of issues, but Tokyo always claimed to treat through this ministry the governments of formerly sovereign states, 'puppet-states', and Western colonies declared 'independent', such as Burma, quite equally.[32]

Of course, in the case of Thailand, it was not Dr Pridi who finally responded to this 'common-cause', Asian solidarity approach, but Marshal Phibun Songkhram, already Thai Premier since 1938. Having publicly maintained the Thai profile of determined resistance to any foreign encroachment on Thai territory until almost the last moment, he then absented himself from the Thai capital on the eve of the arrival of the Japanese troops en route from Cambodia to Singapore on 8 December 1941, by the 21st had arranged the full alliance between Thailand and Japan, and on 25 January 1942, forthrightly declared war on both Britain and the United States. To the Japanese at the time, he gave the impression that this had always been his intention, but that unwilling cabinet colleagues and members of the Thai ruling élite had had to be persuaded by the deteriorating international situation. Post-war, by contrast, when it was instead victorious Western powers that needed to be appeased, and when he was hoping to return to the power he had lost in 1944 as a result of Japan's declining fortunes in the war, and which he actually managed to do 1948–57, he claimed that his had been just an unwilling reaction to *force majeure*.

In 1967, E.T. Flood took the view that even Phibun had been 'pro-Japanese', and that the alliance of 21 December 1941 had been the realisation of something long planned, indeed a promise that he had made to Japanese Minister Yatabe way back on 20 June 1933, at the climax of the coup he organised to secure the 1932 Revolution. Of course, this was in the context of a very negative view of 1930s Japanese policies, and tantamount to characterising Phibun as a traitor to his own country, even though Flood also notes the general consensus amongst Phibun's contemporaries that he was not only a nationalist but a patriot through and through.[33]

By contrast, Bruce Reynolds, who most recently assessed these developments, stresses his dissatisfaction with Flood's view, explains his willingness because of it to trace the story of Thai–Japanese relations back as far as 1932, and argues that Flood depended far too heavily on self-serving or otherwise untrustworthy Japanese sources. For him, 'survivalist instinct and the prospect of Japanese victory...inspired the decision by Thai Prime Minister Phibun Songkhram to join Japan's side in the war', and this at quite a late stage.[34]

Again, Sir Andrew Gilchrist, a British diplomat present in Bangkok at the time of the outbreak of the Far Eastern War, takes the view that Phibun deliberately absented himself from the Thai capital because he wanted to avoid the Japanese approaches to make common cause against the Western colonial powers. In his view, Phibun probably expected an effective British resistance to the Japanese advance down through the Malay Peninsula, and simply wished to allow time for this to happen. Of course almost certainly this was what Churchill, Britain's prime minister since May 1940, also expected, only to be sorely disappointed, principally due to the remarkable organisation of the Japanese.[35]

Finally, however, W.L. Swan argues that:

> important postwar Siamese [Thai] memoirs and reminiscences have not been forthright in their rendering of events [*sic*] with Japan at the beginning of the war, and that the Siamese [Thai] government, especially Phibun, was ready to commit Siam [Thailand] totally to the Japanese side by the second day of the war.

He also adds in explanation of this conclusion, that as of December 1941:

> Phibun's inclination was towards Japan, and he certainly knew that when Japan went to war it would be to rid East Asia of the West. If Japan won, Siam would have to accommodate itself to a new order in Asia, but that new order also offered Siam the opportunity to build a Greater Thailand which, in cooperation with Japan, could become the most significant nation in Southeast Asia.[36]

Such an interpretation Swan deliberately sets up alongside the view that 'the Siamese were not the reluctant Japanese ally as has come to be commonly accepted since the war', and Reynolds, writing shortly after Swan to whom he pays tribute in various respects, was evidently also concerned to combat his revisionism as well as the older Flood interpretation at the other extreme.

Thus the historical verdict is to say the least unclear. But what Thailand's stance was in December 1941 is not the principal concern of this chapter. What is significant about it is what it says of Japan's claims to represent broader Asian feeling rather than mere self-aggrandisement. Certainly it seems that there was support in Thailand at least for a broad crusade against Western hegemonism in Asia, and even that it was Phibun rather than the Japanese who was the self-aggrandiser. And Phibun was a popular leader at least amongst the educated Bangkok élite, almost the sole politicised element in the country. Meanwhile Reynolds throws his own conclusions into doubt when he cites the aforementioned Thai deputy premier Adun, who set the tone of the critical Thai cabinet debate on the morning of 8 December 1941, declaring:

> We see that with the great powers like America and Britain, the Japanese don't hesitate at all to attack them straight away. But it was just the opposite for Thailand. They came and handed us a proposition. It was as if they were willing to listen to us a bit, even though Thailand is a very small country. My feeling is that since Japan doesn't dare [!] attack us as it's doing to America and Britain [it] means that the policy of the Japanese government is not to cause any trouble between Asian peoples. Otherwise their declaration that they were helping the peoples of Asia would mean nothing...It means they respect us as Asian people.[37]

Longer historical perspective is anyhow patently necessary, as Reynolds himself recognised. But this does not only required detailed consideration of the origins of the 1932–3 'revolution', and appreciation of the ideological stance of Dr Pridi, who if he failed to secure practical leadership of his country other than by, ironically, renewed Western intervention after the war's end in 1945, nonetheless acted as intellectual mentor to his whole 1930s generation, in terms of anti-Westernism as much as anything.[38] More than that, arguably, it requires an awareness of the threat, and indeed impact, of Western imperialism so far as that whole neo-colonial entity known as 'Siam' was concerned. As evidence presented above indicates, not only 'Siam' but also Japan too had its basic political and social constitution severely distorted by the dominance secured by Western powers in Asia in the second half of the nineteenth century. And if many of the consequent changes made in the two countries were laudable not only from a Western but a local viewpoint (though that would always be a difficult distinction to make) the sense in both countries of having been *forced* to make such changes was always bound to affect the way the changes were viewed.

Another, more general, conclusion to be drawn from the overall story of modern Thai–Japanese relations, is that it was perhaps Thailand (or 'Siam') rather than Japan which was generally the prime mover. This appears to apply for the earliest period, the 1880s, for the early 1920s, when King Wachirawut sought vainly to be invited on a state visit to Japan,[39] and perhaps even the early 1930s, when Phahon and Phibun, following their coup of June 1933, went to Yatabe, the Japanese Minister, in search of support against the expected renewed

Anglo–French intervention on behalf of the old 'absolute monarchy' regime. Even the 1890s appear to feature Thai activity at least as great as that of Japan, with Thai Foreign Minister, Prince Thewawong (Devawongse) taking the initiative in offering an unequal treaty relationship to Japan.[40] And this simply anticipates Dr Sun's offer of the 21 Demands concessions to Japan in 1915. In other words, in most respects up to the 1930s, in line with the acclaim heaped on her for inflicting the first defeats by an Asian country on a Western power in the Russo-Japanese war of 1904–5, Japan was invariably seen as a highly desirable ally if not a protector, to be seduced into action on behalf of others almost oblivious to her own interests. And whatever the attitude of Chinese leaders in the 1930s, there seems good reason to suppose that the Thai of that decade welcomed the new balance of power created in consequence of the rise of Japan. More than that of course, a wide range of other South-East Asian nationalist leaders fighting colonial powers for self-determination welcomed the arrival of the Japanese in 1941–2. This does not mean that, then or before, the Japanese did agree to take action except when it suited them. But if thereafter, many such nationalist leaders felt that independence did not come as quickly as they had hoped, and that their interests were subordinated to those of Japan in its desperate struggle to resist the inevitable counterattack of the colonial powers – and in Burma 'The Longest War'[41] might be viewed simply as Britain's last successful colonial war, designed so far as Britain was concerned, merely to restore empire – in reality, this was no more than they might have expected, given the almost total inadequacy of the aid they were capable of affording to the Japanese.[42]

One final historiographical point needs making. 1989 was the double centenary of the great French Revolution, and in one of the commemorative volumes, *The Permanent Revolution*, Geoffrey Best declares variously:

> The new missionary practice was correspondingly uncompromising. The French, it was soon discovered, had a mission, a calling, the duty as well as the right to give other peoples the benefits of the same experience they had given themselves. Beginning as 'liberation', it was in practice scarcely distinguishable from domination.

> In vain did French propagandists deploy the argument used later by the Soviet Union, that its protégés should be glad to make sacrifices to keep their only possible protector in business. What the French called liberation, and what, indeed, met with a welcome from Francophile minorities in most countries, was experienced by their national majorities as oppression and exploitation.

And finally,

> But in another light France was a bully and a parasite. Disagreeable experiences of invasion and occupation by French armies – *la grande nation,* in the form of *la nation armée* – had the effect of catalysing and militarizing national

sentiment, to such effect that by the time France's armies were at last confined to their homeland, Europe's nationalisms were more mature and violent than they might otherwise have been.[43]

Ever since Elsbree it has been conventional wisdom that Japan's role in catalysing the self-determination of pre-war colonial South-East Asia, and thereby also southern Asia and Africa subsequently, could be considered no better than accidental or incidental.[44] But the above comments at once pose the question of the comparability of French actions in Europe in the 1790s, and those of Japan in Eastern Asia in the 1940s. Time has created the consensus that the French revolution represents a permanent social and political change on at least a Europe-wide basis when contemporary opinion in many of France's neighbours, not least in Britain, saw it as no more than French national aggrandisement aimed at a French Europe-wide hegemony. Moreover, if this last became more credible with the advent of Napoleon, nonetheless his lasting achievement was to spread the ideals of the revolution in a way that perhaps the revolutionaries of the 1790s themselves never managed to, and that also needs to be borne in mind when judging Japan, still only half a century after her critical role in destroying Western imperial hegemony in the non-Western world.

Of course, there was no extraneous, extra-European force with which the French revolutionaries had to deal, not even, at that time, a Russian one if it could be called extra-European. On the other hand, Japan was and is as near a unique society as any in the world, thanks to its geography and consequent history, which have left it with minimal historical links, and therefore little claim to speak more generally for its region, Eastern Asia. By contrast, France was always an integral part of Europe and the European tradition. But notwithstanding these caveats, there is enough in the Japanese pan-Asianist tradition, brought out particularly by the story of the relationship with Thailand, to require recognition of a positive, idealistic contribution behind the inception of Japan's 1941–5 war, alongside the relatively negative, self-defence considerations prompted by the exigencies of the early 1930s.

## NOTES

1. Joseph Frankel introduction to N. Sheahan (ed.), *New York Times Pentagon Papers* (New York, 1973) p. 647.
2. See Nigel Brailey, *Thailand and the Fall of Singapore: A Frustrated Asian Revolution* (Boulder and London, 1986) pp. 101–2; or Gary Hess, *The United States Emergence as a Southeast Asian Power, 1940–1950* (Columbia, NY, 1987).
3. Direk Jayanama, *Siam and World War II*, trans. Jane Keyes (Bangkok, 1978) pp. 113. A fuller version appears in W.L. Swan, 'Japanese Economic Relations with

Siam, Aspects of their Historical Development 1884–1942,' (PhD thesis, Australian National University, 1986) appendix, pp. 247–8.

4.  Brailey, *Thailand and the Fall of Singapore*, p. 100.

5.  For this fudge, see Nigel Brailey 'Southeast Asia and Japan's Road to War', in the *Historical Journal* 30:4 (1987) pp. 995–1011. For Pridi's subsequent efforts to undermine French colonial rule in Indo-China, see Brailey *Thailand and the Fall of Singapore*, pp. 121–3. And it should be noted that while the United States refused to recognise Thailand's declaration of war on 25 January 1942, Britain accepted it, and maintained a strongly punitive line almost up to the final peace settlement of 1 January 1946.

6.  Iida Junzo, 'Japan's Relations with Independent Siam up to 1933: Prelude to Pan-Asian Solidarity', PhD thesis (University of Bristol, 1991) pp. 4–8, 247–9.

7.  Norman himself in his *The Peoples and Politics of the Far East* (London, 1895) pp. 398–9, was commenting on a recent article in the *St James Gazette*. Interestingly, he was already raising the prospect of a Japan desirous of 'a parallel to the Monroe Doctrine for the Far East, with herself at its centre', although this was mainly in terms of 'reorganizing' China, and not yet as a threat to European colonial possessions in Southeast Asia.

8.  See especially H. Conroy, *The Japanese Seizure of Korea 1873–1910* (Philadelphia, 1960); and Ivan Morris, *The Nobility of Failure* (London, 1975). Cf. also Key Hiuk-kim, *The Last Phase of the East Asian World Order...1860–1882* (California, 1980).

9.  Iida, 'Japan's Relations with Independent Siam'. The Tokyo Geographical Society had been showing an interest in Siam as early as 1884. Satow Diaries, 17 November 1884, 30/33/15/8, Public Record Office, Kew.

10. For Inagaki's career see especially Iida, 'Japan's Relations with Independent Siam' also his 'Inagaki Manjiro, an early Japanese Economic Expansionist' (forthcoming article), and Brailey, 'Sir Ernest Satow, Japan and Asia: the Trials of a Diplomat in the Age of High Imperialism', *Historical Journal* 35, 1 (March 1992), pp. 115–50.

11. Already by the end of 1904, Inagaki had been expected to take over as Minister in Seoul from Hayashi Gonsuke, who was to replace Uchida Yasuya in Peking. Iida, 'Inagaki Manjiro...'.

12. The demands were for a set of concessions first *offered* to Japan by Dr Sun Yat-sen in the hope of enlisting support against the Western-backed President Yüan Shih-k'ai. See E.P. Young, 'Chinese Leaders and Japanese Aid in the Early Republic', pp. 124–39 in Akira Iriye (ed.), *The Chinese and the Japanese* (New Jersey, 1980). American hostility derived particularly after 1905 from Japanese exclusion of Western economic interests from Manchuria, widely viewed as a kind of new Eldorado.

13. As the depression was born in the West, and spread to the East thanks to the creation of a global economy over the previous fifty years or more, through the development of the Western imperial world hegemony, it seems appropriate to call it 'the West's Great Depression'.

14. The significance of Japan's isolation for its 1930s policy-making is widely attested to. See especially G.R. Storry, *Japan and the Decline of the West in Asia, 1894–1943* (London, 1979), and Akira Iriye, *The Second World War in Asia and the Pacific* (London, 1987).

15. See for example, E.T. Flood, 'Japan's Relations with Thailand, 1928–41', PhD thesis (University of Washington, 1967); W.L. Swan, 'Japanese Economic Relations with Siam' and his 'Thai-Japanese Relations at the Start of the Pacific War'. *Journal of South-East Asian Studies* XVII: 2 (Sept 1987), pp. 270–93; E.B. Reynolds, 'Ambivalent Allies: Japan and Thailand 1941–1945', PhD thesis (University of Hawaii, 1988), and Iida Junzo, 'Japan's Relations with Independent Siam'. See also Chai-wat Kamchoo and Reynolds (eds), *Thai-Japanese Relations in Historical*

*Perspective* (Bangkok, 1988). Here and elsewhere, Reynolds has been the author of a whole series of articles and essays stemming from his PhD thesis, most recently his 'Imperial Japan's Cultural Program in Thailand,' in G.K. Goodman (ed.), *Japanese Cultural Policies in Southeast Asia during World War 2* (London, 1991), pp. 93–116.

16. For the context to this, see especially G.L. Gong, *The 'Standard of Civilization' in International Society* (London, 1984).

17. Yet leading members of the Absolute Monarchy regime such as Princes Boworadet, Burachat and Sawat, were already,before 1932, in the habit of anticipating the collapse of the Western colonial empires in Asia. See British Minister J. Dormer to Henderson, 16 March, 30 June 1931, FO 371/15531, and to Simon, 11 Jan 1934, FO 422/90. And it should be noted that both the Absolute Monarchy regime in February 1932, and that of Phya Mano attempting a restoration of the Absolute Monarchy at the time of the Lytton Report debate in February 1933, declined to vote against Japan at the League of Nations. For other evidence of the sympathy between various Thai and Japanese interests at this time, see Flood, 'Japan's Relations with Thailand' and Iida, 'Japan's Relations with Independent Siam'.

18. D. Mackillop of the Foreign Office, 6 August 1932, commenting on a report from Bangkok Chargé d'Affaires F.H. Johns of 30 June, FO 371/16261, described it perhaps somewhat condescendingly as 'one of the most interesting (if hardly one of the most important) by-products of the world economic crisis'.

19. See the Taiheiyō Sensō e no Michi series, trans. and edited by J. Morley et al. as *Japan's Road to the Pacific War*, esp. vol. 3, *The China Quagmire* (New York, 1983).

20. M. Peattie, *Ishiwara Kanji and Japan's Confrontation with the West* (Princeton, 1975) chap 8. Of course, more than anyone else, Ishiwara had been responsible earlier for antagonising the Chinese through the Mukden Incident of September 1931, which led to the creation of the Japanese Manchukuo 'puppet-state' in 1932. This detached from China an area controlled since the 1911 Revolution by the Chang warlords, apparently for fear that it would otherwise fall under the sway of the Soviet Union.

21. G.M. Wilson, *Radical Nationalist in Japan: Kita Ikki, 1883–1937* (Cambridge, Mass., 1969).

22. See for example M.B. Jansen, *The Japanese and Sun Yat-sen* (Cambridge, Mass., 1954), and Miyazaki Toten, *My Thirty-Three Years Dream*, trans. Eto Shinkichi and M.B. Jansen (Princeton, 1982).

23. See especially G.W. Skinner, *Chinese Society in Thailand: An Analytical History* (Ithaca, NY, 1957), for the continuity of Thai attitudes.

24. B.A. Batson, *The End of the Absolute Monarchy in Siam* (Singapore, 1984), p. 304.

25. See Brailey, *Thailand the Fall of Singapore*, pp. 74–6.

26. Ibid., p. 87. For a good example of contemporary anti-Japanese innuendo and propaganda, see E. Robertson, *The Japanese File* (Singapore, 1979). Cf. Tsuji Masanobu, *Singapore: The Japanese Version* (London, 1984), and also Fujiwara Iwaichi, *F. Kikan: Japanese Army Intelligence Operations in Southeast Asia during World War II*, trans. Akashi Yoji (Hong Kong, 1983), esp. p. 299.

27. See Flood, 'Japan's Relations with Thailand'; N. Tarling, 'King Prajadhipok and the Apple Cart: British Attitudes towards the 1932 Revolution'. *Journal of the Siam Society* 64: 2 (1976).

28. Iida, 'Japan's Relations with Independent Siam', pp. 236–7.

29. Flood, 'Japan's Relations with Thailand', pp. 456–563; Reynolds, 'Ambivalent Allies' 139–52. Japanese policy was doubtless influenced in part by a concern to appease its own ally and Vichy France's master, Nazi Germany.

30. See note 6 above for its 1890s origins. Another parallel with American policy is the use of the word 'quagmire' to represent 1930s China where Japan intervened, like 1960s Vietnam where the US was involved. Cf. note 19.

31. Oka Yoshitake, *Konoe Fumimaro: A Political Biography* (Tokyo, 1972, trans. 1983), pp. 99–100.

32. Direk, *Siam and WWII* p. 90, Thai foreign minister before, during, and after the war, notes that 'As for Manchukuo, China, the Philippines, Indochina [Vietnam?], Siam and Burma, these countries would either have been given their independence, or continued respect would have been shown for their sovereignty. However, Japan would have made certain claims for special privileges, especially in regard to military bases, together possibly with agreements for military and political aid. Economically, countries within the Greater East Asia Co-Prosperity Sphere would have been prosperous and self-sufficient, producing the maximum from their resources, but would have had to agree to buy products they could not produce themselves from other countries within the Co-Prosperity Sphere.' However he has already noted earlier, p. 85, that with the foundation of the Greater East Asia Ministry, absorbing the earlier Overseas (Colonies) Ministry, as he saw it a gap had begun to open in Japanese policy between idealised theory and everyday practice: 'The establishment of the Greater East Asia Ministry was only a first step in expanding Japan's influence and authority over this part of the world, and it was now [1942?] clear that Japan's object in building up the Greater East Asia Co-Prosperity Sphere was none other than to bring this region under her "protectorship" and "leadership"'. See J.J. Stephan, *Hawaii under the Rising Sun: Japan's Plans for Conquest after Pearl Harbor* (Honolulu, 1984) pp. 78–80, 136–8, who claims deliberate Japanese vagueness in defining the Sphere's geographical scope and political structure, and Joyce Lebra, *Japan's Greater East Asia Co-Prosperity Sphere in World War II* (Kuala Lumpur, 1975), who argues, on p. x, that 'Inchoate goals toward South-East Asia meant that the structure of the Greater East Asia Co-Prosperity Sphere was highly divergent from one country to the next. Lack of coordination between agencies and offices within the military establishment regarding a given country was the rule.

33. Flood, 'Japan's Relations with Thailand'.

34. Reynolds, 'Ambivalent Allies', pp. xxiii, viii.

35. Sir A. Gilchrist, 'Diplomacy and Disaster: Thailand and the British Empire in 1941', *Asian Affairs* XIII (October 1982), pp. 249–64. See also A. Stewart, *The Underrated Enemy* (London, 1987).

36. Swan, 'Japanese Economic Relations with Siam', abstract and pp. 149–50.

37. Reynolds, 'Ambivalent Allies', pp. 747–8 and fn. 1., based on Swan, 'Japanese Economic Relations with Siam' pp. 246–8. Reynolds's own title, 'Ambivalent Allies', recalls C. Thorne's *Allies of a Kind: The United States, Britain, and the War against Japan, 1941–45* (London, 1978), and that Anglo-American alliance is still far from being considered meaningless.

38. Brailey *Thailand and the Fall of Singapore*, esp. pp. 39–42, and P. Fistie, *Sous-development et Utopie au Siam* (Paris, 1969).

39. Iida, 'Japan's Relations with Independent Siam', also reproduced as 'King Wachirawut, Thai Nationalism and Taisho Japan', in I. Nish (ed.), *Japan–Thailand Relations* (LSE ST/ICERD Discussion Paper 228), 1991.

40. Iida, 'Japan's Relations with Independent Siam', chap. 4.

41. See Louis Allen, *The Longest War* (London, 1984), esp. pp. 557–68, which places much emphasis on Burmese nationalist hero Aung San's initial total devotion to the Japanese, and by contrast, the unwillingness of the originally more cautious Dr Ba Maw to ever disavow them.

42. Phibun's wartime sensitivity about the Japanese might be viewed in a similar light, contributing to his refusal to attend the November 1943 Greater East Asia premiers' conference in Tokyo. Cf. Reynolds, 'Ambivalent Allies', pp. 530–9.

43. G. Best, 'The French Revolution and Human Rights' in Best (ed.), *The Permanent Revolution: The French Revolution and its Legacy, 1789–1989* (London, 1989), pp. 106–7. Conor Cruise O'Brien in his 'Nationalism and the French Revolution', ibid., pp. 7–48, also dwells very interestingly on the French ambivalence over *republiques-soeurs* and non-French *patriotes* as opposed to France's own expansionist *frontieres naturelles* claims, based on J. Godechot, *La Grande Nation: l'expansion revolutionnaire de la France dans le monde, 1789–1799* (Paris, 1956).

44. W.H. Elsbree, *Japan's Role in Southeast Asian Nationalist Movements* (New York, 1953). See also H. Grimal, *Decolonization: the British, French, Dutch and Belgian Empires 1919–1963* (London, 1978; original Paris edn, 1965).

# 8 The China Theatre and the Pacific War

## Wenzhao Tao

Japan had already been engaged upon an aggressive war with China for four and a half years when the Pacific War began suddenly in December 1941. Japan, together with Germany and Italy, finally stepped onto the road towards world domination. China's War of Resistance against Japanese militarism now became part of the worldwide anti-Axis group.

In the immediate aftermath of the Japanese attack on Pearl Harbor, Chiang Kai-shek, the President of the Supreme Committee of National Defence of China, proposed a military alliance between the Allies, to include China, the United States, Britain, Australia, the Netherlands, Canada and New Zealand. On 23 December 1941, American, British and Chinese military representatives met in Chongqing. Nearly a week later, following an initiative by US President Franklin D. Roosevelt, Britain, the Netherlands and the United States agreed to establish, the China theatre, with Chiang as its Supreme Commander. In January 1942, General Joseph Stilwell was appointed as the US military representative in China who would also act as Chief of Staff to the Supreme Commander of the China theatre as well as the Commander of the US Army Air Force in China, Burma and India. Stilwell's task was to 'increase the effectiveness of United States assistance to the Chinese Government for the prosecution of the war and to assist in improving the combat efficiency of the Chinese Army'.[1] This marked the beginning of the wartime collaboration between China and the Allies. This chapter deals with the relationship between the United States, Britain and China and examines the role of China in defeating Japan during the Pacific War.

In May 1943, the United States Chiefs of Staff summarised American war aims as follows: 'a. In cooperation with Russia and [the] lesser allies to force an unconditional surrender of the Axis in Europe; b. Simultaneously, in cooperation with our allies, to maintain and extend unremitting pressure against Japan in the Pacific and from China; c. Thereafter, in cooperation with other Pacific powers and if possible with Russia, to combine the full resources of the United States and Great Britain to force the unconditional surrender of Japan.'[2] Between 1942 and mid 1943, the United States leadership regarded it as essential to keep China active in the war in order both to contain as many Japanese troops on mainland China as possible and to secure Chinese air bases which would allow the Allies to strike at Japan's mainland.

General Stilwell arrived in Chongqing, the Nationalist Government's capital, in early March 1942 to take over the command of the Chinese Army, which was then fighting in Burma. However, a serious difference of opinion between Stilwell and Chiang soon emerged at a meeting on 10 March. General Stilwell regarded the defence of Burma as more important to China than to Britain, since China's lines of communication would be cut off if Burma was lost; however, Chiang did not agree. The Generalissimo told Stilwell that:

> China was fighting in Burma originally to defend Rangoon. With the fall of Rangoon, the whole situation has changed and it is no longer necessary for the Chinese army to stay there. Japan may launch an attack from Vietnam on Yunnan by taking advantage of the weak defences of that province. We should, therefore, transfer the Chinese troops in Burma to Yunnan and to the Yangtze Basin.

Chiang also pointed out that China had sent her best forces, the 5th and 6th Armies, to Burma and that he would not like to see them defeated there.[3]

As a result of the Japanese seizure of Burma in May, China's land and sea communications with the Allies were interdicted and the only remaining supply line was by air between upper Assam and the plateau of Yunnan over the Indo-Burmese mountains (the Hump). This air corridor was extremely dangerous and was described by pilots as 'the skyway to hell'. Unarmed cargo carriers crossed 500 miles of uncharted mountains and jungles at a height of 20 000 feet in the face of possible Japanese air attacks, tropical monsoons and Tibetan ice. In any case, the amount of supplies which could be carried by air cargo over the Hump was very limited, for instance only a few dozen tons per month initially, which was totally inadequate for the China theatre. Meanwhile, thousands of tons of lend-lease materiel which should have been brought to China was piling up in India. General Stilwell and the Operations Division of the US War Department agreed that 'it [was] of the utmost importance to again start a flow of munitions through Rangoon into China'. They also concluded that it would be difficult to keep China in the war unless the Burma Road was reopened. In July 1942, General Stilwell set out his plan for retaking Burma, which proposed that Britain should concentrate naval forces in the Bay of Bengal to make an Allied landing at Rangoon possible, while at the same time the British army should invade Burma via the Chindwin River towards Shwebo and Mandalay. Secondly, the plan required China to attack in the Lashio area, then to advance on Liolem and Mandalay. Thirdly, the United States would provide strong air cover for these operations and American troops, if available, should join the British troops in attacking across the Chindwin river or in retaking Rangoon. According to Stilwell, if Burma was to be retaken successfully, some 30 000 tons of materiel would have to be shipped through Rangoon to China and then the situation in China would then improve dramatically over the six months.[4]

Chiang Kai-shek approved Stilwell's plan for the recapture of Burma and at a meeting with Lauchlin Currie, Roosevelt's administrative assistant, Chiang asked him to recommend the plan to the President. At Chiang's request, General Shang

Zhen, Director of the Foreign Affairs Bureau of the National Military Council, told Stilwell how important the British amphibious operations in the Bay of Bengal would be to the success of the Burma Campaign. According to the Chinese General, the key to the success of the Burma Campaign depended on

> whether the British can allocate and transfer enough naval and air force to control the Bay of Bengal and regain air and sea control in the Burma area, which would block Japanese reinforcement from Malaya and Singapore through Rangoon. If this can be done, the Burma Campaign is quite simple and can be successful.[5]

The Joint Chiefs of Staff (JCS) accepted Stilwell's plan in principle and the Combined (Anglo-American) Chiefs of Staff (CCS) discussed it on 25 August 1942. American military leaders were afraid that, without any visible Allied assistance to China, China might make a separate peace with Japan and the JCS recommended that Burma campaign should therefore take place in the next dry season, that is from October 1942 to May 1943.[6] However, the British Chiefs of Staff wanted to concentrate Britain's resources on defeating Germany in Europe. Britain did not want to lose India, but she seemed more interested in retaining her control over India and regaining her other lost colonies in South-East Asia than in defeating Japan. British military leaders did not want the Americans to fight in their former colonies, in case the United States, having defeated the Japanese, seized control of them for herself. Nor did the British want the Chinese to fight in Burma, since this might encourage the rise of Asian nationalism there. Instead, the British leadership believed that Burma should be retaken solely by British forces and then restored to British rule. Thus, the British Chiefs of Staff could not support Stilwell's plan as it stood.

In September 1942, at a meeting of the Combined Chiefs of Staff, the British argued that it was unlikely that their troops and amphibious forces would be available for the Burma offensive before April 1943. The monsoon season would start in May and therefore October 1943 would be the earliest time to launch the campaign. Stilwell then proposed a revised plan designed to retake North Burma, which would allow the Chinese to rebuild the Ledo Road and resume land transportation between China and India. When Stilwell's revised plan was discussed at CCS meetings between 19 and 21 November 1942, the British representative would not agree to the North Burma campaign either.

However, General Stilwell persisted with his plan to retake Burma. On 23 December 1942, he sent a memorandum to the Chinese Foreign Minister, T.V. Soong, and the Chief of Staff, He Yingqin, which suggested that Chinese troops in India and Yunnan province attack Burma from both east and west on 1 March 1943, while British troops mount an offensive at Akyab and along the Chindwin river. The proposal did not include an amphibious operation by Britain in the Bay of Bengal. Chiang Kai-shek opposed a plan which differed very significantly from Stilwell's original plan of July 1942. Chiang wrote to President Roosevelt on 28 December 1942:

> While two months ago General Wavell promised me to send seven British divisions from India to join the Burma campaign, the General, however, recently stated that he could mobilize only three divisions for a limited offensive at Akyab and along the Chindwin... I think it really regrettable if the Burma campaign was cancelled because of Britain's refusal to fulfil her promises... I beg you to urge the British to change their minds on this. China, which has been fighting Japan for five and a half years, is seriously weakened militarily and economically, and the Chinese Army and the people cannot afford to risk a second defeat in Burma.[7]

President Roosevelt replied on 2 January 1943 that he would talk to Churchill about the Burma Campaign privately during the forthcoming Casablanca Conference.

At the Conference, which opened on 14 January, the Burma Campaign was one of the major items on the agenda. United States military leaders were resolved to force the British into launching the Burma campaign, code-named ANAKIM, in the autumn of 1943. In the meantime, American forces were engaged in prolonged and costly fighting with the Japanese in Guadalcanal and New Guinea. United States military leaders were convinced that the only economical way of defeating Japan was to utilise the enormous manpower of China against Japan. Ernest J. King, Commander in Chief of the US fleet, said at the Conference that:

> In the European Theatre, Russia was most advantageously placed for dealing with Germany in view of her geopolitical position and manpower; in the Pacific, China bore a similar relation to the Japanese. It should be our basic policy to provide the manpower resources of Russia and China with the necessary equipment to enable them to fight.

He considered ANAKIM a step in this direction. US Army Chief General George Marshall was also in favour of utilising Chinese manpower, as 'the present operations in the South Pacific are tremendously expensive in merchant vessels, naval vessels and escorts'. General Marshall continued that 'unless Anakim could be undertaken ... a situation might arise in the Pacific at any time that would necessitate the United States regretfully withdrawing from their commitments in the European Theatre.[8] Marshall's threat was nothing more than a bluff, since he also argued strongly for the concentration of Allied air and ground forces for a cross-Channel invasion to defeat Germany at the earliest possible date. The British were compelled to compromise and the CCS agreed to prepare for the ANAKIM operation, which was to begin on 15 November 1943. The actual decision to launch the Burma offensive was to be made by the CCS in the summer of 1943.

After the Casablanca Conference, Roosevelt and Churchill sent General H.H. Arnold and Marshal Sir John Dill to China in order to report the outcome of the Conference to Chiang. Arnold and Dill also went to see Generals Wavell and Stilwell in India and the four generals agreed that ANAKIM should be waged from November 1943 to May 1944. They also discussed broad operational plans whereby the Chinese Army in India would advance toward Ledo, while 11 Chinese divisions in Yunnan province (the Chinese Expeditionary Force, Yoke Force, or Y-Force) would advance towards Lashio. Three Indian divisions would launch an attack along the Chindwin River. Mandalay would be the immediate target for the ground forces, which should retake Rangoon in January 1944, with the British navy blockading Rangoon from the sea.

The Trident Conference between Churchill and Roosevelt in Washington in May demonstrated, however, that Anglo-American differences about ANAKIM still continued. United States strategic thinking was reflected in the JCS's document of 14 May 1943 on 'The Strategic Plan for the Defeat of Japan'. Under this plan, American forces would drive across the Pacific and take the Philippines, and then move towards the Hong Kong area, while Allied troops in the Chinese-Burma-Indian theatre would first seize Burma and then advance towards Hong Kong from that direction. Two allied group forces were thus to converge in the area of Hong Kong and from there they would drive into Japanese occupied north China and would launch a 'sustained, systematic and large scale [air] offensive against Japan itself', which might cause Japan to surrender. Even if this did not happen, allied strategic bombing from bases in China would undermine Japan's military-industrial resources and the morale of her people which would then make an Allied landing on the mainland of Japan a feasible proposition. The plan stated that 'an air offensive on the required scale can only be conducted from bases in China'.[9] Thus it was clear that the importance of the China theatre lay in airbases from whence the United States would undertake aerial offensives against Japan's mainland, although the United States Chiefs of Staff believed it essential for the Allies to retake Burma or at least to open the land supply route to China.

However, at the Trident Conference, British leaders now rejected ANAKIM. British Prime Minister Winston Churchill prepared a long document to elaborate Britain's attitude towards this operation. He 'hated jungles' and 'going into swampy jungles to fight the Japanese is like going into the water to fight a shark. It is better to entice him into a trap or catch him on a hook and then demolish him with axes after hauling him out on to dry land.' The way to 'deceive and entrap the shark', Churchill suggested, would be to abandon ANAKIM and instead launch amphibious operations in Sumatra and on the Malayan peninsula.[10] The British Chiefs also argued against ANAKIM for a number of reasons: it would be very difficult to attack Rangoon from the sea, while keeping Allied troops in north Burma supplied would be a tremendous logistical problem. Moreover, the jungle would prevent the use of modern weapons, while the monsoon would limit the length of time in which military operations could be sustained there. In conclusion, the British Chiefs recommended the cancellation of ANAKIM. They thought that the best way to keep China in the war would be to expand both the number of cargo flights across the Hump and the size of General Chennault's air forces for the defence of China.

General Stilwell and General Chennault also attended the Conference. These two differed in their approach to operations in the China theatre. Chennault was enthusiastic about strategic bombing against Japan from China. He had once stated that if he was given one hundred aircraft, he would probably defeat Japan within six months or at most within a year.[11] Stilwell, on the other hand, claimed that the efficiency of Chinese troops should be improved so that they would be able to recapture Burma. Chiang Kai-shek favoured Chennault's idea of expanding his air force, since Stilwell's plan for the reorganisation of the Chinese Army might endanger Chiang's personal control over it.

T.V. Soong also was at the Conference to discuss the issue with the CCS. This was one of the few occasions during the Pacific War when the Chinese actually participated in the CCS's discussions. Soong sided with Chennault's air strategy. The Chinese foreign minister stated that he appreciated that Stilwell and Chennault, although differing in their approaches, were both trying to help China. Soong insisted, however, that Chiang Kai-shek, who was, after all, the Supreme Commander of the China theatre, felt strongly about the need to expand the Allied air forces in China. This would contribute towards strengthening not only the morale of the Chinese Army but also in defending Chongqing. Soong also mentioned that Stilwell's doubts about the efficiency of the Chinese Army were too pessimistic. During the Trident Conference, Soong was instructed by Chiang to insist on mounting operation ANAKIM as had already been decided at the Casablanca Conference in January 1943. Soong was also told to demand that the maintenance of British naval supremacy in the Bay of Bengal and the recapture of Rangoon were both essential if ANAKIM was to be successful. Thus, Soong opposed the North Burma campaign plan and he informed the Anglo-American representatives that if this conference decided to abandon ANAKIM, the Chinese people would completely lose confidence in the Western allies.[12]

As it transpired, because of persistent British opposition, the Trident Conference decided that ANAKIM should be pigeonholed. The final campaign in Burma was now set for 1944–5. Chiang Kai-shek was disappointed by this outcome. Partly to console Chiang, Roosevelt decided to increase deliveries over the Hump from 3400 tons to 7000 tons monthly by 1 July 1943, and to 10 000 tons monthly by 1 September 1943. The United States Chiefs of Staff also suggested on 20 May 1943 that '[t]hough the opening of the Burma Road was a symbol to China, it might be possible to convince them that an air route would achieve the same results.'[13]

General George Marshall and other American military leaders remained strongly in favour of a major British operation in the Bay of Bengal. They thought that the British must be persuaded to commit themselves to the original timing and scale of the Burma campaign. This was one of the goals the United States Chiefs wanted to achieve at the Quadrant Conference in Quebec in August 1943. At a CCS meeting on 14 August, General Marshall argued his case:

> There seemed to be four issues which must be decided. Firstly, what was the value of Chinese troops; secondly, could we afford to take so little action with regard to China that the present government would fall; thirdly, if we employed only air forces from China, would not the Japanese reactions be so strong as to cut the line of communication to them, and, fourthly, in an operation through China was it essential to capture a port for [the] heavy build up of supplies and thus link up with naval operations across the Pacific?

General Arnold stated that from the air force point of view, the opening of the Burma Road was essential, together with a port on the east coast of China through which the air forces could be adequately supplied.[14] Their British counterparts remained opposed to counter-offensives in southern Burma. Churchill pointed out that 'a campaign through Rangoon up the Irrawaddy to Mandalay and beyond would be most detrimental and disadvantageous' to the British. He thought that such an offensive would give the British nothing except 'the future right to trail through the swamps and jungles of Burma'.[15] Consequently, at the Quebec Conference, the question of British amphibious operations in southern Burma remained undecided.

By mid-1943, the American naval and military situation in the Pacific had begun to improve. By then, American superiority by sea and air gave the initiative to the United States. Especially after the United States began to employ an island-hopping strategy, Japanese forces found it very hard to defend Japan's conquests in the vast Pacific ocean.[16] In the meantime, in Europe, Germany's advance in Russia was checked at Stalingrad in February 1943, while Italy surrendered in August of that year. In the light of this favourable strategic situation, United States military leaders anticipated that Germany would surrender in the autumn of 1944, while Japan could be defeated twelve months later.

The US Operation Divisions of the War Department concluded on 18 October 1943 that the final campaign against Japan should be launched from American-seized strategic points in the Pacific rather than from mainland Asia. Furthermore, on 8 November 1943, the Joint Strategic Survey Committee proposed that '[t]he key to [the] early defeat of Japan lies in all-out operations through the Central Pacific with supporting operations on the Northern and Southern flanks'.[17] American strategic planners began to attach less importance to the China theatre in the defeat of Japan even before the Cairo Conference met on 22 November 1943.

Chiang Kai-shek now participated for the first time in an Allied summit conference. The Cairo Declaration solemnly proclaimed that 'all the territories Japan has stolen from China, such as Manchuria, Formosa, and the Pescadores, shall be restored' to China at the end of the war. This was an important international pledge of the restoration of China's territorial integrity and China's diplomacy reached its zenith at Cairo. Chiang asked the United States to arm and train 90 Chinese divisions to open an offensive in Burma before the onset of the monsoon in 1944. The Generalissimo also set target dates for the recapture of Hong Kong, Canton and Shanghai. Chiang repeated how important amphibious operations across the Bay of Bengal (now code-named BUCCANEER) would be in preventing Japanese reinforcements reaching Burma. President Roosevelt was sympathetic, since, despite his instructions, the deliveries over the Hump had not increased much. Therefore, while the British remained hesitant about BUCCANEER, Roosevelt proposed the Chinese that the operation would be launched in March 1944.

At the Teheran Conference immediately following the first Cairo Conference, Churchill, under strong pressure from Stalin and Roosevelt, agreed to launch the cross-channel invasion, code-named OVERLORD, in May 1944. Stalin also promised at Teheran that once Germany was defeated, Soviet forces in Siberia would be substantially increased and that the Soviets would participate in the final defeat of Japan.[18] After Teheran, the Anglo-American leaders returned to Cairo to continue their discussions. Churchill argued that BUCCANEER must be postponed until the autumn of 1944 for two reasons: First, Stalin's pledge to enter the war with Japan meant that the Allies would have bases in Siberia to launch strategic bombing attacks on Japan. These bases would be an improvement on those China had to offer. Secondly, the decision to launch OVERLORD precluded the possibility that the British could assemble the necessary amphibious forces for BUCCANEER.[19] Roosevelt and the American chiefs were reluctant to break their promise to Chiang Kai-shek and the President was 'stubborn as a mule for four days', but he then gave in. In a letter to Chiang on 5 December 1943 Roosevelt proposed two alternatives: either to go ahead with the North Burma Campaign, codenamed TARZAN, without large-scale amphibious operations in the Bay of Bengal, or to postpone BUCCANEER until November 1944.[20] Chiang Kai-shek remained opposed to the North Burma campaign and he replied on 17 December that he preferred to delay BUCCANEER. At the same time, he requested a billion-dollar loan from the US, the further expansion of Chennault's air force and an increase in deliveries over the Hump.

The North Burma campaign was already under way in late October 1943 and the Chinese army in India won initial battles in the Hukawng Valley. On 19 December, Chiang appointed General Stilwell as Commander-in-Chief of the Chinese Army in India. From his past experience, Stilwell knew only too well that the Chinese generals would not obey him without definite instructions from Chiang. He also knew that he could not achieve a successful North Burma campaign without the Chinese Expeditionary Force crossing the Salween River and joining the campaign. In a radio communication with General Marshall on

19 December 1943, Stilwell proposed that the President should persuade Chiang to allow the use of the Y-Force for the North Burma Campaign. Accordingly, Roosevelt pressed Chiang to agree to cooperate in telegrams on 20 and 29 December 1943 and on 14 January 1944, warning Chiang that the United States might decrease lend-lease supplies to China if Chiang Kai-shek did not agreed on the use of the Expeditionary (Y-Force). Chiang remained stubborn and in letters on 23 December and 9 January to Roosevelt, the Chinese leader repeatedly pointed out that:

> Without considerable amphibious force landing in southern Burma, the offensive of ground forces in northern Burma is doomed to failure. Indeed, I cannot agree with this operation plan. In spite of this I have already handed over to General Stilwell the Chinese Army in India which can be used in the Burma Campaign. I think this may not affect the China theatre....Judging from the recent military arrangements, the Allied powers are neglecting the defence of China and this has caused serious impacts on China's confidence in the Allies.[21]

In early March 1944, Japan launched an attack on Imphal in India. Lord Louis Mountbatten, the Supreme Allied South-East Asia Commander, sent a long telegram to Washington and London on 17 March, requesting that Chiang Kai–shek be pressed to act. Accordingly, Roosevelt made a renewed request to the Chinese leader for the use of the Y-Force in the Allied campaign in Burma. However, Chiang replied on 27 March that, in the light of the precarious military situation in Yunnan, he could not agree to move the Expeditionary Force to Burma, but he offered to send reinforcements to join the Chinese Army in India.

In April 1944, Stilwell reported to the President on the worsening Allied military situation in Burma and on 3 April, Roosevelt again appealed to Chiang:

> we have during the past year, been equipping and training your Yoke Forces. If they are not to be used in the common cause our most strenuous [and] extensive efforts to fly in equipment and to furnish instructional personnel have not been justified.[22]

A week later, General Marshall instructed Stilwell to stop lend-lease shipments to the Y-Forces unless these forces were moved to Burma. General Stilwell told his Chief of Staff General Hearn to comply with this at once. When he heard of this new development, General Heyingqin asked General Hearn to wait two more days. On 14 April 1943, Chiang Kai shek at last gave his consent for the Y-Forces to move into Burma. The following day, these forces crossed the Salween River and advanced towards Tengchong and Longling and launched a fierce attack against the Japanese 56th Division.

With the successful progress of the American offensives in the Pacific, United States military planners re-examined their strategy for defeating Japan. A report produced by the Joint Strategic Survey Committee on 16 February 1944 stated that the ultimate objective of the Pacific strategy was to crack 'the Japanese Citadel' – Japan, Korea, Manchuria and Shantung. To achieve this, 'the primary effort ... should be made from the East, across the Central Pacific' to recapture Luzon, Formosa and the China coast, with Formosa as a centre of the area for attacking the citadel of Japan. Operations in other areas, such as the South-West Pacific, the North Pacific, China and Burma should thus be regarded as of secondary importance to the 'primary effort'.

China remained one of the major bases for the strategic bombing of Japan's mainland; however, there was now a difference between the February 1944 plan and the 'strategic plan' of May 1943. The China coast was supposed to be retaken by the westward advance of the American forces in the Central Pacific rather than by Chinese troops. On 12 March 1944, the Joint Chiefs of Staff informed General MacArthur and Admiral Nimitz that 'the most feasible approach to the Formosa-Luzon-China area is by way of [the] Mariana-Carolines-Palau-Mindanao area.' Two months later, the Joint Strategic Survey Committee wrote that the May 1943 strategy of converging operations towards the Hong Kong area was 'no longer a sound concept'. The report continued that '[our] progress and capabilities in the advance from the East and Southeast have exceeded expectations', although the planners still regarded a British effort from the south-west as essential.[23] Thus, US military planners produced a new strategy, that is, one of converging operations towards Luzon-Taiwan and the Japanese home islands from three directions, i.e. a United States advance from the east and south-east and a British advance from the south-west.

Accordingly, under this new strategic plan, the United States no longer considered the equipping and training of the Chinese forces as of primary importance and the policy of 'keeping China in the war' had lost its substance. All the United States wanted from China was for her to remain in the war and for the Nationalist Government to remain in power so that the country would not degenerate into chaos. Stilwell's mission also changed significantly. Marshall wrote to Stilwell on 27 May 1944 that Stilwell's 'paramount mission in [the] China Theatre for the immediate future is to conduct such military operations as will most effectively support the main effort in the Pacific', that is, to support the Hump lift and its security, and to increase its capacity.[24]

However, this did not alter the fact that the US military chiefs remained anxious to retake north Burma and to open the Ledo Road. They thought that north Burma could be retaken by the advance of the Allied forces to the line Kalewa–Shwebo–Katha–Lashio, and that the rest of Burma as well as other Japanese-occupied territories would fall after an Allied lodgement had been secured in the Formosa-China coast-Luzon area. The Allied counter-offensive in Burma began in September 1944.

By the summer of 1944, Allied offensive against Germany and Japan had made substantial progress. The United States seizure of the Marianas meant that these islands could be used as bases for long-range bombers (B-29s) to attack Japan's mainland directly. It was becoming increasingly clear to United States military leaders that 'America's least expensive course of action is to continue and intensify the air and sea blockade, with an intensified bombardment of Japan's war industry, and at the same time to reoccupy the Philippines'.[25]

One school of thought has argued that after Stilwell's recall in October 1944, the United States left the China theatre in limbo. However, this is debatable. The allied capture of the Myitkyina airfield in May 1944 opened a shorter supply route at a lower altitude, so that the tonnage over the Hump increased steadily. In January 1945 the Ledo Road was opened, and the oil pipeline began to operate. Lend-lease supplies were delivered by air, through the new road, and by the oil pipeline from January to August 1945. These amounted to 496 900 short tons in total, compared with the amount of some 416 860 tons delivered during the previous two years.[26] With these supplies General Albert Wedemeyer, who had replaced General Stilwell, was in a better position to speed up the process of equipping and training the Chinese troops. In November 1944, Lieutenant Colonel George Elsey, Roosevelt's administrative assistant, wrote a long and comprehensive report on US–China relations during the war. The report stated that 'the Soviet decision at Cairo to enter the war against Japan after the defeat of Germany reduced the value of China as a base for future operations, but this did not affect the determination of the President to support China.'[27] As the Pacific War was moving towards its end, American political considerations about the future of post-war China became increasingly important in the minds of US decision-makers.

Assessing the military value of the China theatre in Allied strategy and the actual role China played in the war with Japan are two totally different things. However, the following observations might be useful.

First, it was the China Theatre that tied down the largest number of Japanese troops throughout the Pacific War. At the outbreak of the War, 36 out of 62 divisions, as well as 42 out of 58 independent composite brigades, were engaged in China, while there were only 10 divisions plus three composite brigades fighting in the Pacific. In November 1943, when the situation in the Pacific worsened for the Japanese, there were still 39 out of the total of 70 divisions, together with 11 out of 22 brigades, in China. At the time of Japan's surrender in August 1945, nearly 45 per cent of the total Japanese armed forces were in China (except for north-east China.)[28]

That the China theatre kept such a large number of Japanese military effectives engaged facilitated the Allied victory over Japan. It delayed the outbreak of the Pacific War, which broke out after four and a half years of war in China. This was not because Japan did not want to expand the war earlier, but because, since she had become bogged down in China, Japan did not feel strong enough to expand the war into other areas. In July 1940, the Japanese Government approved a strategy which emphasised that Japan should devote herself, among other things, to winning the war in China and that while the war was continuing in China, Japan should be careful not to provoke the other powers.[29] Nevertheless, Japan did launch the Pacific War before ending the war with China. This was because Japanese expansionist hardliners became more influential in determining the nation's military actions. As late as in November 1941, General Marshall, Admiral Harold Stark, the Chief of Naval Operations and other military leaders agreed that the United States was unprepared for war both in the Atlantic and the Pacific theatres. They wanted very much to avoid war in East Asia and 'to do all in our power ... to delay this to the last moment'.[30] Had the Pacific War broken out earlier, the Allies would certainly have been faced with considerable problems.

Moreover, the ongoing Sino-Japanese war (even after the outbreak of the Pacific War) helped to disrupt the Axis' strategic plans. Japan initially planned to attack Australia, Ceylon and West Asia, apparently in coordination with Germany. Had this ambitious Axis plan materialised, the situation for the Allies would have been extremely difficult. The failure to achieve these aims was mainly because the bulk of Japanese forces were pinned down in the China theatre.

Indeed, Roosevelt and Churchill were well aware of this. During the Cairo Conference, Roosevelt told his son that: 'Without China, if China goes under, how many divisions of Japanese troops ... will be freed – to do what? Take Australia, take India – and it's as ripe as a plum for the picking. Move straight on to the Middle East ... '[31] Churchill estimated in April 1942 that 'at least fifteen and perhaps twenty Japanese divisions would be freed by the collapse of China. Thereafter a major invasion of India would indeed be possible'. He continued that should the Japanese become dominant in the western Indian Ocean oil supplies would be interrupted, and this would result in the collapse of the Allied position in the Middle East.[32]

The continuation of the Sino-Japanese war also eased Japanese pressure on the Allied forces in the Pacific. As a result, much of the Japanese army could not be used in the Pacific at all during the course of the war. Admiral Nimitz told a meeting of the Combined Chiefs of Staff in March 1944 that he felt it essential to make the most of the Allied sea and air superiority in the Pacific and to avoid for as long as possible fighting the Japanese army on land. If one takes the examples of US experience in land operations in the Bonins and the Ryukyus, it is clear why the United States wanted so much to avoid costly land battles with the Japanese troops.[33]

The second role of the China theatre was that it consumed, rather than enriched, Japan's strength. It is understood in China that Japan wanted to use China's abundant resources of material and manpower in order to wage her 'Sacred Great East Asia War'. However, this intention of 'supporting the war by the war' never materialised because of China's unremitting resistance against the Japanese. From October 1938, after the fall of Guangzhou and Wuhan, Japan made a great effort to pursue a policy of 'securing the occupied areas and ensuring safety there'. The Japanese troops waged ruthless 'mopping up' campaigns in north China and 'clearing up' campaigns in east and central China. But all these Japanese 'campaigns for public order' failed to annihilate the Eighth Route Army and the New Fourth Army led by the Chinese Communist Party. Between 1936 and 1938 a number of American journalists, scholars and servicemen, including Edgar Snow, Owen Lattimore and Evans Carlson, visited Chinese bases in north-west, north and east China. According to them, in those areas which Japan claimed to have occupied, Japan controlled only the key railway lines and road communications, and the cities, while the rest of the area was effectively run by the Chinese community. They saw Chinese administration at work in Chinese-operated factories, banks, arsenals, schools and farm cooperatives, and also in the mobilisation of partisan troops. J. Clayton Miller, an American historian, who visited central Hebei in spring 1938, stressed that Chinese guerrilla warfare against the Japanese was organised in a comprehensive manner, penetrating the community behind the enemy's lines politically, socially, economically and militarily. He concluded that 'Japan's efforts to conquer North China will meet with insuperable obstacles'.[34] In spring 1945, a member of the US Army Observer Group wrote: 'our past consideration that this territory is Japanese occupied should be revised. The Japanese holds only a thin skeleton; the rest of the area is controlled by forces on our side.'[35] Thus, the China theatre certainly reduced Japanese war capabilities considerably.

Thirdly, the China theatre provided convenient bases for the US air force. The main air bases were located in Jinhua, Lishui, Yushan, Quzhou in Zhejiang Province, Jianou in Fujian Province, Enshi, Laohekou in Hubei Province, Hengyang, Lingling, Zhijiang, Baoqing in Hunan Province, Ganzhou, Suichuan in Jiangzi Province, Nanxiong in Guangdong Province, Xi'an, Ankang, Hanzhong in Shannxi Province, Chengdu, Liangshan, Baishiyi in Sichuan Province, Kunming, Yinan, Zhanyi, Luliang in Yunnan Province, and Guilin and Liuzhou in Guangxi Province. In April 1942, US B-25 bombers made the first air assault on the Japanese home islands. The bombers took off from an aircraft carrier in the Pacific and landed at the airfields in Zhejiang Province after the attack. On 15 June 1944 the Japanese islands came under fierce bombardment by Chengdu-based B-29s, while strategic bombing by Superfortresses based on the Marianas began five months later on 24 November 1944. The Chinese-based joint Sino-American air forces made a considerable contribution to the Allied victory by destroying Japanese transport facilities and military installations. For instance, between 15 November 1944 and 15 May 1945, the 14th Air Force shot down 1634 enemy airplanes.[36] In 1944, Japan made a final effort to destroy the Allied air bases by carrying out the so-called Ichigo Operation.

Fourthly, China's resistance to the Japanese invasion helped to boost the morale of other Asian peoples in their struggle against Japan. Those South Asian peoples, who had been under Western rule before the outbreak of the Pacific War, were determined to obtain independence from their Western rulers. Japan exploited these anti-Western feelings and promised Asian nationalists to liberate their countries and to help them to obtain national independence in due course. Although this was purely Japanese propaganda, some nationalist leaders, including Achemed Soekarno, believed the Japanese promises. Consequently, they initially cooperated with the Japanese. During the first Burma campaign in the spring of 1942, it was the Japanese troops rather than Allied forces who received help from the indigenous Burmese. Thus, China's resistance was noteworthy and the Allies were well aware of this. The Joint US Intelligence Committee reported on 1 July 1942 that:

Chinese resistance has adversely affected Japan's prestige and is constantly damaging to Japan's morale. Collapse of this resistance would therefore be helpful to Japan and, at the same time, would adversely affect the morale and prestige of the United Nations.

The Committee also concluded, in another report on 4 August 1944, that 'the significance of Asiatics resisting the encroachments of other Asiatics is of tremendous political and psychological importance'.[37]

Lastly, the China theatre made a valuable contribution to Allied strategic resources, including tin, tungsten and antimony. Moreover, Chinese intelligence about the deployment of Japanese troops in China was also useful to the US Office of Strategic Service, while at the same time China provided Allied forces with food and labour in return for US lend-lease aid.

Japanese militarism was defeated by the joint efforts of the Chinese, Americans, British, Russians and the peace-loving peoples of all Asian countries, and the efforts made by the peoples of each country against Japan should therefore be acknowledged. China received help from the Allies, but she also contributed to the Allied cause of defeating Japan in a variety of ways. China made great national sacrifices and a considerable contribution to the Pacific War. This should be fairly evaluated in the history of the Second World War.

## NOTES

1. Charles F. Romanus and Riley Sunderland, *Stilwell's Mission to China* (Washington, DC: US Government Printing Office, 1953) p. 74.
2. The Combined Chiefs of Staff [CCS] 83rd mtg, 7 May 1943, Annex A. RG 218, Records of Joints Chiefs of Staff, Box 170, National Archives and Records Administration, Washington DC (hereafter cited as NARA).
3. Zhongguo guomindang zhongyang weiyuanhui dangshi weiyuanhui (Committee on Party History of the Central Committee of the Kuomintang), Zhonghua minguo zhongyao shiliao chubian-duiri kangzhan shiqi, 3: Zhanshi waijiao (*Important*

*Historical Documents of the Republic of China – The Period of the War of Resistance against Japan* 3: *Diplomatic Relations during the War* (hereafter cited as *Diplomatic Relations*) (Taipei, 1981), vol. III, pp. 568–9.

4. Romanus and Sunderland, *Stilwell's Mission*, p. 179.
5. *Diplomatic Relations*, p. 623.
6. Romanus and Sunderland, *Stilwell's Mission*, p. 223.
7. Liang Jingchun, Shidiwei shijian (*The Stilwell Incident*) (Taipei, 1971) p. 101.
8. CCS 58th and 59th mtgs, 16 and 17 January 1943, RG 219, Box 169, NARA.
9. Michael Kublin, *The Role of China in American Military Strategy from Pearl Harbor to the Fall of 1944* (Ann Arbor, Michigan: University Microfilms International, 1984) pp. 147–8.
10. Winston S. Churchill, *The Second World War, vol. IV, The Hinge of Fate* (London: Cassell, 1951) pp. 702–3. 708.
11. Romanus and Sunderland, *Stilwell's Mission*, pp. 252–3.
12. *Diplomatic Relations*, pp. 225–30.
13. CCS 90th mtg, 20 May 1943, RG 218, Box 170, NARA.
14. CCS 107th mtg, 14 August 1943, RG 218, Box 170, NARA.
15. Winston Churchill, *The Second World War, vol. V, Closing the Ring* (London, 1952) pp. 78–9.
16. For General Tojo's appreciation of America's leapfrogging strategy, see Samuel E. Morison, *History of the United States Naval Operations in World War II*, vol. VI, (Boston: Little, Brown, 1950) p. 225.
17. Romanus and Sunderland, *Stilwell's Command Problem* (Washington, DC: USGPO, 1956), pp. 53–5.
18. W. Averell Harriman and Elle Abel, *Special Envoy to Churchill and Stalin, 1941–1946* (New York: Random House, 1975) p. 266.
19. Herbert Feis, *The China Tangle* (Princeton: Princeton University Press, 1953) p. 118.
20. *Foreign Relations of the United States, 1943, China* (Washington DC: USGPO, 1957) p. 178.
21. *Diplomatic Relations*, vol. 3, pp. 289–93.
22. Romanus and Sunderland, *Stilwell's Command Problem*, pp. 310–12.
23. Grance P. Hayes, *The History of the Joint Chiefs of Staff in World War II: The War against Japan* (Annapolis, Maryland: Naval Institute Press, 1982) pp. 551, 559; Joint Strategic Survey Committee 'Policies, Combined Planning for the Defeat of Japan', 12 May 1944, RG218, Box 170, NARA.
24. Romanus and Sunderland, *Stilwell's Command Problem*, pp. 363–4.
25. JCS 172nd mtg, 5 September 1944, Box 196, RG218, NARA.
26. US Department of State, *United States Relations with China with special reference to the period 1944–1949* (Washington DC: USGPO, 1949) p. 27; Arthur Young, *China and Helping Hands* (Cambridge, Mass. Harvard University Press, 1963) p. 340.
27. George Elsey, 'The President and US Aid to China' p. 54. Roosevelt commented that 'it [the report] is excellent'. Box 165, Map Room Files, Franklin Delano Roosevelt Library, Hyde Park, New York.
28. T. Hattori, *The Complete History of the Great East Asian War* (Tokyo, 1953) vol. 1, pp. 328–30; He Yingqin, *the History of Eight Year Japanese Aggression against China and China's Resistance War* (Taipei, 1982) p. 355.
29. Hattori, *The Complete History*, p. 54.
30. Herbert Feis, *The Road to Pearl Harbor: The Coming of the War between the United States and Japan* (Princeton: Princeton University Press, 1950) p. 300.
31. Elliot Roosevelt, *As He Saw It* (New York: Duell, Sloan & Pearce, 1946) p. 53.

32. Churchill, *The Second World War*, vol. IV, pp. 161–4 ff.
33. Hattori, *The Complete History*, pp. 135, 144.
34. J. Clayton Miller, 'The Chinese Still Rule North China' *Amerasia*, 7:7 (September 1938), pp. 336–45.
35. Joseph W. Esherick (ed), *Lost Chance in China: The World War II Despatches of John S. Service* (New York: Vintage Books, 1974) p. 246.
36. Anna Chennault, *Chennault and the Flying Tigers* (New York: Vintage Books, 1974) p. 246.
37. Joint US Intelligence Committee's report 'Chinese Capabilities', 1 July 1942, and 'The Political Effect of Present Japanese Operations in China', 4 August 1944, both in Box 563, RG 218, NARA.

# Part IV
# International Relations during the War

# 9 The German–Japanese Alliance in the Second World War[*]

## Bernd Martin

The Pacific War converted the German war in Europe and North Africa and the Japanese localised conflict in China into worldwide conflagration.[1] The conclusion of the Tripartite Pact of 26 September 1940 led the Americans to believe that global war had now become inevitable.[2]

Neither the Reich's revisionism, officially contained within Europe, nor Japan's aggressive pursuit of a new order in East Asia would necessarily have led to global war. Nevertheless, the political strategies of both Germany and Japan in the 1930s to create their own self-sufficient spheres of influence threatened the security of the victorious powers of the First World War. In restructuring their societies on authoritarian patterns by recourse to nationalist ideologies, both Germany and Japan sought to become world powers, by force, if necessary.[3]

Throughout the inter-war years the doctrinal communism of an externally and internally enfeebled Soviet Union was far less of a challenge to the liberal-capitalist Western democracies and their much postulated individual freedoms than the united front of a transnational fascist system in which the individual was superseded by communal interests and the omnipotent state regulated all public and economic matters. When, therefore, the Western countries united against fascist provocations they acted essentially on socio-political principles, as well as, naturally, for power and economic interests; conversely, internal-political norms and deliberations of power were fundamental to the joining of forces of Germany, Japan and Italy.

The former socio-imperialism of the Western colonial powers (the United States included) was being restated in a new, more radical form in the revisionist states which still felt dissatisfied with the outcome of the last world-wide conflict. Of these, fascist Italy – economically backward, a 'late-comer' if compared to Britain and the United States – was the first to attempt to realise a premodernistic state-concept by applying rigid repressive methods internally and adopting an aggressive stance externally. Germany and Japan, socially and economically in near collapse after the Great Depression, followed suit. It is therefore far more likely that the German–Japanese understanding in the Second World War was the result of internal political parallels and not of international diplomatic movements. In Japan, an affinity with Germany had been consciously sought since Meiji times, culminating in the widely promulgated fascist 'kindred spirit', which came to an abrupt end in 1945.[4]

## FROM POLAND TO PEARL HARBOR

At the announcement of Hitler's deal with Stalin in August 1939, the Hiranuma cabinet resigned and recalled Japan's ambassador, General Oshima, from Berlin. Oshima was one of the most prominent exponents of a Japanese–German alliance. German–Japanese relations were at zero point.[5] In 1939, the first requirement for a change of status of this nature would have been the termination of the Chinese war. But withdrawal from China, even a *modus vivendi* worked out with the Western powers in the China question, on which Britain was ready to make extensive concessions, would at once have revived the troublesome, army-borne protest movement of the 'agrarian socialism from below' and would have unsettled the entire Japanese socio-political order. The continuation of the old order, and of the privileges of a small but powerful élite, was inextricably linked with its fortunes in the Chinese war. Once committed to the course of creating a 'new order' in the Far East and of occupying the positions vacated by the Western powers, there was no option open for the Tokyo leaders but to go on. Only the successful conclusion of the war would preserve the Imperial system and its supporting state ideology (*Kokutai*)[6]; in much the same way as the national-socialist and the Italian fascist system could only survive if the ideological war was won. The inability to compromise, to make an arrangement with the opponent or to achieve a timely end of hostilities, the failure to recognise an inevitable capitulation, were characteristics of the three fascist countries, which bound them much more closely than any pact agreements.

Apart from resigning, the Japanese leadership's only option was to make a renewed approach to Germany. The military success of the Germans in Poland had won admiration in the Japanese army command, and naval and industrial circles, who favoured a settlement with the Western powers, were beginning to wonder how strong the established European colonial powers really were. Moreover, after the conclusion of the armistice with Russia strained Japanese–Soviet relations had, thanks to German intervention, considerably eased, so that the establishment of a German–Japanese front became more acceptable both in Tokyo and in Berlin. Foreign Minister Ribbentrop, whose world-political design[7] of an Eurasian landbloc was primarily intended to check world-wide British domination, did, in any event, agree with the notions held in radical Japanese circles by those who were quite willing to pay for southern expansion at the price of a war with Britain and the Netherlands. Germany's policies and war strategies were increasingly involving Japan in the conflict with the Western powers.

The capitulation of the Dutch army and the confidently expected success of the German campaign in France offered German foreign politics a good opportunity to encourage Japan to strike into South-East Asia and enter the war against Britain. Germany's waiver of claims on the Dutch East Indies (20 May 1940)[8] was in fact a blank cheque to Japan to proceed with the conquest of South-East Asia. Ribbentrop had also yielded to the Japanese demand for the strict protection of its own future empire against 'white power' encroachments. The Japanese temptation to step into the old colonial powers' legacy under cover of the European war proved irresistible, the more so as it was with the explicit consent of Germany, the victor power. After the French defeat, Japanese troops moved into the northern part of Indo-China – ostensibly to cut off the arms supplies to Chiang Kai-shek, strategically to push ahead with the southern expansion.[9] However, America could not be deceived and, with its first embargo measures, signalled its intention to take a firm stance against Japanese expansion. The contours of the future military fronts in the Far East were becoming visible.

Meanwhile in Japan the army was urging the political reorganisation of the country in accordance with the pattern set by the German National Socialist victors, as well as the conclusion of a military alliance with Germany in order to secure the future Japanese sphere of power. When Prince Konoye returned as Prime Minister on 22 July 1940, the external and internal political change was finally set in motion.[10] The government programme – announced in terms of a 'Greater East Asia Co-Prosperity Sphere' – restressed Imperial Japan's demands for the creation of a greater Asian political and economic region, for whose welfare it required the Reich's protection. On Japanese premises only the help of the German Reich could restrain the Americans from a military engagement in South-East Asia, and eject the British from their colonial positions.

The Japanese proposals for a new approach were rejected in Berlin as sheer opportunism as long as the German leadership saw a chance for a political agreement with Britain.[11] After the end of the campaign in France, Hitler sought an arrangement with the Aryan brother-nation with a view to future global co-domination: the rule of the 'white man' would be consolidated in the Far East, and the United States confined to their own American double-continent. Following the unequivocal British rejection of any such deal, and the unfavourable course (for the Germans) of the Battle of Britain, Hitler, supported by naval, diplomatic and overseas trading circles, ultimately decided to settle for the Japanese alternative. A special envoy hastened to Tokyo, and the treaty was drawn up, principally to keep the USA out of the war and mutually to recognise each others' prospective spheres of power. In the treaty settlements Japan had to reveal for the first time the geographical extent of its future empire: it embraced Australia and India in the south and the eastern most Soviet provinces in the north-east. With these boundaries formally recognised by the German side, the Japanese dream of global power seemed to lie within its grasp. However, it was not possible for the Germans to reach agreement with the Japanese leadership on a joint military conduct of the war. In secret supplementary clauses each partner had reserved the option for single-handed operations.[12] The loudly promulgated Military Alliance turned out to be little more than a worthless 'defence agreement with loopholes'.

The United States was not intimidated; it continued to support China demonstratively and it tightened up the trade embargos *vis-à-vis* Japan.[13] President

Roosevelt gladly used the Tripartite Pact for indicting the three 'have-nots' for world conspiracy, and for mobilising his largely isolationist American public for the impending war. The Japanese and German foreign ministers' attempt to bring the Soviet Union into the pact had foundered because of exaggerated Soviet demands.[14] The Soviet Union wanted to be treated as an equal power and it declined to expand to the south merely at the bidding of its two neighbouring partners. Foreign Minister Molotov's remarks to that effect during his Berlin visit in November 1940 only served to harden Hitler's anti-Bolshevist views and his secret intention to attack the Soviet Union.[15] The Tripartite Pact therefore accelerated the drift towards a global war. Further, a German declaration of war upon Russia would interrupt the lines of communication and hinder the contractually agreed liaison, so, in turn, leading to uncoordinated, and ultimately incompatible military lines of offensive.

Whilst the German forces were preparing for the planned war of extermination in Russia, Japan's Foreign Minister Matsuoka signed a Treaty of Neutrality in Moscow (13 April 1941) as a foreign political deal to safeguard the country's northern flank during the planned southern operations. Following the German attack, only Foreign Minister Ribbentrop and his Japanese colleague argued strictly in the spirit of the Continental Eurasian Axis when they demanded Japan's immediate intervention so as to uphold the continental connection, even across a defeated Russia.[16] But neither end of the military axis would take diplomatic advice: Hitler and his over-confident generals declined 'yellow' assistance; in Japan the political and military leaders chose to ignore their diplomats altogether and, in voting for the immediate resumption of the southern offensive, initiated the occupation of South Indo-China. The Imperial Conference[17] suspended for the time being any decision about Japan's entry into the Russian war and this cautious attitude seemed justified when the German offensive was held up for almost a month outside Smolensk.

Divided, each facing a different enemy, Germany and Japan were moving diagonally away from each other both geographically and ideologically long before the latter's entry into the war with the West. The United States reacted to the new Japanese offensive in South-East Asia by enacting a total trade embargo (26 July 1941) and by freezing Japanese assets. Since more than 40 per cent of Japanese overseas trading related to the US, and since Japan – poor in natural resources – was for the production of war materials almost entirely dependent on American supplies of oil and scrap-metals, the total trade embargo effectively strangled Japanese industrial and armament output. The Imperial naval command could easily foresee when lack of fuel would dock its ships. From the end of July 1941 the decisions about war and peace in the Pacific were made in the United States.[18]

As early as September 1941 the Konoye cabinet passed a conditional war-resolution[19] but had to resign in the face of the declining hope of a political agreement. The succeeding cabinet, headed by Prime Minister General Tōjō made a last attempt at mediating between the warring factions, but resolved at the same time that military measures would be initiated if agreement failed. This brought the recently much-abused German partner back into the field.[20] Berlin and Rome had to be consulted to achieve if possible a simultaneous entry into the war against the US and an agreement with both partners that no separate peace treaties would be sought. Tokyo thought to arrange a negotiated peace in the Russian war[21] so that the communication lines between the two theatres of war could be restored.

Ribbentrop was evasive but not discouraging when first approached on this subject by the Japanese. The German leaders were well aware that the Russian 'Blitzkrieg' had failed, and even Hitler himself seems to have expressed doubt in private conversation, about the outcome of the Russian war. Alternative strategies – like that of a German–Japanese maritime pincer-operation against British Near East positions – were again becoming important. Besides, Germany was hopeful that war in the Pacific might shift the entire American war potential there and away from Britain. And a renewal of the Russian campaign would also have a better chance if the US was in the war but far from Europe. Authorised by Hitler, Ribbentrop therefore replied to the written enquiry from Japan that the German Reich also was prepared to declare war upon the United States. About 60 hours before hostilities started, and without prior knowledge of Japanese war strategies or war aims, Germany and Italy had transmitted to the Japanese a written promise that they would join the war.[22] Although the German pledge usefully reinforced Japan's northern flank while its fleet had set course for Hawaii, it had no bearing on Japan's decision to go to war. No joint military strategies or even strategical master plans existed.

## WORLD WAR AND COMBINED WARFARE: INCOMPATIBLE MILITARY AND POLITICAL AIMS

The Japanese global strategy was not produced until 20 October 1941 and proved to be no blueprint for global domination.[23] Hastily drawn up, the strategic plan incorporated defensive elements: military opposition to America's overwhelming political and economic force; shock attacks against the fleets of hostile nations; elimination of American, British and Dutch military bases; occupation, as security, of certain territories; defensive measures against repossession of their holdings, by former colonial powers and whose boundaries were to determine the, yet unspecified, demarcation line of the area under occupation; enforced American recognition, by a peace settlement, of the East Asian Commonwealth Sphere. The planners excluded possible American counter-offensives. Britain was – in accordance with the German view – already defeated and its empire on the point of collapse.[24] Logistical agreement with Germany was therefore superfluous. The hostilities simultaneously started at various and widely distant fronts from the Pacific island of Guam to British Malaya, and the exhilarating initial victories were demonstrative of such overwhelming Japanese strength that outside help could be dispensed with. Within a few weeks Phase I of the plan – the conquest of American positions and the reversal of the British forces – had been achieved. In a second phase the British key fortress of Singapore was to fall and the Dutch East Indies and British Burma would be occupied.[25]

Preoccupied with their own problems at the Russian front, the triumph in the Far East suited the German leaders, who agreed to meet Japan's wishes although these negated the concept of combined warfare.[26] Hitler's determination not to invite Japan into his Russian war was unchanged, despite the first ominous setbacks to his Russian campaign and despite the representations of his foreign minister. Also, the army command was unwilling to fight the Russian war with the help of a country that was totally outside its own continental orbit. Only the navy devoted some thought to integrated strategies and revived its old alternative strategy – a concentration of forces against British positions in Suez and the Near East – but, being the weakest and least influential arm of the three services the navy remained unheard. Torn between admiration and envy of Japan's successes the German leaders themselves were little inclined to effect military agreements with the Japanese.

Both the actual military situation and the ideological power concepts – to create a Great Germanic Empire in Europe and a Greater East Asia Co–Prosperity Sphere – suited the purposes of both powers, more especially the Japanese, to achieve a contractual definition of each sphere of dominance. Within a week of the successful raid on Pearl Harbor General Oshima (who had returned as ambassador to Berlin) had submitted a draft agreement on firmer military cooperation, which in reality amounted to division rather than cooperation. On Japanese notions the dividing line between the two zones of operation (or zones of influence) should coincide with longitude 70° East, at approximately Karachi/the Indus estuary. This was rejected by the German Foreign Office and by the German navy. Division at this geographical point allocated India to the Japanese and precluded naval operations in that area. But clear separation met the wishes of Hitler, who was then deeply involved in his war on the eastern front. The treaty was consequently signed in Berlin on 18 January 1942.[27] The negotiated boundaries were soon to prove an unsurmountable obstacle to coordinated political decisions: on the liberation of India[28] or on naval strategies in those waters. Even the crossing of this boundary line by supply cruisers or blockade runners required tedious prior consultation. Japan, Germany and Italy had set out to give the world a new order. They had loudly publicised their claim and had confirmed it in secretly negotiated pacts. But when it came to the point, the three 'rising young nations' had neither the will nor the strength to redesign the existing world order.

The first half of 1942 was perhaps best suited for combined military operations in the form of either a joint campaign against the Soviet Union or, alternatively, a naval pincer-operation against British Middle East and Indian positions, recently reinforced with American troops. Both operations together would have overstrained even their combined resources but a concerted effort in the first half-year at either one or the other front might well have succeeded. On strategical deployments of this kind, however, the opinions of the respective upper echelons of Germany habitually clashed and *Führer*-decisions had to paper over the differences. In the absence of an all-powerful dictator, the discord among Japanese leaders was apt to result in strategical half-measures and empty compromise. Quite unlike their adversaries – this chance alliance of Western capitalism and Eastern communism – the 'fascist' powers were unable to compromise internally or cooperate externally. The 'prerogative of the strongest', contained in the National-Socialist and Italian fascist ideologies, as also in the missionary fervour of the Yamato race (*Kokutai*), produced in all three nations egoistic, compartmentalised thinking and foreign-political 'sacro egoismo' guidelines. Inability to compromise internally and to cooperate on a rational basis became the hallmarks of all three 'fascist' states.

The issue of a united front against the Soviet Union is a case in point:[29] in Berlin the foreign ministry untiringly propagated Japan's entry into war against Russia to Japanese diplomats and military attachés. No unreasonable course of actions for Ribbentrop to take, in view of the critical war situation, but shared by nobody else. Hitler himself continued to dislike the idea of the 'yellows' fighting in his own Germanic war of destiny in the east. In fact, he even warned Japan not to dissipate its strength. Hitler's growing detachment from his Japanese partner shows in the infrequency of his contacts with Japanese representatives: the *Führer* saw the Japanese ambassador perhaps twice on formal occasions after the Japanese declaration of war and then not again for a whole year. However, on 21 January 1943, with the Stalingrad disaster at near-culmination point, Hitler again summoned the Japanese ambassador to him to convey the urgent request that Japan should finally enter the war against the Soviet Union,[30] to which Tokyo replied belatedly in March and predictably in the negative.

In view of the disparity within the German leadership – Hitler's attitude was fully shared by the army supreme command and supported by the navy, eager to introduce its own alternative strategic plans – Tokyo did not feel particularly obliged to launch an attack against the Soviet east provinces.

To the Imperial navy, bent upon its southward strategy, the British and American navies remained the major adversaries. Military alliance against Russia was therefore incompatible with the Japanese primary war aim of driving the Western powers out of East Asia. Since the German war of attrition in Russia was diverting German resources from the war with the Anglo-American powers, the naval command had consistently urged its cessation. For the sophisticated technology of the Japanese carrier fleet the free transfer of war materials and technology with the highly developed armament industry of the Reich was of vital importance in order to prevail against the equally highly technologically sophisticated American forces. And in the wake of the defeat in the Midway aircraft carrier battle in June 1942, an American counter-offensive and hence an extended war loomed larger.

Japan's maritime *Blitzkrieg* concept had failed after seven months of victorious advance, and global defensive politics against the Americans regained significance. The Japanese navy – supported by the Foreign Ministry and, after autumn 1942, by the army – consequently became the driving force behind a German–Soviet peace settlement.[31] The entire Japanese leadership made this the main element of its foreign policy for the remaining three years of the war. In numerous official and unofficial initiatives Japan attempted in Berlin and Moscow to bring the combatants to the conference table, to re-establish the Eurasian bloc and at least obtain a balance of power with Britain and the United States in this battle of the continents. But all Japanese efforts remained disregarded; moreover, since Moscow regularly informed the Western powers of each new initiative, the coalition between the USA and Soviet Russia was strengthened rather than weakened. On the German side, Hitler clung dogmatically to his decisive racist war in the east and refused even to discuss a negotiated peace in Russia. Even Russia's readiness for talks, and several feelers in this direction in Stockholm,[32] were diverted on Hitler's instructions, whilst Ribbentrop, and later Goebbels and Himmler, saw ending the war in the east as the only chance of rescuing the Reich and National Socialism. The question of the Soviet Union was to be decisive for Germany's and Japan's defeat, the differing, ideologically founded strategies of the Tripartite Pact powers towards the Soviet Union being primarily responsible for the collapse of the German–Japanese alliance.

The failure to cooperate across the Indian Ocean[33] was, in the face of this, of secondary importance. Ten days after the start of war in the Pacific – regarded with envy by the German navy – high-ranking Japanese naval officers met with Commander-in-Chief Admiral Raeder to discuss mutual plans for the first time. Important naval officers in Tokyo also were positively inclined towards a connection of both powers in the Indian Ocean. Plans, studies and reports were made in Berlin and Tokyo. When the British stronghold of Singapore capitulated in February 1942, and it was apparent that Japan would succeed in occupying Burma and the Dutch Indies, the question in Tokyo concerned further expansive strikes. The naval staff officers had three main alternatives to choose from: an offensive in the Indian Ocean, towards Australia, or towards the American Midway Islands. As the Germans would not commit themselves to an attack by Rommel's Afrikakorps on Suez, the most promising alternative was only partially pursued.

At the beginning of April a Japanese taskforce arrived in the Indian Ocean. The presence of heavily armed Japanese units opposite Colombo, Ceylon, and the ensuing bombardment on 5 April 1942 caused panic reactions among the Western powers. The British Eastern Fleet relinquished the ocean area and sought protection from the superior might of the Japanese fleet in harbours in East

Africa. The Indian Ocean, even India itself as the jewel of the British Crown, lay open to the tripartite states. However, the Japanese force turned back as its ships were needed for scattered attacks against Australia and Midway. When two months later the Germans, after the fall of Tobruk on 20 June 1942, opened their offensive against Suez, the Japanese fleet had suffered defeats at Port Moresby (New Guinea) and Midway and was in no position to undertake any extensive naval operations. The attempts at combined maritime warfare foundered in Germany primarily through Hitler's obstinacy and the absolute priority given to the land war against Russia. On the Japanese side, carelessness and the lack of a strategic concept, leading to a wastage of potential and then to the first naval defeats of the Imperial Navy, were responsible for the failure of the Singapore-Suez connection.

Separation of the respective zones of warfare and influence in the Indian ocean by 70° longitude was a further, more strongly political, hindrance to German–Japanese cooperation. The German navy and foreign office kept jealous watch against any disregard of the demarcation line by the Japanese fleet. When the Japanese wanted to launch an offensive against Madagascar,[34] which lay in the sphere claimed by Germany, it was stifled in the planning phase by massive German objections. Also, in the question of the future role of India, the demarcation agreement proved to be a hindrance to cooperation.

German foreign and military policy however maintained strong interest in the Indian subcontinent,[35] despite its allocation to the Japanese. One of the most prominent Indian politicians, the leader of the radical wing of the Indian independence movement, Subhas Chandra Bose, was in German custody; with his help it was possible to found an Indian exile organisation and Indian armed units. A declaration of freedom prepared by the Germans was wrecked by the distrust of the Japanese. When, however, somewhat later the Japanese wanted to garnish their successful naval offensives in the Indian Ocean with a political declaration on future freedom for India, the German side found such action premature, and refused. In August 1942 the worst internal rioting in India's colonial history broke out, in which Congress demanded that Britain relinquish the country. But the Japanese were no longer capable of encouraging the disturbances by spectacular military actions. Germany also, whose troops at this time were held north of the Caucasus, was incapable of influencing the internal situation in India. The possible dislodgement of India from the Britain empire through concentrated combined operations by the tripartite states failed equally from their own egoistic power interests.

## TRADE RELATIONS AND TECHNOLOGICAL TRANSFER

The exchange of industrial goods and raw materials between the German Reich and the Japanese Empire was regulated by a 'Commercial and Shipping Treaty' dating back to 1927.[36] All attempts to renew this agreement according to the new political situation, and changing demands of industry in the 1930s, failed even while communication lines – the Trans-Siberian railway and merchant shipping – were yet undisturbed by war activities. It was not before January 1943 when surface transportation even by blockade runners had almost ended that a new 'Treaty on Economic Cooperation' was signed, of course, to no effect. Like all the political agreements, the Anti-Comintern pact of 1936, the Tripartite pact of 1940 and the No-Separate-Peace agreement of 11 December 1941, were mainly designed to bluff the adversaries of the Fascist New World Order, all commercial arrangements and technical contracts aimed at similar propaganda effects. Lacking real substance, these treaties were supposed to cover up weakness and shortcomings on both sides. Mistrust, envy and even perfidy, together with an outspoken racial feeling of superiority were characteristic of German–Japanese trade relations, especially for the period of combined warfare. The greediness of the have-nots and their inability to come to terms, or even to communicate in a frank way, were best revealed in their commercial talks during the war.

As both countries lacked natural resources for their industry, highly developed in Germany, less so in Japan, they could hardly be regarded as complementary trading partners. Since the nineteenth century German industry had been looking to China as Germany's future market for exporting commodities in exchange for the import of raw materials, for example special ores, and foodstuffs such as soya beans. While German–Chinese barter trade boomed on the eve of the war in 1937, with Germany ranking second in China's over-all foreign trade,[37] commercial relations between the newly allied nations of Hitler's Germany and Imperial Japan made up about 0.6 per cent of all German imports, while, on the other hand, the share of German goods exported to Japan was 1.8 per cent of Germany's total export volume.[38] German merchants complained continually about Japanese bureaucratic restrictions and trade limitations. 'Receiving a lot of friendship, but very few import licences'[39] was quite a common saying among the German community in Japan.

The situation did not change for the better, as German politicians had hoped, when the Reich gave up its dominant trade position in China, acknowledging the special necessities of Japanese warfare on the Asian mainland. Even German diplomatic recognition of Japan's puppet-state of Manchuria [Manchukuo] in March 1938[40] with the intention of improving trade relations with this agrarian-surplus region brought nothing. The New Order of East Asia was to be dominated politically and economically by Japan. Tokyo planned to become the hub of a closed economic sphere[41] where no white nation, not even the befriended Germans, would be granted special privileges. This stubborn Japanese attitude, to expel German trade from all Japanese controlled or occupied areas of the 'Greater East Asia Co-Prosperity Sphere', as well as Japan's constant refusal to compensate German firms for their losses, prevailed until September 1943.[42] Then, eventually, Japan, with her industry almost wrecked, invited Germany, who was suffering severe military setbacks on all fronts, to participate in the reconstruction of East Asia, which by then had developed into a 'Greater East Asia Robbery Sphere'.

Despite the low volume of bilateral trade some significant technical cooperation did exist between the two countries. Since Germany's industry during and after the First World War was far more advanced than Japan's, which basically remained an agrarian country, this exchange soon turned into a unilateral technical transfer from Germany to Japan. Although Japanese industry had been modernised after English and American patterns during the Meiji period (1868–1912),[43] the Empire was forced from 1930 onward, due to rising tensions with the Western powers, to rely on Germany as a model regarding technical and industrial developments.

The high standard of German armaments had attracted Japanese army and navy groups as early as during the Great War. Sharing in the Allied victory over Germany, Japan had requested and was granted German reparations in the form of captured weapons and naval units. Seven German submarines, several different types of aircraft, and one complete airship, as well as sets of motors and samples of special equipment, were delivered free of charge to the Japanese. In most cases the equipment, for example the planes and the submarines, were dismantled for the purpose of studying their construction and put together again with some improvements. The Japanese Navy even managed to acquire the newest construction plans for submarines no longer to be built in German shipyards, and engaged five German civilian experts and one former German submarine commander for about six years at the naval station in Kobe. There, the first Japanese submarine-cruisers (I-1 to I-4) were eventually launched from the Kawasaki shipyards.[44]

German aviation greatly influenced the development of Japanese planes during the inter-war period. As under the Treaty of Versailles the construction of fighter-planes and bombers was forbidden to Germany, German aircraft pioneers welcomed the Japanese aircraft engineers and shared their knowledge with the curious visitors from the Far East. All prominent German aircraft firms, like Messerschmitt, Junkers, Heinkel and Dornier, provided technical help to the Japanese. Dornier and Kawasaki even went as far as to conclude a partnership treaty for 10 years which allowed the Japanese to construct and build German planes under licence. German engineers and technicians helped with the construction of the first Japanese all-metal plane built with duralumin.[45]

After the abrogation of the Versailles Treaty by the National-Socialist Government the new and highly advanced German air force attracted the Japanese the most. An order for more than 70 Heinkel 111 bombers had finally to be cancelled as the German authorities refused the required export permit in order to give priority to German rearmament. Japanese proposals for a joint construction plant in Japan for the production of a revised model of the German Me-109 fighter plane were declined for the same reason. But in both cases plans and blueprints reached construction bureaus in Japan, often with the help of industrial espionage, and greatly influenced the development of the respective Japanese models. From 1936 onward, Junkers sold their models to Japan and as late as 1941 managed to have four planes (Ju-86) transported via the Trans-Siberian railroad to Germany's ally in the Far East. Japanese aircraft engineers were trained in Junkers' plants. Aircraft engines with fuel injection like the famous Daimler Benz motors were sold to Japan (altogether 601 units) and later built under licence by the firms of Aichi and Kawasaki.[46]

Furthermore, German expertise helped the Japanese develop lightweight alloys for the fabrication of tin plate as did German know-how with the introduction of the Thomas process in steel production.[47] Collaboration and technological transfer could also be found in the field of electronics, radio transmitters, wireless sets, and valves before the outbreak of the war.[48] There is no question that Germany helped Japanese rearmament. But the German share is difficult to assess, since the Western democracies, until the abrogation of the American–Japanese Commercial Treaty by Washington in July 1939, did the same. Last but not least some Italian technological help in aircraft production should be mentioned and evaluated as well.

Most prominent as middleman between the Japanese military, especially the Imperial Navy, and German firms was a businessman and arms-broker from Freiburg, Dr Friedrich-Wilhelm Hack.[49] His conduct as a businessman was typical of the contacts and semi-legal contracts between the Germans and the Japanese during the pre-war period. His political influence in shaping the military alliance between the two outcast nations has been almost forgotten. Serving as an adviser to the South Manchurian Railway before the outbreak of the First World War, Hack acquired a knowledge of spoken Japanese. During the war the young businessman served as an interpreter with the besieged German garrison at Tsingtau, where he was taken prisoner by the Japanese. During his five-year internment Hack improved his language skills, and used them for contacts with Japanese officers and business people. When released, Hack was made chief of the first Japanese trade delegation to visit Germany after the Great War. Together with Albert Schinzinger, formerly Krupp's representative in Japan and afterwards His Majesty's Consul General in Berlin, Hack founded an export-firm, Schinzinger und Hack, dealing with the legal and illegal export of arms and technical devices. Hack specialised in military aviation and brought about most of the aforementioned contacts between the German aircraft industry and its Japanese counterparts.[50] It was he, a business go-between and a founding member of the German–Japanese Society in Berlin, who elaborated together with his Japanese acquaintances the idea of a closer alliance between the Empire and the re-emerging German Reich. Eventually in 1935 Hack introduced high-ranking Japanese military leaders, including Admiral Yamamoto and Military Attaché General Oshima, to Ribbentrop, then Hitler's personal adviser in foreign affairs. In return for this mediation Hack was entrusted with the talks on an anti-Soviet military alliance which he successfully concluded with his Japanese counterparts as early as November 1935. Disappointed with Hitler's politics he got into trouble with the Nazi regime, was arrested, set free owing to diplomatic pressure by the Japanese Embassy and finally left Germany for Switzerland. There he again served as a middleman between the American Office of Strategic Services (Allen Dulles) and the Japanese during the entire war and in the end helped to mediate Japan's surrender in 1945.

But in 1939, with the conclusion of the Hitler–Stalin Pact and the outbreak of war in Europe, political and economic relations between Japan and Germany almost came to an end. The talks for a new commercial treaty, which had continued since the beginning of 1939, were suspended by the Japanese Government because of 'undesirable political developments in Europe'. Shipment of urgently needed raw materials, like rubber, tin and quinine from Japanese ports to Vladivostok for rail-transport to Germany was stopped by the Japanese authorities. Hampering German trade and helping British commerce became the guideline of Japan's economic foreign policy at that time.[51] This attitude did not change much even after the fall of France. Despite improving political relations and the signing of the formal military alliance, the Tripartite Pact, in September 1940, Japan did not fulfil her obligations with respect to economic aid. Allotments of rubber, granted by the Vichy government to the German side, could not be shipped from Indo-China because of Japan's refusal of assistance.

Numerous complaints by German firms, diplomats and military men from Tokyo reached the Foreign Office in Berlin, which, of course, had to react to the unfriendly and egoistic Japanese behaviour. When Japanese delegations from the Imperial Army and Navy visited Germany at the beginning of 1941, an official warning was issued on 11 February 1941: 'All Japanese wishes which come close to industrial espionage or look like technological transfer should be declined at once'.[52] But despite this policy of retaliation, the Japanese naval mission arriving by special ship in Bilbao (Spain) managed to buy or get hold of many samples of weaponry, especially electronic devices.[53] The shipment in the *Asaka Maru*, which safely arrived at her Japanese home port, was the last transfer of technological hardware from Germany to Japan before land communication was interrupted by the German attack on Soviet Russia.

However, with the arrival of a German trade delegation (Wohlthat mission) in Tokyo in March 1941 and Matsuoka's visit to Berlin the following month, German imports from East Asia improved. Transit on the Trans-Siberian railroad[54] reached its peak during the last two months before the war started. Special trains transported huge quantities of rubber from Vladivostok to the German–Soviet border station at Brest-Litovsk. There, because of different railway gauges, the shipment had to be transferred to German freight-cars. The amount of rubber transported over the land route was sufficient for tyre-production in the following years. With the interruption of this route German–Japanese trade came virtually to an end before the blockade-runners started in the darkness of the long winter nights. However, only 11 ships out of 15 starting from Japan reached French ports on the Atlantic, and sailing in the other direction only five ships managed to reach Japanese home waters in the winter of 1941–2.[55]

During the summer of 1942 when sea transportation had to be suspended again, expectations about future trade were running high in Tokyo as well as in Berlin. With victory apparently close at hand the Japanese diplomats in Berlin proposed a kind of barter trade on a large scale.[56] Ambassador Oshima handed in a list requesting German credit of over one million yen in order to buy machine tools and samples of technically advanced German weaponry. The Japanese also showed interest in hydrogenation in order to produce synthetic oil, although the oil-fields of the Dutch East Indies lay open for exploitation by them.[57] Therefore, the Japanese promise to provide Germany with all the raw materials needed for armament and civilian production did not sound very convincing. Japan obviously lacked the ships needed to transport the riches of the South to the Japanese homeland. This shortage in shipping facilities was revealed to the Germans when the Japanese asked for more than a million tons of steel and half a million tons of shipping at the end of August 1942.[58] At that time hopes of defeating the British in the Near East and establishing a new communication line via the Suez Canal ran high, but actually no traffic between the two spheres existed.

Talks about a new trade agreement were taken up simultaneously in Tokyo and Berlin. Numerous proposals which appeared unrealistic, were made, and many drafts were outlined, but their fundamental differences could not be overcome. Gaining victory after victory in South-East Asia, the Japanese flatly refused to share their booty with their German ally. Tokyo insisted on monopolising the entire trade of the region. Therefore, German firms were neither to be compensated for their losses nor were they to enjoy special status under Japanese rule. German direct trade with the former colonies of the Western powers was to be eliminated. Once and for all, the white man's rule was to come to an end. Another issue the protection of German designs and licences for production in Japan, could not be solved either. Claiming an inferior technical status as compared with Germany, Japan wanted these rights free of charge for military as well as for civilian production. Within their community of fate the Japanese felt Germany should demonstrate its generosity and supply Japanese industry with all the patents and blueprints it needed to win the war and establish Japan's leading position in East Asia. It was only on Hitler's direct orders that these obstacles on the way to an agreement were removed. The German *Führer* blamed the British for the loss of a whole continent to the white race and admonished German firms to cooperate with Japan and even to abandon all former special rights in East Asia. Finally, the new trade agreement was signed on 20 January 1943,[59] but it had no practical results. While the new Fascist nations were struggling over their respective spheres of economic interest and the conditions of future trade, the few blockade-runners leaving Europe for East Asia carried less cargo than ballast. German industry did not consent to Hitler's verdict and still refused to send samples and plans to Japan without payment for the licences. As no agreement could be reached the ships went on their last voyage half-empty.[60] With these embarrassing results surface communication by blockade-runners came to an end.

The whole issue of Japanese payment for German rights and patents reached a new dimension when Hitler presented two brand-new German submarines to the Japanese Navy the day after the commercial treaty had been signed.[61] The German Navy together with German firms specialising in submarine construction tried in vain to dissuade Hitler from handling over these samples of Germany's latest technical advancement to the Japanese. It was thought they would be unable to copy these ships for production. The submarine with a German crew arrived safely in Japan, while the second, with a Japanese crew, was lost on her voyage. The Imperial Navy had the submarine dismantled in one of its dockyards where navy experts carefully studied the new German devices – the electronic equipment, the special pumps, the engine and the design of the periscope. Although Japanese industry at that time lacked both the proficiency and the material to build this type of submarine, they wanted to acquire all the patents for military as well as for civilian use. As Hitler wanted to encourage the Japanese Navy to take up submarine warfare against Anglo-American communication lines in the Pacific and the Indian Ocean, he at once consented to Japanese wishes. All patents and devices concerning the submarine should be given as a further gift from the *Führer* to the Japanese. Unanimously German firms criticised Hitler's decision as 'sacrificing the whole technical standard of German industry for nothing'[62] and insisted on the Japanese paying at least for other patents and production under licence.

Now the Japanese tried to tip the scales in their favour by presenting some gifts to the German Navy. The unwanted presents shipped by Japanese submarine-cruisers to French Atlantic ports did not fill German navy personnel with enthusiasm for their Japanese comrades. The German admirality mocked this new method of compensation and drew an unfavourable balance for the Japanese side. The value of the new submarines and licences for special engines and bomb igniters totalled 36 million Reichsmark, the Japanese 'presents' amounting to a mere 90 000 Reichsmark.[63] It was again up to the *Führer* himself to solve this controversial issue which by then had become a burden to bilateral relations. On an explicit order from Hitler a 'Technical Exchange Agreement' was worked out and finally signed on 2 March 1944.[64] The provisions of the new treaty resembled those of the lend-lease agreements between the United States and her dependent allies. All technical devices and German patents should be given on request to Japan without charge. After final victory payment should be settled on the basis of a final balance. But since both countries lost the war no payment was made at all. Under the obligations of this new treaty the German chemical trust IG-Farben was compelled to convey all patents regarding hydrogenation of coal for the purpose of obtaining synthetic oil to Japanese industry free of charge until as late as January 1945.[65]

Technological transfer, therefore, from Germany to Japan peaked in 1944 after the signing of the agreement. Now the Japanese Navy sent transport submarines with rubber to Europe in order to carry home blueprints and samples of the latest German technical devices. A complete radar set (the Würzburg model) reached Japan in 1944 as did new technology for welding metals.[66] The technique for welding a ship's hull together, instead of riveting the steel plates, which was taken over from the Germans, turned out to be of great importance to the Japanese shipbuilding industry after the war. The Japanese were also very much concerned about further development of their fighter planes in order to stop the Americans' advance from one island to the next in the south-west Pacific. The rocket propelled Messerschmitt 163, which could use chemical fuels, and the German turbo-jet fighter, the Messerschmitt 262, were both revised and rebuilt in Japan. At the end of the war 19 prototypes of the Japanese jet-fighter 'Kikka' were ready for combat use.[67]

With the invasion of the Reich by the victorious armies of the anti-Hitler coalition at the beginning of 1945, German and Japanese naval experts together worked out a plan to have Germany's top rocket-technology (V2) and shipbuilding engineers evacuated to Japan by submarine. This 'Action Paper Clip' to benefit the Japanese ally (rather than the American adversary) started in April 1945, when a delegation of 27 experts left the doomed Reich for Japan.[68] However, the submarine had to surrender after the German capitulation and delivered the engineers directly into American custody.

A final assessment of German technical help and technological transfer with regard to Japan's industrial development after the war seems almost impossible. The German influence should neither be exaggerated nor minimised. Japanese industry was fairly well advanced at the outbreak of the Pacific War and further developed on its own under severe pressure from America. While Japan needed 'hardware' from the West during the inter-war period in order to compete with Western standards, the armament industry needed 'software' during the war in order to construct and build the most modern weaponry, for example fighter planes, ships, and tankers for oil transportation from South-East Asia. The greatest advances by Japanese industry were stimulated by the Japanese government and industrialists themselves. Structural reforms, like the establishment of the 'Munitions Ministry' in 1943, a forerunner to the powerful Ministry of International Trade and Industry (MITI)'[69] in the 1950s, had a greater impact on Japan's economic miracle than the technological transfer from Germany during the war. But a final evaluation of this critical topic should be made by Japanese scholars with the help of Japanese source material.

CONCLUSION

Within less than a year of separate fighting, both Germany and Japan were in retreat. Within a further year the Japanese leaders drew political consequences from the collapse of the military alliance and declared the East Asian theatre of war to be fully independent from the European.[70] For both authoritarian systems there remained a separate defeat; in both, the leaders in Berlin and Tokyo were incapable of ending an increasingly forlorn war; and in both, the civilian populations were subjected to great losses and suffering.

Germany and Japan as proponents of new world orders – the one as saviour of the Occident from the communist threat, the other as saviour of the colonised peoples of Asia from the white man's yoke – collapsed in 1945; whereas Italy, seen as the unreliable third power in the pact, had already removed itself in 1943 from the unstable fascist alliance. Mercifully for the populations of these countries and for those of their opponents, a successful, pragmatical cooperation on a totalitarian basis requiring war, destruction and subjugation as means of execution, proved impossible. A combined creed of unscrupulous, arbitrary power politics proved an inadequate basis for united warfare. In almost five years of military alliance, Germany and Japan acted together only once – when both aggressor states were compelled in 1945 to capitulate to their combined adversaries.

However, the world war started by Germany and Japan has not had only negative results for the two countries. On the ruins of the old orders – in Japan the semi-feudal imperial system and in Germany the degenerate authoritarian Prussian state – lay the opportunity for both to build new social and political forms. The complete military defeat and moral discredit of their political systems achieved by force what the two latecomer nations alone from their own efforts could not: integration within the western world.

An epoch of forced socio-political change had already begun in Japan and in Germany during the war, the start of a new social structure which admittedly could only develop afterwards. The war economy had stimulated innovations – in Japan even more than in Germany – which were to come to fruition in the following phase of rebuilding. It later proved favourable also, that, during the war, mobility and improvisation were demanded from the population in general. The breakdown in 1945 was the necessary drastic rupture in both countries, the prerequisite for the start into the modern world of mass democracy. The socio-political deformations, manifest in rigid perseverance in reactionary social systems, the socio-political quarantine in both countries and the chiliastic expectation of an historical standstill in the thousand-year-Reich was first felt by Japan and Germany themselves, with their nationalist totalitarian regimes and internal suppression. The world was drawn into the vortex of the past global war before this catastrophic development was forcibly terminated.

NOTES

\* For monographs on the Berlin–Tokyo axis in the Second World War see Bernd Martin, *Deutschland und Japan im Zweiten Weltkrieg. Vom Angriff auf Pearl Harbour bis zur deutschen Kapitulation* (Göttingen, 1969); Japanese liberal translation by the

Air Force Academy, Japanese Self-Defence Forces (Tokyo, 1969), and Johanna Menzel-Meskill, *Hitler and Japan. The Hollow Alliance* (New York, 1966). There is no Japanese study on the war alliance but only one on the Tripartite Pact by Masaki Miyake, *Nichi-Doku-I sangoku dōmei no kenkyū*. With an English summary (Tokyo, 1975).

1. Peter Herde, *Pearl Harbor. 7 Dezember 1941. Der Ausbruch des Krieges zwischen Japan und den Vereinigten Staaten und die Ausweitung des europäischen Krieges zum Weltkrieg* (Darmstadt, 1980). For a concise study on the origins of the Pacific War see Akira Iriye, *The origins of the Second World War in Asia and the Pacific War* (London, 1989), for Germany's role see Bernd Martin, 'Germany and Pearl Harbor. The German–Japanese Alliance and the Outbreak of the War in the Pacific' in Chihiro Hosoya and Akira Iriye, (eds), *Fifty Years After. The Pacific War Re-examined* (Tokyo and New York, forthcoming).

2. On the Tripartite Pact see Theo Sommer, *Deutschland und Japan zwischen den Mächten. Vom Antikominternpakt zum Dreimächtepakt* (Tübingen, 1962); Chihiro Hosoya 'The Tripartite Pact, 1939–1940' in James W. Morley (ed.), *Deterrent Diplomacy. Japan, Germany and the USSR, 1935–1940* (New York, 1976) pp. 179–258, and Ian Nish, (ed.), *The Tripartite Pact of 1940: Japan, Germany and Italy* (London, 1984).

3. For a comparison of the three 'Fascist' countries see Bernd Martin 'Zur Tauglichkeit eines übergreifenden Faschismusbegriffes. Ein Vergleich zwischen Japan, Italien und Deutschland', *Vierteljahrshefte für Zeitgeschichte* 29, Heft 1 (1981).

4. Bernd Martin 'The German Role in the Modernization of Japan. The Pitfall of Blind Acculturation' *Oriens Extremus* 33, Heft 1 (1980).

5. Bernd Martin 'German–Japanese Relations after the Hitler–Stalin-Pact', in David W. Pike (ed.), *The Opening of the Second World War* (New York and Bern, 1992).

6. For the Japanese political system, and the role of the Tenno see Klaus Antoni, *Der Himmlische Herrscher und sein Staat* (München, 1991).

7. Wolfgang Michalka, *Ribbentrop und die deutsche Weltpolitik 1933–1940* (München, 1980).

8. *Documents on German Foreign Policy* Series D, Vol. XI, Document No. 280 (London, 1949). (Hereafter cited as DGFP).

9. James W. Morley (ed.), *The Fateful Choice, Japan's Advance into South-East Asia, 1939–1941* (New York, 1980).

10. For Matsuoka's and Konoe's policy towards Germany see Gerhard Krebs, *Japans Deutschlandpolitik 1935–1941. Eine Studie zur Vorgeschichte des Pazifischen Krieges* (Hamburg, 1984).

11. On the peace issue see Bernd Martin, *Friedensinitiativen und Machtpolitik im Zweiten Weltkrieg 1939–1942*, 2nd edition (Düsseldorf, 1976).

12. Cf. note 2 above. For the text of the treaty, which was drawn in English, and of the secret clauses, in English too, see Sommer, *Deutschland und Japan* pp. 398ff and 514f.

13. Paul W. Schroeder, *The Axis Alliance and Japanese–American Relations*, 3rd edition (Ithaca, 1963).

14. DGFP, D, XI Document No. 404 (Soviet demands). On Japanese–Soviet relations see Hubertus Lupke, *Japans Rußlandpolitik von 1939–1941* (Frankfurt am Main, 1962) and George A. Lensen, *The Strange Neutrality. Soviet–Japanese Relations during the Second World War* (Tallahassee, Fla., 1972).

15. German classical study on the preparations for the attack on the Soviet Union: Andreas Hillgruber, *Hitlers Strategie. Politik und Kriegführung 1940/41* (Frankfurt am Main, 1965).

16. Gerhard Krebs 'Japan und der deutsch–sowjetische Krieg 1941' in Bernd Wegner, ed., *Zwei Wege nach Moskau. Vom Hitler–Stalin-Pakt zum 'Unternehmen Barbarossa'* (München, 1991) pp. 564, 583; also Bernd Martin, *Japan and Barbarossa* paper, University of Waterloo, Ontario, Center for Soviet Studies, 18 May 1991 (forthcoming).

17. Imperial Conference 2 July 1941. Nobutake Ike (ed), *Japan's Decision for War. Records of the 1941 Policy Conferences* (Stanford, Calif. 1967) pp. 77–90.

18. For the origins of Pearl Harbor see the recent study by Hilary Conroy and Harry Wray (eds), *Pearl Harbor Re-examined. Prologue to the Pacific War* (Honolulu, 1990).

19. Imperial Conference 6 September 1941. See Ike, *Japan's Decision for War* pp. 133–66.

20. Cf. Martin, *'Germany and Pearl Harbor'*.

21. Gerhard Krebs 'Japanische Vermittlungsversuche im deutsch–sowjetischen Krieg 1941–1945', in Josef Kreiner and Regine Mathias, eds., *Deutschland–Japan in der Zwischenkriegszeit* (Bonn, 1990) pp. 239–88.

22. For the German decision to declare war on the United States see Jürgen Rohwer and Ernst Jäckel (eds), *Kriegswende Dezember 1941* (Frankfurt am Main, 1981); for the preceding talks with the Japanese, Bernd Martin, *Deutschland und Japan*, pp. 26–45.

23. Takushiro Hattori, *The Complete History of the Greater East Asia War* (Tokyo, 1953), American translation, unpublished, copy on microfilm). The semi-official account of an insider – Hattori was member of the Japanese General Staff.

24. Kiyoshi Ikeda 'The Road to Singapore: Japan's View of Britain 1922–1941', in T.G. Fraser and Peter Lowe (eds), *Conflict and Amity in East Asia. Essays in Honour of Ian Nish* (London, 1992) pp. 30–46.

25. For the military events see Louis Morton, *The War in the Pacific. Strategy and Command: The First Two Years*, Washington, DC, 1962); a more popular account by E.P. Hoyt, *Japan's War. The Great Pacific Conflict* (London, 1987).

26. On strategic plans for coalition warfare, see Martin, *Deutschland und Japan*, pp. 129–51.

27. Ibid., pp. 46–54. For the Japanese draft and the final text see ibid, pp. 230–4.

28. Ibid., pp. 61–80 and Milan Hauner, *India in Axis Strategy* (Stuttgart, 1981).

29. Martin, *Deutschland und Japan*, pp. 94–121.

30. Ibid., p. 173.

31. Ibid., pp. 110–21, and Krebs, 'Japanische Vermittlungsversuche'.

32. On Soviet–German peace talks in Stockholm see Bernd Martin 'Deutsch–sowjetische Sondierungen über einen separaten Friedensschluss im Zweiten Weltkrieg. Bericht und Dokumentation', in Inge Auerbach et al. (eds), *Felder und Vorfelder russischer Geschichte. Studien zu Ehren von Peter Scheibert* (Freiburg, 1985) pp. 280–309.

33. See Martin, *Deutschland und Japan*, pp. 135ff.

34. Ibid., pp. 81–8.

35. Cf. note 28 above.

36. *Reichsgesetzblatt* 1927, Teil II, pp. 1087–100 (27. November 1927). For an overview see: Erich Pauer 'Die wirtschaftlichen Beziehungen zwischen Japan und Deutschland 1900–1945', in Josef Kreiner (ed.), *Deutschland–Japan. Historische Kontakte* (Bonn, 1984) pp. 161–210.

37. William C. Kirby, *Germany and Republican China* (Stanford, Calif., 1984) and Udo Ratenhof, *Die Chinapolitik des Deutschen Reiches 1871–1945. Wirtschaft-Rüstung-Militär* (Boppard, 1985).

172     *Bernd Martin*

38. Pauer, 'Die wirtschaftlichen Beziehungen', p. 191.
39. Ibid., p. 201 ... daß man zwar 'viel Freundschaft erhalte, aber nur wenige Einfuhrgenehmigungen'.
40. Hitler's announcement in his Reichstag speech of 20 February 1938. For the shift in German Far Eastern policy from China to Japan see John P. Fox, *Germany and the Far Eastern Crisis 1931–1938* (Oxford, 1982).
41. Michael A. Barnhart, *Japan Prepares for Total War. The Search for Economic Security 1919–1941* (Ithaca, 1987).
42. Decision of liaison-conference of 25 September 1943. See Hattori The Complete *History*. III (6) pp. 16f.
43. Olivia Checkland, *Britain's Encounter with Meiji-Japan, 1868–1912* (London, 1989) and Foster R. Dulles, *Yankees and Samurai. America's Role in the Emergence of Modern Japan, 1791–1900* (New York, 1965).
44. For the technological transfer from Germany to Japan from 1850 until present times see the recent collection of essays edited by Erich Pauer, *Technologietransfer Deutschland–Japan. Von 1850 bis zur Gegenwart* (München, 1992). For the forced deliveries after 1918 see Erich Pauer 'Deutsche Ingenieure in Japan, japanische Ingenieure in Deutschland' in Josef Kreiner and Regine Mathias, eds., *Deutschland–Japan*, pp. 289–324.
45. Ibid., p. 299 ff.
46. Hans-Joachim Braun 'Technologietransfer im Flugzeugbau zwischen Deutschland und Japan 1936–1945' in Josef Kreiner and Regine Mathias, *Deutschland–Japan*, pp. 325–40.
47. Pauer, 'Deutsche Ingenieure', pp. 312 ff.
48. Ibid., pp. 306 and 317.
49. Hack was born in 1887 in Freiburg and died in Zürich in 1949. His business transactions are still mysterious. He is better known in Japan than in Germany where only one article – full of mistakes – was written on him: 'Der geheimnisvolle Doktor Hack' in *Frankfurter Allgemeine Zeitung*, 31 August 1965. The account in this text is mainly based on Hack's private papers, which the author obtained from Hack's nephew in 1970. Most of these papers which will be published in 1993, deal with the origins of the Anti-Comintern pact.
50. These contacts are mentioned by John W.M. Chapman, 'Japan and German Naval Policy, 1919–1945', in Kreiner, ed., *Deutschland–Japan*, pp. 235f.
51. Martin, 'German–Japanese Relations after the Hitler–Stalin Pact'.
52. 'Es sind grundsätzlich alle japanischen Wünsche abzulehnen, die einer Industriespionage oder Industrieverschleppung gleichkommen' quoted in Pauer, 'Deutsche Ingenieure in Japan ...'. p. 317.
53. John W.M. Chapman, 'The Have-Nots go to War. The Economic and Technological Basis of the German Alliance with Japan' in Ian Nish, (ed.), *The Tripartite Pact*, pp. 25–73.
54. For the transit via the Soviet Union see: Heinrich Schwendemann, *Die wirtschaftliche Zusammenarbeit zwischen dem Deutschen Reich und der Sowjetunion von 1939 bis 1941 – Alternativve zu Hitlers Ostprogramm?* (Berlin, 1993).
55. Martin, *Deutschland–Japan*, p. 158.
56. Ibid., pp. 161ff.
57. (31 August 1942). Ibid., pp. 166.
58. For the long talks preceding the trade agreement see ibid., pp. 251–5.
59. Ibid., p. 170.
60. Ibid., pp. 207ff. On the whole issue see also the file 'German Submarine Materials', Box 370, in the Library of Congress, Manuscript Division, Washington DC.

61. Note by Wiehl, Head of the Economic Department of the Foreign Office, from 29 April 1943 ('Kostenlose Preisgabe des gesamten technischen Entwicklungsstandes der deutschen Industrie') Martin, *Deutschland–Japan*, p. 210.

62. 'Letter from OKM (German Naval High Command) to Foreign Office from 20 November 1943' in German Submarine Materials, Box 370, (see note 60).

63. Martin, *Deutschland–Japan*, p. 211. For the full text see ibid., p. 331.

64. Ibid., p. 212.

65. Pauer 'Deutsche Ingenieure ...', p. 319.

66. Braun, 'Technologietransfer im Flugzeugbau ...' in Kreiner and Mathias (eds), *Deutschland–Japan*, pp. 337f.

67. Martin, *Deutschland und Japan*, p. 212f.

68. Bernd Martin 'Japans Kriegswirtschaft' in Friedrich Forstmeier und Hans-Erich Volkmann (eds), *Kriegswirtschaft und Rüstung 1939–1945* (Düsseldorf, 1977), pp. 256–86, and on social change in Japan during the last war by the same author, 'Sozialer Wandel in Japan während des *Zweiten Weltkrieges und seine Folgen für die Nachkriegszeit*', in Waclaw Dlugoborski, (ed.), *Zweiter Weltkrieg und sozialer Wandel* (Göttingen, 1981) pp. 364–84.

69. Chalmers Johnson, *MITI and the Japanese Miracle. The Growth of Industrial Policy, 1925–1975* (Stanford, 1982).

70. Bernd Martin 'Die Einschätzung der Lage Deutschlands aus japanischer Sicht: Japans Abkehr vom Bündnis und seine Hinwendung auf Ostasien (1943–1945)', in Manfred Messerschmidt (ed), *Die Zukunft des Reiches. Gegner, Verbündete und Neutrale 1943* (Bonn, 1990) pp. 127–46 (Decision of the liaison–conference of 25 September 1943).

# 10 Britain, the Commonwealth and Pacific Security

## Peter Lowe

In January 1911 the Australian paper, the *Bulletin*, published a cartoon by Norman Lindsay. The caption, 'Sleeping at his Homework', depicted a fair-haired boy asleep at his desk while an oriental militarist of sinister appearance stood at his side, a samurai sword in his left hand and a bottle of ink in his right hand, the ink miraculously flowing from the bottle on to the boy's unfinished homework in the approximate outline of the Commonwealth of Australia. The boy's supposedly sturdy chair was labelled, 'False Security'. Translating the none too subtle meaning, the cartoon connoted the youth as Australia, the venerable chair as the imperial government in London, and the oriental soldier as the fast growing and unrestrained ambition of Japan: the promising, yet somewhat naive Australia would experience bitter disillusionment when imperial assurances collapsed amidst the complacency or stupidity of the imperial authorities[1] This cartoon was published just over thirty years before the outbreak of the Pacific War. This demonstrates the protracted nature of apprehension concerning the rise of Japan felt in the British dominions before 1914. Australia and New Zealand feared Japan, Canada disliked Japan, and South Africa was remote but dubious. On one level Norman Lindsay's cartoon was prophetic but at the time it was published there was no likelihood of Japan tearing up the Anglo-Japanese alliance in order to pursue an expansionist policy in the Pacific.[2] In a longer perspective, however, Lindsay's cartoon was justified: increasing numbers in the southern dominions became uneasy at the trend of British defence policy and believed, in 1940–1, that 'false security' was an extremely accurate definition of the dilemma they faced.

The fundamental problem facing the Commonwealth was that it could not be defended effectively and parts of it possibly could not be defended at all if confronted with a foe of sufficient tenacity. Advocates of empire before 1914, such as Lord Rosebery, Joseph Chamberlain and Lord Milner, sought to discover a solution to imperial cohesion but without success. The combined pressures caused by the losses in the First World War, the brittle nature of European stability, the growth of British commitments in the Middle East, the decline in defence capabilities, severely limited what could be done to defend the Commonwealth. Yet British ministers and officials nurtured the illusion that when the crunch came, British forces would somehow respond. The emotional ties with the dominions, together with the belief that Britain must act like a great power, allowed for no other response. British policy-makers became 'economical with the truth'. The irony was compounded by the fact that even they did not appreciate the extent of the 'economising' until 15 February 1942: the trauma of the surrender of Singapore liquidated continuing delusions.[3] British ministers recognised the pressures pushing the dominions towards greater independence after 1919 and they wished to work harmoniously with their Commonwealth colleagues if possible; despite the exasperation caused by individual members, notably Eire under Eamon de Valera's sinuous direction, and the difficulties arising from the approach of prominent politicians, such as Mackenzie King of Canada and General J.B.M. Hertzog of South Africa, it was argued that the Commonwealth must be held together. If it fragmented, Britain would be left entirely on its own pending an American commitment to intervene: it must be recalled that the Commonwealth stood alone in 1940, after the fall of France, until the United States involved itself indirectly and then directly during 1941.[4] It was necessary, too, to keep in mind the impact of the evolving relationship with the Commonwealth upon India.

As regards the outlook of individual dominions, Canada was obsessed with the importance of working closely with the United States and of maintaining reasonable cohesion between English and French Canada. Mackenzie King was concerned, down to September 1939, with obviating Canadian involvement in binding commitments before absolutely necessary and subsequently with keeping unity in Canada during the European war. King was not particularly interested in the Pacific crisis and felt that only the Americans could deal effectively with Japan.[5] The Union of South Africa was the least concerned but the South African contribution was sometimes more significant because of the great prestige enjoyed by General J.C. Smuts. Smuts sent reflective assessments to Churchill on various occasions: the principal themes comprised avoiding undue appeasement of Japan and not advancing too far ahead of the United States. Smuts attached profound significance to fostering a cordial relationship with the USA since his experience in London during the Great War.[6] New Zealand showed deep loyalty to the 'mother country' and was disinclined to criticise imperial decision-making. However, the visible expansion in Japanese power and the alarm manifested in Australia led New Zealand ministers to convey their anxiety more strongly on occasions.[7] Australia was the most profoundly affected. Australians were influenced by economic, strategic and racial aspects. The 'White Australia' policy must be preserved and a Japanese challenge contained. Justified doubts were entertained as to whether Britain's policy of dispatching a fleet to Singapore, if Japanese actions necessitated it, would prove viable. Relations between Britain and Australia were strained severely between 1939 and 1941 as Australian representatives tried to elicit solid guarantees from their British counterparts with little success. At the same time Australia's own policy towards Japan was ambivalent and in a number of respects mirrored the uncertainties in British policy. Australian governments did not desire war, for Australia would be particularly vulnerable in a situation where neither Britain nor the United States would give convincing promises of support. Robert Menzies personified the old approach of close cooperation with Britain until he became involved in sharp exchanges with Churchill. John Curtin, the leader of the Labour party, who succeeded Menzies and Fadden as prime minister during the latter part of 1941, was more overtly critical and was regarded as a thorn in Britain's side (but a lesser thorn than Dr Evatt was to prove).[8] .

This study focuses upon British policy regarding Pacific security in 1940 and 1941 and then considers the situation during the Pacific conflict: the relationship between Britain and the dominions was tense for constitutional and strategic reasons. British ministers and officials held the characteristic Whitehall view that the dominions should realise that the British knew what was in their best interests and this should be accepted. There was a failure to understand that the dominions now expected prompt, genuine consultation and not a half-hearted version after the event. Churchill fervently believed in the Commonwealth but it was *his* version which prevailed: sadly this bore diminishing resemblance to the reality he dealt with. He deemed war in the Pacific to be remote and became irritated by the expression of contrary views.[9] The outlook of the British chiefs of staff was determined by the wholly inadequate resources available to them. They were endeavouring to cope with grave crises in Europe and the Middle East, as well as the Far East and the Pacific and could not conceivably find the requisite resources.[10] Like their American counterparts, the British defence chiefs wished to postpone conflict with Japan for as long as feasible. Indeed exchanges between the chiefs and the Foreign Office comprised a dialogue of the deaf with the latter protesting at the evasiveness of the defence chiefs while the former bemoaned the lack of realism in the Office. The chiefs urged a negotiated solution to the crisis in Tientsin in 1939, and to the crisis over the Burma Road in 1940, and hoped, during the American–Japanese talks in 1941 that war against Japan could be deferred into 1942.[11] In July 1940 the chiefs produced a new appraisal of Asian and Pacific defence problems, the first reassessment for over three years. For several years doubts had grown in the dominions over the intention in London to send a fleet to Singapore, and these had been fully borne out by the embarrassed statements forthcoming from Neville Chamberlain and Lord Chatfield in June to July 1939.[12] The European crisis was so severe in 1940 as to render it impossible to send a fleet. The chiefs admitted, in effect, that the Commonwealth could not be defended and that short-term requirements meant that a political agreement with Japan should be reached. The Foreign Office reacted very sceptically.[13] The defence chiefs anticipated a pattern of creeping advance, whereby Japanese forces moved into Indo-China or Thailand and subsequently into the Dutch East Indies before proceeding against Singapore. Commonwealth defence viability rendered agreement with the Netherlands government-in-exile upon full cooperation extremely desirable.

Therefore, in 1940–1 the chiefs of staff held that the Commonwealth should be defended through achieving much closer cooperation between Britain, Australia,

New Zealand, the Dutch East Indies, and the United States. This should be realised through more effective direction in Singapore with the holding of defence conferences at which each country should be represented. This was sensible subject to two important qualifications: Britain must guarantee the integrity of the Dutch East Indies and the US must be induced to guarantee support for the British and the Dutch. Both proved impossible to resolve positively until just before the Japanese attacks on Malaya and Pearl Harbor. The geographical location of the East Indies was central to the defence of the Commonwealth; it was inconceivable that Britain should allow Japan to occupy the East Indies for this would nullify the whole basis of British policy. The question of Britain's attitude to cooperation with the East Indies developed during the 1930s and assumed urgency in 1940 with the German invasion of the Netherlands. Churchill's initial reaction when he became prime minister was that the British should promise to defend the East Indies.[14] The first sea lord, Admiral Sir Dudley Pound, was dominated by global commitments and the inability of the Royal Navy to fulfil them. Pound convinced his service colleagues and Churchill that no definitive undertaking could be entered into unless the United States extended a guarantee to Britain. Australia was ambivalent, wishing to sustain the East Indies yet not wishing to precipitate war. Churchill supported the Admiralty's reasoning and repeatedly blocked the attempts of Halifax and Eden to secure a British guarantee.[15] The situation could best be described as tragi-comic. It did considerable damage to relations with the Dutch and handicapped defence coordination.

Attempts were made to strengthen British defence coordination in 1940–1. A series of regional conferences met in Singapore attended by Commonwealth countries concerned, plus the Dutch, with American observers. The first, in October 1940, was chaired by the C-in-C, China station, Vice-Admiral Sir Geoffrey Layton. Hong Kong, Malaya, British Borneo, Burma, and the East Indies or Timor were regarded as the obvious Japanese targets. The Japanese would probably invade Pacific islands and assail trade routes. Australia and New Zealand might be attacked but this was not likely at first. The total inadequacy of British power was emphasised.[16] The fears so intensely felt in Australia and New Zealand were entirely warranted in the light of stark depiction of defence weakness. Indeed it was too stark for the joint planning staff in London. While approving the report, the planning staff censured the undue pessimism it radiated – 'they have in particular tended to over-estimate the minimum air forces necessary for reasonable security'.[17] The planning staff added, giving hostages to fortune in so doing, that 'The Japanese have never fought against a first-class Power in the air and we have no reason to believe that their operations would be any more effective than those of the Italians'.[18]

In January and February 1941 highly important talks took place in Washington between the American chiefs of staff and representatives of the British defence chiefs. The British underlined the value of the Middle East and Far East to the Allies' global strategy.[19] Australia and New Zealand must be protected adequately. The Americans envisaged their Pacific fleet severing Japanese communications and cooperating in the defence of the Philippines. The British emphasised how important an American contribution would be in restoring confidence in the dominions. The Americans resisted British efforts to commit them to a common command.[20] The main disagreement arose from diverging attitudes to Singapore. The British placed the stress upon the Commonwealth:

> Just as the United States strategy has to take account of the integrity of their Western seabords so British strategy must always be influenced by similar factors in the Dominions of Australia and New Zealand, to whom we are bound, not only by the bond of kinship and a common citizenship, but by specific undertakings to defend them. But the retention of a Fleet base in the Far East means far more than that. We are a maritime Commonwealth, whose various Dominions and Colonies are held together by the communications and trade routes across the oceans of the world...[21]

The prestige and morale of the Commonwealth rested upon the defence of Singapore.

The US staff committee emphasised political complexities domestically, which made it difficult to accept binding commitments. In the event of war with Japan Anglo-American strategy would be primarily defensive, concentrating on holding the Malay barrier and applying an economic blockade against Japan. Sir Robert Craigie warned perceptively in February 1941 against the danger of adopting a 'Maginot line mentality' as regards Singapore.[22] The same thought struck the Americans: Singapore had become an obsession for the British: 'Its value as a symbol has become so great that its capture by Japan would be a serious blow. But many severe blows have been taken by these various nations and other severe blows can be absorbed without leading to final disaster.'[23]

Alarm in Australia and New Zealand grew rapidly in 1940–1 and was expressed by two prime ministers, Robert Menzies and Peter Fraser. Menzies travelled to London and stayed for lengthy exchanges, especially regarding the Middle East and Far East/Pacific. Menzies stressed how vulnerable the southern dominions felt in the face of rapid Japanese expansion. Churchill reiterated the promises made in his famous 'kith and kin' telegram of 23 December 1940 that if the dominions were gravely menaced, then British forces would be switched to the Pacific as a priority. The Australian defence chiefs warned of the threat to sea communications and to continued Australian participation in the Middle East.[24] Menzies expressed fundamental criticisms of British strategy in Asia and the Pacific; he pressed for concrete assurances that plans would be devised to accomplish the withdrawal of Australian forces from the Middle East if the situation worsened in the Pacific. Churchill saw the Middle East as essential to world strategy against the Axis powers.[25] Menzies caused annoyance by making a speech in which he advocated endeavouring to meet Japanese grievances so as to obviate war. Esler Dening observed that Menzies should have discovered by now that a dictator could not be brought off: it was best to continue applying diplomatic pressure in the hope that Japan would be deterred from advancing. R.A. Butler commented, with quiet satisfaction, that Menzies would come to realise that the conduct of foreign policy was a more delicate operation than his 'lively intelligence' had appreciated. Butler added sharply and prophetically that Menzies might be torpedoed at home.[26] Menzies left London with no more confidence in the direction of British policy than when he had arrived; Fraser felt similarly but New Zealand was more restrained in its statements.

Further defence discussions and conferences were held in Singapore between February and April 1941. More positive arrangements for coordination between the British, Australians and Dutch were provided for; relations with the Dutch were still hindered by Churchill's refusal to guarantee defence of the East Indies. Local defence personnel from the Commonwealth and the East Indies desired comprehensive coordination and deprecated the tardiness of their political masters in resolving problems, but the local planners underestimated Japan's ability to launch simultaneous attacks against their opponents in the Pacific and South-East Asia; they succumbed in part to their own propaganda regarding the advances supposedly made in strengthening defences.[27] The C-in-C, Far East, Air Chief Marshal Sir Robert Brooke-Popham, was broadly satisfied but felt the dominions could have been more fully represented: the same applied to the US. Brooke-Popham visited Australia but was not impressed with the ability of Australian politicians.[28] The American chiefs of staff held that the Singapore conferences intruded into delicate political areas outside their terms of reference; they felt that undue attention was paid to protecting the sea communications of the Commonwealth.

The Commonwealth was kept largely in ignorance of developments in the Washington talks between the US and Japan. Britain itself knew little, for Cordell Hull, the American secretary of state, insisted on pursuing 'exploratory' discussions before a full stage of negotiations could be reached. Churchill urged Roosevelt to issue a tough warning to Japan against new acts of aggression. When the president was dissuaded by Hull, Churchill issued his own warning, castigating Japanese expansion in China for carrying with it, 'carnage, ruin and corruption'.[29] The principal reservation from the dominions at this point emanated from General Smuts who asked whether the US was ready for war adding that, if not, the Commonwealth would have to bear the brunt of the struggle in its early stages; Smuts deprecated 'language which may touch [the] face of Japan and provoke conflict for which America is perhaps not ready?'[30] In Australia Menzies fell from office, and after the brief interval of the Fadden government, John Curtin became prime minister. The Labour government was far more critical of Britain and relations between Churchill and Curtin became very acrimonious. An elderly Australian politician, Sir Earle Page, had already been sent to London by Fadden to represent his government's views. Page conveyed Australian alarm at meetings of the war cabinet. He condemned the weak Commonwealth air strength in Malaya and was told by Churchill that the Soviet Union and the Middle East came first.[31] Page further urged guaranteeing the Dutch East Indies and supporting the Soviet Union if Japan moved north.[32] He expressed doubts over the British policy of leaving the US to handle the talks with Japan. The British defence chiefs assured Page that military and air strength should be adequate for holding Japan. Churchill and the chiefs remarked on the absence of 'extreme danger' in the Pacific.[33] Churchill did not wish to divert resources from the principal theatres of war. He considered Australian fears to be exaggerated. He told Page that he did not consider a Japanese invasion of Australia to be feasible; however, if it materialised, then he would redeem past promises and sacrifice the Middle East. Churchill's one move to reassure the dominions was the disastrous decision to dispatch the *Prince of Wales* and the *Repulse* as a token presence which would supposedly impress the Japanese. Precisely the reverse effect was achieved when the two ships were sunk by Japanese planes on the third day of the Pacific War.

Before discussing the impact of the Pacific War itself, it is important to ask how much influence was exerted by the dominions over the formulation of British policy before December 1941. Dominion prime ministers each emphasised the necessity of working as closely as possible with the United States; this was continuously brought out in messages from King, Smuts, Menzies, Curtin and Fraser. However, this was already fully grasped in London so it reinforced a basic aim of British policy. Smuts and Menzies urged a balanced approach in handling Japan. Menzies was worried that Australia could be forced to the forefront of conflict in the Pacific without much support from Britain and possibly without an indication of American participation. Australian apprehension pushed Britain towards closing the Burma Road for a three-month period in July 1940, although the chief determinant was the desperate situation in Europe. British efforts to strengthen defence coordination in 1940–1 were again affected by representations from the southern dominions. *The Prince of Wales* and the *Repulse* were sent, in part, to encourage Australia and New Zealand. It would be fair to say that dominion pressures intensified British endeavours to square the circle; this was also influenced by strategic and political factors concerning India. Anglo-American relations, the necessity of propping up China, and obligations to the Commonwealth each merged, sometimes complementing each other and sometimes conflicting. The dominions were not satisfied with the frequency or efficacy of consultation. In the Pacific context this did not particularly worry King or Smuts but it angered Menzies and Curtin. Menzies did not carry his criticisms too far, perhaps because he harboured ambitions to play a role in British politics as Smuts had done in the latter part of the First World War. Curtin had few inhibitions and an acerbic tone came to characterise communications between Canberra and London.

In December 1941 the acid test for Commonwealth security in the Pacific arrived. Canadian interest was initially promoted by the significant involvement of Canadian troops in the forlorn defence of Hong Kong. Thereafter, Mackenzie King saw himself fulfilling a 'watching brief' hinging on his concern for Canada's interests in the framework of Anglo-American relations. Smuts believed that the Second World War in total would stimulate the trend towards increasing independence in the dominions. No doubt Smuts was influenced by the peculiar situation in South Africa where he faced a greater threat to the moderate policies he espoused than did the leader of any other dominion. Smuts possessed an acute grasp of overall world trends. He saw close Anglo-American harmony as the key but wished to see a distinct role for the Commonwealth to be created in the new era. In Australia and New Zealand Curtin and Fraser believed that they had to prevent panic and stabilise a situation in which many were prone to hysteria. The American consul in Adelaide commented, immediately after the loss of the *Prince of Wales* and the *Repulse*, that ordinary people were 'the closest to actual panic that I had ever seen'.[34] The relentless series of Japanese successes in the first phase of the war was extremely traumatic and it took a lengthy period to surmount apprehension concerning an actual invasion of Australia. Not surprisingly recrimination against Britain for allowing such a terrible threat to confront Australia was vocal. It was best illustrated in the famous press interview at the end of December 1941 in which Curtin spoke of the long-standing ties of affection to Britain now having been replaced by a realistic understanding that Australian security depended upon the US for fulfilment. In one sense this may be seen as part of a longer term development in which Australia and New Zealand were incorporated within the American defence system: the conclusion of the Anzus treaty in 1951 was foreshadowed by Curtin's words a decade earlier. However, as will be seen, enthusiasm for the US diminished in the latter part of the war. Protests at lack of consultation between London and the dominions were voiced in Canberra and Wellington. Little was known of Churchill's discussions in Washington at the 'Arcadia' conference in late December 1941 and early January 1942. Churchill reluctantly accepted the creation of the ABDA (American-British-Dutch-Australian) command headed by Wavell. The creation of such a vast command area demonstrated the lack of sufficient solidity in the pre-war conferences.[35]

The catastrophic outcome of the Malayan campaign gravely undermined remaining Australian faith in British strategy. Relations were soured further by arguments over responsibility for the defeat; this was not helped by the disputed hasty departure from Singapore of the Australian commander, General Bennett, shortly before the surrender. General Pownall's comments in his diary were the same as those prevailing in Australia: 'we were frankly out-generalled, outwitted and outfought. It is a great disaster, one of the worst in our history, and a great blow to the honour and prestige of the Army'.[36] During 1942 and 1943 the southern dominions looked to Washington for leadership, to Churchill's ire. The Pacific War Council was established in Washington in April 1942; this afforded comfort and encouragement in Australia and New Zealand. Ironically the War

Council was later perceived as a nominal body without sufficient authority. Roosevelt set up the War Council reluctantly but then made clear his intention to dominate it by presiding over its weekly meeting in 1942. Dr Herbert Evatt was important in influencing Australian policy heavily in 1942 and 1943 but the Pacific War Council achieved much less in terms of coordinating policy than Evatt had hoped in March 1942.[37] Roosevelt told Winant, the ambassador in London, in June 1942 that his chairmanship permitted him to control its deliberations and that 'he told stories' at its meetings.[38] In 1943 the Council met less often, about once or twice a month, and its final meeting occurred in January 1944.[39]

With the Japanese forces in the Philippines on the verge of victory, General Douglas MacArthur departed on Roosevelt's orders, in March 1942, to establish his command in Australia. This greatly encouraged Australians; they would have been less happy had they known that Roosevelt had stated privately that it would be preferable to lose Australia and New Zealand rather than contribute to the collapse of the Soviet Union.[40] MacArthur was the most eminent general in the American army, a former chief of the general staff who had worked on the defence of the Philippines after retiring from the US army. He was a man of immense vigour, dynamism, and commitment, capable of inspiring deep trust but also the reverse. He was very much a 'political general'. He had various contacts within Congress and entertained political ambition: he was a possible future Republican presidential candidate.[41] Up to a point MacArthur and the southern dominions shared common aims: they wanted far greater recognition of the Pacific theatre with a corresponding increase in resources allocated to it. MacArthur publicly praised the Australian contribution and his relationship with Curtin was cordial in 1942–3. In private, as Christopher Thorne has shown, MacArthur was frequently critical of Australian prowess.[42] He believed in supporting Australia, since its survival was fundamental to his aspirations. He supported the British Commonwealth for the same reason: its recovery in the Pacific region was inseparable from the political ambition of MacArthur. Naturally he wanted the US to become the chief power in East Asia and the Pacific after the war, which inevitably connoted a junior role for the Commonwealth. When Australian and New Zealand ministers discerned the more overt expression of these opinions in the latter part of the war, so their reservations over American policy increased.

At the beginning of 1943 Japanese expansion reached its greatest point in New Guinea. Despite the result of the battles of the Coral Sea and Midway, Australian fear of a Japanese invasion persisted. By the summer of 1943 the apprehension abated: now leaders in the southern dominions began to express anxiety over ultimate American intentions. MacArthur's solid and avuncular qualities appeared unduly paternalistic, if not arrogant: the proximity of the 1944 election accentuated MacArthur's inclination to squeeze all he could out of Washington. Roosevelt, in turn, was wary in case MacArthur turned out to be his Republican opponent or exerted particular influence in the campaign. American visitors to Australia referred to American commercial objectives after the war, sometimes alluding to the British Commonwealth in critical terms, implying that it belonged to the past and had no future. Curtin and Fraser had no desire to see Australia and New Zealand regarded as commercial outlets for American economic ambition. Curtin's tone towards Britain became less abrasive and his relations with Churchill at last warmed. He told Churchill that the Americans saw themselves as winning the Pacific War essentially on their own.[43] For his part Churchill described Curtin in 1944 as having been the most positive of the Commonwealth prime ministers at a recent conference.[44] A further factor was injected by the ambitious Evatt, minister of external affairs. Evatt wanted to be the next leader of the Labour party and seized every opportunity (and some occasions that were not) to press Australia's case. A conference between Australia and New Zealand met in January 1944 as Evatt's instigation; it urged the creation of a regional defence zone and an international commission for the south Pacific.[45] Just as the dominions contemplated a new, more assertive role for the Commonwealth, so British ministers saw the Commonwealth as important in Britain's capacity as a world power following the end of the Pacific war. It was uncertain how American policy would evolve after Roosevelt's death in April 1945; the Commonwealth would be valuable in the contingencies both of the US retreating from world power or becoming too overbearing a force. Churchill and Attlee were fully alive to the necessity of playing a more interventionist part. Of course, the British army was making a major contribution to Japanese defeat in Burma where the Japanese army experienced its biggest defeat on land during the Pacific war.[46] This was conveniently forgotten by Americans imbued with their own impressive achievements in the Pacific. The Royal Navy reappeared in the final phase of the war: its Pacific fleet arrived in Australian waters at the end of 1944. American naval chiefs, notably Admiral Ernest J. King, did not deem British participation to be necessary but Roosevelt was insistent for political reasons.

In broad terms the US dominated the concluding stages of the war as vigorously as they had done earlier on. It was essentially Truman's decision to use the atomic bomb against Japan in August 1945. Notwithstanding the doubts of his own chiefs of staff and of Churchill over adhering to the policy of unconditional surrender, Truman moved decisively to terminate the Pacific War. The dominions regretted the absence of consultation during the Potsdam conference. Australian ministers were annoyed from 1943 onwards at MacArthur's reluctance to give more prominence to the role of Australian forces.[47] Now they demanded, on 11 August 1945, that the Showa Emperor should not be immune from prosecution for war crimes and responsibility for Japan's aggression. They were not reassured by Truman's concession that the Emperor did not have to sign the surrender document.[48] Curtin died in July 1945 and was succeeded by Ben Chifley who did not possess his predecessor's experience. Evatt worked zealously in 1944–5 to promote a new position for the

Commonwealth. Evatt and Fraser urged Britain, in April 1945, to replace its colonies under trusteeship as a recognition of the qualities expected in the new era. It was scarcely surprising that Anthony Eden termed Evatt 'tiresome' and Fraser 'woolly'.[49] The impending end of the war – even though it was widely believed that this would not be accomplished until 1946 – concentrated attention in the dominions on the future of the colonial empires so comprehensively discredited by the speed with which Japanese forces captured them in 1942. Britain wholly supported the return of the Dutch and the French to their empires in the East Indies and Indo-China for two reasons: the British wanted to regain their own colonial territories and it was important to sustain the Netherlands and France as part of the policy of restoring a devastated Europe. Australia was very interested in the future of the East Indies. Dutch ministers suspected that Britain and Australia wished to meddle in the East Indies to the detriment of the aims laid down by those now returning to The Hague. These fears were not justified in the case of the British but Evatt desired to establish Australian influence in the East Indies.[50] Evatt's restless activity concerned the American government early in 1944 when it was reported that he wanted to secure Australian sovereignty over the Fiji, Solomons, and New Hebrides Islands.[51] Cordell Hull informed Curtin in April 1944 that the US did not like Evatt's attitude.[52]

In a work dealing with his contribution to the negotiation of the Anzus treaty and the Colombo Plan, Sir Percy Spender assessed the factors leading to the conclusion of Anzus in 1951. He wrote of his own farsightedness in appreciating since 1938 that, with the best will in the world, Britain would or could do little to help Australia in a world struggle of unprecedented dimensions.[53] Spender remarked dismissively of the efforts of his predecessors during the 1940s: 'The concept of Pacific security had been talked about at different times over the decade before 1950 but nothing had resulted, unless one were to suggest that the Australia–New Zealand Agreement of 1944, or anything done under it, added anything of substance to the joint or separate security of either country'.[54] The Pacific war sharpened awareness of regional defence commitments. While attempts were being made to inject new vigour into the Commonwealth, not least because of the momentous developments concerning the Indian sub-continent, Australia and New Zealand understood the political and economic pressures compelling British concentration primarily upon Europe. It took longer for New Zealand's leaders and opinion to adjust, since they were so wedded to dependence on Britain.[55] In 1946 American policy towards the south Pacific changed radically: planning in Washington demoted the south Pacific to relative insignificance and it was unlikely that American forces would be concerned with this region.[56] Australia and New Zealand were alarmed at the possibility of a revived Japanese military threat once the allied occupation ended. The growth of the Cold War after 1947 heightened awareness of a potential communist menace: in addition, the communist threat rendered it more likely that the Americans might encourage Japanese rearmament. Whatever reservations the southern dominions held regarding American political and commercial designs, they recognised that their defence against Japanese militarism or Soviet/Chinese communism could only be avoided through entering into a binding commitment with the US. Spender observed that Australian opinion had become more mature in the light of its experience between 1941 and 1945 and that the kind of accusations of 'disloyalty', made against him in 1938, when he had warned against relying too heavily on Britain, were no longer uttered.[57] Indeed the strength of his statement is underlined by the fact that it was a Liberal government led by Menzies that entered into the Anzus pact in 1951. The Labour government in Britain reluctantly acquiesced in a regional arrangement from which Britain was excluded and in which its historic role was clearly occupied by the United States. Churchill's reaction in opposition was incandescent and he vowed to remove this slur on British leadership in the Commonwealth.

It proved to be a bitter issue for the Conservative government when Churchill returned to office in October 1951 and one in which he was forced to concede defeat. There was a certain irony in Churchill's stand, since he had emphasised to the dominions and the Dutch in 1940–1 that the US must assume leadership in the Pacific region. The conclusion of the Anzus treaty was an essential part of the arrangements for providing for security in East Asia and the Pacific during the 1950s and after: it was imperative in order to convince Australia and New Zealand of the necessity for a liberal peace treaty. John Foster Dulles revealed great subtlety and skill in reconciling the divergent elements involved in the peace treaty and security arrangements.[58] The Anzus treaty provided better assurance for Australia and New Zealand than they had enjoyed since the early years of the twentieth century. Ironically in the 1980s it was not Australia but New Zealand which so rocked the boat as to bring the functioning of Anzus to a low ebb, if not a halt, by objecting to American ships carrying nuclear weapons visiting New Zealand ports. If the respective leaders of 1941 could have returned to observe Pacific security nearly half a century later, it would have been this that would have shocked them more than anything else. The world had indeed turned upside down.

## NOTES

1.   *Bulletin*, 10 January 1911.
2.   See Ian Nish, The *Anglo-Japanese Alliance* (London, 1966) and *Alliance in Decline* (London, 1972).
3.   For assessments of British decline and of the 'Singapore strategy', see W.D. McIntyre, *The Rise and Fall of the Singapore Naval Base* (London, 1979) and Paul Haggie, *Britannia at Bay* (Oxford, 1981).

4. For analyses of Roosevelt's policy, see J.M. Burns, *Roosevelt: the Soldier of Freedom* (London, 1971) and R.A. Dallek, *Franklin D. Roosevelt and American Foreign Policy, 1932–1945* (Oxford, 1979).

5. For a discussion of Canadian policy, see James Eayrs, *In Defence of Canada*, 2 vols, paperback edition (Toronto, 1964, 1965).

6. The most satisfactory discussion of Smuts's role and of his endeavours to reconcile domestic and international priorities is to be found in Sir Keith Hancock, *Smuts: the Fields of Force, 1919–1950* (Cambridge, 1970).

7. For a discussion of New Zealand's policy, see Keith Sinclair, *Walter Nash* (Auckland, 1976), pp. 198–236.

8. For assessments of Australian society and politics before, during and after the Pacific war, see Stuart Macintyre and Geoffrey Bolton, *The Oxford History of Australia*, vols. 4 and 5 (Oxford, 1986 and 1990).

9. For a discussion of Churchill's views towards Japan, over a generation, see Peter Lowe, 'Winston Churchill and Japan, 1914–1942', in J.W.M. Chapman (ed.), *Proceedings of the British Association for Japanese Studies*, vol. 6, part 1 (1981), pp. 39–47, 236–7.

10. For a judicious analysis of British defence policy before September 1939, see N.H. Gibbs, *Grand Strategy*, vol. 1 (London, 1976). For the personal views of a defence planner in Whitehall who later had to meet the Japanese onslaught in 1941–2, see Brian Bond (ed.), *Chief of Staff: the Diaries of Lieutenant-General Sir Henry Pownall, 1933–1944*, 2 vols, (London, 1974).

11. For a discussion of these issues, see Peter Lowe, *Great Britain and the Origins of the Pacific War* (Oxford, 1977).

12. See Lowe, *Origins*, pp. 93–5.

13. 'The situation in the Far East in the event of Japanese intervention against us', report by chiefs of staff committee, 31 July 1940, COS (40) 592, WP (40) 302, Cab. 66/10. See also copy in FO files, FO371/24708/3765.

14. See Lowe, *Origins*, p. 164.

15. Ibid., pp. 165–7, 248–50.

16. Report of the Singapore Defence Conference, 1940, Cab. 80/24.

17. 'Far East Tactical Appreciation and Report of Singapore Defence Conference', report by joint planning staff, 1 January 1941, Cab. 79/8.

18. Ibid., appendix 2.

19. 'British–United States staff conversations', BUS(J) 41 (6), 'Relative Importance of the Middle and Far East Theatres', 31 January 1941, Cab. 99/5.

20. Lowe, *Origins*, p. 192.

21. 'The Far East: Appreciation by the United Kingdom Delegation', 11 February 1941, BUS(J) (41)13, Cab. 99/5.

22. Craigie to FO, 3 February 1941, FO 371/27740/11540.

23. 'Statement by the United States staff committee: The United States Military Position in the Far East', 19 February 1941, BUS(J) (41)16, Cab. 99/5.

24. 'Appreciation of the situation in the Far East by the Australian Chiefs of Staff', note by the secretary, 22 February 1941', enclosed in Fadden to Casey, 19 February 1941, BUS (41) 17, Cab. 99/5.

25. Chiefs of Staff committee, 'Visit of the Australian Prime Minister: Reply by Chiefs of Staff to memorandum by the Prime Minister of Australia', 11 April 1941, Cab. 80/27.

26. Minutes by Dening, 5 March, and Butler, 6 March, 1941 FO371/27774/1601/54/61.

27. Lowe, *Origins*, pp. 204–5.

28. Ibid. p. 207.

29.  Ibid. p. 242.
30.  Union of South Africa to Dominions Office, 29 August 1941, FO 371/27910/8621.
31.  War Cabinet conclusions, confidential annexe, 5 November 1941, 109(41)2, Cab. 65/24.
32.  Ibid., 12 November 1941, 112(41)1, Cab. 65/24.
33.  Ibid.
34.  Cited Christopher Thorne, *Allies of a Kind* (London, 1978), p. 252.
35.  For the deliberations in Washington, see '"Arcadia": Record of Proceedings, Washington War Conference, December 1941–January 1942', Cab. 99/17.
36.  Bond (ed.), *Chief of Staff*, 2, p. 85, entry for 13 February 1942.
37.  R.J. Bell, *Unequal Allies: Australian–American Relations and the Pacific War* (Melbourne, 1977), pp. 60–4.
38.  Ibid., p. 64.
39.  Ibid., p. 61.
40.  Ibid., p. 75.
41.  See D. Clayton James, *The Years of MacArthur*, vol. 2 (London, 1975).
42.  C. Thorne, 'MacArthur, Australia and the British', *Australian Outlook* (April and August 1975).
43.  Thorne, *Allies of a Kind*, p. 479.
44.  Bell, *Unequal Allies*, p. 163.
45.  Thorne, *Allies of a Kind*, p. 480.
46.  See Louis Allen, *Burma: the Longest War* (London, 1984) for an outstanding analysis of the savage struggle in Burma.
47.  Bell, *Unequal Allies*, p. 178. See also Trevor Reese, *Australia, New Zealand and the United States: a Survey of International Relations, 1941–1968* (Oxford, 1969).
48.  Bell, *Unequal Allies*, pp. 118–19.
49.  Thorne, *Allies of a Kind*, p. 602.
50.  For a discussion of Australian interest in the Dutch East Indies, see Thorne, *Allies of a Kind*, pp. 366, 460, 481.
51.  Bell, *Unequal Allies*, p. 111.
52.  Ibid., pp. 155–6.
53.  Sir Percy Spender, *Exercises in Diplomacy* (Sydney, 1969), p. 24.
54.  Ibid., p. 21.
55.  For an admirable account of the process of adjustment, see Ann Trotter, *New Zealand and Japan, 1945–1952: the Occupation and the Peace Treaty* (London, 1990).
56.  Bell, *Unequal Allies*, p. 167.
57.  Spender, *Exercises*, p. 24.
58.  See Peter Lowe, 'Great Britain and the Japanese Peace Treaty, 1951', in P. Lowe and H.J. Moeshart (eds), *Western Interactions with Japan: Expansion, the Armed Forces and Readjustment, 1859–1956* (Folkestone, 1990) pp. 91–104.

# Part V
# Termination of the War, August 1945

# 11 Hiroshima: A Strategy of Shock
## Lawrence Freedman and Saki Dockrill

Nuclear weapons have only been used in anger twice since their explosive power was proved in July 1945. A few weeks after the New Mexico test two bombs were dropped on the Japanese cities of Hiroshima and Nagasaki. Hundreds more have been tested but none has been used since.

The unique nature of this event and its association with the conclusion of the Pacific War immediately sparked off a debate which may never be properly concluded. A widespread Japanese appreciation of the destruction of these two cities remains that this was a move that was more criminal than strategic, only loosely related to the preceding years of war. Thus the comprehensive study by the Committee for the Compilation of Materials on Damage Caused by the Atomic Bomb in Hiroshima and Nagasaki,[1] contains almost every scrap of information relating to the bombings, including an extensive discussion of the outrage prompted by the impact of Hiroshima and Nagasaki and the consequent protest movements, but only minimal reference to why the weapons were used. This discussion extends to two separate paragraphs. In one it is stated that:

> the A-Bomb attacks were needed not so much against Japan – already on the brink of surrender and no longer capable of mounting an effective counter-offensive – as to establish clearly America's postwar international position and strategic supremacy in the anticipated cold war setting. One tragedy of Hiroshima and Nagasaki is that this historically unprecedented devastation of human society stemmed from essentially experimental and political aims.[2]

In another paragraph this argument is repeated, citing as authorities two dated Western studies, one of which is by a communist,[3] and the other by Patrick Blackett who in 1948 was the first to assert that the atomic bombing was the first shot in the Cold War rather than the last in the Pacific War,[4] and a 1968 Japanese study. As the anniversary of the outbreak of the Pacific War approached, and the Japanese Diet moved to pass a motion apologising for initiating the war with the surprise attack on Pearl Harbor, there were suggestions that it would be appropriate if the United States reciprocated with an apology for Hiroshima and Nagasaki, a notion to which President Bush gave short shrift.

Those in Japan doubting the necessity of the atomic bombing have been able to cite in support a series of Western studies which have argued that (a) the war would have ended anyway without recourse to an invasion of Japan, (b) there were realistic alternatives to the actual use of the bomb against civilian targets, in particular a staged demonstration of its power, (c) all this was known to the

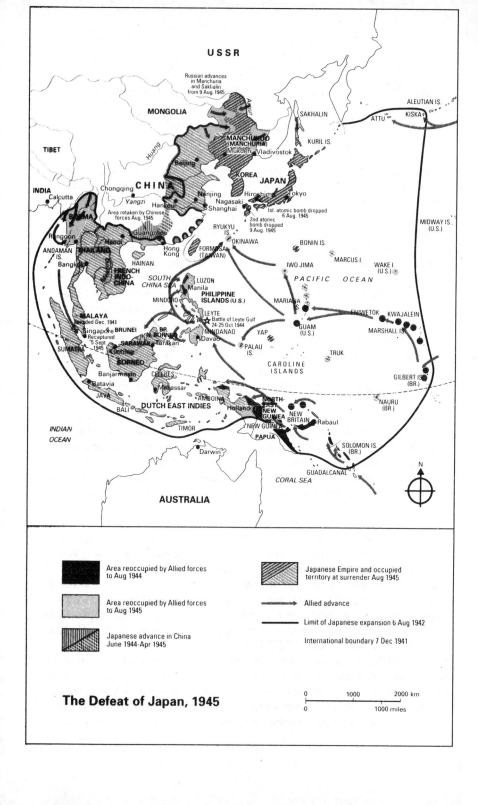

**The Defeat of Japan, 1945**

Area reoccupied by Allied forces to Aug 1944

Area reoccupied by Allied forces to Aug 1945

Japanese advance in China June 1944-Apr 1945

Japanese Empire and occupied territory at surrender Aug 1945

Allied advance

Limit of Japanese expansion 6 Aug 1942

International boundary 7 Dec 1941

| 0 | 1000 | 2000 km |
| 0 | 1000 miles | |

USSR

MONGOLIA

TIBET

INDIA
Calcutta

Russian advances in Manchuria and Sakhalin from 9 Aug 1945

Amur

SAKHALIN

ALEUTIAN IS.

KISKA
ATTU

MANCHUKUO (MANCHURIA)
Mukden · Vladivostok

KURIL IS.

Huang

Beijing

CHINA
Chongqing
Yangzi
Hankou

BURMA

Rangoon

ANDAMAN IS.

THAILAND
Bangkok

Nanjing
Shanghai

Area retaken by Chinese forces Aug 1945

Hanoi
Guangzhou

FRENCH INDO-CHINA

HAINAN

SOUTH CHINA SEA

Hong Kong

KOREA    JAPAN
Hiroshima   Tokyo
Nagasaki

1st atomic bomb dropped 6 Aug 1945

2nd atomic bomb dropped 9 Aug 1945

RYUKYU IS.

FORMOSA (TAIWAN)

OKINAWA

BONIN IS.

MIDWAY IS. (U.S.)

MARCUS I.

IWO JIMA

WAKE I. (U.S.)

PACIFIC OCEAN

MALAYA
Invaded Dec. 1941
Singapore
Recaptured 5 Sept 1945

BRUNEI

SARAWAK

LUZON
Manila

PHILIPPINE ISLANDS (U.S.)

MINDORO

BR. N. BORNEO
Tarakan

LEYTE
Battle of Leyte Gulf 24-25 Oct 1944

MARIANA

ENIWETOK
KWAJALEIN

MARSHALL IS.

SUMATRA

Kuching

BORNEO

MINDANAO
Davao

YAP

GUAM (U.S.)

PALAU IS.

TRUK

CAROLINE ISLANDS

GILBERT IS. (BR.)

Banjarmasin

CELEBES
Makassar

AMBOINA
Hollandia

NORTH-EAST NEW GUINEA

NEW BRITAIN
Rabaul

NAURU (BR.)

JAVA
Batavia

BALI

DUTCH EAST INDIES

TIMOR

NEW GUINEA

PAPUA

SOLOMON IS. (BR.)

INDIAN OCEAN

Darwin

GUADALCANAL

CORAL SEA

N

AUSTRALIA

Truman administration, yet (d) it still persevered because it wanted to strengthen its hand in its post-war dealings with the Soviet Union. This line of argument is now largely discredited among Western historians.[5]

With hindsight the likelihood of an early Japanese surrender is acknowledged (although *how* early remains moot), and the sensitivity of American policy-makers to their developing struggle with the Soviet Union is undoubted. Nonetheless, the weight of evidence supports the view that the primary motive for the atomic bombing remained the defeat of Japan and that a demonstration shot was discounted because there was no confidence that it would work.

It is not our intention in this chapter to rehearse once more this familiar debate. Rather we intend to look more closely at the question of the manner of the atomic bombing. Our contention is that it reflected a clear and coherent strategy of 'shock'. This was the only strategy that made much sense in the military circumstances of August 1945. It was reflected in the stress on the spectacle of a nuclear detonation and the consequent tactics of cryptic warning and inconspicuous delivery. For these reasons, and contrary to the hopes of at least some of those responsible, it also maximised the association of the bomb with mass destruction. We further argue that in practice it worked: the available evidence suggests that Japanese policy-makers were caught off guard by the news of Hiroshima and that, despite the best efforts of the hardliners, they never recovered their balance. Although the two developments remain hard to disentangle, the bombing may well have been more important in prompting the Japanese surrender than the entry of Russia into the war.

By the time that the United States began to consider seriously the employment of the first atomic bombs they were influenced by two critical factors: the limited number of weapons available and the limited number of targets left.

In April 1944 General Leslie Groves, in charge of the Manhattan Project, had informed General Marshall that several plutonium implosion bombs with a yield of between 0.7 and 1.5 kilotons might be available between March and June 1945. However, by the turn of the year Grove had been obliged to report that these hopes had been 'dissipated by scientific difficulties which we have not as yet been able to solve'.[6] By the summer of 1945 it was clear that there were going to be very few weapons available.

It is important to note that prior to the New Mexico test of July 1945 this comparatively low-yield estimate remained the best judgement and influenced the first considerations of the weapon's employment.[7] With the uranium gun-type weapon, the type eventually used over Hiroshima, estimates were more confident at between five and 15 kilotons. It was only after it became apparent that the normal yield of the implosion bomb would exceed 0.5 kilotons that its use became 'subject to considerations of high-level policy'. At or below that level, it would simply have been handed over to the military for use without restriction.[8] By the summer of 1945 the atom bombs were seen as single city-busters, but the confidence in this capability was quite recent.

There remained a lack of knowledge of the bomb's effects. This has been commented on in the literature as providing an experimental motive for the bomb. Certainly, this was one of Groves's criteria in deciding on a target. In practice it carried little weight. Most notoriously we have Groves favouring Kyoto as a target because, inter alia, it was large enough for the bomb damage to 'run out within the city' and so provide a 'firm understanding' of its destructive power, but this did not override Stimson's political sensitivity to the cultural importance of Kyoto. Equally, against the experimental criterion Nagasaki was a poor target. There was, as General Farrell, Groves's deputy, recalled, disagreement about it on the grounds that:

> the city was not a proper shape and dimension for the large bombs. It was long and narrow and was confined between two ranges of hills that would deflect the blast effect of the bombs. Also it had been very seriously bombed on several occasions before and it would be difficult to measure the effects of the atomic bomb in view of the previous damage.[9]

One of the first meetings to discuss the possible use of the bomb in 1943 considered as a possible target the Japanese fleet concentrated at Truk. This would have added attraction as a sort of retribution for Pearl Harbor. But by the time the bomb was ready the fleet did not exist.[10] Of course, at this time the priority targets would still have been German.

In 1944 there was some discussion of the possibility of tactical nuclear use. The weapons might be used as part of a force invading the Japanese mainland. General Marshall told David Lilienthal in 1947 that:

> We knew that the Japanese were determined and fanatical, like the Morros, and we thought we would have had to exterminate them, almost man for man. So we thought the bomb would be a wonderful weapon as a protection and preparation for landings.

Lilienthal records the number '12' in his diary, although in a later interview the number '9' was given by Marshall. The idea appears to have been to attack defences during the early stages of invasion with remaining bombs saved for Japanese reserves.[11] On the other hand Herbert Feis says there were no serious discussions of this in memos or directives.[12] This in itself may not be surprising as details would have been kept very close until senior commanders had to be told. However it had clearly not been taken very far because, as far as Lilienthal could tell, Marshall had not considered the effect of radioactivity on allied personnel. Marshall himself admitted that these plans were hatched when the real potential of the bomb was not known, and this was probably around the time when the invasion was first being seriously considered during the summer of 1944, which was probably also the last point at which a stock of 9–12 bombs would at all have appeared feasible.

In a recent article, Barton Bernstein appears to confuse these thoughts of Marshall with some that occurred to him and a number of people concerned with planning for the November invasion of Kyushu, after the power of the bomb had become known as a result of its initial employment but before the Japanese surrender.[13] It does seem from Bernstein's work that at this point consideration did turn to 'tactical use'. For the purposes of this analysis, however, the key point is that this concept did not influence consideration of the initial use of the bomb.

By the summer of 1945, absent the atomic bombs, the strategic question was whether the remorseless air campaign plus the blockade currently being conducted against Japan would bring about surrender or whether this would require a full-scale invasion, to which American policy-makers looked forward with deep foreboding. To hasten Japanese surrender the Truman leadership sought to commit the Soviet Union to the war (so as to tie down Japanese forces in China) and considered the possibility of hints to Tokyo that the Emperor's position might be respected in the event of an early surrender.

The awareness of the availability of a viable atomic bomb did not make a material difference to any element of this strategy, except possibly the bombing campaign. Planning for the invasion continued while the meeting of the 'big three' was under way at Potsdam, where Truman received news of the first successful test. Stalin was still urged to join the war and the possibility was again explored of conveying to Japanese war leaders the thought that not all honour would be lost through surrender.

Even with regard to the air war against Japan operations were only slightly affected, mainly in terms of preserving some serious civilian targets. General Curtis LeMay, who had been conducting the campaign, expected to run out of targets by October 'when there wouldn't really be much to work on except probably railroads or something of that sort'.[14]

The preoccupation of the historians' debate with the necessity of using the bomb has meant that it has been judged strategically against the prospective invasion rather than the actual air bombardment under way at the time and with which it was unavoidably linked in the minds of policy-makers. While the theorists of strategic bombardment had been left with a 'not proven' verdict following the air campaign against Germany, the raids against Japan were seen by those responsible as an opportunity to prove the independent worth of a strategic bombing force. In April LeMay wrote:

> I am influenced by the conviction that the present stage of development in the air war against Japan presents the AAF for the first time with the opportunity of proving the power of the strategic air arm. I consider that for the first time strategic air bombardment faces a situation in which its strength is proportionate to the magnitude of its task. I feel that the destruction of Japan's ability to wage war is within the capability of this command.[15]

The American distaste for area bombing had evaporated in the face of a set of Japanese targets marked by the complex intermingling of industry and society and fire-prone wooden structures. One only has to recall the most damaging single raid – the March 1945 attack on Tokyo which left nearly 80 000 dead and 300 000 buildings destroyed. Nobody involved in the decision on the atomic bombs could have seen themselves as setting new precedents for mass destruction in scale – only in efficiency. Indeed the appreciation of the bomb's potential should be seen in the light of a growing uneasiness among some senior policy-makers over the conduct of the air war.

If the atomic bomb was to be seen simply as an extension of the air campaign then its necessity was doubtful. LeMay was of this view. He believed that the conventional campaign of strategic bombardment would bring about a Japanese surrender of its own accord and he saw no reason to see the atomic bombs as anything other than a supplement. We have already noted his view, which there is no reason to doubt, that the destruction of all Japanese targets was in reach. The conventional raids did not stop as a prelude to the introduction of the bomb: they continued up to the very moment of Japan's surrender. Indeed when discussion first began with regard to the choice of targets for the bomb, the 20th Air Force was noted to be

> operating primarily to laying waste all the main Japanese cities, and that they do not propose to save some important primary target for us if it interferes with the operation of the war from their point of view.

It was planning to increase its delivery of conventional bombs to 100 000 tons a month by the end of the year.[16]

At issue here was Japan's pain threshold, which by this stage in the war was judged to be high. General Arnold, recorded in his memoirs his perception that there was nothing special about the atomic bombing other than the extra weight of destruction and thus his 'surprise' at Japan's 'abrupt surrender': 'We had figured we would probably have to drop four atomic bombs or increase the destructiveness of our Super Fortress missions by adding the heavy bombers from Europe.'[17] Military leaders not linked to the air campaign, who were also unconvinced by its value and discomforted by its ferocity, were unlikely to change their mind on being told of even more powerful bombs. Eisenhower's distaste for the atomic bomb has been regularly cited, although there is now doubt as to the extent of his actual opposition (and that of other military leaders). The point is largely that they showed no enthusiasm for the bomb.[18] General MacArthur, Supreme Commander in the Pacific, seems to have seen little need for its use.

Military leaders, however, played a limited role in the decision-making. Few of them were well informed on the bomb and they were not consulted by the key decision-makers. Far more influential in shaping decisions on the bomb's use were those responsible for its design and production. They did perhaps, as has often been suggested, have a special stake in their efforts being shown to bear fruit. For our purposes more relevant is their sense of the special quality of an atomic explosion and the awe which it might be expected to produce in all those who might witness it.

President Truman appears never either to have doubted that the bomb should be used if available or to have entered into any extended discussion of the strategic concept which might govern its use. In fact there was little debate anywhere over this matter. While it was probably discussed informally a number of times, the employment concept was actually forged in four meetings, apparently without great dissent, and only once reappraised under pressure from those scientists who argued that a demonstration shot was a feasible and much more desirable option.

The basic concept was that mentioned by Stimson in his 1947 memoir:

I felt that to extract a genuine surrender from the Emperor and his military advisers, they must be administered a tremendous shock which would carry convincing proof of our power to destroy the Empire.

He described it as more than a weapon of terrible destruction; it was 'a psychological weapon'. Stimson also associated Marshall with this view. He was 'emphatic in his insistence on the shock value of the new weapon'.[19]

The idea of the atomic bomb, at least in its initial use, as a psychological weapon, seems to have come from Robert Oppenheimer. This is an inference from Oppenheimer's critical role at the key meetings convened to discuss the bomb's use in April and May 1945.

The first meeting, of which little is known, was at the Military Policy Committee (effectively the board of management of the Manhattan Project). The second meeting, at which General Groves transmitted the results of the first was of a Target Committee. This had been set up under Groves and met in April 1945 at the Pentagon. It consisted of two air force officers and five scientists and was chaired by Groves's Deputy, Thomas Farrell. The title of the Committee indicated its responsibility: to identify the most appropriate targets and the most effective form of attack. Groves brought with him criteria which presumably had been discussed at the Military Policy Committee:

I had set as the governing factor that the targets chosen should be places the bombing of which would meet adversely affect the will of the Japanese people to continue the war. Beyond that, they should be military in nature, consisting either of important headquarters of troop concentrations, or centers of production of military equipment and supplies. To enable us to assess accurately the effects of the bomb, the targets should not have been previously damaged by air raids. It was also desirable that the first target be of such size that the damage would be confined within it, so that we could more definitely determine the power of the bomb.[20]

This ordering describes the eventual priority attached to these various criteria. Inevitably much of the speculation by historians relates to the way in which various cities found themselves earmarked for possible annihilation. Those on this Committee were not likely to reflect overmuch on the first criterion – 'adversely affecting the will of the Japanese people' as this was standard air force speak for area bombing, and there was no disputing that their task was to find a substantial civilian area, with some military role (which most in practice had) that had been left relatively unscathed. This required evaluating a number of cities against a variety of practical issues.

On 10 and 11 May this Committee met again at Los Alamos, with a formidable group of scientists present including Oppenheimer. It was Oppenheimer who set the agenda with a list of topics. The bulk of these were technical, concerning height of detonation, reports on weather, gadget jettisoning and moving on to questions of rehearsals and safety. More critical however were items E and F, 'Psychological Factors in Target Selection' and 'Use Against Military Objectives' respectively.[21] The main conclusion reached on the latter question was that the full impact of the weapon would be lost if only a discrete military target was attacked: 'it should be located in a much larger area subject to blast damage'. More thought was given to the former question concerning 'psychological factors'. The minutes identify two aspects of this:

> (1) obtaining the greatest psychological effect against Japan and (2) making the initial use sufficiently spectacular for the importance of the weapon to be internationally recognized when publicity on it is released.

The 'shock value' of this weapon thus had both short-term and long-term consequences and it was vital that both be maximised. When targets were discussed against these two criteria, shock might be derived from different features: thus Kyoto because the people there were 'more highly intelligent and hence better able to appreciate the significance of the weapon', Hiroshima because of the fraction of the city that would probably be destroyed, and the Emperor's Palace in Tokyo because of its status, although here there was a problem in that there could be no pretence that there was a military target close by.

The next critical meeting took place on Monday 31 May. This was the Interim Committee, set up to discuss the wider implications of the bomb which, almost by the way, addressed its actual employment. It included Secretary of War Henry Stimson and James Byrnes, soon to be Secretary of State. Also involved were a series of key luminaries of the scientific establishment who had been associated with the project since its inception, such as Vannevar Bush and James Conant. Robert Oppenheimer, General Groves and General Marshall were invited to attend.[22]

The Committee had one preliminary meeting before this fateful gathering.[23] At this second meeting the nature of the 'psychological factor' became more precise, again with Oppenheimer's prompting. After it had been noted that the effect of one bomb would not be different from 'any Air Corps strike of current dimensions', Oppenheimer interjected:

the visual effect of an atomic bombing would be tremendous. It would be accompanied by a brilliant luminescence which would rise to a height of 10 000 to 20 000 feet.

It was on the basis of this spectacular quality that those considering the use of the bomb stressed its shock value. The report records how:

After much discussion concerning various types of targets and effects to be produced, the Secretary expressed the conclusion, on which there was general agreement, that we could not give the Japanese any warning, that we could not concentrate on a civilian area, but that we should seek to make a profound psychological impression on as many Japanese as possible. At the suggestion of Dr Conant the Secretary agreed that the most desirable target would be a vital war plant employing a large number of workers and closely surrounded by workers' houses.

Note now how Groves's original criterion – 'to adversely affect the will of the Japanese people to continue the war' – had turned into making a 'profound psychological impression'. This formulation also reinforced the view that, in some way, the members of the committee had shifted discussion away from crude mass destruction. There is little record of the debate at the meeting, but we know that the President himself, Stimson and Marshall were all uneasy with regard to making civilians targets and had been thinking on how best to avoid this in the days before this meeting. On 29 May Marshall had told Stimson that he hoped the weapon 'might first be used against straight military objectives such as a large naval installation' and only later, if necessary, against 'large manufacturing areas', and only then after adequate warning.[24] We know too of Stimson's own conversations with his diary and with his President of his anxiety to spare civilians, and Truman's own conviction – sustained long after the bomb had been dropped – that it was directed at a large military target.

All this contradicted the logic of the target committee and the formulation agreed at the Interim Committee is best seen as a face-saving device. Stimson's only real influence on this matter exercised later was to spare Kyoto – whose people, it will be recalled, the Target Committee judged to be 'more intelligent and hence better able to appreciate the significance of the weapon'.

The tension in Stimson's position was adequately illustrated in his conversation with Truman a week after the Interim Committee's meeting. On the one hand he objected strenuously to continued area bombing. On the other:

I was a little fearful that before we could get ready the Air Force might have Japan so thoroughly bombed out that the new weapon [the atomic bomb] would not have a chance to show its strength.

In practice, and despite the talk of military targets and psychological impact, the stress on the shock value of the weapon ensured that civilian casualties would be maximised. This is evident with regard to two issues also discussed by the Interim Committee. The first recorded in the minutes is of Oppenheimer's suggestion that the psychological impact be maximised by several strikes at the same time: Groves objected because this would require a rush job, the extra knowledge of the bomb's effects gained through successive blasts would be lost and 'the effect would not be sufficiently distinct from our regular Air Force bombing program'. Groves too understood now that this was not simply going to be an extension of the 20th Air Force's campaign.

The second issue was discussed over lunch and is not mentioned in the minutes. According to Arthur Compton he raised the possibility with Stimson of a 'non-military demonstration of the bomb's effects' and he broadened the discussion. The main obstacles to this course were soon identified: if prior warning were given there could be interference with the detonation; a failure following a great advertisement would be wholly counter-productive; a detonation on uninhabited territory might not impress those who most needed to be impressed. This discussion lasted ten minutes.

Despite the difficulty of devising a convincing demonstration, the scientific panel of the committee was asked to see if one could be found. Their efforts then merged with those of the Franck Committee of concerned scientists anxious to find any way of avoiding mass destruction.[25] As the Interim Committee observed at its next meeting after reviewing the issue: 'the difficulties of making a purely technical demonstration that would find its way into Japan's controlling councils were indeed great.'

Most important of all was the lack of warning. This was critical to the whole strategy. A general warning, already made credible enough by the air campaign, had been issued at Potsdam which threatened 'prompt and utter destruction' if there was no unconditional surrender. As Marshall observed: 'It's no good warning them. If you warn them there's no surprise. And the only way to produce shock is surprise.'[26] Groves made the same point. He claimed not to understand how 'anyone could ignore the importance of the effect on the Japanese people and their government of the overwhelming surprise of the bomb'.[27] A lack of specific warning also reduced the risk of the whole thing turning out to be a dud after being heralded as a spectacular instrument of destruction. Of the members of the Interim Committee only Ralph Bard, towards the end of June, became uneasy with regard to the lack of warning and suggested that this policy be reversed.[28]

The tactics of the attack involved distracting the attention of any Japanese air defences by carrying out other air raids on the same day and by using a single, unescorted plane on the assumption that the Japanese would take no notice of a lone plane flying at high altitude. If anything it would be taken to be a reconnaissance plane. Despite this assumption they still expected relatively moderate casualties on the basis of people taking shelter. Oppenheimer had estimated that 20 000 would die. This was one of his few calculations that was grossly in error.

Butow's classic study – *Japan's Decision to Surrender* – correctly points out that the dropping of the two atomic bombs on Japan, together with the Soviet entry into the war 'did not produce the decision' to end the war, but that they created an 'unusual atmosphere' in Tokyo, which facilitated Japan's hurried decision to accept the Potsdam declaration on 15 August 1945.[29]

Before the first atomic bomb was dropped on 6 August, most Japanese decision makers, including the Emperor, Prime Minister Admiral Suzuki Kantarō, Foreign Minister Tōgō Shigenori and many Japanese overseas diplomats, the Director of the Cabinet Board of Information, Shimomura Hiroshi (Kainan) and Navy Minister Yonai Mitsumasa agreed that Japan must end the war and thereby accept defeat.[30] Two interrelated problems remained unresolved: first, Japan's leaders were uneasy about what the price of a decision to surrender would be, since they did not want Japan's termination of the war to bring about her complete downfall – in other words, the extermination of Japan as an entity, the so-called *Kokutai*. They feared that Japan might be eliminated as a nation-state as a result of its unconditional surrender. The *sine qua non* of the continued existence of Japan meant, for these leaders, the preservation of the Imperial system.

The second problem was how to achieve a consensus among the top decision-makers – the Prime Minister, the Foreign Minister, the Navy and War Ministers and the Naval and Army Chiefs of General Staff – for the surrender of Japan. Except for Yonai, the other military leaders, particularly in the army, believed that Japan should continue to fight on the mainland. If the Prime Minister overrode this military opinion, the Army Minister might resign from the Cabinet, and if the Army did not recommend a new Army Minister, the classic pattern of the dissolution of the Cabinet would be repeated. Similarly, those military leaders – although they were aware of Japan's appalling military weaknesses – still had to take account of the feelings of their middle-echelon officers, since, otherwise, there might be a repetition of the army revolts of the 1930s. Thus, the unity of the Japanese decision-making system depended upon a delicate balance between a powerful military hierarchy which was, at the same time, vulnerable to the actions of its subordinates.[31]

Consequently, before Japan decided to surrender, there were a number of uncertainties about the post-war future of the Imperial system under the Potsdam declaration and these tended to stiffen the attitudes of those who supported a final stand on the mainland. The Japanese leaders were unable to overcome the deadlock. Moreover, there remained the hope – albeit declining – that the Soviet Union, which had remained neutral in the Pacific War, might be persuaded to act as a mediator and enable Japan to extract more favourable terms than unconditional surrender from the Western Allies.[32] Thus, after the Potsdam declaration, Tokyo adopted a 'wait and see' policy, but this was complicated by the time factor. The situation in Japan was deteriorating rapidly in 1945, with shortages of food and other necessities (salt, sugar, soap, clothing, rice, etc.), an inability to produce aircraft and military equipment of all kinds and the scarcity of strategic materials, the declining morale of the Japanese people, especially as a result of American strategic bombings ('guests', as the regular bombing missions were called by the desperate Japanese public).[33] In the light of all this, it was clear that, as Louis Allen has pointed out, 'by any rational calculation ... the time was months overdue for Japan to sue for peace'.[34] Certainly, some Japanese ministers and officials were increasingly pessimistic about the prospects for the maintenance of public order if the war continued until the autumn of 1945 and beyond.

As the sequence of events leading to the decision to surrender on 15 August is well known, our focus is on the initial Japanese reaction to the first atomic bomb dropped on Hiroshima, and we will try to examine the importance of the impact of the American use of atomic bombs on the minds of the Japanese leaders at that time.

Lieutenant-Colonel Ōya of the General Staff was sent to Hiroshima at the end of June 1945 to re-organise the information/intelligence section dealing with Anglo-American affairs in the Headquarters of the Second General Army. Ōya originally intended to stay in Hiroshima for a short time, but he was asked to remain in the section until 15 August. On 6 August, the weather in the Hiroshima area was fine and warm, with a temperature of 26.7C. About seven in the morning, he heard an air-raid warning, but then recalled the all-clear sounding at about eight o'clock. According to Hattori, the warning was withdrawn about 7.30 am, but Japan's radio broadcast another warning at about eight that there were two B-29 bombers flying over Hiroshima which were probably on reconnaissance. Ōya was already working in the office and at 8.15 am he heard the noise of the B-29 bombers, and wondered why the air-raid warning had been withdrawn. He stood up and walked to the window behind his desk to look out. He saw two B-29 bombers flying due north-north-west, and he believed that they were flying away from Hiroshima city. He went back to his desk to continue his work, while other officers continued to watch the two aeroplanes from the office windows. Then Ōya suddenly felt a tremendous shock and he sensed a terrific flash of light. He was blown out of his desk chair for a distance of about 2–3 metres and saw blood pouring from the bodies of the seven or so other officers. Of course he had no idea what was happening, but he remembered one of the officers, Captain Ishi, saying that 'this might be an atomic bomb'. Ōya knew that the Americans employed two methods of bombing: in the case of strategic bombing, they tended to use a large number of small incendiary shells, while for battlefield attacks, they used more powerful 'special new types of bombs'. However, he did not then believe that the weapons used at Hiroshima were atomic bombs.[35]

The Special Intelligence Section in the army General Headquarters, which had been established in July 1943 and was attached to the Chief of the General Staff of the Army, claimed that as early as May 1945 they were aware of some interesting American air activity, which might have been connected to the Hiroshima bombing.[36] Given their lack of radar, Special Intelligence had to rely on a radio direction-ranging apparatus (*Hōkō Tanchiki*) to follow up the movements of enemy planes through their radio signals. The special information section was unable to decode the contents of these signals, except for very simple communications, but they were able to identify roughly the number of enemy planes in a flight and the direction in which these planes were flying.[37] The Special Intelligence section noted in mid-May 1945 that one B-29 plane, flying from Hawaii to the Saipan area, despatched a unusually long telegraph to Washington. By mid-June, it became clear that this plane belonged to a small squadron of about 10–12 aircraft. From the end of June this plane, sometimes alone, sometimes with two to three others, flew over the sea near Tenian island in the Marianas and by mid-July, they were flying around the Japanese mainland before returning to an air base on Tenian island. The Special Intelligence Section assumed that this was 'some sort of training', but could not identify what it was for. Separate from the Special Intelligence Section, the 6th division of the Intelligence Department of the Army General Staff in charge of Anglo-American affairs was aware that 'there was a new experiment in New Mexico on 16 July', but they did not connect this with an atomic bomb explosion.[38]

About three in the morning of 6 August, the Special Intelligence Section intercepted a brief signal to Washington from an American aircraft. About one hour later, another signal from a group of 2–3 planes to an American base on Iwo island was monitored, which apparently stated that 'we are flying to our target.' This information did concern the intelligence officials, but no further radio messages were detected until 7.20 on the same morning, when both the Navy and Army intelligence intercepted a signal from a B-29 bomber, which was on its way to the Sea of Harima after flying to Hiroshima from the Bungo Channel, situated between Shikoku and Kyushu islands. This plane was not accompanied by other American planes, as was often the case with American weather reconnaissance squadrons, and this apparently solo flight puzzled the Japanese officials, who continued to monitor the Bungo Channel in the expectation that other American planes were following the first. Even more unusual, however, was that, at about 8.06, two B-29s appeared from the opposite side of the Bungo Channel, and flew towards Hiroshima. The Japanese Intelligence Community realised that they had been outmanoeuvred, but it was now too late to take any precautions against these enemy intruders.[39]

At 8.30 – about 15 minutes after the American bomb was dropped on Hiroshima – Kure navy depot in the Hiroshima prefecture reported to the Navy Ministry in Tokyo that the enemy had dropped an enormously destructive bomb.[40] Just after 10.00 on that morning, the War Ministry in Tokyo received a report from Hiroshima which stated that, given the information that the United States had been developing a new type of bomb, 'this must be it'. Neither of these sources, however, identified this 'new type of bomb' as an atomic device.[41]

During the afternoon of 7 August, an emergency meeting of key Japanese Cabinet ministers took place after President Harry Truman had publicly stated that the bomb which the United States had dropped on Hiroshima was an atomic weapon. However, War Minister Anami contended that, because the Army had not yet begun a thorough investigation into the circumstances at Hiroshima, they did not want to admit that Hiroshima had been subjected to an atomic attack. The Army General Staff was to send a group of investigators to Hiroshima, headed by Lieutenant-General Arisue.[42]

In the meantime, the Army persistently rejected any reference to the words 'atomic bomb' in Hiroshima in public announcements and there was a heated debate between the Army Headquarters and the Board of Information as to how the public were to be informed of the disaster that had taken place in the city. The information bureau argued that the public must be told the truth so that they could be psychologically prepared for a new phase of modern warfare, while the Army feared that such an announcement would destroy public morale.[43] Consequently, the radio merely announced at 15.30 on 7 August that a few B-29 bombers had dropped 'a new type of bomb' on Hiroshima and which had caused a fair amount of damage and many casualties.[44] The next day, the major newspapers, *Asahi*, *Yomiuri*, and *Mainichi*, reported on similar lines.[45]

Because of engine trouble in their plane, the despatch of the Arisue mission to Hiroshima was delayed by one day and the mission did not arrive in the city until about noon on 8 August, more than two days after the bombing had taken place.[46] In the early hours of 9 August, Chief Cabinet Secretary Sakomizu received the news about the Soviet entry into the war with Japan. Sakomizu felt as if 'the earth was shaking'. Tōgō urged the Prime Minister to end the war as soon as possible. The Emperor told Marquis Kido, the Lord Keeper of the Privy Seal, 'now that the Soviets have entered the war with Japan, there was urgent need to resolve the problem of a ceasefire' and Hirohito asked Kido to convey this Imperial message to Suzuki.[47]

The six members of the Supreme War Direction Council met at 10.30 am on 9 August 1945, followed by two Cabinet meetings from 14.30 till 22.00. During the Supreme War Direction Council meeting, the Japanese leaders were informed that a second atomic bomb had been dropped on Nagasaki. Except for the Navy Minister, the military leaders remained opposed to accepting the Potsdam declaration. The Army Minister insisted that Japan was still able to fight a victorious battle on the mainland. Given this division of opinion, Prime Minister Suzuki asked the Emperor to decide on the matter. The Imperial conference convened at 23.50 and Hirohito informed the leaders of his decision that Japan must accept the Potsdam declaration but on the understanding that its acceptance must not involve the elimination of the Imperial system.[48] As we know, it would require a second Imperial decision on 14 August before Japan finally surrendered, and this decision was broadcast to the Japanese people by the Emperor on 15 August 1945.

Because of the delay to Arisue's mission (his report was completed on 10 August and it identified the bomb dropped on Hiroshima as an atomic one),[49] and because of the subsequent Soviet entry into the war before the Japanese leadership had time to clarify their views on the effects of the dropping of the first bomb, it is difficult to separate the impact of the atomic bombs on Japan's final decision to make peace from the effect of the Soviet entry into the war on that decision. However, the following observations suggest that the impact of the atomic bombs was of crucial importance to, and in some respects possibly even decisive in, Japan's decision in favour of a ceasefire.

First, between the dropping of the first atomic bomb and the Soviet entry, the Emperor and his close advisers believed that Japan must now end the war. Prime Minister Admiral Suzuki, on learning of Truman's statement on 7 August that Hiroshima had been the target of an atomic bomb, was awed by the American achievement and he argued 'unequivocally' that Japan must sue for peace.[50] Prince Konoye also took the new development seriously and told Marquis Kido that the war should be ended immediately.[51] As soon as he heard the news Shimomura sent a message to the Prime Minister that it was imperative that Japan decided on peace.[52] When Foreign Minister Tōgō reported to the Emperor during the afternoon of 8 August that the bomb provided an overwhelming motive for Japan to end the war, Hirohito entirely agreed, telling the Foreign Minister that 'now that this kind of weapon had been used in the war, it was even more impossible for Japan to continue the war'. He continued:

Japan could no longer afford to talk about the conditions of her surrender terms. She must aim for a speedy resolution of the war.[53]

Thus, before the Arisue mission's final report and before the Soviet Union declared war, the peace faction had resolved on a speedy ceasefire.

Secondly, while it was true that the Soviet entry into the war had shattered any lingering hope that the Soviet Union might mediate a negotiated peace between Japan and the Allies, many civilian leaders, who were shocked by the Soviet action, were already thinking of a ceasefire. Moreover, Foreign Minister Tōgō and his diplomats overseas had not placed much faith in the Soviet Union as a mediator.[54] Similarly, the Army was well aware that the Russians were preparing for war in the East and had been transferring troops from Europe to the Far East since February 1945. Moscow's declaration in April 1945 that it would not renew the neutrality pact with Japan, followed by Germany's unconditional surrender in May, seemed to prove the Soviet Union's ultimate intentions. The Soviet entry so soon after the dropping of the atomic bomb on Hiroshima added to the distress of the Japanese and also upset the Army's plan for the final battle on the mainland which involved transferring some 250 000 men and weapons from Manchuria to mainland Japan. Nonetheless, the imminent opening of hostilities by the USSR was not unexpected – indeed, the Army thought that it was merely 'a matter of time' before Moscow decided to enter the war against Japan.[55]

Thirdly, in comparison to the Soviet entry, the atomic bomb took Japan's leaders completely by surprise, since Army General Headquarters had concluded optimistically that the Americans would be unable to complete their research on atomic weapons before the end of the war.[56] A section of the Japanese Army had also been trying desperately, but without success, to develop atomic weapons.

As early as April 1940, Major General Yasuda Takeo, then director of the Institute of Aviation Technology in the Army, instructed his staff to work on the atomic bomb. His decision was partially influenced by German progress in this field. The Army's research was directed by Dr Nishina, head of the Institute of Physical and Chemical Research.[57] Three years later, in March 1943, Yasuda reported to General Tōjō that it might be possible for Japan to produce atomic weapons in the near future. General Tōjō, knowing that the Americans were also making progress with this weapon, believed that 'the atomic weapons might decide the outcome of the present war with the United States'.[58]

Accordingly, Tōjō ordered Yasuda to promote the research and development of atomic bombs vigorously and the Army's aviation centre, in collaboration with Dr Nishina's research office, took the first official step towards developing atomic weapons. The codename was 'Ni-gō' research – 'Ni' was derived from the first two letters of Dr Nishina's surname. This is why when Tōjō first learned of the Hiroshima bombing, he realised that this must be caused by the detonation of an atomic bomb.[59]

However, the Japanese scientists were unable to produce a chain reaction. Nor did Dr Nishina succeed in splitting the two uranium isotopes, 235 and 238. Uranium was in short supply and he asked the Army to obtain at least 2 tons for his research programme. The search for uranium only seriously began in 1943. As Japan produced so little, Captain Kawashima investigated gold mines near Seoul, Korea, but he discovered that the mines contained only a small quantity (one could obtain about a dozen uranium isotopes, each the size of the tip of the fifth finger, from 24 cubic square inches of ore).[60] The Army also hoped to obtain some from Germany, as Czechoslovakia, then under German occupation, was reputed to produce good quality uranium. After difficult negotiations, Nazi Germany agreed to give about two tons of uranium to Japan, which would be transported there by two submarines, despatched to Japan for this purpose. One never arrived in Japan, and the other was unable to sail after Germany surrendered in May 1945. Accordingly, the 'Ni-gō' research made slow progress, and finally, the Army had to abandon atomic research altogether in the spring of 1945, when intensive air raids on Tokyo and Osaka destroyed a number of research centres working on atomic bombs.[61] The Navy, too, was involved in atomic research, but they soon realised that they could achieve little before the end of the war and switched their efforts to the development of radio beams. This research also was never completed.[62] Of course, given the secrecy attached to atomic weapons research, most Japanese civilian leaders and military officials knew nothing about the project. However, Army General Headquarters claimed that they had already suspected, before the final Arisue report came, that an atomic bomb had been dropped on Hiroshima.[63] Nevertheless, the Army leaders deliberately underestimated the amount of damage caused by the bomb and were reluctant to give much information either to the civilian leaders or to the public (the latter did not know the full truth about the atomic bomb until after Japan's surrender).[64]

The reality was that the military could do nothing to counter the threat of atomic bombardment, except to suggest some defensive measures, which included (1) a rapid evacuation of the populace into shelters if even one enemy plane was sighted over Japan's air sphere; (2) to order the people to cover their bodies with sufficient clothing, preferably with white outer clothes, and not to expose their skin to radiation; (3) always to carry some ointment for burns; and (4) in the event of evacuation, to make sure that fires were not started by carelessly discarding lighted cigarettes, leaving on kitchen stoves, etc.[65]

While the Army contended that these measures would be sufficient to counter the effects of atomic bombs, they soon shifted from an underestimation to an overestimation of the ability of the United States to produce these weapons. At the Cabinet meeting on 9 August, War Minister Anami, who had obtained some information from an American prisoner of war, told the Ministers that:

> One atomic bomb could destroy 6 square miles, which was equivalent to 2000 B-29s each with 300 conventional bombs of 500 pounds each ... the Americans appeared to have one hundred atomic bombs ... while they could drop three per day. The next target might well be Tokyo.[66]

Thus the Army's surprise at the American achievement in atomic technology in contrast to Japan's inability to reach even the initial level of atomic research, their consequent reluctance to use the words, 'atomic bomb' in any public announcements, (whereas the news of the Soviet Union's entry into the war was reported in headlines of the major newspapers on 10 August), their ready acceptance that the Americans possessed about 100 atomic bombs, all suggested the depth of the shock of the atomic bomb on the minds of the military leaders.

Finally, and as the American leaders had anticipated, whatever the impact of the Soviet invasion of Manchuria and Sakhalin may have been, it was *indirect*, whereas the atomic bomb demonstrated *directly* to Japan's leaders that the United States could totally devastate her mainland. The fact that one single bomb could kill and injure 130 000 human beings instantly, as was initially reported, exposed the already appalling military weakness of Japan to the entire leadership of the country.[67]

Of course, the impact of the atomic bomb cannot be discussed in isolation and can be seen as the final phase of the cumulative damage already inflicted on mainland Japan by the intensive American air raids which began during the autumn of 1944. Given that Manchuria and Japan's other occupied territories were still regarded as 'outside land' [*gaichi*], as opposed to Japan's mainland which was referred as 'inside land' [*naichi*], the people of Japan were faced with the military reality of war for the first time when the United States began to bomb their homeland.

Prior to the dropping of the two atomic bombs, American strategic bombing had already killed some 665 000 people and destroyed 20 per cent of civilian housing in Japan.[68] After a massive air raid on 25 May 1945, the Army leaders were attacked by Cabinet ministers for their inability to find any measures to counter the American bombers. The Imperial Palace also caught fire and as a result War Minister Anami nearly resigned.[69] In May, an exhibition of weapons for the national volunteer army was held at the Prime Minister's office. Prime Minister Suzuki and other ministers were disgusted with the poor quality of the weapons on display. These included bamboo spears, bows and arrows, and pistols with only 50 per cent accuracy, which fired pieces of iron instead of bullets, which were by then hard to obtain.[70] The shortage and poor quality of these weapons were compounded by the untrained manpower available to deploy them – men who were either too young or too old to be in the regular forces.[71] Cabinet ministers feared that a tired and hungry populace might become defiant and that public disorder might result.[72]

Thus, the atomic bombs helped to bring home on a much larger scale to those Japan's leaders, who were already seeking a means to end the war, how potentially catastrophic Japan's situation was. At the same time, the military radicals, who could not conceive that Japan was on the verge of defeat, were angered by the growing official consensus about the need to accept the Potsdam declaration. However, the military leaders now had more power over their subordinates, since the Emperor, who was the Supreme Commander of the Japanese Armed Forces, had twice decided in favour of Japan's surrender at the Imperial Conference. War Minister Anami, the Chief of the General Staff Umezu and General Tōjō, the former Prime Minister, all refused to collaborate with plans for a *coup d'état* by the younger middle-echelon officers. On the night of 14 August, an attempted military coup by the radicals, designed to prevent any appeal for peace from the Imperial Palace and to steal the recording of the Emperor's announcement of Japan's acceptance of the Potsdam declaration, collapsed ignominiously.[73]

In conclusion, the atomic bombs succeeded in the American aim of shocking Japan into surrender. While it is difficult to separate the impact of the atomic bomb from the subsequent blow of the Soviet entry into the war, or to isolate completely the effects of the dropping of the atomic bombs from the cumulative effects of American strategic bombing, the events from 6 to 9 August 1945 helped to expedite the Japanese decision-making process, which was notoriously complicated and time-consuming, and finally led to Japan's decision to terminate the war. Japanese leaders were not only awed by the American ability to produce atomic bombs during the war, but were also taken by surprise when one was dropped on

Hiroshima. The nature of shock was more direct than the news about the Soviet entry, which itself dramatically exposed Japan's appalling military weakness.

Indeed, Japan would probably have used the new weapons during the war if her atomic research had succeeded. Colonel Ogata, then a military aide-de-camp to His Majesty, believed, when he heard the news of Hiroshima, that 'if Japan had possessed atomic weapons, she could have attacked the United States, which might have changed the phase of the war in Japan's favour'. The view was, as Kojima has discussed, also echoed by some civilian leaders.[74] Those Japanese leaders who were desperate to avoid defeat or unconditional surrender would have taken any steps to avoid either alternative. Seen in this light, lingering Japanese criticisms about the American use of the atomic bomb (most of whose awful side effects were then unknown to United States leadership) are ill founded.[75] Conversely, the United States can claim that her use of the atomic bomb was in the end justifiable in that Japan also intended to use such weapons during the war if and when they became available.

## NOTES

1. The Committee for the Compilation of Materials on Damage caused by the Atomic Bomb in Hiroshima and Nagasaki, *Hiroshima and Nagasaki: The Physical, Medical, and Social Effects of the Atomic Bombings* (London: Hutchinson, 1981).
2. Ibid., p. 335.
3. J.S. Allen, *Atomic Imperialism: The State, Monopoly and the Bomb* (New York: International Publishers, 1952).
4. P.M.S. Blackett, *Military and Political Consequences of Atomic Energy* (London: Turnstile Press, 1948).
5. Gar Alperovitz, *Atomic Diplomacy: Hiroshima and Potsdam; The Use of the Atomic Bomb and the American Confrontation with Soviet Power* (New York: Vintage, 1985) still keeps the revisionist flag flying although his thesis is not taken very seriously now. For a spirited exchange involving a television producer who does, see Sheila Kerr, 'Alperovitz, Timewatch and the Bomb', *Intelligence and National Security* 5:3 (July 1990), and Robert Marshall, 'The Atomic Bomb and the Lag in the Historical Understanding', *Intelligence and National Security* 6:2 (April 1991), with rejoinders by S. Kerr, G. Warner and D. Cameron Watt. For the contrasting view, see the essays by Alperovitz and Warner in David Carlton and Herbert Levine (ed.), *The Cold War Debated* (London: McGraw-Hill, 1988).
6. Richard G. Hewlett and Oscar Anderson, *The New World 1939–1946*, vol. 1 of a History of the USAEC (Pennsylvania: Pennsylvania State University Press, 1962) pp. 254, 322.
7. Letters to *Science* Magazine, 2 December 1959.
8. Arthur Compton, *Atomic Quest* (New York: Harper, 1950) p. 234.
9. See Leslie Groves, *Now It Can Be Told: The Story of the Manhattan Project* (New York: Harper & Row, 1962), pp. 272–3; L. Giovannitti and F. Freed, *The Decision to Drop the Bomb* (London: Methuen, 1967) pp. 247–8.
10. Hewlett and Anderson, *The New World*, p. 253.

210        *Lawrence Freedman and Saki Dockrill*

11.  The Journals of David E. Lilienthal, vol. 2, *The Atomic Energy Years, 1945–1950* (London: Harper & Row, 1964) pp. 198–9; John P. Sutherland, 'The Story General Marshall Told Me' *US News & World Report*, 2 November 1959, p. 53.
12.  Herbert Feis, *The Atomic Bomb and the End of World War II* (Princeton: Princeton University Press, 1966) p. 10.
13.  Barton Bernstein, 'Eclipsed by Hiroshima and Nagasaki: Early Thinking about Tactical Nuclear Weapons', *International Security* 15:4 (Spring 1991).
14.  Giovannitti and Freed, *The Decision to Drop the Bomb*, p. 36.
15.  Quoted in ibid., p. 35.
16.  Views of Air Force Colonel on Target Committee, cited in Richard Rhodes, *The Making of the Atomic Bomb* (London: Simon & Schuster, 1986) p. 627.
17.  General H.H. Arnold, *Global Mission* (London: Hutchinson, 1951) p. 260.
18.  Barton J. Bernstein, 'Ike and Hiroshima: Did He Oppose It?', *The Journal of Strategic Studies* 10:3 (September 1987).
19.  Henry Stimson and McGeorge Bundy, *On Active Service in Peace and War*, (London: Hutchinson, 1948) pp. 364, 369–70, 373.
20.  Groves, *Now It Can Be Told*, p. 267.
21.  Rhodes, *The Making of the Atomic Bomb*, p. 631. The full document is reproduced in Michael B. Stoff, Jonathan F. Fanton and R. Hal Williams, *The Manhattan Project: A Documentary Introduction to the Atomic Age* (New York: McGraw Hill, 1991) pp. 97–103.
22.  Other members were Ralph Bard, William Clayton, Karl Compton, George Harrison. Among those invited to attend were Enrico Fermi, Arthur Compton, E.O. Lawrence, Harvey Bundy and Arthur Page.
23.  The minutes are found in Stoff, et al., *The Manhattan Project*, pp. 105–20.
24.  Cited in Bernstein, 'Eclipsed by Hiroshima', p. 156.
25.  Compton, *Atomic Quest*, pp. 236–44. This was the strategy, rather than the direct attack, that had been proposed with the clearest eye on the post-war world.
26.  Giovannitti and Freed, *The Decision to Drop the Bomb*, p. 36.
27.  Groves, *Now It Can Be Told*, p. 266.
28.  On the question of warning, see McGeorge Bundy, *Danger and Survival: Choices about the Bomb in the First Fifty Years* (New York: Random House, 1988) pp. 172–7.
29.  Robert Butow, *Japan's Decision to Surrender* (Stanford: Stanford University Press, 1954) p. 231. Despite the ever-growing literature on this subject, there have been relatively few articles from the Japanese perspective published in English. See Sadao Asada, 'Japanese Perceptions of the A-Bomb Decision, 1945–1980' Joe C. Dixon (ed.), *The American Military and the Far East – Proceedings of the Ninth Military History Symposium, United States Air Force Academy, 1–3 October 1980* (Washington DC: United States Air Force Academy and Office Air Force History Headquarters, 1980) pp. 200–19.
30.  Tōgō Shigenori, *Jidai no Ichimen* (Memoirs), (Tokyo: Hara, 1989) pp. 330–42; Butow, *The Decision to Surrender*, pp. 104–111ff; The Ministry of Foreign Affairs (ed.), *Dai'niji Sekai Taisen Shūsen Shiroku* (The historical record of the termination of the Second World War) vol. 2, (Tokyo: Yamate, 1990) pp. 448–66. (Hereafter cited as *Shiroku*).
31.  S. Hayashi, *Taiheiyō Sensō* (The Pacific War), (Tokyo: Chuokoron, 1980) pp. 438–52 ff; H. Suzuki (ed.) *Memoirs of Suzuki Kantarō* (Tokyo: Jiji, 1985) pp. 275–93; for Japanese civil-military relations, see S. Dockrill, 'Hirohito, the Emperor's Army and Pearl Harbor', *Review of International Studies* 18 (1992), pp. 319–33.
32.  For instance, the subject was discussed at a meeting of the Supreme Council for the Direction of War on 11 May 1945, see *Shiroku*, pp. 448–64; Hayashi, *Taiheiyō Sensō*, pp. 442–4.
33.  Hayashi, *Taiheiyō Sensō*, p. 406.

34. Louis Allen, 'Japan Surrenders: Reason and Unreason in August 1945', unpublished Conference paper presented at the Second Strategy Conference at the US Army War College, Carlisle Barracks, Pennsylvania, 7–10 February 1991.
35. For Ōya's oral history, on 11 Feb 1976, see The Army Record: Hondo - Seibu-204. The Army Archives, The Institute for National Defence Studies, the Self-Defence Agency, Tokyo. We are grateful to the Japanese Self-Defence Agency, and especially Mr Ōya for allowing us to quote from Mr Ōya's oral history concerning his experiences in Hiroshima.
36. Eizo Hori, *Daihon'ei-Sanbō no Jōhō Senki* (The record of the war of Intelligence at the Army General Staff) (Tokyo: Bungei Shunju, 1989) pp. 208–14. For the recent study on Japanese Intelligence, see Louis Allen, 'Japanese Intelligence Systems' *Journal of Contemporary History* 22:4 (October 1987), pp. 547–62: J. Chapman, 'Japanese Intelligence, 1918–1945: A Suitable Case for Treatment' in Christopher Andrew and Jeremy Noakes (eds), *Intelligence and International Relations 1900–1945*, Exeter Studies in History no. 15 (Exeter: University of Exeter, 1987) pp. 145–90; Edward Drea, 'Reading Each Other's Mail: Japanese Communication Intelligence 1920–1941', *The Journal of Military History* 55:2 (April 1991), pp. 185–96; H. Iwashima, *Jōhōsen ni Kanpai Shita Nihon: Rikugun Angō 'Shinwa' no Hakai* (Tokyo: Hara, 1984).
37. Hori, *Jōhō*, pp. 211–13.
38. Ibid, pp. 213–16; Ronald Spector, *Eagle against the Sun* (Harmondsworth and New York: Penguin, 1987) pp. 554–5.
39. Hori, *Jōhō*, pp. 216–19; William Craig, *The Fall of Japan* (Harmondsworth: Penguin, 1979) pp. 69–71.
40. K. Han'dō, *Seidan-Ten'nō to Suzuki Kantarō* (A Sacred Decision: the Emperor and Suzuki) (Tokyo: Bungeishunjū, 1988) p. 330.
41. The Military History Section, The Self-Defence Agency (eds), *Sensi Sōsho vol. 19 - Hondo Bōkū Sakusen* (the Strategy for the air defence of mainland Japan), (Tokyo: Asagumo, 1968) p. 628. (Hereafter cited as *Sōsho, vol. 19).*
42. Ibid, p. 635; Hayashi, *Taiheiyō Sensō*, pp. 456–7.
43. See Shimomura, *Shūsenki* (The Record of the Termination of the War), (Tokyo: Kamakura bunko, 1948) pp. 97–8; See also *Shiroku*, pp. 734–5; Yomiuri (ed.), *Shōwashi no Ten'nō* (The Emperor during the Showa era) vol. 7, (Tokyo: Yomiuri, 1972) p. 228.
44. The Military History Section the Self-Defence Agency (ed.), *Hondo Kessen Junbi (2) -Sensi Sōsho, vol. 57* (Preparations for the decisive battle on the mainland) (Tokyo: Asagumo, 1972) p. 578. (Hereafter cited as *Sōsho, vol. 57.)*
45. See *Mainichi*, 8 August 1945; *Asahi*, 8 August 1945; *Yomiuri*, 8 August 1945; for the Soviet entry, see *Asahi*, 10 August 1945.
46. *Sōsho, vol. 19*, p. 635.
47. K. Kido, *Kido Diaries*, vol. 2, (Tokyo: Tokyo University Press, 1966), p. 1223; Hayashi, *Taiheiyō Sensō*, p. 458.
48. *Shiroku*, pp. 760–85; Kido, *Kido Diaries*, pp. 1223–4.
49. *Sōsho, vol. 57*, p. 579.
50. Suzuki (ed.), *Memoirs*, p. 294.
51. Kido, *Diaries*, p. 1222; Hayashi, *Taiheiyō Sensō*, pp. 456–7; T. Yabe (ed.), *Konoe Fumimaro* (Biography of Prince Konoe), vol. 2 (Tokyo: Konoe Fumimaro Denki Hensan Kanko-kai, 1952) p. 565.
52. *Showa no Ten'nō*, vol. 7, pp. 207–8.
53. Tōgō, *Memoirs*, pp. 355–6. Han'dō, *Seidan*, p. 335.
54. Tōgō, *Memoirs*, pp. 327–42ff; *Shiroku*, pp. 448–66ff; See also Sato, Ambassador to Moscow to the Ministry of Foreign Affairs, tels. 1143, 1328, 1416, 8 June, 12, July 1945, ibid., pp. 634–44; Butow, *Japan's Decision to Surrender*, pp. 104–11.

55.   *Sōsho, vol. 57*, pp. 580–2; see also Mizumachi minute (undated), 'Japanese preparations as of February 1945 for a possible war with the Soviet Union', File 1003, Army Archives 56, the Institute for National Defense Studies, Tokyo.
56.   *Shiroku*, pp. 731–2; Suzuki (ed.), *Memoirs*, p. 294.
57.   *Sōsho, vol. 19*, p. 631.
58.   *Sōsho, vol. 19*, p. 632; M. Hosaka, *Tōjō Hideki to Ten'nō no Jidai* (H. Tōjō and the Emperor's era), vol. 2 (Tokyo: Bunshun, 1988) pp. 102, 202.
59.   For the outline of Japan's atomic research, see *Sōsho vol. 19*, pp. 631–2.
60.   *Sōsho, vol. 19*, p. 633.
61.   Ibid., pp. 633–5.
62.   *Shōwashi no Ten'nō*, 7, p. 243; *Sōsho vol. 19*, p. 635.
63.   Ibid., pp. 635.
64.   *Shōwashi no Ten'nō*, vol. 7, p. 228; *Shiroku*, pp. 727, 734–37; Shimomura, *Shūsenki* pp. 96–9; *Sōsho, vol. 19*, p. 635; *Sōsho, vol. 57*, p. 578.
65.   See for instance, *Asahi*, 9 and 10 August 1945; *Sōsho vol. 19*, pp. 641–2.
66.   *Shiroku*, p. 778.
67.   Noboru Kojima, *Ten'nō* vol. 5, (Tokyo: Bunshun, 1988) p. 278.
68.   Hayashi, *Taiheiyō Sensō*, pp. 405–6.
69.   Kojima, *Ten'nō* vol. 5, p. 214–8; Han'dō, *Seidan*, pp. 264–7; *Shōwa no Ten'nō* vol. 7, pp. 158–60.
70.   Ibid., p. 162; N. Kojima *Taiheiyō Sensō* (The Pacific War), vol. 2, (Tokyo: Chuko, 1988) pp. 334–5.
71.   Akira Fujiwara, *Nihon Gunjishi* (Japanese Military History) vol. 1, (Tokyo Nihon Hyōronsha, 1987) pp. 237–61ff; Jun'ichiro Kisaka, *Taiheiyō Sensō*, (Tokyo: Shoga'kan, 1989), p. 394.
72.   *Shōwa no Ten'nō*, vol. 7, pp. 177–80; *Tōgō, Memoirs*, p. 342; *Shiroku*, pp. 730–1, 766–7.
73.   Tōgō, *Memoirs*, p. 345; *Shiroku*, pp. 798–812; *Shōwa no Ten'nō*, vol. 7, pp. 177–8, 181–3, 228, 289; Hosaka, *Tōjō*, vol. 2, pp. 204–11; Shimomura, *Shusenki*, p. 50; Yuzuru Sanematsu, *Yonai Mitsumasa* (Tokyo: Yomiuri, 1990) pp. 365–401.
74.   Kojima, *Ten'nō* vol. 5, p. 279; Admiral Koshiro Oikawa, who served as Navy Minister between September 1941 and September 1942, also believed, in the aftermath of the battle of Okinawa, that Japan might have to use the new weapon. See the record of an interview with Itoh (undated, c. 1958), in 1-Shūsenshori (problems on the termination of the Pacific War)-4, Navy Archives, 10, the Institute of the National Defence Studies, Tokyo.
75.   However, during the immediate period after Japan's surrender, the statistics showed that more people believed that the war was 'Japan's own fault' than those who blamed the Americans for their action at Hiroshima and Nagasaki. See Asada, *'Japanese Perceptions'* p. 202. More recently, a school of thought has suggested that while the Americans often say 'Remember Pearl Harbor', the Japanese do not equate the causes (Pearl Harbor) and the results (Hiroshima). See Shin Itonaga, 'Beikaigun no Tainichi Sensō Keikaku' (The US Navy's War Planning against Japan' in Ikuhiko Hata (ed.), *Shinjuwan wa Moeru* (Pearl Harbor Burning), vol. 1 (Tokyo: Hara, 1991) p. 102.

# Part VI
# Conclusions

# 12  The Legacy of the 'Pacific War' as Seen from Europe
## Saki Dockrill

Historians have adopted differing views on the study of recent history. Some consider it premature to examine a war which took place *only* fifty years ago. However, compared with the voluminous studies of the Second World War in Europe, most of which are available in English, one might ask why the literature of the Pacific War has been so neglected in English publications. Moreover, post-war Germany has been integrated into the Western community through the Council of Europe, NATO, the Western European Union and the European Economic Community, and it has become a leading economic and political power in Europe. Now that Germany has become united, she is expected to play an even more powerful role in the European Community, while the political influence of the United States in Europe is certainly declining. It is true that there remains a legacy of lingering bitterness and apprehension about Germany's growing power and fears that she might once again dominate Europe. However, it cannot be denied that post-war Germany has established herself as a respected member of the European community. On the other hand, the image of post-war Japan remains uneven and unbalanced. Japan is seen as a massive economic power, which, however, lacks the ability to influence international events as in the case of the recent Gulf War – and the decency to admit the appalling consequences of her military aggression in Asia and the Pacific. Japan's economic success is not accepted as entirely the product of her own efforts. It has been pointed out that she has benefited from United States protection of her military security and from massive US aid of about 20 billion dollars between 1945 and 1951, compared with about 30 billion dollars to Western European countries at large between 1946 and 1951.[1] Apart from the interest of Britain and Western Europe in forging economic cooperation with Japan and other Asian countries, these countries lie 'too far' to the east to excite much European interest in their histories or cultures. The gap between European perceptions of post-war Germany and post-war Japan remains a wide one.

That post-war Japanese governments have, after 47 years, been unsuccessful in building up confidence in her peaceful intentions in the countries Japan invaded in Asia, is *partly* the result of the international environment in which Japan found herself in the post-war period. Germany was occupied and remained divided for 45 years, but European reconciliation with the West Germans was hastened by the impact of the Cold War. The integration of Western Europe, including West Germany, came to be seen as imperative if the Communist threat was to be resisted.[2] It was true that negotiating with the ex-enemy did cause bitterness and antagonism between the West Germans and their potential allies in Western Europe. For instance, it took five years of negotiations with the Federal Republic of Germany before she became the fifteenth member of NATO in 1955. The memories of the Third Reich remained so vivid that the West Germans themselves were initially reluctant to rearm their nation, while the European allies feared a resurgent Germany once she was allowed to rearm. It took six years after 1949 before the sovereignty of the Federal Republic of Germany was restored, although her reunification remained unachieved until 1990 and her military occupation by the three victorious Western powers finally came to an end on 5 May 1955.[3] Nevertheless, during these years, the West German government attended numerous meetings and conferences with its former enemies, including France and Britain, which laid the foundations for Germany's post-war relationship with the rest of Western Europe.

On the other hand, the Cold War in Asia isolated Japan from mainland China and North Korea and from the victorious European powers. It is true that Japan was able to rearm much earlier (in 1950) than West Germany and she secured the restoration of her sovereignty in April 1952, three years earlier than West Germany. These diplomatic achievements were secured without any genuine reconciliation or even regular meetings with the leaders of her Asian neighbours. The Cold War in Asia led only to the creation of close links between Japan and the United States and made it seen as if the 1941–5 war had been waged only between the United States and Japan.[4] The relations of even these two countries have been strained recently by trade frictions and there still remains a lack of mutual understanding over the causes and consequences of the recent war.[5]

During the Yalta Conference in February 1945, the Allied powers (the United States, Britain and the Soviet Union) agreed that Germany must pay reparations 'in kind' rather than in money in order to avoid a repetition of the bitter experiences of the 1920s. It is well known that the Russians, who fought the Germans almost alone between 1941 and 1944 and who suffered enormous casualties, were ruthless in extracting reparations from both West and East Germany. The Soviet Union occupied eastern Germany and set up an East German government in 1949. The Russians were at last presented with the opportunity of punishing their former enemy, whereas China, a major victim of the Asian War, neither played a major role in Japan's occupation nor received much in the way of reparations from Japan. Here lay the seeds of China's continuing suspicious of Japan after 1945. Roosevelt regarded China as a future leading power in Asia and assured Chiang Kai-shek during the Cairo Conference in November 1943 that, among other things, China should be given a role in the occupation of Japan, an offer which was, however, rejected by Chiang on the ground that 'it would be too great a burden for China to bear'. In the end, Chiang had to promise to send about three Chinese divisions to occupy Japan, although these never materialised, as Chiang was by 1945 fully preoccupied in fighting the Chinese Communists.[6]

In the immediate post-war years from 1945 to 1949, China was embroiled in a civil war, while the rest of the world became divided between the Western bloc under the United States and the Eastern bloc under the Soviet Union. In the meantime, United States efforts to unite China and to encourage her to emerge as an Asian great power were frustrated and the US was instead compelled, under the pressure of the Cold War, to reconstruct Japan as anti-Communist bulwark in Asia. Accordingly, United States occupation policy became, as in post-war West Germany, less punitive and more concerned to promote Japan's economic recovery. The so-called 'reverse course' in US occupation policy in Japan took place after 1948 and the United States allowed Japan to discontinue all reparation payments in 1949.[7] By that time, China, the Netherlands, the Philippines and Britain had obtained only 30 per cent of the provisional reparations they had been promised.[8]

In September 1951, Japan concluded a peace treaty with 48 countries, but the Soviet Union, China, Taiwan, North Korea, India and Burma did not sign it, while Indonesia later refused to ratify the treaty. The reparation provisions [article 14] of the San Francisco Peace Treaty stated that Japan should pay reparations to those Allied and Asian countries who had suffered damage and destruction as a result of her military aggression. However, the article also contained a premise that, in view of her current economic weakness, Japan could not be expected to pay off her reparation bills completely. Thus, the article concluded that, while Japan should enter into negotiations with those countries who had expressed a desire for reparations, other countries should waive their reparations claims. This lenient provision was understandably unpopular among Japan's Asian victims – the Philippines, Burma and Indonesia – while Australia and New Zealand were reluctant to sign the Peace Treaty.[9]

The United States was thus pressing for Japan's former enemies to accept little or no reparation from Japan, while the United States herself began to provide massive economic and military assistance to the Asian third world countries (including India). Between 1951 and 1954, the United States concluded a number of defensive alliances with Asian countries, including a defence pact with New Zealand and Australia (ANZUS) in 1951, with South Korea in 1953, with France, Britain, Australia, New Zealand, Thailand, the Philippines and Pakistan (the South-East Asia Treaty Organisation (SEATO) in September 1954 and later that year with the Nationalist Chinese government in Taiwan.[10] For the Americans, these pacts were designed to counter the Eastern bloc more effectively by helping those Asian countries to reconstruct themselves economically and militarily. However, these alliances and the US aid that accompanied them made it difficult for Asian countries to oppose the lenient American policy towards Japan's reparations. In a sense, therefore, United States financial and technical assistance partially replaced Japan's reparations obligations.

On the other hand, Japan's efforts to reconcile herself with neighbouring countries and with her other former enemies were conducted bilaterally in a way which was hardly seen by Asia as a whole as attempts at seeking a genuine reconciliation. Japan concluded reparation agreements with South Vietnam (1959), Burma (1954 and 1963), the Philippines (1956) and Indonesia (1958). With other countries, including Laos (1959), Cambodia (1959), Thailand (1955, 1962), Malaysia (1962) and Singapore (1967), Japan concluded economic agreements, which were intended to replace her liabilities for reparations in kind. A separate peace treaty was also concluded with the Republic of Korea in April 1952. Nearly ten years later, in 1963, a Japanese–South Korean treaty to form a 'fundamental relationship' was signed. This provided South Korea with economic assistance in return for the abandonment of Korea's claim for Japanese reparations. The bulk of Koreans living in Japan after 1945 (more than two million at the time of Japan's defeat) had not chosen to come to Japan: they had been either forcibly transported from Korea as cheap labour or drafted into the Imperial Army (36 million Koreans served in the Japanese Army during the war). However, under the San Francisco Peace Treaty, these Koreans had to accept an automatic change of nationality from Japanese to Korean. Consequently, Korean veterans and their families living in Japan were not entitled to war veterans' pensions. Japan has signed no formal reparations agreement with North Korea. It was not until September 1972 that Japan and the People's Republic of China signed a communiqué whereby China waived her right to demand reparations from Japan.[11] It is true that the impact of the Cold War on relations between the countries of Asia, the preoccupation of the Europeans with closer unity, the growing American influence in Asian military and economic affairs, the conclusion of the mutual defence treaty between the United States and Japan at the time of the signature of San Francisco Peace Treaty, and Japan's geographically isolated position by comparison with Germany, all contributed to separating Japan from Europe in the post-war world, putting Japan further under the shadow of the United States.

However, more importantly, Japan does not now appear, in the eyes of her former enemies, to be making any tangible efforts to deal with the consequences of her military aggression before 1945. On the contrary Japanese officials seem to prefer to provide them with economic assistance rather than pay them reparations. Now that the Cold War is over, Japan is not expected to pay so much attention to advice from Washington about her foreign and defence policies. In other words, she has acquired more leverage in her diplomacy and she 'needs to be drawn into a web of wider relationships within [Japan's] own region and outside'.[12] The present Japanese Emperor visited China in October 1992, the first time such a visit had been made since the Pacific War. This provided Japan with the opportunity of moving towards a reconciliation with China, which would be apparent to the rest of the world. While the Emperor stated that 'my country inflicted great sufferings on the people of China', he only 'deeply deplore[d]' this. In Japan the statement seems to have been received favourably in that it made it clear for the first time that 'Japan caused China's sufferings'. However,

British newspapers merely commented, 'Akihito offers no apology to China', or 'Emperor expressed grief at China War'.[13] Prior to the Emperor's trip, Japanese officials made it clear that 'it was not to be undertaken with a view to apologising to the Chinese',[14] and this probably explains why he said no more.

Japan is now facing a flood of criticism from Asian countries for her failure to pay compensation for their wartime suffering. Those who suffered include the survivors of between 700 000 and two million Chinese who were brought to Japan as forced labour; 43 000 Koreans used as forced labour and who remain on Sakhalin; about 80 000–200 000 Asian women (80 per cent Koreans) sent to Japanese battlefields elsewhere in China and South-East Asia as 'comfort women'; survivors of 250 000 Asians (Thais, Burmese, Malayans, Indonesians and Vietnamese) who were used to build the Burma railway, and 148 Koreans convicted as war criminals, having been forced to obey Japanese officers; and about 100 000 Koreans who suffered from the effect of atomic radiation in Hiroshima or Nagasaki.[15] The atomic bombs and their appalling effects on human bodies have been the major influence on Japan's peace and anti-nuclear movements. It is therefore astonishing that the Japanese government did not, until very recently, inform those Korean families that their loved ones were killed during the bombing nor has it extended any medical help or compensation to those Koreans who are still suffering from the consequences of the atomic bombs.[16]

Overall, the Japanese government's attitude towards acknowledging its responsibility for compensation in these cases is, at best, grudging, merely reiterating the official position that Japan has completed her reparation obligations.[17] Thus, post-war Japanese governments, unlike those of Germany, do not seem to be willing to resolve in a constructive manner the problems arising from Japan's military aggression in the past. This is the second factor which has contributed to increasing overseas suspicions about Japan's sincerity.

In Japan, there has been an incessant flow of publications on the subject of the Pacific War (although this has not reached the level in terms of quality and perhaps quantity of American reappraisals of the Vietnam War). Historical surveys and analyses, memoirs, video films, biographies, including some books translated from English, have been produced on an even larger scale since the death of Hirohito in January 1989. Most of the books which are available to general readers in paperback are more outspoken than Japanese officials in admitting Japan's fatal mistakes in the recent past, while leading newspapers regularly criticise the lacklustre attitudes of politicians and officials towards Japan's war guilt. Moreover, the Japanese public are generally well informed of overseas criticism about these Japanese attitudes. For conscientious and intelligent Japanese, this situation is very frustrating in that they are caught between the condemnation of her wartime actions from other countries and the slow response to this condemnation by Japanese officials. This is reflected in the growing number of grassroots civilian groups who are pressing the government to take reparations and compensation issues more seriously.

A lawyer who has been working on the reparations issue has stated in a leading newspaper that Japan's economic growth has been at the cost of evading her reparation obligations and has suggested that she should now face up to her responsibilities for her aggression in Asia. A Japanese female university professor has also commented, in the same vein, that 'it is nonsense that Japan, who was not even able to look after her past, financially and humanely, could talk about her international contribution to world peace'.[18] In other words, in Japan, there seem to be many 'Professor Fischers' – those who are prepared to be self-critical, objective and courageous about her role in the Pacific–Asian War. At the moment, these outspoken comments have not led to any major revisionism equivalent to the 'Fischer controversy', nor have they been much commented on by the West.[19]

The third reason why the Japanese do not appear to feel genuinely guilty about their past military aggression is that Emperor Hirohito remained on the throne for over 44 years after the war. The subject of responsibility for the war has been a long-running one in post-war Japanese society, but no consensus has yet been reached as to who was really responsible. This contrasted with the situation in Germany and the rest of Europe, where Adolf Hitler was blamed for causing the Second World War in Europe. In Japan, there were many who might have been responsible: the military leaders or the middle echelons of the Army, or a weak civilian leadership, or the Emperor, or the Japanese people as a whole.[20] Having been unable to pin down exactly who was responsible for the War, and given that Japanese society tends to prefer to use ambiguous language rather than to express matters in cut and dried terms, the Japanese public seems to be persuaded that a collective sense of guilt must be accepted by all Japanese. As one leading newspaper reminded its readers at the time of Hirohito's death:

> the end of Shōwa as a result of the death of Hirohito should not be regarded as the end of debate about Japan's responsibility for the war and that Japan should realise that no other nation but Japan needed to reflect upon Japan's sins in the past.[21]

This is indeed a very enlightened but depressing message for younger Japanese.

Hirohito apparently expressed at least three times his desire to abdicate as a means of atoning for the nation's responsibility for the war, first on 29 August 1945, then in November 1948, and finally in the aftermath of Japan's signature of the peace treaty in September 1951. However, just as before 1945 his opinions had usually been ignored by the leaders of Imperial Japan, his desire to admit his responsibility after the war was frustrated by various factors.[22] That the death of Hirohito in 1989 raised once again in Japan the question of his role in wartime politics and in the causes of the war reflects the confusion and frustration in the minds of contemporary Japanese about the advantages and disadvantages of Hirothito's remaining on the throne. Most importantly, for neighbouring countries and the other Allied powers who suffered from Imperial Japan's aggression, Hirohito's continuation on the throne increased their suspicions of post-war Japan. The Japanese press reported mixed overseas responses to Hirohito's death: the People's Republic of China received the news calmly, while the general mood in South Korea, the Philippines, Australia and Taiwan was critical of Hirohito.[23] His position within the internal Imperial decision-making system was not well known outside Japan. Most non-Japanese believed that Hirohito was behind the war, because he was widely depicted as being the same authoritarian figure as Hitler. It would have been well if Hirohito had abdicated as he so wished, if not in 1945, but in September 1951 at the latest.[24]

The situation was made worse by the vague concept that the Emperor's status after 1945 has a purely symbolic one. He was, under the new constitution, to be the non-political representative of the nation, derived 'from the will of the people with whom resides sovereign power'. This involved, in theory, a drastic change from the role of the Emperor under the old constitution, whereby he was the Supreme Commander as well as the supreme authority in Japan, and a dilemma arose because the same Emperor who was said to have approved Japan's wars in the past had now become a non-political monarch. Hirohito was apparently aware of this. The Emperor is said to have expressed his apologies for Imperial Japan's aggression before 1945, to the leaders of the Philippines and South Korea in private conversations because these seemed to be the only occasions when the Emperor could express his personal opinion without the intervention of officials of the government and the Imperial Court.[25] When it came to official statements by Hirohito, drafted by governmental and court officials, they were innocuous and contained evasive expressions, such as the 'unfortunate event between the countries', thereby increasing suspicions about the Emperor's sincerity in Japan as well as abroad. Japanese officials, however, are of the opinion that the Emperor is not supposed to play a political role under the new constitution, and is not therefore entitled to give his apologies for what Imperial Japan did during the war.

However, these official attitudes sometimes contradict the concept of the Emperor as a non-political symbol. For instance, the Ministry of Foreign Affairs, and sometimes right-wing politicians, use the word *Genshu* (or 'sovereign' in the English translation)[26] which in 1988 caused a stir in the Diet and in the British press. During the visit to China of Akihito (who succeeded to the throne after his father's death in 1989), the nationally owned Japanese broadcast NHK news, used the word *Genshu* at least three times on 24 October 1992, and there were numerous phone calls to the NHK, pointing out this mistake. The official comment was that 'if one looks at the Emperor's job of entertaining overseas officials, he could be seen as *Genshu* in this respect', while opposition parties protested about the use of a term which was contained in the pre-1945 constitution.[27]

Similarly, other nations apparently continue to regard the Emperor as a kind of sovereign, and ambassadors to Japan present their credentials to the Emperor, rather than to the Prime Minister. Japanese governments have never protested about this, rather accepting it as custom.[28] In February 1989, the Government invited many high officials and politicians from overseas countries to the funeral of Hirohito. These guests would not have gone through the painfully slow funeral ceremony, which took place in freezing cold and wet weather, unless they were convinced that the Emperor was more than the mere symbol of Japan.[29]

The Emperor's role under the new constitution, let alone Hirohito's role before 1945, falls into a grey area in Japanese history, and debates on the subject are likely to continue in Japan. If this is the case, it will be even more difficult for other nations to understand the role of the Emperor and therefore Japan's attitude towards the Pacific War. Moreover, despite the quantity of newspaper coverage and the increased number of publications about the recent history of Japan, one contemporary school textbook, for example, contains only four sentences explaining the role of the post-war Emperor, while eight cover his predecessors' position in general terms between 1868 and 1945, Emperor Hirohito being mentioned only once before 1945. Only 18 pages or so describe the events between 1931 and 1945 – out of a total 362 pages.[30] This no doubt contributes to the indifference of the younger generation to the issue, while many are probably confused as to why the media publish special coverage of the Pacific War at least in August and December each year. One Emeritus Professor has written to a leading newspaper to propose that the teaching of Japanese history should be divided into two, to be taught by two different teachers: one from the ancient to the modern period, the other concentrating on the twentieth century only. These two courses must start simultaneously at the beginning of the academic year. He also proposes the creation of a national war museum, dealing solely with the Pacific War, because existing museums are interested only in the ancient period or in arts and culture.[31]

In conclusion, Japan's attitude towards the Pacific War can be divided roughly into two: on the official level there appears to be no interest in encouraging the Japanese public to face up to the subject; on the contrary, successive Japanese governments have been ever more anxious to play down public interest in this question. Japanese officials apparently prefer to wait until neighbouring countries lose interest in their experiences with Imperial Japan with the passage of time, while emphasising that Japan is now embarking on a new era by the recent passage of a bill through the Diet, which, despite the Constitution, allows Japanese troops to cooperate with United Nations Peace-Keeping Forces. The right-wing group, of course, regards the official attitude towards the Pacific War and the role of the Emperor as being too soft.

On other and more informal levels, there exists a level of resistance within society against the non-committal attitude of Japanese officials. The Press, television programmes and grassroots group try to remind the general public of recent Japanese history. In the preface of a paperback on 'Japanese War Compensation' by a grassroots group, the editor encourages the Japanese to look back on their own past and subsequent problems seriously, otherwise 'she will never be able to obtain confidence from the world community'.[32]

It remains to be seen how and when these internal pressures change official attitudes. However, all the external factors: the end of the Cold War, the consequent decline in US influence over Asian affairs, the growing pressures from her neighbouring countries on Japan to tackle the consequences of the War, suggest that it is now time for Japan to face up to her recent history. Just as this volume is intended as a first step towards an international approach to the subject of the War in Asia and in the Pacific, the legacy of the Pacific War is now beginning to be examined more carefully by the wider Asian community.

## NOTES

1. S. Yoshizawa, *Nihon Gaikōshi* (Japanese diplomatic history), vol. 29 (Tokyo: Kashima Kenkyusho Press, 1973) p. 71; Foster Dulles's minute (for the President), 6 September 1953, *Foreign Relations of the United States 1952–54*, vol. 2 (Washington, DC: US Government Printing Office 1984) p. 458. See also Henry Pelling, *Britain and the Marshall Plan* (London: Macmillan, 1988).

2. See, for instance, Olav Riste (ed.), *Western Security: The Formative Years* (Oslo: Norwegian University Press, 1985); F. Heller and John Gillingham (eds), *NATO: The Forming of the Atlantic Alliance and the Integration of Europe* (London and New York: Macmillan, 1992).

3. For the process of West Germany's integration into NATO, see Saki Dockrill, *Britain's Policy for West German Rearmament, 1950–1955* (New York and Cambridge: Cambridge University Press, 1991); Thomas Schwartz, *America's Germany* (Cambridge, Mass: Harvard University Press, 1991).

4. See A. Iriye, 'Continuities in US–Japanese Relations 1941–1949' in Nagai and Iriye (eds), *The Origins of the Cold War in Asia* (New York and Tokyo: Columbia University Press, 1977); Michael Schaller, *The American Occupation of Japan – The Origins of the Cold War in Asia* (New York and Oxford: Oxford University Press, 1985).

5. For instance, see George Friedman and Meredith Lebard, *The Coming War with Japan* (New York: St. Martin's Press, 1991); *The Observer*, 8 December 1991; *The Independent*, 7 December 1991.

6. Keith Sainsbury, *The Turning Point* (Oxford and New York: Oxford University Press, 1985) p. 189; A. Yamagiwa, 'China's policy for an Occupied Japan' in R. Sodei (ed.), *Sekaishi no nakano Nihon Senryō* (The Allied Occupation of Japan in World History) (Tokyo: Nihon Hyoronsha, 1985) p. 290.

7. I. Hata, 'The occupation of Japan, 1945–52; in Joe C. Dixon (ed.), *The American Military and the Far East* (Washington, DC: United States Air Force Academy, 1980) pp. 92–108.

8. A. Utsumi, H. Tanaka et al., *Sengo Hoshō* (Japan's War Compensation), (Tokyo: Nashi no kisha, 1992) table 25.

9. Evelyn Colbert, *Southeast Asia in International Politics 1941–56* (Ithaca and London: Cornell University Press, 1977) pp. 174–6; See also Yoshizawa, *Japanese Diplomatic History*, vol. 29; For the San Francisco Peace Treaty of 1951, K.

Nishimura, *Japanese Diplomatic History,* vol. 27 (Tokyo: Kashima Kenkyusho Press, 1974) pp. 397–420.

10. See Saki Dockrill, *Controversy and Compromise: Eisenhower's New Look Military Doctrine, 1953–1961* (to be published by North Carolina University Press) see Chapters 2 and 8.

11. For Japan's post-war settlement with a number of Asian countries, see Yoshizawa, *Japanese Diplomatic History,* vols 28 and 29; see also Utsumi, Tanaka et al., *The Japanese War Compensation.*

12. *The Observer,* 8 December 1991.

13. *The Asahi,* 24 October 1992; *The Guardian,* 24 October 1992; *The Times,* 24 October 1992; *The Independent,* 24 October 1992.

14. *The Asahi,* 24 October 1992.

15. For the recent claims by Asian victims, see *The Asahi,* 24 December 1991, 5 January 1992; *The Guardian,* 17 and 20 January 1992; *The Asahi,* 1, 10 and 12 August 1992; Utsumi, Tanaka et al., *The Japanese War Compensation.*

16. *The Asahi,* 10 August 1992.

17. See official views stated in *The Asahi,* 5 January and 10 August 1992.

18. *The Asahi,* 5 January 1992.

19. For a summary of the Fischer controversy, see Fritz Fischer, *World Power or Decline – The Controversy over 'Germany's Aims in the First World War* (London: Weidenfeld & Nicolson, 1975). Originally published in German under the title *Weltmacht oder Niedergang* in 1965 by Europäische Verlagsanstalt, Frankfurt am Main.

20. Recent studies in English on Hirohito, see Thomas Crump, *The Death of an Emperor* (Oxford and New York: Oxford University Press 1991); see also Saki Dockrill, 'Hirohito, the Emperor's Army and Pearl Harbor' *Review of International Studies* 18, (1992), pp. 319–33 and Stephen Large, *Emperor Hirohito and Showa Japan* (London and New York: Routledge, 1992).

21. *The Asahi,* 9 January 1989.

22. H. Takahashi, *Shocho Ten'nō* (The Emperor as a symbol) (Tokyo: Iwanami shinsho, 1988) pp. 18–59; see also S. Iriye, *Iriye Jiūchōno shuki* (Iriye Grand Chamberlain's Daries), entries of 11 May and 17 August 1948 printed in *The Asahi* 1 February 1989, and entry of 2 May 1951 in *The Asahi,* 3 February 1989.

23. *The Asahi,* 7 January 1989.

24. For a concise study on the Emperor's legal position under the post-war constitution, see K. Yokota, *Kenpō to Ten'nō sei* (The Constitution and the Imperial System) (Tokyo: Iwanami shinsho, 1990).

25. Takahashi, *Shocho Ten'nō,* pp. 98–10 ff.

26. See, *The Asahi,* 16 January 1989.

27. *The Asahi,* 25 October 1992.

28. *The Asahi,* 16 January 1989.

29. Tokyo Television (ed.), *Shōgen: Watashi no Shōwashi* (Witness history of the Showa Period), vol. 5 (Tokyo: Bunshun bunko, 1989) pp. 3–6.

30. See, for instance, M. Inoue et al., *Nihonshi* (Japanese History), (Tokyo: Yamakawa Press, 1989).

31. *The Asahi,* 15 August 1992.

32. See Utsumi, Tenaka et al., *The Japanese War Compensation,* p. i.

# Select Bibliography

The place of publication is London or New York, unless otherwise stated. The list is in general confined to published secondary works mentioned in the text.

Allen, J.S., *Atomic Imperialism: The State, Monopoly and the Bomb* (1952).
Allen, L., 'The Campaigns in Asia and the Pacific', *Journal of Strategic Studies* 13:1 (March 1990).
____, *Sittang: The Last Battle* (1973).
____, *The End of the War in Asia* (1976).
____, *Burma: the Longest War, 1942–45* (1984).
____, 'Japanese Intelligence Systems', *Journal of Contemporary History* 22:4 (October 1987).
Alperovitz, G.A., *Atomic Diplomacy* (1985).
Andrew, C. and Noakes, J. (eds), *Intelligence and International Relations 1900–1945* (Exeter, 1987).
Antoni, *K., Der Himmlische Herrscher und sein Staat* (München, 1980).
Arnold, Gen. H.H., *Global Mission* (1951).
Asada, S., 'Japanese Perceptions of the A-Bomb Decision, 1945–1980' in Dixon, J.C., (ed.) *The American Military and the Far East – Proceedings of the Ninth Military History Symposium, United States Air Force Academy*, 1–3 October 1980 (Washington DC, 1980).
Auerbach, I. et al. (eds), *Felder und Vorfelder russischer Geschichte: Studien zu Ehren von Peter Scheibert* (Freiburg, 1985).
Bacevich, A.J., *Diplomat in Khaki: Major-General Frank McCoy and American Foreign Policy, 1898–1949* (Kansas, 1989).
Ballard, G. St. V., *On ULTRA Active Service: The Story of Australia's Signals Intelligence Operations during World* War II (Richmond, 1991).
Bamba, N., *Japanese Diplomacy in a Dilemma: New Light on Japan's China Policy, 1924–9* (Kyoto, 1972).
Barker, A.J., *The March on Delhi* (1963).
Barnhart, M.A., *Japan Prepares for Total War: The Search for Economic Security 1919–1941* (1987).
Batson, B.A. *The End of the Absolute Monarchy in Siam* (Singapore, 1984).
Bell, R.J., *Unequal Allies: Australian–American Relations and the Pacific War* (Melbourne, 1977).
Bennett, G. 'British Policy in the Far East, 1933–6: Treasury and Foreign Office', *Modern Asian Studies* 25 (1991).

Bernstein, B., 'Eclipsed by Hiroshima and Nagasaki: Early thinking about Tactical Nuclear Weapons' *International Security* 15:4 (Spring 1991).

____, 'Ike and Hiroshima: Did He Oppose It?', *Journal of Strategic Studies* 10:3 (September 1987).

Best, G., 'The French Revolution and Human Rights' in Best (ed.), *The Permanent Revolution: The French Revolution and its Legacy, 1789–1989* (1989).

Bidwell, S., *The Chindit War: The Campaign in Burma, 1944* (1979).

Blackett, P.M.S., *Military and Political Consequences of Atomic Energy* (1948).

Bond, B. *British Military Policy between the Two World Wars* (1980).

____(ed.), *Chief of Staff: The Diaries of Lietenant-General Sir Henry Pownall, II, 1940–44* (1974).

Borg, D. and Okamoto, S. (eds), *Pearl Harbor as History* (1973).

Brailey, N., *Thailand and the Fall of Singapore: A Frustrated Asian Revolution* (1986).

____, 'Southeast Asia and Japan's Road to War', *Historical Journal*, 30:4 (1987).

____, 'Sir Ernest Satow, Japan and Asia: The Trials of a Diplomat in the Age of High Imperialism', *Historical Journal* 35:1 (March 1992).

Braun, H.J., 'Technologietransfer im Flugzeugbau zwischen Deutschland und Japan 1936–1945' in Kreiner and Mathias (eds), *Deutschland und Japan in der Zwischenkriegszeit* (Bonn, 1990).

Buell, T.B., *The Quiet Warrior* (Boston, 1974).

Bundy, M., *Danger and Survival: Choices about the Bomb in the First Fifty Years* (1988).

Burns, J.M. *Roosevelt: The Soldier of Freedom* (1971).

Butow, R.J.C., *Japan's Decision to Surrender* (Stanford, 1954).

Callahan, R., *Burma: 1942–1945* (1978).

Calvert, M., *Prisoners of Hope* (1952).

Calvocoressi, P., Wint, G., and Pritchard, R.J., *Total War: The Causes and Courses of the Second World War*, 2nd rev. edn (1989).

Carlton, D. and Levine H. (eds), *The Cold War Debated* (1988).

Channon, H., *Chips: The Diaries of Sir Henry Channon* (1967).

Chapman, J.W.M., 'The Have-Nots go to War: The Economic and Technological Basis of the German Alliance with Japan' in Nish, I. (ed.), *The Tripartite Pact* (1984).

____, 'Japan and German Naval Policy, 1919–1945', in Kreiner, J. (ed.), *Deutschland–Japan Historische Kontakte* (Bonn, 1984).

____, (ed.) *Proceedings of the British Association for Japanese Studies*, vol. 6 part 1 (1981).

____, 'Japanese Intelligence, 1918–1945: A Suitable Case for Treatment', in Andrew, C. and Noakes, J. (eds). *Intelligence and International Relations 1900–1945* (Exeter, 1987).

Checkland, O., *Britain's Encounter with Meiji-Japan, 1868–1912* (1989).

Chennault, A., *Chennault and the Flying Tigers* (1974).

Churchill, W.S., *The Second World War: The Grand Alliance* (1950).

___, *The Second World War: The Hinge of Fate* (1951).

___, *The Second World War: Closing the Ring* (1952).

Clifford, N.B., *Retreat From China: British Policy in the Far East, 1937–1941* (1967).

Compton, A., *Atomic Quest* (1950).

Cohen, E.A., 'Churchill and Coalition Strategy in World War II', in Kennedy, P. (ed.), *Grand Strategies in War and Peace* (1991).

Colbert, E., *Southeast Asia in International Politics, 1941–56* (1977).

Conroy, H. and Wray, H. (eds) *Pearl Harbor Reexamined: Prologue to the Pacific War* (1991)

___, *The Japanese Seizure of Korea 1873–1910* (Philadelphia, 1960).

Cosgrove, P., *Churchill at War, I: Alone, 1939–40* (1974).

Costello, J., *Ten Days that Saved the West* (1991).

Craig, W., *The Fall of Japan* (1979).

Crump, T., *The Death of the Emperor* (1991).

Dallek, R., *Franklin D. Roosevelt and American Foreign Policy, 1932–45* (1979).

Dilks, D. (ed.), *Retreat from Power – Studies in Britain's Foreign Policy of the Twentieth Century, 1906–1939* (1981).

___(ed.), *The Diaries of Sir Alexander Cadogan, 1938–1945* (1971).

Dixon, J.C. (ed.), *The American Military and the Far East – Proceedings of the Ninth Military History Symposium, United States Air Force Academy, 1–3 October 1980* (Washington DC, 1980).

Dockrill, S., 'Hirohito, the Emperor's Army and Pearl Harbor', *Review of International Studies* 18 (1992).

___, *Britain's Policy for West German Rearmament 1950–55* (Cambridge, 1991).

Dower, J., *Empire and Aftermath: Yoshida Shigeru and the Japanese Experience, 1878–1954* (1988).

Drea, E.J., 'Ultra Intelligence and General Douglas MacArthur's Leap to Hollandia, January–April 1944', *Intelligence and National Security* 5:2 (April 1990).

___, *MacArthur's ULTRA: Codebreaking and the War Against Japan* (Kansas, 1991).

___, 'Reading Each Other's Mail: Japanese Communication Intelligence 1920–41' *Journal of Military History* 55:2 (April 1991).

Dulles, F.R., *Yankees and Samurai: American's Role in the Emergence of Modern Japan, 1791–1900* (1965).

Eayres, J., *In Defence of Canada*, 2 vols (Toronto, 1964, 1965).

Endicott, S.L., *Diplomacy and Enterprise: British China Policy, 1933–7* (Manchester, 1975).

Ephron, D., 'An American Cryptanalyst in Australia', *Cryptologia* (October 1985).

Ersbree, W.H., *Japan's Role in Southeast Asian Nationalist Movements* (1953).

Esherick, J.W. (eds), *Lost Chance in China: The World War II. Despatches of John S. Service* (1974).

Evans, G. and Brett-James, A., *Imphal: A Flower on Lofty Heights* (1962).

Feis, H. *The China Tangle* (Princeton, 1953).

_____, *The Road to Pearl Harbor: The Coming of the War between the United States and Japan* (Princeton, 1950).

_____, *The Atomic Bomb and the End of the World War II* (Princeton, 1966).

Finnegan, J., 'Grim Fate for Station 6', *Military History* (October, 1986).

Fischer, F., *World Power or Decline – The Controversy over 'Germany's Aims in the First World War'* (1975).

Fistie, P., *Sous-développement et Utopie au Siam* (Paris, 1969).

Fox, J.P., *Germany and the Far Eastern Crisis 1931–1938* (Oxford, 1982).

Frank, R.B., *Guadalcanal* (1990).

Fraser T.G. and Lowe, P. (eds), *Conflict and Amity in East Asia: Essays in Honour of Ian Nish* (1992).

Friedman, G. and Lebard, M., *The Coming War with Japan* (1991).

Fujiwara, A., *Nihon Gunjishi* (Tokyo, 1987).

Fujiwara, I.F., *Kikan: Japanese Army Intelligence Operations in Southeast Asia during World War II*, trans. by Yoji, A. (Hong Kong, 1983).

Fukudome, S., *Shikan Shinjuwan Kogeki* (Tokyo, 1955).

Gardner, B. *Churchill in his Time: A Study in a Reputation, 1939–1945* (1968).

Gibbs, N.H., *Grand Strategy*, vol. 1 (1976).

Gilbert, M., *Finest Hour: Winston S. Churchill 1919–1941* (1983).

_____, *Road to Victory: Winston S. Churchill, 1941–1945* (1986).

Gilchrist, Sir A., 'Diplomacy and Disaster: Thailand and the British Empire in 1941', *Asian Affairs*, XIII (October 1982).

Giovannitti L. and Freed, F., *The Decision to Drop the Bomb* (1967).

Godechot, J., *La Grande Nation: l'expansion révolutionnaire de la France dans le monde, 1789–1799* (Paris, 1956).

Goodman, G.K. (ed.), *Japanese Cultural Policies in Southeast Asia during World War 2* (1991).

Gong, G.L., *The 'Standard of Civilisation' in International Society* (1984).

Greenfield, K.R., *Command Decisions* (Washington, DC, 1960).

Grimal, H., *Decolonization: the British, French, Dutch and Belgian Empires, 1919–1963* (1978).

Groves, L., *Now It Can Be Told: The Story of the Manhattan Project* (1962).

Haggie, P., *Britannia at Bay* (1981).

Hancock, Sir K., *Smuts: The Felds of Force, 1919–1950* (Cambridge, 1970).

Han'dō, K., *Seidan-Ten'nō to Suzuki Kantarō* (Tokyo, 1988).

Harriman, W.A. and Abel, E., *Special Envoy to Churchill and Stalin 1941–1946* (1975).

Hata, I., *Taiheiyō Kokusai Kankei-shi* (Tokyo, 1971).

____, *Shōwashi no gunjintachi* (Tokyo, 1982).

____, (ed.) *Shinjuwan wa Moeru* (Tokyo, 1991).

____, 'The occupation of Japan, 1945–52', in Dixon, J.C. (ed.) *The American Military and the Far East* (Washington, DC, 1980).

Hatano, S., 'Leith Ross no Kyokuto Hōmon to Nihon', *Kokusi Seiji* 58 (1977).

Hattori, T., *Dai Tōa Sensō Zenshi* (Tokyo, 1953).

Hauner, M., *India in Axis Strategy* (Stuttgart, 1981).

Hayes, G.P., *The History of the Joint Chiefs of Staff in World War II: The War against Japan* (Annapolis, 1982).

Hayashi, S., *Taiheiyō Sensō*, (Tokyo, 1980).

Heinrichs, W.H., 'The Role of the U.S. Navy' in Borg, D. and Okamoto, S. (eds), *Pearl Harbor as History* (1973).

Heller, F. and Gillingham, J. (eds) *NATO: The Forming of the Atlantic Alliance and the Integration of Europe* (1992).

Herde, P., *Pearl Harbor, 7 Dezember 1941: Der Ausbruch des Krieges zwischen Japan und den Vereinigten Staaten und die Ausweitung des europäischen Krieges zum Weltkrieg* (Darmstadt, 1980).

Hess, G., *The United States Emergence as a Southeast Asian Power, 1940–1950* (1987).

Hewlett, R.G. and Anderson, O., *The New World 1939–46*, vol. 1 of *a History of the USAEG* (Pennsylvania, 1962).

Hillgruber, A., *Hitlers Strategie: Politik und Kriegführung, 1940–1941* (Frankfurt am Main, 1965).

Hori, E., *Daihon'ei-Sanbō no Jōhō Senki* (Tokyo, 1989).

Horner, D.M., *High Command: Australia and Allied Strategy, 1939–1945* (Canberra, 1982).

Hosaka, M., *Tōjō Hideki to Ten'nō no Jidai* (Tokyo, 1988).

Hosoya, C., 'Britain and the United States in Japan's View', 1919–37' in Nish, I. (ed.), *Anglo-Japanese Alienation, 1919–1952* (1982).

____, '1934-nen no Nichi-Ei Fukashin Kyōtei Mondai', *Kokusai Seiji* 58 (1977).

____, 'The Tripartite Pact, 1939–1940', in Morley, J. (ed.) *Deterrent Diplomacy: Japan, Germany and the USSR, 1935–1940* (1976).

Hough, R., *Former Naval Person: Churchill and the Wars at Sea* (1985).

Howard, M. 'British Military Preparations for the Second World War' in David Dilks (ed.) *Retreat from Power – Studies in Britain's Foreign Policy of the Twentieth Century, 1906–1939* (1981).

Hoyt, E.P., *Japan's War: The Great Pacific Conflict* (1987).

Ike, N., *Japan's Decision for War: Records of the 1941 Policy Conferences* (Stanford, 1967).

Ikeda, K., 'The Road to Singapore: Japan's View of Britain, 1922–1941' in Fraser, T.G. and Lowe, P. (eds) *Conflict and Amity in East Asia: Essays in Honour of Ian Nish* (1992).

Inoki, M., *Hyoden Yoshida Shigeru*, 4 vols (Tokyo, 1981).

Iriye, A., *The Origins of the Second World War in Asia and the Pacific* (1987).

\_\_\_\_(ed.), *The Chinese and the Japanese* (New Jersey, 1980).

\_\_\_\_, Nichibei Sensō (Tokyo, 1978).

\_\_\_\_, 'Continuities in US–Japanese Relations 1941–1949' in Nagai, Y. and Iriye, (eds) *The Origins of the Cold War in Asia* (1977).

Itonaga, S., 'Beikaigun no Tainichi Sensō Keikaku' in Hata, I. (ed.) *Shinjuwan wa Moeru* (Tokyo, 1991).

Iwashima, H., *Johosen ni Kanpai Shita Nihon: Rikugun Angō "Shinwa" no Hakai* (Tokyo: 1984).

James, D.C., *The Years of MacArthur, 1941–1945* (1975).

\_\_\_\_, 'American and Japanese Strategies in the Pacific War' in Paret, P. (ed.), *Makers of Modern Strategy* (Princeton, 1986).

James, R.R., *Churchill: A Study in Failure* (1970).

Jansen, M.B., *The Japanese and Sun Yat-sen* (Cambridge, Mass., 1954).

Jayanama, D., *Siam and World War II*, trans. by Keyes, J. (Bangkok, 1978).

Johnson, C., *MITI and the Japanese Miracle: The Growth of Industrial Policy, 1925–1975* (Stanford, 1982).

Kahn, D., *The Codebreakers: The Story of Secret Writing* (1967).

Kamaga, K., 'Nihon rikugun angō wa "antai" datta', *Shogen: Rekishi to Jimbutsu: Hiroku: Taiheiyō Sensō* (Tokyo, September 1984).

Kennedy, M.D., *Estrangement of Great Britain and Japan, 1917–35* (Manchester, 1969).

Kennedy, P.M. (ed.), *Grand Strategies in War and Peace* (1991).

Kerr, S., 'Alperovitz, Timewatch and the Bomb' *Intelligence and National Security* 5:3 (July 1990).

Key, H., *The Last Phase of the East Asian World Ortder, 1860–1882* (California, 1980).

Khamchoo, C., and Reynolds, E.B., (eds), *Thai–Japanese Relations in Historical Perspective* (Bangkok, 1988).

Kibata, Y., 'Igirisu no tai-Nichi seisaku, 1934', *Kyoyo gakka kiyo* (1977).

Kido, K., *Kido Diaries*, (Tokyo, 1966).

Kimball, F., The Juggler – Franklin Roosevelt as Wartime Statesman (Princeton, 1991).

King and Whitehall, *Fleet Admiral King* (1952).

Kinvig, C., *River Kwai Railway: The Story of the Burma-Siam Railroad* (1992).

Kirby, W.C., *Germany and Republican China* (Stanford, 1984).

Kisaka, J. *Taiheiyō Sensō* (Tokyo 1989)

Kojima, N., Ten'nō (Tokyo, 1988).

\_\_\_\_, *Taiheiyō Sensō* (Tokyo, 1988).

Krebs, G., *Japans Deutschlandpolitik 1935–1941: Eine Studie zur Vorgeschichte des Pazifischen Krieges* (Hamburg, 1984).

\_\_\_\_, 'Japan und der deutsch–sowjetische Krieg 1941' in Wegner, B. (ed.), *Zwei Wege nach Moskau: Vom Hitler–Stalin-Pakt zum 'Unternehmen Barbarossa'* (München, 1991).

_____, 'Japanische Vermittlungsversuche im deutsch–sowjetischen Krieg 1941–1945; in Kreiner, J., and Mathias, R. (eds), *Deutschland–Japan in der Zwischenkriegszeit* (Bonn, 1990).

Kreiner, J., and Mathias, R. (eds), *Deutschland–Japan in der Zwischenkriegszeit* (Bonn, 1990).

_____, *Deutschland–Japan Historische Kontakte* (Bonn, 1984).

Kublin, M., *The Role of China in American Military Strategy from Pearl Harbor to the Fall of 1944* (Michigan, 1984).

Kurihara, K. (ed.), *Ningen Yoshida Shigeru* (Tokyo, 1991).

Lamb, R., *Churchill as War Leader: Right or Wrong* (1991).

_____, *The Ghosts of Peace, 1935–1945* (1987).

Large, S., *Emperor Hirohito and Shōwa Japan* (1992).

Lebra, J., *Japan's Greater East Asia Co-Prosperity Sphere in World War II* (Kuala Lumpur, 1975).

Lensen, G.A., *The Strange Neutrality: Soviet–Japanese Relations during the Second World War* (Florida, 1972).

Lewin, R., *Slim: The Standard-bearer: A Biography of Field Marshall the Viscount Slim* (1976).

Lilienthal, D.E., *The Atomic Energy Years 1945–1950* (1964).

Love, R.W., 'Ernest Joseph King, Jr', in Love, R.W. (ed.) *The Chiefs of Naval Operations* (Annapolis, 1983).

Lowe, P., *Great Britain and the Origins of the Pacific War: A Study of British Policy in East Asia 1937–41* (1977).

_____, 'Winston Churchill and Japan, 1914–1942' in Chapman, J.W.M. (ed.), *Proceedings of the British Association for the Japanese Studies* vol. 6 part 1 (1981).

_____, 'Great Britain and the Japanese Peace Treaty, 1951' in Lowe, P. and Moeshart, H.J. (eds), *Western Interactions with Japan: Expansion, the Armed Forces and Readjustment, 1859–1956* (Folkestone, 1990).

Lupke, H., *Japans Russlandpolitik von 1934–1941* (Frankfurt am Main, 1962).

Macintyre, S. and Bolton, G., *The Oxford History of Australia*, vols. 4 and 5, (Oxford, 1986, 1990).

Marder, A.J. 'Winston is Back: Churchill at the Admiralty, 1939–1940' *English Historical Review*, Supplement V (1972).

Martin, B., *Deutschland und Japan im Zweiten Weltkrieg: Vom Angriff auf Pearl Harbor bis zur deutschen Kapitulation* (Göttingen, 1969).

_____, 'Zur Tauglichkeit eines übergreifenden Faschismusbegriffes: Ein Vergleich zwischen Japan, Italien und Deutschland' *Vierteljahrshefte für Zeitgeschichte* 29:1 (1981).

_____, 'The German Role in the Modernization of Japan: The Pitfall of Blind Acculturation', *Oriens Extremus* 33:1 (1980).

_____, 'German–Japanese Relations after the Hitler–Stalin Pact' in Pike, D.W. (ed.), *The Opening of the Second World War* (1992).

_____, *Friedensinitiativen und Machtpolitik im Zweiten Weltkrieg, 1939–1942* (Düsseldorf, 1976).

_____, 'Deutsch-sowjetische Sondierungen über einen separaten Friedensschluss im Zweiten Weltkrieg: Bericht und Dokumentation', in Augerbach, I. et al. (eds), *Felder und Vorfelder russischer Geschichte: Studien zu Ehren von Peter Scheibert* (Freiburg, 1985).

_____, 'Japans Kriegswirtschaft' in Forstmeier, F. and Volkmann, H.E. (eds), *Kriegswirtschaft und Rüstung 1939–1945* (Düsseldorf, 1977).

_____, 'Sozialer Wandel in Japan während des Zweiten Weltkrieges und seine Folgen für die Nachkriegszeit' in Dlugoborski, W. (ed.), *Zweiter Weltkrieg und sozialer Wandel* (Göttingen, 1981).

_____, 'Die Einschätzung der Lage Deutschlands aus japanischer Sicht: Japans Abkehr vom Bündnis und seine Hinwendung auf Ostasien (1943–1945) in Messerschmidt, M. (ed.) *Die Zunkunft des Reiches: Gegner, Verbündete und Neutrale 1943* (Bonn, 1990).

Master, J. *The Road Past Mandalay* (1961).

Matloff, M. and Snell, E.M., *Strategic Planning for Coalition Warfare, 1941–1942* (Washington, DC, 1953).

Matsushita, Y., *Mizuno Hironori* (Tokyo: 1950).

McIntyre, W.D., *The Rise and Fall of the Singapore Naval Base* (1979).

McKercher, B.J.M., 'Our Most Dangerous Enemy: Great Britain Pre-eminent in the 1930s', *International History Review* 13 (1991).

Menzel-Meskill, J., *Hitler and Japan: The Hollow Alliance* (1966).

Messerschmidt, M. (ed.), *Die Zunkunft des Reiches: Gegner, Verbündete und Neutrale 1943* (Bonn, 1990).

Michalka, W., *Ribbentrop und die deutsche Weltpolitik 1933–1940* (München, 1980).

Miller, J.C., 'The Chinese Still Rule North China', *Amerasia*, 7:7 (September 1938).

Miyake, M., *Nichi-Doku-I sangoku dōmei no kenkyū* (Tokyo, 1975).

Montgomery, B., *Shenton of Singapore: Governor and Prisoner of War* (1984).

Morley, J. (ed.), *The China Quagmire* (1983).

_____(ed.), *Deterrent Diplomacy: Japan, Germany and the USSR, 1935–1940* (1976).

_____(ed.), *The Fateful Choice: Japan's Advance into South-East Asia, 1939–1941* (1980).

Morison, S.E., *History of United States Naval Operations in World War II: The Rising Sun in the Pacific* (1968).

_____, *Strategy and Compromise* (Boston, 1958).

_____, *Breaking the Bismarcks Barrier* (Boston, 1950).

Morris, I., *The Nobility of Failure* (1975).

Morton, L., *The War in the Pacific: Strategy and Command: The First Two Years* (Washington, DC, 1962).

Nish, I. (ed.), *Anglo-Japanese Alienation, 1919–1952: Papers of the Anglo-Japanese Conference on the History of the Second World War* (1982).

____, *Alliance in Decline: A Study in Anglo-Japanese Relations, 1908–23* (1972).

____, *Japan's Struggle with Internationalism: Japan, China and the League of Nations, 1931–3* (1992).

____, 'Mr Yoshida at the London Embassy, 1936–8', *Bulletin of the Japan Society* (1979).

____, (ed.), *The Tripartite Pact of 1940: Japan, Germany and Italy* (1984).

____, *The Anglo-Japanese Alliance* (1966).

Nishimura, K., Japanese Diplomatic History, vol. 27 (Tokyo, 1974).

Norman, Sir H., *The Peoples and Politics of the Far East* (1895).

Northedge, F.S., *The Troubled Giant: Britain among the Great Powers, 1916–1939* (1966).

Ogata, S., *Defiance in Manchuria, 1931–2* (Berkeley, 1964).

Oka, Y., *Konoe Fumimaro: A Political Biography* (Tokyo, 1972: trans. 1983).

Oudendyk, W.J., *Ways and By-ways in Diplomacy* (1939).

Paret, P. (ed.), *Makers of Modern Strategy* (Princeton, 1986).

Parker, F.D., 'The Unsolved Messages of Pearl Harbor', *Cryptologia* (October, 1991).

Parkinson, R., *Blood, Toil, Tears and Sweat* (1973).

Parrish, T., *The Ultra Americans: The U.S. Role in Breaking the Nazi Codes* (1984).

Pauer, E. 'Die wirtschaftlichen Beziehungen zwischen Japan und Deutschland 1900–1945', Kreiner, J. (ed.), *Deutschland–Japan Historische Kontakte* (Bonn, 1984).

____, *Technologietransfer Deutschland–Japan: von 1850-vis zur Gegenwart* (München, 1992).

____, 'Deutsche Ingenieure in Japan: japanische Ingenieure in Deutschland', in Kreiner and Mathias (eds), *Deutschland–Japan in der Zwischenkriegszeit* (Bonn, 1990).

Peattie, M., *Ishiwara Kanji and Japan's Confrontation with the West* (Princeton, 1975).

Pelling, H., *Britain and the Marshall Plan* (1988).

Pelz, S.E., *Race to Pearl Harbor* (Cambridge, Mass., 1974).

Pike, D.W. (ed.), *The Opening of the Second World War* (1992)

Pogue, F.C., *George C. Marshall: Ordeal and Hope* (1967).

Pritchard, R.J., 'The Far East as an Influence on the Chamberlain Government's Pre-War European Policies' *Millennium: Journal of International Studies*, 2:3, (1973–4).

____, *Far Eastern Influences upon British Strategy towards the Great Powers, 1937–1939* (1987).

____, and Zaide, S.M. (ed), *The Tokyo Trial: Proceedings of the International Military Tribunal for the Far East* (1981).

Ratenhof, U., *Die Chinapolitik des Deutschen Reiches 1871–1945: Wirtschaft-Rüstung-Militär* (Boppard, 1985).

Reese, T., *Australia, New Zealand and the United States: A Survey of International Relations, 1941–1968* (Oxford, 1969).

Reynolds, E.B., 'Imperial Japan's Cultural Program in Thailand', in Goodman, G.K. (ed.), *Japanese Cultural Policies in Southeast Asia during World War 2* (1991).

Rhodes, R., *The Making of the Atomic Bomb* (1986).

Riste, O. (ed.), *Western Security: the Formative Years* (Oslo, 1985).

Robertson, E., *The Japanese File* (Singapore, 1979).

Rohwer, J. and Jäckel (eds), *Kriegswende Dezember 1941* (Frankfurt am Main, 1981).

Romanus, C.F. and Sunderland, R., *Stilwell's Mission to China* (Washington, DC, 1953).

Roosevelt, E., *As He Saw It* (1946).

Roskill, S.K., *Hankey: Man of Secrets*, III, (1974).

Sainsbury, K., *The Turning Point* (1985).

Sanematsu, Y., *Yonai Mitsumasa* (Tokyo, 1990).

Schaller, M., *The American Occupation of Japan – The Origins of the Cold War in Asia* (1985).

Schroeder, P.W., *The Axis Alliance and Japanese – American Relations* (1963).

Schwartz, T., *America's Germany* (Cambridge, Mass., 1991).

Sheahan, N., *New York Times Pentagon Papers* (1973).

Shimomura, K., *Shūsenki* (Tokyo, 1948).

Simmon, I., *Too Little, Too Late* (1970).

Sinclair, K., *Walter Nash* (Auckland, 1976).

Skinner, G.W., *Chinese Society in Thailand: an Analytical History* (1957)

Slim, Field-Marshal Sir William, *Defeat into Victory* (1956).

Smith, R.R., *The Approach to the Philippines* (Washington, DC, 1953).

Sodei, R. (ed.), *Sekaishi no nakano Nihon senryō* (Tokyo, 1985).

Sommer, T. *Deutschland und Japan zwischen den Mächten: Vom Antikominternpakt zum Dreimächtepakt* (Tübingen, 1962).

Spector, R.H., 'Fifty Years Ago: Views of World War II', *Washington Post Book World*, XIX, (December, 1989).

____, *Eagle Against the Sun: The American War with Japan* (1985).

Spencer, Sir P., *Exercises in Diplomacy* (Sydney, 1969).

Stephan, J.J., *Hawaii Under the Rising Sun* (Honolulu, 1984).

Stewart A., *The Underrated Enemy* (1987)

____, 'Luzon Versus Formosa', in Greenfield, K.R., *Command Decisions* (Washington, DC, 1960).

Stimson, H. and Bundy, M., *On Active Service in Peace and War* (1948).

Storry, G.R., *Japan and the Decline of the West in Asia, 1894–1979*.

Sutherland, J.P., 'The Story General Marshall Told Me' *U.S. News and World Report* (2 November 1959).

Suzuki, H. (ed.), *Memoirs of Suzuki Kantaro* (Tokyo, 1985).

Swan, W.L., 'Thai-Japanese Relations at the Start of the Pacific War', *Journal of South East Asian Studies* XVII: 2 (September 1987).

Swinson, A., *Four Samurai: A Quartet of Japanese Army Commanders in the Second World War* (1968).

Sykes, C., *Orde Wingate* (1959).

Takagi, S., *Shikan Tahieyō Sensō* (Tokyo, 1969).

Takahashi, H., Shōchō Ten'nō (Tokyo, 1988).

Tarling, N., 'King Prajadhipok and the Apple Cart: British Attitudes towards the 1932 Revolution', *Journal of the Siam Society* 64:2 (1976).

Tedder, Lord, *Air Power in War* (1948).

Thorne, C., *The Far Eastern War* (1986).

____, *Allies of a Kind* (1978).

____, 'MacArthur, Australia and the British', *Australian Outlook* (April and August 1975).

Tōgō, S., *Jidai no ichimen* (Tokyo, 1951).

Toyama, S., 'The Outline of the Armament Expansion of the Imperial Japanese Navy during the Years 1930–41', *Revue Internationale d'Histoire Militaire* 73 (1991).

Trotter, A., *Britain and East Asia 1993–7* (1975).

____, 'Backstage Diplomacy: Britain and Japan in the 1930s' *Journal of Oriental Studies* (Hong Kong), 15 (1977).

____, *New Zealand and Japan, 1945–1952: The Occupation and the Peace Treaty* (1990).

Tsuji, M., *Singapore, the Japanese Version* (1956).

Tucker, D.P., 'Rhapsoday in Purpule: A New History of Pearl Harbor (1)', edited and annotated by Mellen, G., *Cryptologia* (July 1982).

Utsumi, A., Tanaka H., et al., *Sengo Hoshō* (Tokyo, 1992).

Watt, D. Cameron, *How War Came* (1989).

____, *Personalities and Policies* (1965).

Wegner, B. (ed.), *Zwei Wege nach Moskau: Vom Hitler–Stalin-Pakt zum 'Unternehmen Barbarossa'* (München, 1991).

Weigley, R., *The American Way of War* (1973).

Williams, H., *The Manhattan Project: A Documentary Introduction to the Atomic Age* (1991).

Wilmott, J.P., *The Great Crusade* (1990).

Wilson, G.M., *Radical Nationalist in Japan: Kita Ikki, 1883–1937* (Cambridge, Mass., 1969).

Woodburn-Kirby, S., *The War against Japan* I. (1957).

____, *Singapore: The Chain of Disaster* (1971).

Yabe, T., *Konoe Fumimaro* (Tokyo, 1952).

Yamagiwa, A., 'The Republic of China towards an occupied Japan, in Sodei, R. (ed.), *Sekaishi no nakano Nihon Senryō* (Tokyo, 1985).

Yamamoto, C., *Daihon'ei Kaigunbu* (Tokyo, 1974).

Yardley, H.O., *The American Black Chamber* (1981).

Yingqin, H., *The History of Eight Year Japanese Aggression against China and China's Resistance War* (Taipei, 1982).

Yokota, K., *Kenpō to Ten'nō sei* (Tokyo, 1990).

Yoshida, Y., *Whispering Leaves in Grosvenor Square, 1936–7* (1938).

Yoshizawa, K., *Gaikō-60-nen* (Tokyo, 1958).

Yoshizawa, S. *Nihon Gaikōshi* (Tokyo, 1973).

Young, A.M. *Imperial Japan, 1926–38* (1938).

\_\_\_\_, *China and Helping Hands* (Cambridge, Mass., 1963).

Zhanshi, W., *Important Historical Documents of the Republic of China: The Period of the War of Resistance against Japan, 3: Diplomatic Relations during the War* (Taipei, 1981).

# Index